CW00386316

Guide to the
COMMUNITY TRADE MARK

Guide to the
COMMUNITY TRADE MARK

Ruth E. Annand, B.A. (Dunelm), Solicitor

Professor of Law, University of Bristol,
Associate with Humphreys & Co, Bristol

and

Helen E. Norman, LL.M. (Birmingham), Barrister, Gray's Inn

Lecturer in Law, University of Bristol,
Consultant in European Law and Intellectual Property to Townsends,
Solicitors, Swindon

BLACKSTONE
PRESS LIMITED

First published in Great Britain 1998 by Blackstone Press Limited,
Aldine Place, London W12 8AA. Telephone 0181-740 2277

© R. Annand, H. Norman, 1998

ISBN: 1 85431 580 3

Brtish Library Cataloguing in Publication Data
A CIP catalogue record for this book is available from the British Library

Typeset by Style Photosetting Ltd, Mayfield, East Sussex
Printed by Livesey Limited, Shrewsbury Shropshire

Contents

Preface

The authors wish to acknowledge the contribution of Luis-Alfonso Durán of Durán-Corretjer, Barcelona, Spain, towards the Seniority section of chapter 4. The authors would like to express their thanks to Marie Davies and Pat Jones for their help in researching this book.

References to 'he' or 'his' are not intended to be gender specific. The law and practice is stated as at 1 November 1997.

Readers should note the following developments since 1 November 1997:

(a) The decision of the Court of Justice of the European Communities in *Parfums Christian Dior SA* v *Evora BV* (case C-337/95) on 4 November 1997. The Court ruled that under both Article 7(2) of the Trade Marks Directive (the equivalent of Article 13(2) of the Community Trade Mark Regulation (CTMR) and Articles 30 and 36 of the Treaty of Rome, a trade mark owner may not rely on his trade mark rights to prevent a retailer advertising 'original' goods in ways customary to the reseller's sector of trade, unless it is established that such advertising seriously damages the luxury image of the goods.

(b) The decision of the same Court in *Frits Loendersloot* v *George Ballantine & Sons Ltd* (case C-349-95) on 11 November 1997. Here the Court decided that a trade mark owner is entitled to prevent a third party parallel importer from removing and then reaffixing or replacing labels attached to 'original' goods unless:

(i) it is established that the use of the trade mark rights would contribute to artificial partitioning of the markets between Member States;

(ii) it is shown that the relabelling cannot affect the original condition of the product;

(iii) the presentation of the relabelled product is not such as to be liable to damage the reputation of the trade mark and its owner; and

(iv) the person who relabels the products informs the trade mark owner of the relabelling before the relabelled products are put on sale.

(c) The ruling of the Court of Justice in *Sabel BV* v *Puma AG* (case C-251/95) of 11 November 1997. This is to the effect that 'likelihood of confusion' in Article 4(1)(b) of the Trade Marks Directive (the counterpart of Article 8(1)(b) CTMR) includes direct and indirect confusion as to the origin of the goods but not non-origin association as understood in Benelux law. The Court confirmed that the test for likelihood of confusion is a global one which will include, where appropriate, the reputation of the mark acquired on the market. The Court also made clear that confusion is not a requirement for protection against dilution (Articles 4(3), 4(4)(a) and 5(2) of the Directive, Articles 8(5) and 9(1)(c) of the CTMR). The Court did not decide the status of the joint statements by the Council and the Commission entered in the minutes of the Council meetings at which the Directive and CTMR were adopted.

(d)   The Office for Harmonisation in the Internal Market (Trade Marks and Designs) (OHIM) announced in issue 29/97 of the *Community Trade Marks Bulletin*, 24 November 1997, that:

> In order to accelerate the examination procedures to the point of publication, it was decided to suspend temporarily the checking of the seniority claims. Accordingly, the applicatons published from the bulletin no. 29/97 no longer contain the heading 350 [particulars of a seniority claim].

The authority for OHIM's decision is unclear. Publication of a Community trade mark (CTM) application can only take placed once OHIM is satisfied, inter alia, that the conditions of filing are met (Articles 36 and 40 CTMR). OHIM's examination for the conditions of filing must include at least the formal correctness of any seniority claim (Rules 8 and 9 of the Implementing Regulation (IR)). Rule 12(h) of the IR requires the publication of a CTM application to particularise details of an applicable seniority claim.

OHIM's decision impedes, albeit temporarily, one of the advantages of seniority claiming for a CTM application, namely notice to would-be opposers that prior rights of the CTM applicant exist in Member States. For a full account of seniority the reader is referred to chapter 4.

Ruth E. Annand
Helen E. Norman
November 1997

Table of Cases

Table of International Treaties

Table of EU Legislation

Table of Statutes

**TABLE OF SECONDARY
LEGISLATION**

Abbreviations

AR	Commission Regulation (EC) No. 216/96
BTA	Benelux Trademark Act 1971
CTM	Community trade mark
CTMR	Council Regulation (EC) No. 40/94 on the Community Trade Mark
EPC	European Patent Convention
EPO	European Patent Office
FR	Commission Regulation (EC) No. 2869/95
IR	Commission Regulation (EC) No. 2868/95
OHIM	Office for Harmonisation in the Internal Market
OHIM OJ	OHIM *Official Journal*
TRIPs Agreement	Agreement on Trade Related Aspects of Intellectual Property Rights
WIPO	World Intellectual Property Organisation
WTO	World Trade Organisation

Chapter One
Introduction to the Community Trade Mark

It has been said on more than one occasion that 1996 was the 'Year of the Trade Mark'. In that year, three major events took place, namely:

(a)   The coming into force on 1 August 1996 of the Trademark Law Treaty 1994, explained below.

(b)   The coming into force on 1 April 1996 of the Madrid Protocol 1989, to run in parallel to the Madrid Agreement of 1891. For convenience these two Treaties are referred to as 'the Madrid system'. The Madrid system is explained briefly below and more fully in chapter 10.

(c)   The formal opening, on 1 April 1996, of the Office for Harmonisation in the Internal Market (Trade Marks and Designs) (OHIM) for the receipt of applications pursuant to the Community Trade Mark Regulation 1994 (CTMR). The status of OHIM is dealt with further below, along with OHIM's means of communicating with trade mark applicants, opponents and proprietors, and the time limits within which responses to its decisions are required. The significance of the Community system lies in the fact that Community trade marks (CTMs) are effective throughout the whole territory of the European Community.

The cumulative effect of these changes has been to shift the focus of trade mark law from the national to the international arena. In particular, the availability of a single registration of unitary effect throughout the whole of the EC has forced many trade mark owners to rethink their strategy.

Whether the CTM is viewed as merely an enhanced form of regional trade mark, or the first ever example of a truly supranational trade mark right, its popularity has exceeded all expectations. OHIM estimated that some 15,000 CTM applications would be filed in 1996, when in fact almost three times this number were actually received (further statistics are given in chapter 3). Its impact is therefore enormous.

International conventions affecting trade marks

For over a century, the traditional means of obtaining registrable intellectual property rights (that is, patents, trade marks and registered designs), has been to seek registration in every country where the applicant intends to do business. This reflects one of the hallmarks of intellectual property, namely its territorial effect. The need to pursue national registrations exposes the trade mark applicant to multiple application fees, translation and legal representation costs, and the vagaries of differing procedural and substantive rules. Until recently, international intellectual property conventions were concerned principally with assisting the trade mark applicant in obtaining multiple national registrations. A trade mark applicant may still choose to make multiple national filings (see the section entitled 'Strategy' below) but two out of the three developments outlined above mean that this approach need no longer be the norm.

Paris Convention for the Protection of Industrial Property 1883
This is the 'parent' intellectual property convention (and indeed the oldest) and will be referred to throughout this work as 'the Paris Convention'. It has been revised seven times since its completion in 1891 and is open for signature to any country (the list of contracting parties as of 24 October 1997 appears in appendix 1, though for the sake of simplicity the version of the Convention which each country has signed is not indicated). The Convention covers those forms of intellectual property rights obtainable by registration, namely patents, registered designs and trade marks (copyright and unregistered designs are covered by the Berne Copyright Convention of 1886).

Membership of the Convention obliges a country to establish a national patent office and to publish information about its decisions. In relation to trade marks, the Convention obliges its signatories:

(a)   to protect well known marks belonging to nationals of Convention countries (Article 6*bis*);
(b)   to prevent the use and registration of 'armorial bearings, flags and emblems' of the countries of the Convention (Article 6*ter*);
(c)   to provide effective protection against unfair competition (Article 10*bis*); and
(d)   to accept for registration any trade mark which has been duly registered in its country of origin (Article 6*quinquies* — the so-called '*telle-quelle*' obligation).

The wording of the Convention is quite broad, leaving a considerable discretion to its member states as to how they are to implement the above obligations.

The Paris Convention, like most of the international intellectual property conventions, is administered by the World Intellectual Property Organisation (throughout the remainder of this work, WIPO), which is an agency of the United Nations, based in Geneva, established under the terms of its own Convention of 14 July 1967. WIPO's role is to promote intellectual property throughout the world, by educating and encouraging developing countries to adopt their own intellectual property laws and by putting forward proposals for the worldwide harmonisation of national intellectual property legislation. WIPO's role in promoting the development of intellectual property laws may in due course have to be reassessed in the light of the World Trade Organisation and the TRIPs Agreement, discussed below.

The Paris Convention contains two provisions important in practice. These are the principle of national treatment (Article 2) and the system of claiming Convention priority (Article 4).

National treatment   This principle means that each state belonging to the Convention undertakes to give the same treatment to nationals (whether companies or individuals) of other Convention countries as it gives its own nationals. (In the Convention the signatory countries are described as members of a 'Union for the protection of industrial property': Article 1.) An individual or company having the nationality of one of the States of the Convention is guaranteed the basic right to seek registration of its trade marks in every other country belonging to the Convention and, if such rights are granted, to enforce them. The concept of national treatment goes beyond this, however, as by Article 3 of the Convention, protection is also extended to companies and individuals who, though not nationals of a State belonging to the Convention, are domiciled or have a real and effective industrial and commercial establishment in the territory of one of the countries of the Union.

In the context of the Community system, the obligation found in Articles 2 and 3 of the Paris Convention is fulfilled by Article 5 of the CTMR, which is explained in chapter 2.

Convention priority   The system of claiming Convention priority (of more significance in the patent system) means that where an application for a trade mark has been filed in one member country of the Paris Convention, then any application made in another Convention country within the following six months can claim priority from date of the first application, provided it relates to the same subject matter and provided the earlier application is not withdrawn. Consequently, the validity of the second application is not affected by any third-party rights which arise in the meantime.

A claim for Convention priority can be made in respect of a CTM application under Article 29 of the CTMR (see chapter 3).

Trademark Law Treaty 1994
Although the negotiations for this Treaty commenced in 1987 under the auspices of WIPO with the aspiration of reforming the substantive law of trade marks, ultimately it became the vehicle for harmonising formalities. It thus deals with:

(a)   the form and content of an application for registration (for example, it provides that multi-class applications are to be allowed and that service marks must be recognised);
(b)   the appointment of a representative to deal with one or more applications or registrations (for example, it states that a power of attorney can relate to more than one mark and notarisation cannot be demanded); and
(c)   renewal (the standard term of protection is to be 10 years).

The Treaty declares that contracting States may not impose on trade mark applicants or proprietors any requirements over and above those laid down in the Treaty. Although 42 Paris Convention countries were signatories to the Treaty, as of 28 October 1997 only 12 countries had formally acceded to it, five being the minimum number to bring the Treaty into force.

The CTMR already complies with the provisions of the Trademark Law Treaty and it has been proposed that the Community should become a member of the

Treaty in addition to the 15 Member States of the EC who are already signatories to it (see COM (95) 92 final of 27 March 1995, Recommendation for a Council Decision authorising the signing on behalf of the EC of the WIPO Trademark Law Treaty of 27 October 1994).

TRIPs

The Agreement on Trade Related Aspects of Intellectual Property Rights was concluded as part of the Uruguay Round on the renegotiation of the General Agreement on Tariffs and Trade (GATT) in 1994, which in turn established the World Trade Organisation (WTO). The WTO is primarily concerned with developing tariff-free world trade and the obligations found in the TRIPs Agreement can, cynically, be seen as the price a developing country must pay for being able to export its produce worldwide.

The TRIPs Agreement provides for links to be established between the WTO and WIPO. Further, it combines the principle of national treatment found in the Paris Convention with that of most favoured nation treatment (found in the WTO Agreement itself) as an obligation of membership. It also declares its support for the major intellectual property international conventions, requiring its signatory States to accede to the latest versions thereof, and itself lays down minimum standards for the protection of copyright and related rights, trade marks, geographical indications, industrial designs, patents, integrated circuits, and confidential information. Member States are required to provide effective enforcement procedures in respect of those rights. The inducement to amend national intellectual property laws as the price of free trade is the principal reason why the WTO should be seen as a rival to WIPO.

The European Community is a co-signatory along with its 15 Member States to the TRIPs Agreement, the Community having shared competence with the Member States in this matter (see *Opinion 1/94* [1994] ECR I-5267). The CTMR was amended to take account of the Community's obligation to accept CTM applications from nationals of WTO countries which are not members of the Paris Convention (see Regulation (EC) 3288/94 [1994] OJ L 349/83).

A list of members of the World Trade Organisation as at 1 November 1997 appears in appendix 2.

Madrid Agreement for the International Registration of Marks 1891

The Madrid Agreement enables an individual or company established in one of the contracting states, once a 'home' registration has been obtained, to apply to the International Bureau at WIPO for an international trade mark registration. The Bureau will pass on the application to the national trade mark offices of those contracting countries for which the applicant has requested protection. In due course these will be processed and, subject to any objections, will become national 'registrations'. The Madrid system therefore provides a procedural short cut for filing a batch of national applications by means of a single transaction (thus saving on translation and representation costs) but hardly deserves the name of 'international registration'.

Despite its longevity, the Madrid Agreement attracted relatively few members because of its perceived weaknesses (the need for a home registration, the vulnerability of the international registration to 'central attack' on the home registration, the short period of time given to national offices for examination of the application, and the low fees paid for their examinations). In 1989, the Madrid Protocol was agreed. It contains a number of changes which were intended to overcome the deficiencies of the Agreement and hence to make the Madrid system more attractive to countries which had not previously joined (such as the United Kingdom). However, it must be appreciated that the Protocol exists independently of the Agreement, providing its own procedure for the international registration of trade marks. This means that until at least 1 December 2005 the Agreement and Protocol will run as parallel systems, so that there are three groups of members of the Madrid system:

(a) countries which are party only to the Madrid Agreement;
(b) countries which are party only to the Madrid Protocol;
(c) countries which are party to both.

Appendix 3 contains the list of those countries which as of 1 November 1997 are members of the Madrid Agreement and appendix 4 contains the list of those which as of the same date are members of the Protocol. There is a proposal that the European Community should link the CTMR with the Madrid system by means of:

(a) the Community itself becoming a member of the Protocol (see COM (96) 367 final of 22 February 1996, Proposal for a Council Decision approving the accession of the EC to the Madrid Protocol); and

(b) for a CTM to operate as a 'home' registration or application for the purposes of an international application under the Protocol, and for an international applicant to be able to designate the Community as one of its chosen 'countries' (see COM (96) 372 final of 24 July 1996, Proposal for a Council Regulation modifying Council Regulation (EC) No 40/94).

The formal link is expected to be completed in the spring of 1998.

The workings of the Madrid system for the international registration of trade marks are explained more fully in chapter 10.

Arrangement of Nice for the International Classification of Goods and Services 1957

Trade marks have to be registered for specific goods and/or services. The list of items for which a mark is registered is known as the 'specification'. To assist with the registration of and searching for trade marks, the Nice Arrangement divides goods into 34 classes and services into eight classes and provides an alphabetical list of goods and services giving the class in which each product or service is classified. Adoption of the Nice Classification does not bind a country either as to the evaluation of the extent of protection of a trade mark, or to recognise service marks (but recognition of service marks is required by the Trademark Law Treaty).

The Nice Classification is kept constantly up to date by WIPO, with new products being added and old ones being deleted. The seventh version was published in 1996. The Classification is used by OHIM by virtue of Article 28 of the CTMR together with Rule 2 of the Implementing Regulations (IR).

Vienna Agreement Establishing an International Classification of the Figurative Elements of Marks 1973
This establishes a common classification for the figurative elements of marks and comprises a list of sections into which marks consisting of two-dimensional designs or three-dimensional shapes are classified. Its main aim is to facilitate searching but it has no effect on the scope of protection afforded to a mark. Although ratified by only a handful of countries, its influence is widespread and it is used in both the Madrid and Community systems. It is administered by WIPO.

Why a Community trade mark?

Impact of case law
Long before the transitional period for implementing the Treaty of Rome expired, the Court of Justice of the European Communities was obliged to resolve the inherent conflict between the single market and national trade mark rights. In a series of decisions, the Court had to consider several factual situations where the ownership or exploitation of intellectual property created a barrier to trade:

(a)   Parallel registrations by a trade mark owner in each Member State. The territorial effect of such registrations could, in theory, entitle the proprietor to keep out of each Member State not only infringing imports originating from rivals or counterfeiters, but parallel imports placed on the market within the Community by the trade mark owner, or a subsidiary, licensee or distributor acting with the owner's consent; alternatively, contractual arrangements, such as distribution agreements or trade mark licences, could result in the trade mark right being used by a licensee or distributor to keep out parallel imports.

(b)   Use of different brand names for the same product in different countries, thereby impeding parallel imports.

(c)   Differences between national laws concerning what was registrable, the scope of the trade mark right and what amounted to a confusingly similar trade mark.

(d)   The existence of conflicting, independently created, trade marks in the hands of independent enterprises in different Member States.

The solutions adopted by Court of Justice to deal with some (but not all) of these difficulties were as follows:

(a)   The doctrine of exhaustion of rights was developed by the Court of Justice to prevent a proprietor relying on national trade mark rights to keep out of a particular Member State parallel imports from another Member State. The doctrine of exhaustion was held to apply also where trade mark ownership was divided between different members of a corporate group, so that the group was treated as a single entity (*Centrafarm BV* v *Winthrop BV* (case 16/74) [1974] ECR 1183). The doctrine of exhaustion is incorporated into the CTMR by Article 13 thereof, and its application to CTMs is set out in chapter 7.

(b)   Distribution agreements and licences of trade marks were (and are) subject to the controls of EC competition policy (*Établissements Consten SA* v *Commission* (cases 56 and 58/64) [1966] ECR 299). The impact of EC competition policy on CTMs is considered in chapter 9.

(c) Where a trade mark owner chose different trade marks for different Member States, or even different packaging for different Member States, this was held to have the potential effect of partitioning the single market along national boundaries (irrespective of the owner's intentions). Consequently, the conduct of a parallel importer who repackaged the product could not be challenged, unless the repackaging affected the condition of the goods (*Hoffmann-La Roche and Co. AG v Centrafarm Vertriebsgesellschaft Pharmazeutischer Erzeugnisse mbH* (case 102/77) [1978] ECR 1139) or was otherwise defective, of poor quality or untidy (*Bristol-Myers Squibb v Paranova A/S* (cases C-427, 429 and 436/93) [1996] ECR I-3457).

However, the Court of Justice concluded that where, as a result of independent creation, there existed conflicting marks being owned in different Member States by unconnected enterprises (see *Terrapin (Overseas) Ltd v Terranova Industrie C.A. Kapferer and Co.* (case 119/75) [1976] ECR 1039; *Deutsche Renault AG v Audi AG* (case C-317/91) [1993] ECR I-6227) the single market had to give way to national trade mark rights, with the result that each enterprise could keep the other out of its territory.

Legislative solution
In relation to the other cases, listed above, where the territorial nature of trade mark rights conflicted with the philosophy of the single market, the European Community adopted a twofold strategy, namely to harmonise national law whilst at the same time creating a pan-European right.

Origins of the Community legislation   Discussions for the creation of a Community-wide trade mark can be traced back to 1964, when the Commission proposed a Convention for the Community Trade Mark, to run parallel to the Community Patent Convention (although the latter was not agreed until 1975 and has, despite recent attempts to reactivate it, still not been implemented). Further proposals emerged in 1976 in a document entitled 'Memorandum on the creation of a EEC trade mark', Bull EC suppl. 8/76.

However, it was not until 1980 that the Commission adopted the twin-track approach of bringing national laws into line by means of a harmonising Directive whilst at the same time creating a Community-wide right obtainable by registration, a strategy subsequently adopted also in relation to industrial designs. The draft Directive and Regulation published in that year were later revised in 1985 and 1984 respectively.

The First Council Directive to Approximate the laws of the Member States relating to Trade Marks ([1989] OJ L 40/1) was agreed in late 1988 and will be referred to throughout this work as 'the Directive'. This seeks to resolve the problem of the diversity of national law by establishing the basic criteria for registrability, infringement, invalidity and revocation. However, although most Member States have now legislated to bring their national laws into line with the Directive, such legislation will operate in the context of varying legal systems and traditions. Furthermore, linguistic differences between Member States may result in a proposed trade mark receiving different treatment at the hands of different national trade mark registries.

Council Regulation (EC) No. 40/94 on the Community Trade Mark ([1994] OJ L 11/1) was adopted late in 1993 and is referred to throughout this work as 'the CTMR'. In the opinion of the Commission, the creation of a single trade mark for the whole of the Community was the only way to overcome the remaining conflicts between trade marks and the single market, and of stopping a trade mark owner choosing a different mark for different countries (see *Centrafarm BV* v *American Home Products Corporation* (case 3/78) [1978] ECR 1823). The concept of a unitary trade mark (which means that the mark will have the same effect throughout the whole of the EC) also resolves another problem encountered in the earlier case law of the Court, namely where an assignment of national rights results in fragmented ownership of the trade mark among different enterprises in different Member States (*IHT Internationale Heiztechnik GmbH* v *Ideal-Standard GmbH* (case C-9/93) [1994] ECR I-2789).

The objective of the twin-track approach is that the national and Community systems of substantive trade mark law should converge through the unifying mechanism of interpretations given by the Court of Justice of the European Communities pursuant to its preliminary rulings jurisdiction under Article 177 of the Treaty of Rome. The Directive and the CTMR accordingly have many provisions in common, and hence, where appropriate, this book will point out where they share the same wording and where they diverge. It will indicate where there have already been decisions of national courts under the post-harmonisation law, and where key issues of interpretation have already been referred to the Court of Justice.

Legal basis of the CTMR
The CTMR has as its legal basis Article 235 of the Treaty of Rome, the implied powers provision. Any legislation based on this Article has to be agreed by unanimous vote in the Council of Ministers, which may explain why the CTMR took so long to emerge. The significance of the choice of a Regulation as the legislative vehicle for creating a Community-wide right is that under Article 189 of the Treaty of Rome such legislation is directly applicable in all Member States, that is, it has uniform effect throughout the EC and has automatic legal force without the need for intervening national legislation.

Implementation of the CTMR
The CTMR itself makes provision for further implementing legislation (Article 140 CTMR). Accordingly, the following Regulations have since been adopted by the Commission:

(a)   Commission Regulation (EC) No. 2868/95 of 13.12.1995 [1995] OJ L 303/1 (the Implementing Regulation);
(b)   Commission Regulation (EC) No. 2869/95 of 13.12.1995 [1995] OJ L 303/33 (the Fees Regulation); and
(c)   Commission Regulation (EC) No. 216/96 of 5.2.1996 [1996] OJ L 28/11 (the Boards of Appeal Regulation).

These will be referred to throughout this work as the Implementing Regulation (IR), the Fees Regulation (FR) and the Appeal Regulation (AR), the abbreviations being those used by OHIM itself.

OHIM Guidelines
The formal legislative framework of the CTMR will inevitably be supplemented by the practice of OHIM. As is to be expected of any industrial property office, it has published several guidelines already in its own *Official Journal* (hereafter, OHIM OJ), and further are expected. Examination Guidelines were adopted by the President of OHIM by Decision No. EX-96-2 of 26 March 1996 (OHIM OJ 9/96, pp. 1324–46) and Guidelines relating to general provisions on proceedings before OHIM were adopted by the President of OHIM by Decision of 28 October 1996 (OHIM OJ 12/96, pp. 1780–1807). Opposition Proceedings Guidelines have recently been adopted and are to be published in OHIM OJ 10/97. Guidelines relating to the substantive issues of opposition are not expected to issue from OHIM until at least 1998. The OHIM Guidelines contain standard letters which are referred to throughout the book, for example, 'on a 128 communication'.

Assumptions
In preparing this work, it has been assumed that the reader has access to the text of the Directive and of the CTMR, as amended, together with the IR, FR and AR and OHIM's published Guidelines listed above.

Interpretation of the CTMR
As stated above, the only judicial body which can give an authoritative ruling on the interpretation of the Directive and CTMR is the Court of Justice of the European Communities. In the meantime, however, it will often be necessary to put forward suggestions as to the probable meaning of key words and phrases in both documents. Although the final versions of the Directive and CTMR contain major differences from the Commission's initial proposals, it is nevertheless helpful to consider the Commission's thinking by way of understanding the provisions. Accordingly, where necessary, this work will refer to the 'Memorandum on the creation of an EEC trade mark 1976', Bull EC suppl. 8/76 mentioned above and to the Commission's commentary on the earlier drafts of the Directive and CTMR.

There are, however, two further sources of information about the legislative intent behind the Directive and the CTMR.

Recitals In keeping with the requirement of reasoning found in Article 189 of the Treaty of Rome, both the Directive and CTMR contain a series of Recitals. Recitals 1–7 to the Directive state that its goal is to achieve partial harmonisation in areas of substantive trade mark law where the divergence of national law impedes the effective operation of the single market, leaving to Member States the autonomy to determine their own procedural trade mark rules and to apply other domestic laws (such as those relating to unfair competition, civil liability or consumer protection) to trade marks. Other Recitals (8 and 11) deal with the importance of the obligation to use a trade mark and of the role of acquiescence in preventing the exercise of trade mark rights. However, the two most important Recitals to the Directive are 9 and 10, which declare, respectively:

(a) the importance of ensuring that a registered trade mark enjoys the same protection under the legal systems of all the Member States; and

(b)   that the protection to be afforded to registered trade marks reflects the function of trade marks, *which is in particular to guarantee the trade mark as an indication of origin* (emphasis added). Recital 10 goes on to declare that where the registered trade mark and the later sign are identical and the goods and services to which they both relate are identical, such protection must be absolute. Where, however, there is similarity between the mark and the sign and between their respective goods and services, then the scope of protection depends on there being a likelihood of confusion. The Recital then lists the factors to be taken into account in determining whether there is a likelihood of confusion.

Turning to the CTMR, the opening Recitals (1–6) state the reasons why it is necessary to have a Community system of trade marks obtainable by registration alone, the legal basis of the CTMR and the fact that the Community system is intended to coexist with national systems. Recitals 8–10 set out the legislative intent with regard to exhaustion of rights, the requirement of use and the nature of the property right in a CTM, whilst Recitals 11–18 deal with the issues of administration, judicial control over such administration, and the enforcement of CTMs by national courts under the principles of the Brussels Convention on Jurisdiction and the Enforcement of Judgments in Civil and Commercial Matters 1968. Of key concern, however, is Recital 7 to the CTMR, which, making allowance for the different functions performed by each document, is in terms of substance identical to Recital 10 to the Directive, set out above.

The phrase in the Directive and the CTMR, 'the function of which is in particular to guarantee the trade mark as an indication of origin', is likely to become one of the most closely analysed. It begs two questions, namely:

(a)   whether the indication of origin function is the only one to be ascribed to modern trade marks (the presence of the phrase 'in particular' suggests a negative response); and
(b)   if trade marks are to fulfil other functions, what are those functions?

Such questions are not mere academic speculation. The function which the trade mark performs in the modern consumer society has a direct impact on:

(a)   questions of registrability (particularly in relation to merchandising activities, see chapter 2);
(b)   the obligation to make proper use of a trade mark (see chapter 5);
(c)   its liability to revocation for non-use or deceptive use (again, see chapter 5); and
(d)   the scope of protection to be afforded in the infringement action (see chapter 6).

The issue of trade mark function is therefore of key concern to any CTM owner.
Since the ground-breaking work of Frank Schechter (see 'The rational basis of trade mark protection' (1927) 40 Harv L Rev 813), it has generally been accepted that the indication of origin function is outmoded, in that the average consumer neither knows nor cares about the precise identity of the originator of the product. Further, the trade mark cannot truly be treated as an item of property in its own

right, and so cannot be licensed or assigned. It has become customary, instead, to refer to a trade mark as fulfilling three overlapping functions, namely the product differentiation function, the guarantee function and the advertising function.

The CTMR gives express recognition to the product differentiation function by means of its enabling declaration in Article 4 of the CTMR ('signs of which a CTM may consist'; and see Article 2 of the Directive); and to the advertising function by allowing dilution to be pleaded as a ground of opposition to a CTM application (Article 8(5) CTMR) and as a category of infringement (Article 9(1)(c) CTMR). (Articles 4 and 8(5) of the CTMR are explained further in chapter 2 and Article 9(1)(c) of the CTMR in chapter 6.)

However, the Court of Justice has so far given only limited recognition to the guarantee function of trade marks, preferring instead to emphasise the indication of origin function. Although Recital 10 of the Directive and Recital 7 of the CTMR contain the word 'guarantee', the larger phrase in which the word appears is derived from the ruling in *Hoffmann-La Roche and Co. AG v Centrafarm Vertriebsgesellschaft Pharmazeutischer Erzeugnisse mbH* (case 102/77) [1978] ECR 1139, where the Court was concerned only with whether the conduct of a parallel importer broke the connection between the trade mark proprietor and the goods. In *SA CNL-Sucal NV v Hag GF AG* (case C-10/89) [1990] ECR I-3711, the Court stated that a trade mark's essential function would be compromised if its owner could not prevent the circulation of goods bearing a confusingly similar name:

> . . . in this situation consumers would no longer be able to identify with certainty the origin of the marked product and the bad quality of a product for which he is in no way responsible could be attributed to the owner of the right.

There is a further allusion to the guarantee function of the trade mark in similar terms in *IHT Internationale Heiztechnik GmbH v Ideal-Standard GmbH* (case C-9/93) [1994] ECR I-2789. As regards the advertising function, this too has been accorded only a passing mention, such as the Court's statement in *Bristol-Myers Squibb v Paranova* (cases C-427/93 and others) [1996] ECR I-3457 that the trade mark owner can object to defective, poor quality and untidy repackaging; and the recent opinion of Advocate-General Jacobs in *Parfums Christian Dior SA v Evora BV* (case C-337/95) 29 April 1997 to the effect that a trade mark owner should have the right to oppose the use of the mark by a reseller in advertising, where such advertising is liable to damage significantly the reputation of the trade mark and of its owner.

Minutes It is unusual for the deliberations of the Council of Ministers when adopting Community legislation to be made known. Nevertheless, as a result of an article by members of the Benelux delegation, H.R. Furstner and M.C. Geuze, 'The scope of protection of the trade mark law in the Benelux countries and EEC' [1988] BIE 215, reprinted in (1989) ECTA Newsletter No. 15, p. 10, an account of the negotiations leading to the adoption of the Directive became public. Eventually, the OHIM OJ carried the official version of the 'Joint statements by the Council and the Commission entered in the minutes of the Council meeting on the First Council Directive on Trade Marks' (OHIM OJ 5/96, p. 607) and the 'Joint statements by the Council and the Commission entered in the minutes of the Council meeting at which the Regulation on the CTM was adopted' (OHIM OJ 5/96, p. 613). The text carries the warning that 'since the following statements by the Council and the Commission are not part of the legal text they are without prejudice to the interpretation of that text by the Court of Justice of the European Communities', a warning which in view of the Court of Justice's exclusive competence to interpret Community legislation is only right and proper.

Bearing this warning in mind, this work will nevertheless refer the reader, when appropriate, to the minutes, as they frequently shed light on specific words and phrases in the Directive and CTMR. Of particular interest at present, however, is statement 5 in the minutes concerning Articles 4(1)(b) and 5(1)(b) of the Directive and statement 6 in the minutes concerning Articles 8(1)(b) and 9(1)(b) of the CTMR. The two pairs of provisions, in identical form, create:

(a)   the relative ground of refusal, in relation to an application for a national mark or a CTM, where because of its identity with, or similarity to, an earlier trade mark and the identity or similarity of the goods or services covered by the trade marks, *there exists a likelihood of confusion on the part of the public, which includes the likelihood of association with the earlier trade mark* (Article 4(1)(b) Directive and Article 8(1)(b) CTMR, emphasis added); and

(b)   the category of infringing act, in relation to a national mark or CTM, where because of the identity of the alleged infringing sign with, or its similarity to, the trade mark and the identity or similarity of the goods or services covered by the trade mark, and the sign, *there exists a likelihood of confusion on the part of the public, which includes the likelihood of association with the earlier trade mark* (Article 5(1)(b) Directive and Article 9(1)(b) CTMR, emphasis added).

In each case the statement is to the effect that 'the Council and the Commission note that ''likelihood of association'' is a concept which in particular has been developed by Benelux case law'.

The question which this brief pronouncement raises is whether the introduction of 'likelihood of association' into the Directive and CTMR broadens the scope of the trade mark right. This in turn takes the debate back to the matter discussed earlier, namely what is the proper function of the trade mark, bearing in mind the wording of Recital 10 to the Directive and Recital 7 to the CTMR, which are to the effect that the protection to be afforded to registered trade marks reflects the function of trade marks, which is in particular to guarantee the trade mark as an indication of origin.

Attempts so far to rely on the statements have met with a singular lack of success. In the post-harmonisation United Kingdom decision of *Wagamama Ltd* v *City Centre Restaurants plc* [1995] FSR 713, Laddie J rejected various arguments advanced by the plaintiffs in support of their contention that the Benelux view of 'likelihood of association' should be adopted (for a detailed account see chapter 6). (The Benelux view is that, to show infringement, it is not necessary to prove that the potential customer is confused when met with the alleged infringing sign. It suffices if the registered trade mark is 'called to mind'. The net effect of this is to give greater emphasis to the advertising function of trade marks.)

Instead, Laddie J approached the question of interpretation of the key phrase from first principles and concluded that the indication of origin function must govern the scope of the trade mark right, so that the rights of the proprietor against alleged infringers was limited to 'classic infringement':

> If the broader scope were to be adopted, the Directive and our Act would be creating a new type of monopoly not related to the proprietor's trade but in the trade mark itself. Such a monopoly could be likened to a quasi-copyright in the mark. However, unlike copyright, there would be no fixed duration for the right and it would be a true monopoly effective against copyist and non-copyist alike. I can see nothing in the terms of the Directive (or our Act), or in any secondary material which I could legitimately take into account, which would lead me to assume that this was its objective.

'Likelihood of association' is therefore simply a sub-species of 'likelihood of confusion' in which case it adds nothing to the scope of the trade mark right.

Similar thinking is to be found in the opinion of Advocate-General Jacobs in *Sabel BV* v *Puma AG* (case C-251/95) 29 April 1997, a reference to the Court of Justice by the German Bundesgerichtshof seeking guidance on the interpretation of Article 4(1)(b) of the Directive. His view is that it is impermissible to rely on the statements, as the information they reveal is at best ambiguous, so that they are in fact of no assistance. Advocate-General Jacobs's advice to the Court is that the wording of the four provisions mentioned above is quite clear, without the need to refer to extraneous sources. 'Likelihood of confusion' *includes* 'likelihood of association' so that even if under Benelux law the concept stretches the trade mark right beyond its traditional role of indication of origin, it cannot do so for the purposes of the Directive (and therefore, also, the CTMR). It remains to be seen whether the Court of Justice follows this advice.

Office for Harmonisation in the Internal Market

As mentioned at the start of this chapter, one of the principal tasks of the CTMR (now completed) was to provide for the creation of the Community Trade Marks Office (officially and somewhat awkwardly entitled the Office for Harmonisation in the Internal Market (Trade Marks and Designs)). As already indicated, it is referred to throughout this book as 'OHIM'.

Status of OHIM (Articles 111 to 114 CTMR)
OHIM (sited in Alicante, Spain) is a Community body with legal personality, so that it can acquire property and be a party to legal proceedings (Article 111 CTMR). Such personality does not extend outside the Community so that OHIM does not have power to conclude international agreements. It enjoys the normal privileges and immunities accorded to other EC institutions (Article 113 CTMR) and its staff are subject to the EC Staff Regulations (Article 112 CTMR). As a legal personality, it is subject to the same contractual and non-contractual liability as other EC institutions, to be decided by the Court of Justice pursuant to its jurisdiction under Article 215 of the Treaty of Rome (Article 114 CTMR).

Organisation of OHIM (Articles 118 to 124 CTMR)
OHIM is overseen by a President (Article 119(1) CTMR), assisted by one or more Vice-Presidents (Article 119(3) CTMR) (two have in fact been appointed). The

President represents OHIM (Article 111(3) CTMR) and is answerable to the EC Commission for those aspects of the conduct of OHIM which are not subject to judicial review by the Court of First Instance of the European Communities (Article 118 CTMR).

The President and Vice-Presidents have fixed-term appointments, which are renewable. They are subject to the special procedure for the appointment of senior officials found in Article 120 of the CTMR and to the disciplinary control of the Council of Ministers. It should be noted that the same appointment procedure is to be used for the Chairmen of the Boards of Appeal, except that they are subject to the disciplinary control of the Court of Justice (Article 131 CTMR).

The President is empowered, by Article 119 of the CTMR, to take all necessary steps to ensure the functioning of OHIM. This includes the adoption of internal administrative instructions and the publication of notices (several have appeared already in the OHIM OJ). He is also empowered to propose amendments to the CTMR and any of its subsidiary regulations to the Commission, has overall control of the budget and staff, and is to submit an annual report to the Commission, European Parliament and Administrative Board (Article 119(2) CTMR).

The Administrative Board, composed of a representative from each Member State plus one representative from the Commission and assisted by advisers or experts (Article 122 CTMR) deals with the appointment of senior staff, advises the President on matters for which OHIM is responsible and has to be consulted before OHIM adopts any Guidelines for the conduct of business (Article 121 CTMR). The Board, which acts by a simple majority, is expected to meet at least once a year, though additional meetings can be convened by its chairman (who along with its deputy chairman will be one of the Board's members) or by one third of the Member States (Articles 123 and 124 CTMR).

Financial control of OHIM is delegated to the Budget Committee (Articles 133 to 139 CTMR), the composition, chairmanship and meetings of which are subject to the same rules as the Administrative Board. OHIM is subject to the usual cumbersome budgetary procedure of the Community and to the scrutiny of its finances by the EC Court of Auditors.

Decision-making competence (Articles 125 to 132 CTMR)
Under Article 125 of the CTMR, OHIM's decision-making powers are allocated to Examiners (Article 126 CTMR), Opposition Divisions (Article 127 CTMR), Cancellation Divisions (Article 129 CTMR) and an Administration and Legal Division, the latter being responsible under Article 128 of the CTMR for those decisions not falling within the competence of the other three, in particular the making of entries on the Register. Decisions of examiners, the Opposition Divisions, the Cancellation Divisions and the Administration and Legal Division are all subject to an appeal to the Boards of Appeal (Article 130 CTMR), the members of all of which must be independent (Article 131 CTMR). No examiner, member of any of the Divisions or member of any of the Boards of Appeal can take part in a case if he or she has a personal interest therein or has previously been involved as a representative of one of the parties (Article 132 CTMR).

Official publications
OHIM is required to publish periodically the *Community Trade Marks Bulletin* (containing details of CTM applications and registrations as well as any other

matter required to be published under the CTMR) and to publish an *Official Journal* (as mentioned already, the OHIM OJ) containing notices and general information (Article 85 CTMR). OHIM is required to cooperate with the courts or authorities in the Member States (Article 86 CTMR). In particular, national trade mark registries and OHIM are to exchange official publications (Article 87 CTMR).

Languages (Article 115 CTMR)
The working languages of OHIM are Spanish, German, English, French, and Italian (Article 115 CTMR). The OHIM OJ is accordingly published in each of these five languages. However, by virtue of Article 116 of the CTMR, all publications in the *Community Trade Marks Bulletin* together with all entries on the Register of CTMs appear in all of the official languages of the Community (11 in total). The EC's official translation service must be used (Article 117 CTMR).

An application for a CTM can be filed in any of the official languages of the EC but when filing the application, the applicant must indicate a second language which must be one of the languages of OHIM. Oppositions and cancellation proceedings must be in one of the languages of OHIM. Article 115 of the CTMR contains detailed rules for determining which is to be the language of the case where an opponent or applicant for cancellation chooses a language different from that of the first or second language of the applicant. The parties may agree, however, to use any official EC language as the language of the case. The rules are dealt with in greater detail in chapter 3.

Public inspection of the Register and files (Articles 83 and 84 CTMR)
Under Article 83 of the CTMR, OHIM is to keep a Register of CTMs which is open to public inspection. Files kept by OHIM are not open to inspection prior to the publication of an application without the applicant's consent (Article 84 CTMR). However, a third party who has been notified that infringement proceedings will be started against him once a CTM application has been completed, can inspect the files without the applicant's consent. Once an application has been published, files relating to the application can be inspected on request, subject to any restrictions imposed under Rule 88 IR (specifically, papers dealing with whether an OHIM employee is excluded from hearing the case under the terms of Article 132 CTMR, all draft decisions and opinions, and any matter which a party has shown an interest in keeping confidential, subject to the plea of overriding public interest).

Legal representation (Articles 88 and 89 CTMR)
Article 88(1) of the CTMR states that it is not mandatory to be represented before OHIM. However, Article 88(2) provides that businesses which are not domiciled or which do not have either their principal place of business or a real and effective industrial and commercial establishment in the Community must be represented before OHIM, other than when filing an application. Firms which are domiciled or established in the Community, together with related enterprises, may be represented by an employee, who must, however, file a signed authorisation with OHIM (Article 88(3) CTMR).

Representation before OHIM can only be undertaken by legal practitioners qualified in one of the Member States to act in trade mark matters, or professional representatives whose names appear on the list maintained by OHIM. Further details concerning the representation requirements are to be found in chapter 2.

Communications from OHIM

Chapter 3 will explain how a CTM applicant or an opponent of a CTM application can communicate with OHIM. For the sake of convenience, and because it is of general concern, it will be explained here how OHIM communicates with CTM applicants, opponents and proprietors. The method of communication has some bearing on the calculation of time limits, another matter of general concern.

Methods of communication (Rules 61 to 68 IR)

General provisions   The basic principle (found in Rule 61(1) IR) is that notifications made by OHIM shall take the form of the original document. Alternative methods are a certified copy of the original, or a copy bearing OHIM's official seal or a computer printout bearing the official seal. The same provision then anticipates five alternative methods whereby such document is to be sent, namely by post, by hand delivery, by deposit in a postbox at OHIM, by telecopier or other technical means, or by public notification (Rule 61(2) IR).

Postal notifications (Rule 62 IR)   Rule 62(1) of the IR draws a distinction between:

    (a)   notifications of decisions having a time limit for appeal, summonses and other documents as determined by the President;

    (b)   notifications of decisions and other communications which have some other sort of time limit; and

    (c)   'all other communications'.

Notifications having a time limit for appeal are to be sent by registered letter with advice of delivery, notifications of other decisions having time limits are to be sent by registered letter unless the President of OHIM determines otherwise, and all other communications are to be sent by ordinary mail.

Where a registered letter, with or without advice of delivery, is sent, even if the addressee refuses to accept the letter, the notification is deemed to have been delivered to the addressee on the 10th day following its posting, unless the letter fails to reach its destination or arrives late (Rule 61(3) and (4) IR). However, where the notification is sent to an addressee domiciled or established outside the Community who does not have an appointed representative, then notification is to be by ordinary mail to the last known address and is deemed to have been effected on posting (Rule 61(2) IR). Should the circumstances of delivery not be covered by Rules 62(1) to (4), then the law of the State in whose territory notification is made shall apply (Rule 62(5) IR).

The Guidelines relating to general provisions on proceedings before OHIM, OHIM OJ 12/96, p. 1792, indicate that no decisions have been taken by the President concerning what other documents are to be notified by registered letter with advice of delivery and what decisions or other communications may be excluded from notification by registered letter.

Hand delivery (Rule 63 IR)   Rule 63 merely provides for notification to be effected at OHIM's premises by hand delivery to the addressee who is to acknowledge receipt.

Deposit box (Rule 64 IR)   Where the addressee has obtained a deposit box at OHIM, notification may be made by depositing the document therein, with a written record inserted in the files. Notification is deemed to have taken place on the fifth day following deposit. As little interest has been expressed in this method of communication, no decision has yet been taken by the President of OHIM concerning the introduction of postboxes (see the Guidelines relating to general provisions on proceedings before OHIM, OHIM OJ 12/96, p. 1792).

Telecopier or other technical means (Rule 65 IR)   Rule 65 of the IR provides for notification by telecopier to be effected by transmitting the original document or a copy which is in accordance with Rule 61 of the IR. According to the Guidelines relating to general provisions on proceedings before OHIM, OHIM OJ 12/96, p. 1792, notification by electronic means is OHIM's preferred method of communication.

Public notification (Rule 66 IR)   This is considered to be the method of last resort if the address of the addressee cannot be established or if written notification pursuant to Rule 62 of the IR has failed after a second attempt. The only public notification at present envisaged is publication in the *Community Trade Marks Bulletin*. According to Decision No. EX-96-5 of the President of OHIM of 30 July 1996 (OHIM OJ 10/96, p. 1451) the one-month period on the expiry of which the document shall be deemed to have been notified shall start 10 days after the date of issue shown on the *Community Trade Marks Bulletin*.

Notification to representative (Rule 67 IR)   Rule 67(1) provides that where a representative has been appointed notifications shall be addressed to that representative. This applies also to common applications where the first named applicant is deemed to be the common representative under Rule 75 of the IR. Where several representatives have been appointed, notification to any one suffices unless there is a specific address for service; and where several parties have appointed a common representative, notification to that representative is sufficient (Rule 67(2) and (3) IR).

Calculation of time limits (Rules 70 to 72 IR)
Under Article 77 of the CTMR, time limits laid down by the CTMR or the IR are to be calculated from the date of notification of the decision. Under Rule 70(2) of the IR, what matters is when the document in question is *deemed to have been received* (or, in the case of irregularities, when it was *actually* received: Rule 68 IR), with time starting to run on the following day. Time periods are calculated in full years, months, weeks or days (Rule 70(1) IR). Further detail is to be found in Rule 70(3), (4) and (5) on how years, months and weeks are to be calculated.

Where the CTMR or the IR provide for a period to be specified by OHIM, the *minimum* period is to be one month where the addressee is domiciled or has an establishment within the Community and between two and six months if those conditions are not met (Rule 71 IR).

Special provision is made concerning time limits for days on which OHIM is not open for receipt of documents. Any time limit which ends on a day when OHIM is not open for business is automatically extended to the next working day when it is open for the receipt of documents *and* on which ordinary mail is delivered (Rule 72(1) IR). OHIM is open from Monday to Friday excluding public holidays. It publishes a notice annually listing days on which it will not be open for business because of public holidays and days on which it will not receive ordinary mail (see, for example, Decision No. ADM-96-29 of the President of OHIM of 8 November 1996 giving the relevant dates for 1997, OHIM OJ 12/96, p. 1713). Provision is also made in Rule 72(2) of the IR for the President to determine the extension of time limits where there is a dislocation in the delivery of mail in a Member State or between a Member State and OHIM, and in Rule 72(4), in cases where the workings of OHIM are affected by exceptional occurrences such as natural disasters or strikes. Paragraphs (1) and (2) of Rule 72 of the IR are also to apply to dealings with national offices effected under Article 25 of the CTMR.

Restitutio in integrum *(Article 78 CTMR)*
All time limits, whether laid down in the CTMR or in the IR, or whether specified by OHIM in its handling of applications, oppositions or cancellation proceedings, are subject to the general principle of restoration of rights found in Article 78 of the CTMR. *Restitutio in integrum* is fully explained in chapter 8. Throughout this work, whenever any reference is made to the consequences of failing to comply with an OHIM time limit, it is implicit that lost rights may be restored if the conditions of Article 78 of the CTMR can be met, unless otherwise stated.

Strategies for the trade mark applicant

Coexistence with national and international systems
Recital 5 of the CTMR states that the CTM system will not replace the trade mark laws of Member States. There will be no compulsion to register at Community level, indeed many undertakings will not want a Community registration. Small and medium enterprises often have very localised businesses, particular in the service sector. National registration will therefore continue to be a viable option for them and the CTMR does not interfere with this freedom of choice. Equally, a small or medium enterprise with a limited amount of overseas business may wish to utilise the Madrid system (United Kingdom applicants will be restricted to the Madrid Protocol list of countries, see appendix 4) as a convenient short cut to obtaining a batch of national 'registrations'.

Choices available
Nevertheless, a trade mark applicant who wishes to obtain registered trade mark protection in more than one country will have a tactical choice to make. Apart from the consideration of cost and the intended geographical scope of the applicant's marketing operations, much will depend on whether the chosen trade mark is visually and linguistically acceptable in all the Member States of the Community and whether there are any prior Community, regional, national or international registrations blocking the way.

By way of illustration, an intending United Kingdom applicant could do one of the following:

(a)   File separate national applications in countries where it is intended to supply goods or services under the mark. This will entail translation costs and the appointment of local agents to effect the registrations, but has the advantage that each national application can be considered on its merits: failure in one country will not have any repercussions elsewhere.

(b)   File an application for a United Kingdom trade mark and on the basis of that application, or, if it is preferred to wait until the application succeeds, on the basis of the United Kingdom registration, apply for an international registration under the Madrid Protocol. If any of the countries where the applicant does business are not members of the Protocol, then individual national registrations will still need to be sought in those states. Even if the international registration is rejected in one country, it can continue in all the others. Another advantage is that the Madrid system has only two languages (French and English) and does away with the need to appoint agents in each country where the mark is to be protected. Further, because of the strict time limit imposed on national registries for dealing with international registrations, the Madrid route may prove to be a quicker method of obtaining protection than by filing individual national applications. The draw-back is the system of 'central attack'. Rejection of the 'home' United Kingdom application, or loss of the United Kingdom registration in the first five years of the international registration means that the international registration is lost, although it can be transformed into a series of national applications.

(c)   File an application for a CTM at OHIM or at the United Kingdom Trade Marks Registry. Individual national applications will have to be made in any countries outside the EC where business is done. The CTM application will have to be acceptable linguistically in all CTM Member States (what is an invented word in one language could be descriptive, deceptive or contrary to public policy in one or more of the other 10 languages). Further, the CTM application could be barred by a national registration existing in just one of the Member States, or by a used but unregistered mark in another. The CTM registration will be vulnerable at any time to attack by way of cancellation proceedings before OHIM or by way of a counterclaim to infringement proceedings. Such attack, if successful, will destroy the whole CTM, although it is possible to convert it into a national registration under Article 108 of the CTMR.

(d)   Adopt the same strategy as in (b) but at the same time file an application for a CTM. If the CTM application fails, seek conversion and obtain national registrations in individual Member States where possible.

Once the Community has acceded to the Madrid Protocol some time in 1998, the possible permutations become even more complicated. Each of the four options above will still be available, but in addition:

(e)   Relying on a United Kingdom application or registration, it will also be possible to apply for an international registration under the Madrid Protocol, designating the EC as one of the 'countries' where protection is sought, in addition to any other non-EC Member States which are members of the Protocol, with national protection sought for countries outside both the CTM and Madrid systems. The risks here are that the United Kingdom application may not succeed (thereby losing both CTM and international protection) or that OHIM may reject the international registration for the reasons given above.

(f)   It will also be possible to file a CTM application and then use this as the basic application under the Madrid Protocol, designating other non-EC Madrid Protocol states where protection is needed and filing individual national applications in those countries outside both systems as appropriate. The risk here is that the CTM application may be rejected or subsequently lost. Should the loss occur in the first five years of the international registration, the consequences of 'central attack' (outlined above) for the international registration dependent on the CTM will come into play.

Chapter Two
Obtaining Registration of a Community Trade Mark 1:
The Basic Conditions

Who may obtain Community trade mark registration?

Any natural or legal person (Articles 5(1) and 3 CTMR)
Any natural or legal person who falls within the categories listed below may apply
for and own a Community trade mark (CTM) registration (Article 5(1) CTMR).
'Legal persons' are defined as:

> . . . companies or firms and other legal bodies . . . if, under the terms of the law
> governing them, they have the capacity in their own name to have rights and
> obligations of all kinds, to make contracts or accomplish other legal acts and to
> sue and be sued. (Article 3 CTMR)

The definition is intended to cover non-legal entities which are recognised under
the applicable national law as legal persons, for example, the German *offene
Handelsgesellschaft* or the Spanish *sociedades colectivas, sociedades comanditarias* or *sociedades comanditarias por acciones* or the Swedish economic
association *(ek för)* (Explanatory Memorandum to the Draft CTMR, COM (80) 635
final of 19 November 1980, reprinted in Bull EC suppl. 5/80).

United Kingdom partnerships (with the exception of Scottish partnership firms) and
unincorporated bodies or associations are unlikely to qualify within the definition. A
CTM registration must therefore be applied for and owned by the group of natural
persons who are presently members of the partnership or of the unincorporated body or
association, which raises the issue of the need for assignment of the CTM application
or registration each time membership of the group changes. Furthermore, thought must
be given to the identity of the joint proprietor first named in the application for
registration. Article 16(3) of the CTMR provides that property rights in a co-owned
CTM will be governed by the law of the EC Member State where the first-named
proprietor has his seat, domicile or establishment or, if none of the proprietors is
Community-based, Spain (property rights in a CTM are explored in chapter 9). The
latter consideration may assume greater importance in connection with international
partnerships or associations which fall outside the definition of legal person.

OHIM has not yet decided whether to follow the practice of the United Kingdom Trade Marks Registry in accepting applications for registration in the name of the partnership or the unincorporated body or association, or in the name of nominee partners or members (*Trade Marks Registry Work Manual*, ch. 3, paras 4.8–4.13). The efficacy of the United Kingdom practice has been doubted since it is not expressly permitted either by the Trade Marks Act 1994 or by the Trade Marks Rules 1994 (or, indeed, the CTMR or the IR). The safest course to ensure the validity of the CTM in these situations is to apply for registration with a full list of partners or members and to assign the CTM application or registration each time a change occurs.

For the United Kingdom, the definition of legal persons includes private companies limited by share capital, private companies limited by guarantee, public limited companies and organisations incorporated by Act of Parliament or royal charter, for example, universities and professional bodies.

Authorities established under public law are expressly stated in the CTMR to be capable of being proprietors of CTMs (Article 5(1)).

Categories of entitlement (Article 5 CTMR)
The categories of entitled natural and legal persons are as follows (Article 5(1) CTMR):

(a)   nationals of EC Member States;
(b)   nationals of non-EC Member States which are parties to the Paris Convention or to the Agreement Establishing the World Trade Organisation (WTO);
(c)   nationals of States which are not parties to the Paris Convention who are domiciled or have their seat or who have real and effective industrial or commercial establishments within the territory of the Community or of a State which is party to the Paris Convention;
(d)   nationals (not falling within paragraph (c) above) of States which are not parties to the Paris Convention or to the Agreement Establishing the WTO and which accord reciprocal trade mark protection to nationals of all EC Member States.

Stateless persons and refugees, with that formal status, are regarded as nationals of the country in which they have their habitual residence (Article 5(2) CTMR).

OHIM keeps a list of countries which have reciprocal arrangements with EC Member States (OHIM Examination Guidelines, Guideline 3.4, OHIM OJ 9/96, p. 1325). Reciprocity with Taiwan was communicated by the Commission in November 1996 (OHIM OJ 12/96, p. 1717). Generally speaking, applicants who qualify by virtue of paragraph (d) must prove that the trade mark which is sought to be registered as a CTM is registered in the country of origin (Article 5(3) CTMR).

The categories of entitled persons were amended by Council Regulation (EC) 3288/94 of 22 December 1994 ([1994] OJ L 349/83) to comply with the EC's obligations under Article 3 of the TRIPs Agreement. Article 3 embodies the principle of national treatment. The EC must give nationals of all WTO countries the same protection as it accords to nationals of EC Member States. However, in order to comply *fully* with TRIPs Article 3, category (c) should have been extended to allow applications from nationals of other States who are domiciled or who have real and effective industrial or commercial establishments in WTO countries (TRIPs Article 1(3), fn. 1). Interestingly, the Italian-language version, but not the Spanish, German, English or French-language versions, of the amended CTMR (OHIM OJ 1/95, p. 53) contains the required extension to category (c). The OHIM Examination Guidelines also contemplate the required extension to category (c) (Guideline 3.4.1(c), OHIM OJ 9/96, p. 1325). OHIM is aware of the discrepancy and it may be that the CTMR is in need of further amendment.

Lists of parties to the Paris Convention and to the Agreement establishing the WTO appear at appendices 1 and 2 respectively.

The term 'real and effective industrial or commercial establishment' comes from the Paris Convention. The words 'real and effective' were added by the Brussels Revision of 1900 in order to prevent abusive or 'sham' claims to the application of the Convention. There is no universal definition of the term because establishment is determined by the domestic legislation of the Convention country in which protection is claimed. OHIM has indicated that the same term in Article 5(1)(c) of the CTMR will be interpreted liberally to include, for example, branch offices.

Apart from the above qualifications, no other requirements relating directly to the proprietor must be satisfied. In particular, the proprietor need not own the business in which a CTM is to be used (one member of a group of companies can hold the CTM which the other companies in the group use), nor is there any requirement for intention to use. However, applying for a CTM in bad faith — described in the OHIM brochure as 'unfair practices involving lack of good faith on the part of the applicant at the time of filing' — is an absolute ground for invalidating the mark under Article 51(1)(b) of the CTMR.

Non-entitlement to a CTM at the time of registration is an absolute ground for invalidity under Article 51(1)(a) of the CTMR. Where the entitlement criteria are not met subsequent to registration, the CTM is liable to be revoked under Article 50(1)(d) of the CTMR. Revocation and invalidity of a CTM are discussed at chapter 5.

Representation

The need for representation (Article 88(2) CTMR)
Any entitled natural or legal person may *file* an application for registration of a CTM directly with OHIM. But applicants having neither domicile nor a principal place of business nor a real and effective industrial or commercial establishment in the Community *must* appoint a qualified representative to act for them in all other proceedings before OHIM (Article 88(2) CTMR).

Who may be a representative? (Articles 89(1) and 88(3) CTMR)
Representation may only be by (Article 89(1) CTMR):

  (a)   a legal practitioner:

     (i)   qualified in one of the Member States,
     (ii)   with a place of business within the EC,
     (iii) competent in the Member State of qualification to act as a representative in trade mark matters (all Member States except Ireland: Communication No. 1/95

of the President of OHIM on professional representatives of 18 September 1995, OHIM OJ 1/95, p. 16; Communication No. 2/96 of the President of OHIM on professional representatives of 22 March 1996, OHIM OJ 5/96, p. 591); or

(b) a professional representative whose name is entered upon the list maintained by OHIM.

Natural or legal persons who are domiciled or established in the EC may choose to represent themselves (Article 88(1) CTMR) or to be represented by a qualified representative or to act through an employee (Article 88(3) CTMR). As an exception to the rule in Article 88(2) of the CTMR, an employee of a legal person who is domiciled or established in the EC may represent another legal person from outside the EC where there are economic connections between these two legal persons, such as common ownership or control. Thus an American or Japanese company having a European subsidiary could be represented by an employee of that subsidiary (Article 88(3) CTMR).

Authorisations (Articles 88(3) and 89(1) CTMR, Rule 76 IR)
All representatives must file with OHIM a general or an individual authorisation to act (Articles 88(3) and 89(1) CTMR; Rule 76(1) and (2) IR). A general authorisation enables the representative to act in all trade mark transactions of the client before OHIM. It will therefore cover any present and future CTM applications or registrations as well as any proceedings before OHIM to which the client is a party. An individual authorisation is limited to specific proceedings, for example, an individual application or registration or opposition proceeding which must be clearly notified. Identity numbers (equivalent to United Kingdom Trade Marks Registry ADP — automatic data processing — numbers) are issued by OHIM to general representatives and to individual representatives where an individual authorisation relates to several proceedings.

Representatives should complete the official authorisation form (provided pursuant to Rule 83(1)(j) IR) which can be obtained from OHIM or trade marks offices of Member States free of charge. The form may be filed in any of the official languages of OHIM (Spanish, German, English, French, Italian) or in the language of the relevant proceedings where this language is not one of the official languages of OHIM (Rule 76(3) IR and see chapter 3). The form must be signed by (or for legal persons on behalf of) the person giving the authorisation (Rule 76(1) IR). The signature need not be certified (in conformity with Article 8(4) of the Trademark Law Treaty 1994). A seal may be affixed.

Entry on the list of professional representatives (Article 89(2)–(5) CTMR)
To be entered on the list of professional representatives maintained by OHIM a person must (Article 89(2) CTMR):

(a) be a national of one of the Member States;
(b) have a place of business or employment within the Community;
(c) be entitled to act as an agent before the trade marks office of the Member State in which that business or employment is located.

The President of OHIM may grant an exemption to the nationality criterion 'in special circumstances' (Article 89(4)(b) CTMR). It is not yet known what these circumstances might be.

Article 89(2) of the CTMR describes three situations in which a representative will meet the entitlement criterion set out in (c) above:

(a) *Special professional qualification.* In some Member States, for example, Austria, Germany, Spain and Portugal, entitlement to act as an agent in trade mark matters depends on acquiring a special professional qualification.

(b) *Five years' habitual exercise.* In Member States where entitlement to represent clients is not conditional on possessing a special professional qualification, the representative must have habitually acted as an agent before the trade marks office concerned for at least five years. The President of OHIM may grant an exemption to the requirement of five years' habitual exercise if an agent can demonstrate acquisition of the necessary qualification in some other way (Article 89(4)(a) CTMR).

(c) *Recognised professional qualification.* As an alternative to (b) above, some Member States recognise a professional qualification as entitling persons to represent clients before their trade marks offices. Thus, for example, entitlement to practice before the United Kingdom Trade Marks Registry is independent of the requirement of special professional qualification but United Kingdom law recognises the professional qualification of registered trade mark agent (ss. 82 to 88 Trade Marks Act 1994). A United Kingdom registered trade mark agent does not have to satisfy the requirement of five years' habitual exercise.

An application for entry in the list of professional representatives must be made on an individual basis (that is, block applications from firms of trade mark agents are impermissible) and on the official OHIM form. The application form is available in all the official languages of the EC except Greek; there are no professional representatives in Greece and representation in trade mark matters must always be by a legal practitioner. The language in which the form is completed will be the language of any procedure relating to the application, except that where the language is not one of the languages of OHIM (Spanish, German, English, French, Italian), the applicant must specify one of these languages as the language of procedure.

The individual application must be certified by the trade marks office of the relevant Member State (Article 89(3) CTMR). Certification may be by block certification (applying to all representatives listed) notified to OHIM by a Member State's trade mark office, or by individual certification. The United Kingdom Patent Office has no mechanism for providing block certification. Applications must be submitted to the United Kingdom Trade Marks Registry for individual certification and onward transmission to OHIM, if appropriate. Representatives from other Member States (for example, Austria, Germany, Ireland or the Benelux) who are covered by block certification may deal directly with OHIM.

Application forms can be obtained from OHIM or Member States' trade marks offices free of charge. No fee is payable for entry on the list. Forms must be completed in typescript to enable transference of data into OHIM's database — the 'list' is kept in electronic form. Entries on the list of professional representatives are published periodically in the *Official Journal* of OHIM (Rule 78(6) IR). OHIM intends to produce a brochure of professional representatives.

By August 1996, the details of over 4,000 professional representatives had been entered in OHIM's database (letter from the President of OHIM, 14 August 1996). This figure has now risen to over 5,000.

Amendment of the list of professional representatives is governed by Rule 78 of the IR (Article 89(5) CTMR). An entry in the list may be deleted voluntarily at the request of the representative or automatically by OHIM on the death or incapacity of the representative or on the representative no longer meeting the entitlement criteria in Article 89(2) CTMR (see above).

Legal practitioners
Legal practitioners are automatically entitled to represent clients before OHIM. They are not (and do not need to be) entered on the list of professional representatives. However, practitioners who are dually qualified (for example, in the United Kingdom, as solicitors and registered trade mark agents) may be entered on the list if they so wish.

What can be a Community trade mark?

Registration not use (Article 6 CTMR)
A CTM can be obtained only by registration and not by use.

Definition (Article 4 CTMR)
Article 4 of the CTMR states that a CTM may consist of:

any signs capable of being represented graphically, particularly words, including personal names, designs, letters, numerals, the shape of goods or of their packaging, provided that such signs are capable of distinguishing the goods or services of one undertaking from those of other undertakings.

Thus the essential requirements for a CTM are:

(a)   a sign (Why 'any signs' in the plural, when Article 2 of the Directive — which is in similar terms — speaks of 'any sign' in the singular?);

(b)   which is capable of being represented graphically; and

(c)   which is capable of distinguishing the goods or services of one undertaking from those of other undertakings.

The above requirements must also be satisfied for national trade marks registered in EC Member States (Article 2 of the Directive).

Any sign (Article 4 CTMR)
'Sign' is not defined in the CTMR. Dictionary definitions reveal that the word has a wide meaning which covers both visual and sensory mechanisms for conveying information (see, for example, *The Oxford English Reference Dictionary* (1995) and *Collins English Dictionary*, 3rd ed. (1994)).

Article 4 of the CTMR gives as examples of signs that may constitute CTMs: words, including personal names, designs, letters, numerals and the shape of goods or of their packaging. The Commission's Explanatory Memorandum to the Draft CTMR (COM (80) 635 final of 19 November 1980, reprinted in Bull EC suppl. 5/80) confirms that the list is neither exhaustive nor determinative *eiusdem generis* of eligible signs:

> No type of sign is automatically excluded from registration as a Community trade mark. Article [4] lists the types of signs used most frequently by undertakings to identify their goods or services, but *it is not an exhaustive list. It is designed to simplify the adaptation of administrative practices and court judgments to business requirements and to encourage undertakings to apply for Community trade marks.* (Emphasis added)

Similarly, the minutes of the Council meeting at which the CTMR was adopted contain the following joint statement on Article 4:

> The Council and the Commission consider that Article 4 does not rule out the possibility:
> — of registering as a Community trade mark a combination of colours or a single colour;
> — of registering in the future sounds as Community trade marks. (Joint statements by the Council and the Commission of the European Communities entered in the minutes of the Council meeting, at which the Regulation on the Community Trade Mark is adopted on 20 December 1993, OHIM OJ 5/96, p. 613)

The Implementing Regulation acknowledges the possibility of registering colour marks (Rule 3) and there is a box (box 61) for claiming colour on the official form for application for a CTM (see appendix 5).

At the time of writing several CTM applications claiming a single colour or a combination of colours for word and/or device marks, labels and the two-dimensional appearance of product packaging have been accepted and published by OHIM, for example: CTM Application No. 000019216 for the blue MSI letter and device mark; CTM Application No. 000029025 for the red and white ROTPUNKT word and device mark; CTM Application No. 000054841 for Direct Line Insurance plc's 'red telephone' device mark; CTM Application No. 000073718 for the blue, white and black HANNEN ALT label mark; and CTM Application No. 000012930 for the white, blue, light blue and pink two dimensional appearance of the packaging for NIVEA BATH CARE products.

Currently accepted and published CTM applications claiming colour also include:

(a)   several CTM applications claiming two shades of the same colour for LOUIS VUITTON designs, for example: CTM Application Nos. 000015651 and 000015669;

(b)   a CTM application for A RED STRIPE IN THE HEEL OF A MAN'S SHOE: CTM Application No. 000043935; and

(c)   a CTM application 'for the distinctive colouring of a container for liquid foods': CTM Application No. 000068775.

One CTM application claiming the colours of three-dimensional product packaging has been accepted and published by OHIM: CTM Application No. 000031203 for the white, yellow, red, blue and black three-dimensional packaging of the TOBLERONE chocolate bar. To date, there has been no accepted and published application for a CTM which consists of the colour of the goods applied for.

The OHIM Examination Guidelines advise that sound marks are registrable in principle (Guideline 8.2, OHIM OJ 9/96, p. 1331) but give little guidance on how applications for sound marks will be treated. No CTM applications for sound marks have so far been published by OHIM following acceptance.

Three-dimensional marks are expressly mentioned in Article 4 of the CTMR. Registrability extends to the three-dimensional form of goods in respect of which registration is sought, as well as to their packaging:

> The Council and the Commission consider that the word 'shape' [in Article 4] is also intended to cover the three-dimensional form of goods (Joint statements by the Council and the Commission of the European Communities entered in the minutes of the meeting, at which the Regulation on the Community Trade Mark is adopted on 20 December 1993, OHIM OJ 5/96, p. 613).

The logistics of three-dimensional mark applications for registration are set out in Rule 3(4) of the IR and are explored further in Guideline 3.7 of the OHIM Examination Guidelines (OHIM OJ 9/96, p. 1326, see below). Eleven applications for three-dimensional CTMs have been accepted and published by OHIM: three applications for the shapes of snack foods (CTM Application Nos. 000014167, 000014217 and 000013342); three applications for the shapes of the TOBLERONE chocolate bar and its packaging (CTM Application Nos. 000031229, 000031237 and 000031203); an application for the shape of the SCHWARTZ SPICE JAR (CTM Application No. 000033423); an application for the shape of a toaster (CTM Application No. 000048728); an application for the shape of a twenty-three-sided pill (CTM Application No. 000089102); an application for the shape of the CHOCOLATE ORANGE (CTM Application No. 000036459); and an application for a 'sweet in a container' (CTM Application No. 000127308).

The list of registrable signs in the publicity brochure produced by OHIM includes slogans, three-dimensional marks, colours or combinations of colours and sound marks, in particular musical phrases. Several applications for slogans have been published by OHIM following acceptance including: LET HERTZ PUT YOU IN THE DRIVING SEAT for cars, equipment leasing and rental car hire services (CTM Application No. 000037416); PROVIDING SOLUTIONS NOW AND INTO THE NEXT CENTURY! for laser printers (CTM Application No. 000064519); and TOMORROW I STOP SMOKING for tobacco products (CTM Application No. 000084715).

As at November 1997 approximately 6,000 CTM applications have been published by OHIM following acceptance. These indicate that OHIM is operating a flexible policy towards the *form* which a CTM may assume. Non-traditional marks, for example, single colours or combinations of colours, slogans, three-dimensional signs and sounds are registrable as CTMs provided they satisfy the other requirements of Article 4. However, a question mark hovers over the registrability of smells since official documentation on the CTM to date is silent on the issue.

The United Kingdom Trade Marks Registry applies one of the most rigorous standards of examination in the Community. In the 34 months following the introduction on 31 October 1994 of a similar definition of 'trade mark' by s. 1 of the Trade Marks Act 1994, 292 three-dimensional marks, 11 sound marks, two smell marks and one gesture mark have been registered in the United Kingdom Register of Trade Marks.

The majority of three-dimensional registrations are for containers and packaging, for example: the COCA-COLA bottle (UK Registration No. 2000548); the MARTELL bottle (UK Registration No. 2008805); the KODAK GOLD film box (UK Registration No. 2000961); the get-up of BRAND X picture hooks (UK Registration No. 2018783); and the PRITT STICK glue container (UK Registration No. 2013019A). Registrations for the three-dimensional shape of goods include: the CHUBB key (UK Registration No. 2008914); the TOBLERONE chocolate bar (UK Registration No. 2000005); 'the end portion of the head-stock of a guitar' (UK Registration No. 2001531); the Ram Golf Corporation golf club (UK Registration No. 2005630); and the MINI car (UK Registration No. 2002390). The shape of a pale green pill with surface markings has also achieved registration (UK Registration No. 2014334).

The registrations for sound marks include: the MR SHEEN jingle (UK Registration Nos. 2013715 and 2013716); the PC WORLD jingle (UK Registration Nos. 2023711a and 2023711b); 'Air on G-String' for tobacco (UK Registration Nos. 2004529a and 2004529b); British Telecom's 'beeps' on the speaking clock (UK Registration No. 2056092); and ICI's THE SOUND OF A DOG BARKING (UK Registration No. 2007456).

The smell registrations comprise 'the strong smell of bitter beer' in respect of dart flights (UK Registration No. 2000234) and the following registration for a series of smell marks (UK Registration No. 2001416):

The trade mark consists of a floral fragrance/smell as applied to tyres.
The trade mark is a floral fragrance smell.
The trade mark is a floral fragrance/smell reminiscent of roses.
The trade mark is a floral fragrance/smell reminiscent of roses as applied to tyres.

One gesture mark has been registered — the Derbyshire Building Society's 'gesture made by a person by tapping one side of his/her nose with an extended finger, normally the index finger of the hand on the side of the nose being tapped' (UK Registration No. 2012603) — and the ASDA 'pocket tapping gesture' has been applied for and is presently undergoing examination (UK Application No. 2048673).

Registration has also been achieved for single colours, for example: PURPLE for cleaning fluids (UK Registration No. 2009633); COBALT-BLUE 'applied to the bottle as shown on the form of application' for bottled waters (UK Registration No. 2001526); and PINK for fibrous glass insulation (UK Registration No. 2004215 and see the decision of the United States Court of Appeals for the Federal Circuit in *Re Owens-Corning Fiberglas Corporation* (1985) 774 F 2d 1116, 227 USPQ 417). An application for British Petroleum's GREEN (UK Application No. 2012663) has been advertised but is opposed.

Further United Kingdom registrations for unusual marks include: 'the external shape of a dining, restaurant, hotel, entertainment and shopping complex housed inside large-scale beverage cans' (UK Registration No. 2048209); and the layout of the cover page of the DAILY MAIL WEEKEND magazine (UK Registration No. 2002557).

The OHIM Examination Guidelines state that the role of examiners is to facilitate applications for registration within the substantive boundaries of the CTMR (Guideline 2.1, OHIM OJ 9/96, p. 1324). Furthermore examiners should take 'particular account of registrations of trade marks under examination systems in Member States which apply standards of absolute grounds of refusal similar to those in the Regulation' (OHIM Examination Guidelines, Guideline 8.1.4, OHIM OJ 9/96, p. 1330). Such is the case for the United Kingdom.

Indeed, accepted and published CTM applications at the time of writing suggest that it may be easier to register some marks, in particular those consisting of two letters or descriptive signs, as CTMs at OHIM rather than as national trade marks in Member States (see below).

Capable of graphic representation (Article 4 CTMR, Rule 3 IR)
The second requirement in Article 4 of the CTMR is that a sign must be capable of graphic representation.

The requirement is necessary in order to enable interested parties to ascertain the scope of existing CTM rights, either by consulting the *Community Trade Marks Bulletin* or by conducting a search of the Register of CTMs. This means that for the purposes of registration, a CTM must be in a form which can be recorded and published. The requirement also aids owners of earlier marks (see 'Relative grounds for refusal' below) to check the *Bulletin* for conflicting applications for CTMs.

The basic rules governing representation of a CTM are set out in Rule 3 of the IR and summarised at Guideline 3.7 of the OHIM Examination Guidelines (OHIM OJ 9/96, p. 1326).

Rule 3(1) of the IR states that if the applicant does not wish to claim any special graphic feature or colour the mark must be reproduced in normal script, for example, by typing the letters, numerals and signs in the application. The use of small and capital letters is permitted. Paragraphs (2) and (3) of Rule 3 then go on to state that in other cases the application must indicate this fact and the mark must be reproduced on a separate piece of paper. The implication of Rule 3(1) of the IR is that non-stylised word, numeral and letter marks may simply be typed or written into the application form. However, this could be made clearer on the OHIM application form, which requires the applicant to represent anything other than a word mark on a separate sheet and to specify in the application the type of mark applied for (see boxes 55–60).

Where the mark is reproduced on a separate sheet of paper, this must be no larger than A4 size. The space used for the reproduction must not exceed 26.2 cm × 17 cm with a minimum margin of 2.5 cm on the left-hand side. The correct orientation of the mark, if this is not obvious, must be indicated by writing the word 'top' on the reproduction. The reproduction must be of sufficient quality to enable publication of the mark in the *Community Trade Marks Bulletin* in a box 8 cm wide by 16 cm high (8 cm × 8 cm where the mark forms the basis of an international application for registration, see chapter 10). The official position on the subsequent supply of camera-ready copy is unclear. It is necessary to file one copy only of the separate representation of a mark (Decision No. EX-95-1 of the President of OHIM, OHIM OJ 4/95, p. 491). The copy must bear the name and address of the applicant (Rule 3(2) IR).

A three-dimensional mark may be represented either by line drawings or by photographs. Six different perspectives of the mark may be supplied, provided that these fit on the one sheet. The applicant must state on the application form (by checking box 58) that a three-dimensional mark is applied for (Rule 3(4) IR). A written description of the mark is optional (Rule 3(3) IR, boxes 64–5).

The procedure for claiming colour (Rule 3(5) IR) fails to distinguish between a mark consisting:

(a)   exclusively of a colour or colours; and
(b)   colour applied to a shape or a device.

The applicant must indicate on the application form that colour is claimed and must indicate the colour or colours making up the mark (boxes 61–3). There is no requirement that the colour be defined by a Pantone or similar standard. OHIM Examination Guideline 3.7 (OHIM OJ 9/96, p. 1326) advises that 'the applicant is free to use his own description of the colours'. Most published CTM applications have claimed colour merely by reference to the name of the colour, for example, 'Yellow and blue' (CTM Application No. 000012617) although some have utilised the Pantone standard, for example, 'Pantone 375C and pantone 350C' (CTM Application No. 000012880). A reproduction of the mark shown *in colour* must be provided on a separate sheet. Where the mark consists exclusively of colour this will entail supplying a sample of the actual colour applied for. The applicant may include a written description of the mark in the application form (Rule 3(3) IR, boxes 64–5).

The above practice differs from that of the United Kingdom Trade Marks Registry, who will accept a written description of a mark consisting exclusively of colour as an alternative to a sample of the actual colour claimed plus a written description of the mark. A black-and-white representation of a device or a shape mark incorporating colour suffices, provided that this is accompanied by a written description of the colour making up the mark. In either case, the colour must be precisely defined by a Pantone or some other widely known and easily available standard, for example, light green as defined by Pantone standard 1234 (*Trade Marks Registry Work Manual*, ch. 6, 3.1–3.3).

Rule 3 of the IR gives no guidance on the representation of a sound mark other than that it must be on a separate sheet of paper (Rule 3(2) IR). The OHIM Examination Guidelines state that musical notation may be an acceptable form of graphic representation (Guideline 8.2, OHIM OJ 9/96, p. 1331). The applicant must state on the CTM application form that a sound mark is applied for (boxes 59–60). A written description of the sound mark may be added to the form at the applicant's option (Rule 3(3) IR, boxes 64–5). United Kingdom registrations for sound marks have been represented by musical notation and also by written description (see above). The United Kingdom Trade Marks Registry will not accept as graphic representation of sound marks the names of pieces of music, which are considered too imprecise (*Trade Marks Registry Work Manual*, ch. 6, 4.1–4.2).

There is no mention of smell/scent marks in either the IR or the Examination Guidelines. American and United Kingdom practices suggest that a smell/scent mark can be defined adequately in words (*Re Clark* (1990) 17 USPQ 2d 1238; *Trade Marks Registry Work Manual*, ch. 6, 6.1 and the UK registrations described above).

Capable of distinguishing the goods or services of one undertaking from those of other undertakings (Article 4 CTMR)
The interpretation of the third requirement in Article 4 of the CTMR is problematic. It suggests a test of distinctiveness (similar to the test of distinctiveness for Part B marks under s. 10 of the United Kingdom Trade Marks Act 1938) whereas it is, in fact, a test of *validity* (like the nationality conditions set out in Article 5 CTMR).

This is made clear by the absolute grounds for refusal of registration of a CTM, which are based on Article 6*quinquies* of the Paris Convention. Our particular concern is with the grounds contained in Article 7(1)(a) and (b) of the CTMR, which correspond to Article 6*quinquies*A(1) and B(2) of the Paris Convention.

Article 7(1)(a) of the CTMR provides that registration shall be refused to *signs* which do not conform with the requirements of Article 4. Thus, Article 4 embodies the *telle quelle* principle of Article 6*quinquies*A(1) of the Paris Convention (to accept for registration marks registered in other Contracting Parties), that is, Article 4 is an *enabling* provision. But Article 7(1)(a) retains the legitimate right within *telle quelle* to deny registration to those signs which do not qualify as *trade marks* under Community law.

In contrast, Article 7(1)(b) of the CTMR, like its counterpart Article 6*quinquies*B(2) of the Paris Convention, assumes that the sign is a *trade mark* (that is, the sign passes the basic validity test) but provides that the trade mark shall not be registered if, considered on its individual merits, the mark is devoid of any distinctive character. The distinctiveness or otherwise of a particular mark is an issue for Article 7(1)(b) but not Articles 4 and 7(1)(a) of the CTMR.

The third requirement in Article 4 of the CTMR is, therefore, addressing the question whether a sign performs or is intended to perform the function of a trade mark:

> [Article 4] is geared particularly to the question whether the relevant sign is capable of performing the basic function of a trade mark. (Bull EC suppl. 5/80, p. 56)

That function, according to Article 4, is to distinguish the goods or services of one undertaking from those of other undertakings, that is, a product differentiation function. However, it is noted for future discussion that Recital 7 of the Preamble to the CTMR states (in the context of infringement rights) that the function of a CTM is: '. . . *in particular* to guarantee the trade mark as an indication of origin' (emphasis added).

The difference between the requirements that a sign functions as a trade mark and that a trade mark is distinctive can be illustrated by reference to two cases decided under the pre-harmonised United Kingdom trade marks law (Trade Marks Act 1938). Both cases concerned the registrability of single colours for pharmaceutical drugs in tablet form.

In *John Wyeth & Bro. Ltd's Coloured Tablet Trade Mark* [1988] RPC 233, the applicants used the colours blue and yellow to denote respective dosages. Their applications for registration were refused because the colours were not being used as trade marks.

By contrast, in *Smith Kline & French Laboratories Ltd's Cimetidine Trade Mark* [1991] RPC 17, the applicants adduced evidence to show that they adopted the colour pale green in order to distinguish their cimetidine tablets from other tablets for gastric disorders then on the market. Peter Gibson J held that the applicants' pale green colour was a trade mark but that the applicants had failed to demonstrate that it was distinctive of their cimetidine tablets because the use of pale green and similar colours was so common in the pharmaceutical trade.

In *AD2000 Trade Mark* [1997] RPC 168, the applicant for registration under the United Kingdom Trade Marks Act 1994 (which contains similar provisions to Articles 4 and 7(1)(a) and (b) CTMR) argued that if a sign was capable of distinguishing within the definition of a trade mark, then objection could not be taken to the registration of that trade mark on the ground that it was devoid of any distinctive character. The Appointed Person, Geoffrey Hobbs QC, explained the distinction between paras (a) and (b) of s. 3(1) of the 1994 Act (the equivalent of Article 7(1)(a) and (b) CTMR) as follows. In order to be registrable under the 1994 Act a sign must possess the positive features set out in the definition of a trade mark but none of the negative features set out in the absolute grounds for refusal of registration. Thus a sign may satisfy the definition of a trade mark because it is not *incapable* of distinguishing the goods or services of one undertaking from those of other undertakings, but may still not be registrable because it is considered devoid of any distinctive character. While s. 3(1)(a) of the 1994 Act (Article 7(1)(a) CTMR) concerns *signs* which do not qualify as trade marks, s. 3(1)(b) of that Act (Article 7(1)(b) CTMR) concerns *trade marks* which are not distinctive of the goods or services applied for.

It is, however, inevitable that in certain cases objections to registration will be raised both on the ground that a sign is incapable of distinguishing and on the ground that a mark is devoid of any distinctive character. This is recognised by the OHIM Examination Guidelines, which give the example of an application to register the word 'beer' in respect of beer (Guideline 8.1.1, OHIM OJ 9/96, p. 1330).

A complication manifests itself in the form of a proviso to the absolute grounds for refusal to the effect that an objection on the ground, inter alia, that a mark is devoid of any distinctive character can be overcome by evidence showing that the mark has become distinctive of the applicant's goods or services through use (Article 7(3) CTMR). (The proviso also applies to objections raised under Article 7(1)(c) and (d) that a mark is descriptive or generic respectively.)

The proviso does not state that evidence of use, in the form of public and/or trade recognition, cannot be adduced to demonstrate that a sign is capable of performing the function of a trade mark; that is, to overcome an objection that a sign does not conform to the requirements of Article 4 (Article 7(1)(a) CTMR).

Indeed, the practice of the United Kingdom Trade Marks Registry on substantially the same legislation (ss. 1(1) and 3(1)(a) Trade Marks Act 1994) is to require such evidence in the case of applications to register certain forms of non-traditional marks, for example, single colours, smells, some containers and the three-dimensional shape of goods in respect of which registration is sought (*Trade Marks Registry Work Manual*, ch. 6, 2.4, 2.7 and 2.8 and see the majority of the United Kingdom registrations cited above). However, there has been some relaxation of the practice, in particular for sound and shape marks (see, for example, *Trade Marks Journal*, No. 6166, 12 March 1997, p. xvi) since the decision in *AD2000 Trade Mark*.

Disconcertingly, the OHIM Examination Guidelines state that an objection raised under Article 7(1)(a) of the CTMR that a sign is not capable of distinguishing the goods or services of one undertaking from those of other undertakings cannot be overcome 'if it is shown that the trade mark has become distinctive in consequence of use' (Guideline 8.1.2, OHIM OJ 9/96, p. 1330).

The Guidelines suggest the confusion alluded to above between whether a sign functions as a trade mark and distinctiveness. The worry is that certain signs, though 100 per cent distinctive in fact, may be considered incapable *in law* of distinguishing due to a lack of *inherent* distinctiveness. An applicant might then be placed in the invidious position of being able to demonstrate through evidence of use that, say, the laudatory epithet 'perfection' or the colour pink is distinctive of the applicant's goods but not a trade mark. This 'Catch 22' brings to mind Lord Templeman's words in *COCA-COLA Trade Marks* [1986] RPC 421: 'A bottle is a container not a mark'. (The famous COCA-COLA bottle has since been registered under the new United Kingdom Trade Marks Act 1994 (UK Registration No. 2000548) and was the first three-dimensional mark to be placed on the United Kingdom Register.)

It is suggested that this cannot be the correct interpretation of the proviso to the absolute grounds for refusal of registration in Article 7(1). Such an interpretation would defeat the *enabling* purpose of Article 4. As Jacob J stated in *British Sugar plc* v *James Robertson & Sons Ltd* [1996] RPC 281 when confronted with similar argument based on ss. 1(1) and 3(1) of the United Kingdom Trade Marks Act 1994:

> If a mark on its face is non-distinctive (and ordinary descriptive and laudatory words fall into this class) but is shown to have a distinctive character in fact then it must be capable of distinguishing.

Currently accepted and published CTM applications indicate that OHIM will only raise an objection under Article 7(1)(a) of the CTMR where the sign applied for is clearly *incapable* of distinguishing the relevant goods or services (in the sense of *AD2000 Trade Mark*), as in the cited example of 'beer' for beer. For example, unlike their United Kingdom counterparts, the TOBLERONE three-dimensional CTM applications are proceeding without evidence of acquired distinctiveness through use. If such is OHIM's practice, then whether the applicant can adduce evidence to show that his sign is performing a trade mark function becomes a purely academic question.

Goods and services (Article 1(1) CTMR)
A CTM is registrable for both goods and services. No distinction is made in the CTMR between trade marks and service marks, with the term 'Community trade mark' being used synonymously to refer to either (Article 1(1) CTMR).

Controversially, retail store service marks are *not* registrable as CTMs:

The Council and the Commission consider that the activity of retail trading in goods is not as such a service for which a Community trade mark may be registered under this Regulation. (Joint statements by the Council and the Commission of the European Communities entered in the minutes of the meeting, at which the Regulation on the Community Trade Mark is adopted on 20 December 1993, OHIM OJ 5/96, p. 613; and see OHIM Examination Guidelines, Guideline 4.3, OHIM OJ 9/96, p. 1327)

The above rule corresponds with the position in the majority of the Member States including the United Kingdom. Only the Benelux, Italy, Portugal and Sweden permit registration of a mark for 'retail store services' as such.

Can the shape of goods be registered for services?   Two three-dimensional marks registered under the harmonised United Kingdom trade marks law (the Trade Marks Act 1994) raise an interesting point of construction on Article 4 CTMR. The marks are the BRITISH SCHOOL OF MOTORING three-cornered pyramid (UK Registration No. 2000021) and the DIRECT LINE telephone on wheels (UK Registration No. 2000821). Both marks are registered in respect of services and each is distinctive in the United Kingdom for its respective service. But do the marks registered in each case consist of the shape of goods (or of their packaging) as required by s. 1(1) of the United Kingdom Trade Marks Act 1994 or Article 4 of the CTMR? Can the shape of a good (not the subject of the specification for registration) be registered in respect of services? It remains to be seen whether OHIM will follow the United Kingdom Trade Marks Registry's lead.

What cannot be a Community trade mark?

The CTMR presumes that any sign which meets the criteria of Article 4 can be a CTM. The presumption is then limited by express grounds for refusal in subsequent Articles of the CTMR which stipulate what *cannot* be a CTM. The grounds for refusal fall into three categories:

(a)   failure to comply with the conditions of filing and/or entitlement (Articles 36 and 37 CTMR);
(b)   the absolute grounds for refusal of registration (Article 7 CTMR); and
(c)   the relative grounds for refusal of registration (Article 8 CTMR).

OHIM may only examine and, if appropriate, object to an application for CTM registration on grounds (a) and (b). The relative grounds for refusal must be raised by the owner of an earlier conflicting mark or right on opposition.

The remainder of chapter 2 deals with the absolute and relative grounds for refusal of CTM registration. Failure to comply with the conditions of filing and/or entitlement is discussed in the context of registration procedure in chapter 3.

Absolute grounds for refusal of registration

Article 7 CTMR
We have noted that the list of absolute grounds for refusal of registration of a CTM is based to a large extent on Article 6*quinquies* of the Paris Convention and that

failure to meet the validity requirements of Article 4 will result in non-registration (Article 7(1)(a)).

The remaining grounds in Article 7(1) comprise public-interest matters which are considered to stand in the way of the registration of a mark as a CTM, for example, the mark is descriptive, generic or misleading in relation to the goods or services, or the mark is contrary to public order or accepted principles of morality. When applying these grounds each mark should be considered on its individual merits. Article 4 (the enabling provision) requires that a mark is not refused registration merely because, for example, it consists of a geographical name as such although examination may prove that the mark, considered on its individual merits, *is* purely descriptive as to the geographical origin of the goods or services applied for.

Article 7(1) of the CTMR closely follows the wording of Article 3(1) of the Directive (with the exception of Article 7(1)(j) which was added by Council Regulation (EC) No. 3288/94 of 22 December 1994, [1994] OJ L 349/83 in order to comply with Article 23 of the TRIPs Agreement). The absolute grounds for refusal of CTM registration should therefore mirror the absolute grounds for refusal of trade mark registration under national laws of Member States (although there may be a slight variation due to the optional absolute grounds for refusal which Member States are permitted to incorporate into national laws by Article 3(2) of the Directive, for example, that the application for registration of the trade mark was made in bad faith by the applicant; and see the United Kingdom Trade Marks Act 1994, s. 3(6)).

Accordingly the OHIM Examination Guidelines advise (Guideline 8.1.4, OHIM OJ 9/96, p. 1330):

> If a trade mark is already registered in many or all the Member States of the Community this will be an indication to the examiner that absolute grounds for refusal are unlikely to exist. Examiners should take particular account of registrations under examination systems in Member States which apply standards of absolute grounds for refusal similar to those in the Regulation. In neither case will existing registrations be decisive for the examiner but he will have to take them into account.

A further consequence of this congruence in absolute grounds for refusal should be consistency in the practices of OHIM and trade mark offices of Member States in examining applications for the registration of trade marks. However, early indications are that less strict standards are being used by OHIM to judge the registrability of certain signs than in some Member States including the United Kingdom. Perceived differences in practices are discussed in the context of the particular ground.

The absolute grounds for refusal in Article 7(1) are set out below. There may be overlap in any particular case, so that an application for CTM registration may be objected to on one or more of the absolute grounds. OHIM separately details any objections raised, that is, spells out each ground of objection (OHIM Examination Guidelines, Guideline 8.1.2, OHIM OJ 9/96, p. 1330). In applying the absolute grounds for refusal, the examiners consult standard dictionaries in all the official languages of the Community and use 'specialist technical reference material' (OHIM Examination Guidelines, Guideline 8.1.3, OHIM OJ 9/96, p. 1330). As practices develop and reference material is decided on, the OHIM Guidelines will be expanded.

An application for CTM registration must be refused if a ground for objection exists in *any part* of the Community (Article 7(2) CTMR).

Signs which do not conform with the requirements of Article 4 — Article 7(1)(a)
This ground for refusal is discussed above.

The term 'sign' is interpreted broadly to include colours, three-dimensional marks, slogans and sounds. The registrability of smells, tastes and feels and, possibly, gesture and concept marks awaits clarification.

The requirement for graphic representation is likely to pose problems only for applicants for non-traditional marks. The onus is on the applicant or the representative to file a *correct* representation of the mark applied for. Article 44(2) of the CTMR only permits the correction of errors in an application which do not 'substantially change the trade mark'. Applicants submitting line drawings of shape marks or musical notation of sound marks should consider whether facsimile transmission pursuant to Rule 79 of the IR is an appropriate method of filing such applications (although provision is made in Rule 80(2) of the IR for applicants to be notified by OHIM of the receipt of incomplete, illegible or obviously inaccurate faxes). An application for a colour mark may be filed with OHIM by fax and will be deemed to have been received on that date, provided an original reproduction of the mark in colour is filed within one month (Rule 80(1) IR). The United Kingdom Trade Marks Registry does not consider facsimile transmission to be an appropriate method of filing a mark in colour (*Trade Marks Registry Work Manual*, ch. 6, para. 7.1). This may mean submission of the original for applicants choosing to make a CTM application through the United Kingdom Patent Office (see chapter 3).

The requirement that a sign be capable of distinguishing is aimed at ensuring that a CTM performs or is intended to perform the function of product differentiation. It is a low-threshold test of registrability, which, contrary to the suggestion in the OHIM Examination Guidelines (see above), an applicant ought to be able to satisfy, if necessary, by filing appropriate evidence of use.

Trade marks which are devoid of any distinctive character — Article 7(1)(b)
Article 7(1)(b) of the CTMR prohibits the registration of trade marks which are devoid of any distinctive character. The ground is also found in Article 6*quinquies*B(2) of the Paris Convention and Article 3(1)(b) of the Directive.

In *British Sugar plc* v *James Robertson & Sons Ltd* [1996] RPC 281 Jacob J proffered the following definition of 'devoid of any distinctive character' in s. 3(1)(b) of the United Kingdom Trade Marks Act 1994 (implementing Article 3(1)(b) of the Directive) in relation to the trade mark TREAT registered for dessert sauces and syrup:

Next, is 'Treat' within s.3(1)(b)? What does *devoid of any distinctive character* mean? I think the phrase requires consideration of the mark on its own, assuming no use. Is it the sort of word (or other sign) which cannot do the job of distinguishing without first educating the public that it is a trade mark?

The kind of mark (when considered on its individual merits) to which OHIM might be expected to object under Article 7(1)(b) is, for example: a one or two-letter or numeral mark; a single-colour mark (*Smith Kline & French Laboratories Ltd's Cimetidine Trade Mark* [1991] RPC 17); a design or a shape which is considered too simple or too ordinary to be distinctive (for example, a line, a dot or a single star; a red stripe in toothpaste (*Unilever Ltd's (Striped Toothpaste No. 2) Trade Marks* [1987] RPC 13: note, however, that Unilever's United Kingdom application for the shape of a slug of red and white toothpaste is now proceeding to registration because of distinctiveness acquired through use — United Kingdom Application No. 2005137); and a mark which does not consist *exclusively* of a description, a generic sign or a functional shape, but even with the addition of other elements, is considered devoid of any distinctive character.

This is confirmed by the OHIM Examination Guidelines which state at Guideline 8.3 (OHIM OJ 9/96, p. 1331):

> The trade mark must not be devoid of distinctive character and must therefore do more than describe the goods or services whether in words or graphically. A word such as 'wine' in respect of wine is devoid of distinctive character. A trade mark consisting of one or two letters or digits, unless represented in an unusual fashion, would, except in special circumstances, be considered devoid of distinctive character. . . .

> Simple designs such as circles or squares, whether on their own or in conjunction with descriptive elements, are generally considered to be devoid of distinctive character. Single, especially primary colours, of simple designs are usually devoid of distinctive character. Where a trade mark consists of a combination of several elements which on their own would be devoid of distinctive character, the trade mark taken as a whole may have distinctive character.

> However, if the trade mark comprises nothing more than a combination of [a description, a generic sign or a functional shape] it is likely to be devoid of distinctive character.

Nevertheless, OHIM already seems to have created an exception to its own Guideline in the case of two-letter marks. There is a noticeable number of published CTM applications for such marks which have apparently been accepted for registration without evidence of acquired distinctiveness through use (Rule 12(i) of the IR requires the publication of a CTM to contain, where applicable, a statement that the mark has become distinctive through the use which has been made of it). Examples include: A & E for hand tools (CTM Application No. 000022343); and R & A for sound recordings and video tapes (CTM Application No. 000077685). This is contrary at least to United Kingdom Trade Marks Registry Practice (*Trade Marks Registry Work Manual*, ch. 6, para. 6.2).

Stylisation, for example, the use of italics or a fancy typeface, is of itself insufficient to confer distinctive character on a trade mark:

> I am, of course, aware that the words 'Toffee Treat' are written in a fancy way. But then so are many other mere descriptors. One only has to look at how British Sugar write such words as 'meringue mix' or 'golden syrup' to see parallel sorts

of use. I do not think this affects the matter one way or the other. (Jacob J in *British Sugar plc* v *James Robertson & Sons Ltd* [1996] RPC 281 and OHIM Examination Guideline 8.3)

However, where a mark is graphically represented in an unusual or fanciful manner it will not be objected to under Article 7(1)(b). Again the OHIM standard of unusual or fanciful seems to be lower than that applied by the German and United Kingdom trade mark offices (*Trade Marks Journal*, No. 6186, 30 July 1997, p. xiii, citing a recent decision by the 24th German Appeal Senate relating to Article 3(1)(b) of the Directive). As far as one can discern from the publications, the marks EXCELLENT, E & E and H.I.S, each in prominent letters and set against rectangular backgrounds, have, for example, been accepted by OHIM prima facie and without evidence of use (CTM Application Nos. 000043836, 000031591 and 000030817).

The practice of the United Kingdom Trade Marks Registry is to object to common surnames under this head. OHIM has not adopted a similar practice.

Even though a mark might be considered prima facie lacking in distinctive character, it may be registered if the applicant can prove that it has become distinctive of the goods or services for which registration is sought in consequence of the use which has been made of it (Article 7(3) discussed below).

The applicant may be required to disclaim exclusive rights to non-distinctive elements of a mark as a condition of registration (Article 38 CTMR, see chapter 3).

Trade marks which consist exclusively of signs or indications which may serve, in trade, to designate the kind, quality, quantity, intended purpose, value, geographical origin or the time of production of the goods or of rendering of the service, or other characteristics of the goods or service — Article 7(1)(c)

Registration must be refused under Article 7(1)(c) of the CTMR if a trade mark is *purely descriptive*, that is, if it consists *exclusively* of signs or indications which may serve *in trade* to designate particulars of the goods or services concerned as indicated in the ground. Marks which consist of a description and other elements cannot be refused registration under this head, but may be refused registration under Article 7(1)(b) above.

The ground appears to be quite specific about signs which may not be registered, but the final term 'other characteristics of the goods or services' is very broad. This is especially true since all signs are considered in each of the 11 languages of the Community (Article 7(2) CTMR).

The OHIM Examination Guidelines give (at Guideline 8.4.1, OHIM OJ 9/96, p. 1331) the following examples of signs to which examiners should object under Article 7(1)(c):

kind, for example 'light' for low-tar cigarettes;
quality, for example 'premium';
quantity, for example numbers, whether in words or digits, will often describe quantity;
intended purpose, for example 'kitchen' or 'bathroom' for cleaning agents;
value, for example, 'cheapest';

geographical origin, namely the place, whether locality, region or country where the goods are produced or the service is provided or where the relevant public would expect that this would be the case;
the time of production of the goods, for example a particular year for wine or 'fresh each day' for vegetables;
the time of rendering of the service, for example '24-hour banking';
other characteristics of the goods or services, such as 'lead free' for petrol.

The public-policy objective is that trade descriptions should remain in the public domain. Therefore, registration will be refused even where a description as such is not known to the general public and, so far as they are concerned, is not devoid of any distinctive character. By contrast, registration will not be refused to a description which has been 'borrowed' from one trade into another for which it has no relevance:

For example, expressions such as 4 × 3 in building trades refer to the size of products, but might not be common usage to describe a dozen eggs in the retail trade. (OHIM Examination Guidelines, Guideline 8.4.2, OHIM OJ 9/96, p. 1331)

Plenty of precedents exist in Member States for testing the registrability of a descriptive mark by reference to what other traders might wish to use. Article 7(1)(c) of the CTMR is in similar terms to Article 6*quinquies*B(2) of the Paris Convention and is in identical terms to Article 3(1)(c) of the Directive. For example, in the Benelux the mark P20 was not considered registrable for suntanning preparations (*APS v Ultrasun AG* [1996] BIE 60), whereas the mark SNAPPY was accepted for registration in respect of photo and film equipment (Court of Amsterdam, [1984] BIE 188). Similarly, in the United Kingdom the mark SUPERWOUND was refused registration for guitar strings (*SUPERWOUND Trade Mark* [1988] RPC 272), but the mark POUND PUPPIES was accepted for registration in respect of toy dogs (*POUND PUPPIES Trade Mark* [1988] RPC 530). In Germany the mark PRE-MIERE was denied registration for paints and lacquers (*'Premiere'* [1993] GRUR 746), whereas the mark RIGIDITE was allowed registration for compound materials (*RIGIDITE* [1988] GRUR 3798). In Finland the mark INSTALL/1 was refused registration for computers and computer manuals (*Arthur Anderson & Co., Société Coopérative*, Board of Appeal of the Patent Office, No. 27/T93, 21 September 1994), and in France the mark MULTIMEDIA was refused registration for entertainment services (Paris Court of Appeal, decision of 28 September 1994).

A German court (the Landgericht München I) has recently referred questions on the interpretation of Article 3(1)(c) of the Directive (the equivalent of Article 7(1)(c) CTMR) to the European Court of Justice for a ruling, including:

(a)   whether there must be a possibility, likelihood, need or qualified need that other traders might wish to use a mark consisting of a geographical indication;

(b)   whether (a) is affected by the defence to infringement that traders may use a geographical mark to describe the origin of their goods provided that such use is in accordance with honest practices (see chapter 7);

(c)   whether the test for the registrability of geographical indications is the same as for other descriptive signs or whether the test varies according to the need to leave the sign free for other traders' use; and

(d)   in particular, whether the German tribunals' approach of testing the registrability of descriptive signs against acceptance in more than 50 per cent of the trade circles concerned is compatible with Article 3(1)(c) of the Directive (*WSC Windsurfing Chiemsee Produktions- und Vertriebs GmbH* v *Boots- und Segelzubehör Walter Huber* and *WSC Windsurfing Chiemsee Produktions- und Vertriebs GmbH* v *Franz Attenberger* (cases C-108 and 109/97) [1997] OJ C 166/4).

In *Re Trade Mark Applications by Elvis Presley Inc.* [1997] RPC 543 Laddie J decided that three ELVIS marks in respect of toiletries were not registrable under United Kingdom trade marks law. The word 'Elvis' was so well known to the public as the name of the famous singer that other traders would legitimately wish to use the word to describe the characteristics of their memorabilia. In contrast, CTM Applications for BATMAN, BATMOBILE and WONDER-WOMAN for a variety of goods including computer games have been accepted and published by OHIM (CTM Application Nos. 000038174, 000038190 and 000038224).

An objection under Article 7(1)(c) can be overcome by evidence of use showing that the mark is distinctive in fact (Article 7(3) CTMR, see below).

Currently published CTM applications which it might have been difficult to persuade at least the United Kingdom Trade Marks Registrar to accept in the absence of evidence of use include: EURO-HAIR for haircare products, hairpieces and hair salons (CTM Application No. 000011106; compare *EUROLAMB Trade Mark* [1997] RPC 279, *Trade Marks Journal*, No. 6166, 12 March 1997, p. xii); AUTOSAIL for sailboats (CTM Application No. 000011221); LONG-LIFE for rotary tools (CTM Application No. 000033696); 2000+ for sheet metal rolls (CTM Application No. 000035865; compare *AD2000* [1997] RPC 168, *Trade Marks Journal*, No. 6166, 12 March 1997, p. xiii); CAMBRIDGE for stationery and paper goods (CTM Application No. 000033357); RAVEGUM for chewing gum (CTM Application No. 000037937); NETCOOL for computer software (CTM Application No. 000070789; compare *Trade Marks Journal*, No. 6166, 12 March 1997, p. xi); and EXCELFRUIT for fresh fruits and vegetables (CTM Application No. 000005538). None of the cited CTM applications is published with a statement of acquired distinctiveness through use.

Finally, it should be observed that signs and indications under this provision may include not only written descriptions but also descriptions in the form of pictures (for example, a picture of a car for car cleaning products). Furthermore, there is no reason in principle why Article 7(1)(c) of the CTMR should not operate to exclude from registration descriptive colours, shapes, packaging and sensory signs. In France the shape of a bottle was partially refused registration in respect of 'glass packaging for alcoholic drinks' (the registration was allowed for 'glass packaging excepting those for alcoholic drinks') because the shape of the bottle was the usual shape for champagne (Paris Court of Appeal [1995] PIBD 589–III–290).

The OHIM Examination Guidelines are silent as to the treatment of phonetic equivalents of objectionable words which presumably fall within the ambit of the provision. Phonetic equivalents may cause problems to examiners working in the 11 languages of the Community.

Trade marks which consist exclusively of signs or indications which have become customary in the current language or in the bona fide and established practices of the trade — Article 7(1)(d)

Article 7(1)(d) of the CTMR provides an absolute ground for refusal of marks which the trade uses generically, that is, as the name of or the signification for the goods or services for which registration is sought. Examples from United Kingdom case law include 'gramophone' (*Gramophone Co.'s Application* [1910] 2 Ch 423) and 'shredded wheat' (*Shredded Wheat Co. Ltd* v *Kellogg Co. of Great Britain Ltd* (1940) 57 RPC 137); and from United States case law, 'air shuttle' (*Eastern Air Lines* v *New York Air Lines Inc.* (1983) 559 F Supp 1270) and 'turbo diesel' (*Cummins Engine Co.* v *Continental Motors Corp.* (1996) 359 F 2d 892). The OHIM Examination Guidelines point further to the words 'net' and 'network' for computers and to the letter 'L' for driving schools (Guideline 8.5, OHIM OJ 9/96, p. 1331).

The ground applies where the mark consists *exclusively* of a generic trade sign or indication (combination marks may be excluded under Article 7(1)(b) above). The mark is tested against the current language and bona fide and established practices of the particular trade in question.

The objectionable sign need not be a generic word mark. Article 7(1)(d) applies to generic trade colours (for example, white or pale colours for pharmaceutical preparations), generic packaging (for example, a red-coloured lid for decaffeinated coffee), generic devices (for example, bunches of grapes or vine leaves for wine and devices of stars for hotel services), generic picture or portrait marks (the picture of a chef for foodstuffs or restaurant services) and, if there are such things, generic sounds and other sensory signs.

Even though a mark is prima facie excluded from registration by Article 7(1)(d) it may be registered if it is shown to have in fact acquired distinctive character through use (Article 7(3) CTMR, see below).

Equivalent provisions to Article 7(1)(d) of the CTMR are found in Article 6*quinquies*B(2) of the Paris Convention and Article 3(1)(d) of the Directive.

Signs which consist exclusively of: (i) the shape which results from the nature of the goods themselves; or (ii) the shape of goods which is necessary to obtain a technical result; or (iii) the shape which gives substantial value to the goods — Article 7(1)(e)

The justification for Article 7(1)(e) of the CTMR is stated in the Commission's Explanatory Memorandum to the Draft CTMR (CÒM (80) 635 final of 19 November 1980, reprinted in Bull EC suppl. 5/80):

Also, the shape of goods will not be refused registration *unless the fact of registration would make it possible for an undertaking to monopolise that shape to the detriment of its competitors and of consumers* (emphasis added).

Article 7(1)(e) appears to apply to product *shapes* only. However, the following statement indicates that it applies to product *packaging* also:

The Council and the Commission consider that where goods are packaged, the expression 'shape of the goods' [in Article 7(1)(e)] includes the shape of the packaging (Joint statements by the Council and the Commission of the European Communities entered in the minutes of the meeting, at which the Regulation on the Community Trade Mark is adopted on 20 December 1993, OHIM OJ 5/96, p. 613).

The three exclusions contained in Article 7(1)(e) of the CTMR are claimed to be based on the second paragraph of Article 1 of the Benelux Trademark Act 1971 (BTA), as amended (see, for example, C. Gielen and B. Strowel, 'The Benelux Trademark Act: a guide to trademark law in Europe' (1996) 86 TMR 543), which provides:

However, shapes determined by the very nature of the goods or which affect their actual value or produce industrial results cannot be considered marks.

The Benelux Court of Justice held in *Burberrys v Bossi* [1992] NJ 596 that this provision does not apply to two-dimensional designs, in that case the Burberry tartan pattern designs. In the absence of direct authority, it seems fair to assume that the same is true of Article 7(1)(e) of the CTMR. Certainly, the relevant OHIM Examination Guideline speaks only of three-dimensional trade marks (Guideline 8.6, OHIM OJ 9/96, p. 1331).

The Benelux commentators warn against confusion between the requirement for distinctiveness and the exclusion of certain shapes from registrability as CTMs. They point to Article 117(2) of the French Intellectual Property Code as an example of such confusion:

. . . are deprived of any distinctive character:
    (c)   signs made exclusively of a shape which is imposed by the nature or the function of the product, or which gives the latter its substantial value.
    The distinctive character can, with the exception of (c), be acquired by means of usage.

(This provision purports to implement Article 3(1)(e) of the Directive, which is in identical terms to Article 7(1)(e) of the CTMR.)

Like Article 7(1)(a), Article 7(1)(e) of the CTMR opens with the words 'signs which'. By contrast, the other eight grounds for refusal in Article 7(1) commence with the words 'trade marks which'. This makes clear that, like Article 7(1)(a), Article 7(1)(e) is concerned with signs which are incapable of forming the basis of CTMs within the definition in Article 4 (and see 'Capable of distinguishing' above).

The concurrence of protection under intellectual property laws for product shapes or product packaging is apparently irrelevant to the application of Article 7(1)(e) of the CTMR (*Superconfex v Burberrys* (1991) 22 IIC 567).

The shape which results from the nature of the goods themselves Registration must be refused to a sign which consists *exclusively* of the shape which results from the nature of the goods themselves.

It has been suggested that this head might operate to exclude bottles and containers from registration as CTMs. The argument, based on the English House of Lords decision in *COCA-COLA Trade Marks* [1986] RPC 421, runs that since liquid has no shape, an application to register a bottle or a container for liquid as a trade mark must be an application to register the goods themselves.

The OHIM Examination Guidelines expressly reject any such argument at Guideline 8.6 (OHIM OJ 9/95, 1331):

> Quite clearly a liquid can have any shape and the shape of a container for liquids does not arise from the nature of the goods themselves.

However, the document gives no further guidance on how the 'nature of the goods' exception is to be interpreted and applied.

The legislative history of similar wording in the second paragraph of Article 1 of the BTA indicates that the 'nature of the goods' exception is concerned only with shapes which are indispensable to the manufacture or distribution of products. Examples commonly provided include the shape of an umbrella, the shape of a carrier bag and the shape of an egg box. The United Kingdom Trade Marks Registry uses the shape of a toothbrush — needing to have a handle and brushes which are more or less in line with it — as their example of the equivalent exception (*Trade Marks Registry Work Manual*, ch. 6, 2.8). Registration as a trade mark for such basic shapes would obviously permit traders to monopolise the respective goods themselves.

However, arbitrary or fanciful elements may take a particular shape outside the 'nature of the goods' exception. Thus, the District Court of the Hague held that although the rectangular shape of an olive-oil bottle is purely functional, the presence of additional features, namely, grooves and a specially designed handle, meant that the particular bottle in question did not consist *exclusively* of three-dimensional elements which resulted from the nature of the product itself (District Court of the Hague [1992] IER 115). Similarly, OHIM has accepted for registration as a CTM the shape of a 1950s-look toaster with rounded contours (CTM Application No. 000048728).

The shape of goods which is necessary to achieve a technical result   The example of the 'technical result' exception given by the OHIM Examination Guidelines is:

> While the pins in an electric plug are necessary for the plug to work the overall shape of the plug is not determined by this technical requirement (Guideline 8.6, OHIM OJ 9/96, p. 1331).

This example makes clear that the key to application of the exception is *necessity*. If a technical result can be achieved by alternative shapes then the particular shape in question is probably outside the exception. The United Kingdom Trade Marks Registry suggest that the issue must be determined by the *number* of alternative shapes available:

> . . . if a shape is functional it is likely to fall foul of this provision [s. 3(2)(b) of the Trade Marks Act 1994, which is in identical terms to Article 7(1)(e)(ii) of the CTMR]. The fact that there may be two or more shapes which could perform the same function, does not, of itself, mean that one of those shapes can be

registered. However, if a wide range of shapes can perform the same function then the shape is not necessary to achieve the 'technical result' (*Trade Marks Registry Work Manual*, ch. 6, 8.6).

The round shape of a wheel is often given as an example of a shape which is necessary to achieve a technical result within the exception. The shape of the LEGO brick was held not to fall within the 'technical result' exception because of the multiplicity of possible applications which exist for a toy building brick system (*Lego* v *Unica*, Commercial Court of Namur, 4 September 1995, unreported).

The shape which gives substantial value to the goods   The OHIM Examination Guidelines make no comment on this exception.

However, influenced by Benelux precedents on similar wording in Article 1 of the BTA (*ADIDAS* [1986] NJ 285; *Superconfex* v *Burberrys* (1991) 22 IIC 567), it is generally assumed that the 'substantial value' exception directs the tribunal's enquiry into the consumer's motive for buying the goods.

If the consumer purchases the goods primarily because of their eye-appeal, for example, a crystal vase, a set of miniature china houses (District Court of Rotterdam [1982] BIE 193) or a children's bath in the shape of a scallop shell (Court of Appeal den Bosch (1993) Revue de droit intellectuel 238) then the shape is excluded from registration as a CTM.

Conversely, where goods are purchased primarily for reasons unconnected with their eye-appeal, such as taste and comestible value (*VIENETTA-ICE* [1994] IER 16) the 'substantial value' exception does not apply. The exception will also be inapplicable where the goods are bought largely because of the trade mark significance of their shape (*WOKKELS* [1985] BIE 23 — a salty cracker in a spiral shape). Three CTM applications have been accepted and published by OHIM respectively for the horn, star and kangaroo shapes of snack foods (CTM Application Nos. 000014167, 000014217 and 000013342).

Trade marks which are contrary to public policy or to accepted principles of morality — Article 7(1)(f)
Article 7(1)(f) of the CTMR excludes from registration trade marks which are contrary to public policy or to accepted principles of morality. Equivalent grounds for refusal of registration are found in Article 6*quinquies*B(3) of the Paris Convention and Article 3(1)(f) of the Directive.

The trade mark must be judged against prevailing public policy and opinion within the Community. The Examination Guidelines provide only a general indication of how Article 7(1)(f) might be applied by OHIM:

Words or images which are offensive, such as swear words or racially derogatory images, or which are blasphemous are not acceptable. There is a dividing line between this and trade marks which might be considered in bad taste. The latter do not offend this provision (Guideline 8.7, OHIM OJ 9/96, 1331).

In the United Kingdom the mark HALLELUJAH was refused registration for women's clothing (*HALLELUJAH Trade Mark* [1976] RPC 605). The mark MESSIAS was similarly refused registration for articles of clothing in Germany

(*MESSIAS* [1994] GRUR 377). In Greece two device marks of crosses were refused registration for printed matter on the ground that they comprised religious symbols (*Religious Technology Centre*, Decision Nos. 10909/1993 and 10910/1993).

By contrast, the registration of a design for a kilted doll with mimic male genitalia was permitted under a similarly worded provision to Article 7(1)(f) of the CTMR in the United Kingdom Registered Designs Act 1949 (*Masterman's Design* [1991] RPC 89). The Swedish Court of Appeals considered that the mark SCREWING GUM was a funny distortion of the word 'chewing gum' and one which would not cause general offence (Case No. 92–428, Court of Patent Appeals, 24 August 1993).

The accepted and published CTM Application for TOMORROW I STOP SMOKING for tobacco products (CTM Application No. 000084715) is perhaps a little surprising in view of prevailing opinions about smoking.

Trade marks which are of such a nature as to deceive the public, for instance as to the nature, quality or geographical origin of the goods or service — Article 7(1)(g)

Registration must be refused under Article 7(1)(g) of the CTMR if the mark is deceptive of the goods or services applied for. Three instances of deception are mentioned, namely deception as to nature, quality or geographical origin, but the list is not exhaustive. The OHIM Examination Guidelines comment further:

> A trade mark which suggests that goods are made of a particular material, where the material would be a significant factor for a purchaser and where the purchaser would be likely to draw the conclusion that this would be its composition must be objected to if the list of goods is not specific on this point. If, for example, the trade mark gives rise to a real expectation that the goods come from a particular locality, and the list of goods is not specific on this point, then the examiner must object. (Guideline 8.8, OHIM OJ 9/96, pp. 1331–2)

The Guidelines remind examiners that 'the general principle of considering the nature of the trade and its customers has particular application here'.

Examples of marks which have been held to be deceptive of goods or services in Member States include: in the United Kingdom, ORLWOOLA for textile goods (*ORLWOOLA Trade Mark* (1909) 26 RPC 683), SAFEMIX for thermostatically controlled valves (*SAFEMIX Trade Mark* [1978] RPC 397) and ADVOKAAT for an alcoholic drink made in Belgium (*ADVOKAAT Trade Mark* [1978] RPC 252); in Italy, COTONELLE for toilet paper (*Kayersberg SA v Scott Paper Company* (1994) 84 TMR 936); in France, PRILMED for detergents and cleaning preparations (Paris Court of Appeal [1995] PIBD 585–III–190) and CENTRE EURO-PEEN D'EVOLUTION ECONOMIQUE for business rescue and consultancy services ((1995) 85 TMR 84); in the Benelux, CHAMP DE LUX for sparkling wine (*J.Th. van Alst v Institut National des Appellations d'Origine* [1995] BIE 99); and in Finland, DE•NIC for tobacco products containing nicotine (Case No. 3821, DNo. 1825/4/93 of the Supreme Administrative Court, 1 September 1994).

An objection raised on the ground that a mark is deceptive may be overcome by limiting the specification of goods or services in respect of which registration is sought (Article 44(1) CTMR and OHIM Examination Guidelines, Guideline 8.8, OHIM OJ 9/96, pp. 1331–2).

Article 7(1)(g) of the CTMR derives from Article 6*quinquies*B(3) of the Paris Convention and is in the same terms as Article 3(1)(g) of the Directive. Article 3(1) of the Directive is implemented in the United Kingdom by s. 3(3)(b) of the Trade Marks Act 1994. A recent change of practice by the United Kingdom Trade Marks Registry is that objections raised against a mark on grounds of deceptiveness can be overcome by evidence of use showing that the mark is not deceptive in the market place (*Trade Marks Registry Work Manual*, ch. 6, 12.3). The OHIM Examination Guidelines suggest that OHIM will not follow the same practice (Guideline 8.1.2, OHIM OJ 9/96, p. 1330).

Trade marks which have not been authorised by the competent authorities and are to be refused pursuant to Article 6ter of the Paris Convention — Article 7(1)(h)
Article 7(1)(h) of the CTMR excludes from registration as a CTM a State or intergovernmental emblem or symbol unless the applicant has the permission of the organisation concerned. Thus, Article 6*ter* of the Paris Convention provides:

(1)(a) The countries of the Union agree to refuse or to invalidate the registration, and to prohibit by appropriate measures the use, without authorisation by the competent authorities, either as trade marks or as elements of trade marks, of armorial bearings, flags, and other State emblems, of the countries of the Union, official signs and hallmarks indicating control and warranty adopted by them, and any imitation from a heraldic point of view.

(b) The provisions of subparagraph (a), above, shall apply equally to armorial bearings, flags, other emblems, abbreviations, and names, of international intergovernmental organisations of which one or more countries of the Union are members.

OHIM maintains a list of emblems and symbols whose protection has been notified through the International Bureau of WIPO under Article 6*ter* of the Paris Convention. OHIM Examiners will object if the CTM applied for consists of or is similar in heraldic terms to anything from that list unless use has been authorised by the competent authority (OHIM Examination Guidelines, Guideline 8.9, OHIM OJ 9/96, p. 1332).

For example, the Council of Europe will not consent to the registration of a trade mark containing any of the EC or Council of Europe symbols protected by Article 6*ter*. In France, an application to register a sign comprising 12 stars arranged in a circle accompanying the word 'Europresse' was refused on the ground that it was too close to the emblem of the Council of Europe (Paris Court of Appeal, [1993] PIBD 1993-III-493).

Trade marks which include badges, emblems or escutcheons other than those covered by Article 6ter of the Paris Convention and which are of particular public interest, unless the consent of the appropriate authorities to their registration has been given — Article 7(1)(i)
As the OHIM Examination Guidelines comment on Article 7(1)(i) of the CTMR:

Because the Office has no ready source of reference for symbols of particular public interest this will be developed over time as a result of case law. (Guideline 8.10, OHIM OJ 9/96, p. 1332)

Trade marks for wines which contain or consist of a geographical indication identifying wines or for spirits which contain or consist of a geographical indication identifying spirits with respect to such wines or spirits not having that origin — Article 7(1)(j)

This ground for refusal was added to Article 7(1) of the CTMR by Council Regulation (EC) 3288/94 of 22 December 1994 (OJ [1994] L 349/83) to comply with Article 23 of the TRIPs Agreement. There is a certain amount of overlap with Article 7(1)(g) of the CTMR. As for Article 7(1)(g), it may be possible to overcome an objection raised under Article 7(1)(j) by limiting the list of wines or spirits to which the application relates.

Establishing factual distinctiveness — Article 7(3)

Under Article 7(3) of the CTMR, a trade mark which offends Article 7(1)(b), (c) or (d) of the Regulation may still be registered if the trade mark 'has become distinctive in relation to the goods or services for which registration is requested in consequence of the use which has been made of it'. The onus is on the applicant for registration to make the claim and to provide evidence in support of it.

It is apparently not a requirement that the use take place *before* the application for registration of a CTM (compare the compulsory part of Article 3(3) of the Directive). Therefore, distinctive character acquired after the date of filing of a CTM application may be taken into account. Under normal circumstances this would give the applicant a further three months in which to use the trade mark. At present, the period between filing and examination on absolute grounds is much longer because of the number of applications which have been received by OHIM.

The test is whether the trade mark has become distinctive within the Community in consequence of the use made of it. Proof that a trade mark is distinctive *outside* the Community is in itself insufficient to overcome an objection raised under Article 7(1)(b)–(d).

Since there is no requirement that goods or services must have already been provided under the trade mark in the Community, use in advertising within the Community may suffice to establish distinctive character.

Where an objection raised under Article 7(1)(b)–(d) of the CTMR relates to part only of the Community, the applicant's evidence of factual distinctiveness must address, and be assessed in relation to, that part.

The OHIM Examination Guidelines give the following instructions for presenting evidence of use:

The evidence should show the place, time, extent and nature of the use. The evidence may be in the form of documents and items such as packaging, labels, price lists, catalogues, invoices, photographs and advertisements. Statements in writing sworn or affirmed or having similar effect under the law of the State in which the statement is drawn up are another form of evidence. These may come from experts in the trade or trade associations. The results of opinion polls may also be submitted. (Guideline 8.12.1, OHIM OJ 9/96, p. 1332)

Relative grounds for refusal of registration

Article 8 CTMR
The relative grounds for refusal of registration in Article 8 of the CTMR are not raised by OHIM ex officio. They are triggered only on an opposition brought by the proprietor of an earlier trade mark or by the owner of another specified earlier right.

Articles 106 and 107 of the CTMR permit the owner of an earlier trade mark or another earlier right to sue for infringement or oppose the use of a CTM in the Member State to which the earlier trade mark or other earlier right pertains (Articles 106 and 107 are discussed at chapter 4).

Taken together, Articles 8, 106 and 107 of the CTMR mean that there is scope within the CTM system for the negotiated coexistence of CTMs and conflicting national prior rights.

The situations in which a CTM registration can be blocked by a prior-right owner are categorised by Article 8 of the CTMR according to the nature of the prior right concerned.

Earlier trade marks — Article 8(1)
Article 8(1) of the CTMR provides that upon opposition by the proprietor of an earlier trade mark, the CTM applied for shall not be registered:

(a)   if it is identical with the earlier trade mark and the goods or services for which registration is applied for are identical with the goods or services for which the earlier trade mark is protected; or

(b)   if because of its identity with or similarity to the earlier trade mark and the identity or similarity of the goods or services covered by the trade marks there exists a likelihood of confusion on the part of the public in the territory in which the earlier trade mark is protected: the likelihood of confusion includes the likelihood of association with the earlier trade mark.

What is an earlier trade mark? — Article 8(2)
Article 8(2) of the CTMR defines 'earlier trade marks' as:

(a)   CTMs, trade marks registered in a Member State (including the Benelux) and trade marks registered under the Madrid Agreement or the Madrid Protocol having effect in a Member State (see chapter 10), provided these have a date of filing or a date of priority which is earlier than the date of filing or the date of priority of the CTM applied for. For Madrid marks, it suffices that the mark is protected in one Member State only.

(b)   Applications for any of the above trade marks, provided that their application matures into registration.

(c)   Trade marks which are well known in a Member State, 'in the sense in which the words ''well known'' are used in Article 6*bis* of the Paris Convention', at the date of filing or at the date of priority of the CTM applied for.

Well known trade marks   Article 6*bis*(1) of the Paris Convention provides:

The countries of the Union undertake, ex officio if their legislation so permits, or at the request of an interested party, to refuse or to cancel the registration, and to prohibit the use, of a trade mark which constitutes a reproduction, an imitation, or a translation, liable to create confusion, of a mark considered by the competent authority of the country of registration or use to be well known in that country as being already the mark of a person entitled to the benefits of this Convention and used for identical or similar goods.

The Paris Convention does not define the conditions under which a trade mark is to be considered well known for the purposes of Article 6bis. This is left to the competent authority of the country in which protection is sought. However, in the case of Article 8(2)(c) of the CTMR it is unclear whether the appropriate criteria to be applied are those of OHIM or those of the Member State in which the mark is claimed to be well known. No guidance on this issue has yet emerged from OHIM.

Article 8(2)(c) of the CTMR makes clear that the mark must be well known in at least one Member State. It is not sufficient that the mark is well known in the country of origin or elsewhere outside the Community. Article 16(2) of the TRIPs Agreement states that in determining whether a mark is well known: 'Members shall take account of the knowledge of the trade mark in the relevant sector of the public'. This suggests a case-by-case enquiry into the knowledge of actual or potential consumers, whether they be end-users or others in the distribution chain, and not that the mark need be well known to the public at large.

The only requirement under Article 8(2) of the CTMR and Article 6bis of the Paris Convention is that the mark be well known in a Member State. It is generally accepted that the protection of Article 6bis is irrespective of the registration of the trade mark in the country in which protection is sought. However, a notable exception is Article 12 of the Benelux Trademark Act 1971, as amended, which requires registration in the Benelux as a precondition of protection. Modern authority is also moving towards acceptance of the position that a well known mark need not actually have been used in the jurisdiction in which protection is claimed (see, for example, *ConAgra Inc.* v *McCain Foods (Aust) Pty* (1993) 23 IPR 193; *McDonald's Corporation* v *Joburgers Drive-inn Restaurant (Pty) Ltd* [1996] 4 All SA 1 (A) and s. 56 of the United Kingdom Trade Marks Act 1994).

The International Trademark Association recently recommended to the second session of the Committee of Experts on Well Known Marks convened by the World Intellectual Property Organisation (October 1996) first, that protection of well known marks should be irrespective of local registration or use and second, that the following factors should be taken into account when determining whether a mark is well known:

(a)   the amount of local or worldwide recognition of the mark;

(b)   the degree of inherent or acquired distinctiveness of the mark;

(c)   the local or worldwide duration of use and advertising of the mark;

(d)   the local or worldwide geographical scope of the use and the advertising of the mark;

(e)   the local or worldwide quality image that the mark has acquired; and

(f)   the local or worldwide exclusivity of use and registration attained by the mark, and the presence or absence of identical or similar third-party marks validly registered for or used on identical or similar goods and services.

These recommendations have been included in draft provisions which are being considered by WIPO either in the form of a binding international instrument, for example, a Protocol to the Trademark Law Treaty, or a recommendation of the WIPO General Assembly or the Assembly of the Paris Union.

The protection of Article 6*bis* of the Paris Convention has been extended to parties to the Agreement Establishing the WTO by TRIPs Article 2(1).

Identity of marks and goods or services — Article 8(1)(a)
The owner of an earlier trade mark may oppose the registration of a CTM where there is complete identity, that is, where the marks and the goods or services are identical. In such a case the bar to registration is absolute and there is no need for the owner of the earlier trade mark to prove likelihood of confusion.

It is likely that even the smallest difference in the marks will lead to their being considered not identical (see on the same requirement for seniority, OHIM Examination Guidelines, Guideline 6.4, OHIM OJ 9/96, p. 1329 and A. von Mühlendahl, 'Seniority' (1996) ECTA Special Newsletter No. 30, pp. 25–8). Comparison of device and three-dimensional marks is necessarily visual. Two-dimensional marks are not identical to three-dimensional marks and vice versa. If the earlier trade mark is in colour, the later mark will not be identical unless the same colour is claimed. A difference in typeface will not of itself render word marks non-identical. However, a difference in the number or arrangement of letters or digits in word marks will lead to a finding that the marks are not identical. Thus, for example, ORIGINS and ORIGIN were held not to be identical marks by Jacob J in the United Kingdom case of *Origins Natural Resources Inc.* v *Origin Clothing Ltd* [1995] FSR 280.

Partial overlap of goods or services may be overcome by restricting the list of goods or services contained in the CTM application (Article 44(1) CTMR).

Similarity of marks and/or goods or services — Article 8(1)(b)
Article 8(1)(b) of the CTMR provides a relative ground for refusal of registration upon opposition by the proprietor of an earlier trade mark in the following situations:

(a)   Where the earlier trade mark is protected in respect of goods, it will block a later CTM application for:

(i)   an identical mark for similar goods;
(ii)   an identical mark for similar services;
(iii)   a similar mark for identical goods;
(iv)   a similar mark for similar services; and
(v)   a similar mark for similar goods.

(b)   Where the earlier trade mark is protected in respect of services, it will block a later CTM application for:

(i)   an identical mark for similar services;
(ii)   an identical mark for similar goods;
(iii)   a similar mark for identical services;

(iv)   a similar mark for similar goods; and
(v)   a similar mark for similar services.

However, in each case there must exist a likelihood of confusion on the part of the public in the territory in which the earlier trade mark is protected. The likelihood of confusion is expressed to include the likelihood of association with the earlier trade mark.

The scope of protection conferred upon an earlier trade mark by Article 8(1)(b) of the CTMR depends on the answers to the following questions:

(a)   What is the meaning of 'likelihood of confusion [which] includes the likelihood of association with the earlier trade mark'?
(b)   What is the correct approach for the tribunal to adopt in assessing the likelihood of confusion under Article 8(1)(b)?

Including likelihood of association   It seems that the phrase 'likelihood of association' was designed to incorporate into Community and Member States' trade marks laws the protection afforded to registered trade marks under the Benelux law (see, for example, C. Gielen and B. Strowel, 'The Benelux Trademark Act: a guide to trademark law in Europe' (1996) 86 TMR 543 and arguments for the plaintiff in the United Kingdom case of *Wagamama Ltd* v *City Centre Restaurants plc* [1995] FSR 713, both referring to an account of negotiations leading to adoption of the 1988 Directive in H. R. Furstner and M. C. Geuze, 'Scope of protection of the trade mark in the Benelux Countries and EEC harmonisation' [1988] BIE 215, reprinted in (1989) ECTA Newsletter No. 15, p. 10). Thus the words 'likelihood of association' feature not only in the relative grounds for refusal of registration in Article 8(1)(b) of the CTMR and Article 4(1)(b) of the Directive but also in the infringement criteria in Article 9(1)(b) of the CTMR and Article 5(1)(b) of the Directive.

The 'likelihood of association' criterion did not appear in the pre-harmonised version of the BTA 1971. It arose out of the interpretation by the Benelux Court of Justice of the yardstick of 'similarity' between marks in Articles 3 (relative grounds for refusal), 13A (infringement) and 14B (relative grounds for invalidity) of the original version of the 1971 Act. In *UNION/UNION SOLEURE* [1984] BIE 137 the Benelux Court of Justice held that:

The word 'similar' in Articles 3, 13A and 14B must be interpreted to mean that there is similarity between a trade mark and a sign when, taking into account the circumstances of the case and in particular the distinctive power of the trade mark, both the trade mark and the sign, each looked at as a whole and in relation to one another, display such a resemblance orally, visually or conceptually, that for that reason alone it is possible for someone who is confronted with the sign to associate the sign with the trademark.

In *MAASLANDER/WAASLANDER* [1988] BIE 198 the President of the Commercial Court of Brussels confirmed that 'risk of association' was not the same as 'risk of confusion' under Benelux law.

The Benelux concept of similarity, therefore, encompasses more than classical confusion. By concentrating on the mental links which may be evoked by a later trade mark in the mind of the consumer (rather than any connections which the consumer might make between the respective goods or services) the BTA provides a relative ground for refusal of registration in cases of similarity of marks and, or goods or services where there is:

(a)   a likelihood that consumers will believe that goods or services bearing the later mark derive or originate from the same source as goods or services bearing the earlier trade mark (direct confusion as to origin); or

(b)   a likelihood that consumers will believe that goods or services bearing the later mark are produced under licence from the owner of the earlier trade mark (association confusion as to origin); or

(c)   a likelihood that the later mark will cause the consumer to call to mind the earlier trade mark even in the absence of any misapprehension about the source of the respective goods or goods or services (non-origin association).

A case which is often used to illustrate non-origin association in (c) above is the Dutch Supreme Court decision in *MONOPOLY/ANTI-MONOPOLY* [1978] BIE 39 and 43, which concerned competing use for games. The second game was of a totally anti-capitalistic nature and it was improbable that any person would think that the two games originated from the same company. Nevertheless the court ruled that there was similarity. The public when seeing or hearing the word ANTI-MONOPOLY would think of the trade mark MONOPOLY and therefore the risk of association was established.

Two consequences of protecting an earlier trade mark in circumstances of non-origin association are:

(a)   recognition is given to the advertising or goodwill function of a trade mark; and

(b)   protection is afforded against the dilution effect of use of an identical mark for similar goods or services and use of a similar mark for identical or similar goods or services (dilution is discussed more fully below).

A further consequence is that enhanced protection is available against lookalikes, which is important now that colours, shapes and packaging can all be registered as CTMs (see the Benelux case of *ALWAYS/REGINA* [1993] IER 112 and R. Annand, 'Lookalikes under the new United Kingdom Trade Marks Act 1994' (1996) 86 TMR 142).

Support for the proposition that the criterion 'likelihood of confusion [which] includes the likelihood of association' is to be understood in the wider Benelux sense can be found both in the recitals of the preambles to the CTMR and the Directive and in the Joint statements made by the Council and the Commission at the respective times of adoption of the CTMR and the Directive (OHIM OJ 5/96, pp. 613 and 609). Thus, Recital 7 of the Preamble to the CTMR and Recital 10 of the Preamble to the Directive state in almost identical terms:

Whereas the protection afforded by a Community trade mark/the registered trade mark, the function of which is *in particular* to guarantee the trade mark as an indication of origin . . . (emphasis added, the words emphasised suggesting that other functions of a trade mark are recognised)

The Joint statements say of Articles 8(1)(b) and 9(1)(b) of the CTMR and Articles 4(1)(b) and 5(1)(b) of the Directive (that is, the relative ground for refusal and the infringement criterion presently under discussion):

> The Council and the Commission note that 'likelihood of association' is a concept which in particular has been developed by Benelux case law.

Nevertheless, cogent arguments against such an interpretation of the criterion include:

(a)   Likelihood of association is expressed as a subset of likelihood of confusion indicating that the words merely make clear that association as to origin is within the meaning of 'likelihood of confusion'.

(b)   Recent decisions of the European Court of Justice have recognised only the origin and related guarantee functions of a trade mark (*SA CNL-Sucal NV v Hag GF AG* (case C-10/89) [1990] ECR I-3711; *Deutsche Renault AG v Audi AG* (case C-317/91) [1993] ECR I-6227 and *IHT Internationale Heiztechnik GmbH v Ideal-Standard GmbH* (case C-9/93) [1994] ECR I-2789; in the last-mentioned case the European Court of Justice alluded also to the identification function of a trade mark).

These arguments inter alia persuaded Laddie J in *Wagamama Ltd v City Centre Restaurants plc* [1995] FSR 713 to hold that the words 'likelihood of confusion on the part of the public, which includes the likelihood of association with the trade mark' in s. 10(2) of the United Kingdom Trade Marks Act 1994 (implementing the infringement criterion in Article 5(1)(b) of the Directive) embraced only classical confusion, that is, origin confusion or origin association and not non-origin association:

> In my view, the [classical confusion] construction is to be preferred. If the broader scope were to be adopted, the Directive and our Act would be creating a new type of monopoly not related to the proprietor's trade but in the trade mark itself. Such a monopoly could be likened to a quasi-copyright in the mark. However, unlike copyright, there would be no fixed duration for the right and it would be a true monopoly effective against copyist and non-copyist alike.

In the event, infringement was found of the plaintiff's WAGAMAMA mark by the defendant's RAJAMAMA or RAJA MAMA marks on the classical basis.

Laddie J's view was endorsed (*obiter*) by Jacob J in the later English High Court case of *British Sugar plc v James Robertson & Sons Ltd* [1996] RPC 281.

The result is 'stand-off' between the English and the Benelux courts. The latter recently confirmed the correctness of the use of the words 'likelihood of association' only in the post-Directive amended versions of Articles 3 (relative grounds for refusal), 13A (infringement) and 14B (relative grounds for refusal) of the BTA (*Always/Regina* [1993] IER 112).

The issue will shortly be resolved by the ruling of the European Court of Justice in *Sabel BV v Puma AG* (case C-251/95) [1995] OJ C 248/6. The opinion of Advocate-General Jacobs in the case (29 April 1997) is that, while the likelihood of association with an earlier mark is a factor to be taken into account, the registration of a later trade mark can only be opposed under Article 4(1)(b) of the Directive (Article 8(1)(b) CTMR) if there is a genuine and properly substantiated likelihood of *confusion* about the origin of the goods or services in question. A risk that the later trade mark will simply bring the earlier trade mark to mind is insufficient. The Advocate-General's opinion is often, but not always, followed by the European Court of Justice.

OHIM interprets the likelihood of association criterion in Article 8(1)(b) of the CTMR as requiring a mistaken belief on the part of consumers that the goods or services originate from the same or a related undertaking (that is, origin confusion or origin association) (OHIM Examination Guidelines, Guideline 7.5, OHIM OJ 9/96, p. 1330).

Assessing likelihood of confusion   Whatever the outcome of the confusion/association debate, the extent of protection for an earlier trade mark also depends on the strategy for assessment of likelihood of confusion under Article 8(1)(b).

In *British Sugar plc* v *James Robertson & Sons Ltd* [1996] RPC 281 Jacob J indicated that the correct approach was to consider likelihood of confusion only after it had been ascertained that the goods or services and the marks were the same or similar. Applying a formalistic test based on *Jellinek's Application* (1946) 63 RPC 59, which was decided under the United Kingdom Trade Marks Act 1938, he arrived at the bizarre conclusion that, on the one hand, dessert sauces and syrups and, on the other hand, sweet spreads were not similar goods.

Although not strictly necessary to his decision, Jacob J also took the opportunity to restate and slightly amend the test for likelihood of confusion which he had laid down previously in *Origins Natural Resources Inc.* v *Origin Clothing Ltd* [1995] FSR 280. The test was set out in the context of infringement under s. 10(2) of the United Kingdom Trade Marks Act 1994 (implementing Article 5(1)(b) of the Directive and in similar terms to Article 9(1)(b) of the CTMR):

> Section 10 of the Trade Marks Act presupposes that the plaintiff's mark is in use or will come into use. It requires the court to assume the mark of the plaintiff is used in a normal and fair manner in relation to the goods for which it is registered and then to assess a likelihood of confusion in relation to the way the defendant uses its mark, discounting external added matter or circumstances. The comparison is mark for sign.

The test is again based on a case decided under the United Kingdom Trade Marks Act 1938, *Smith Hayden & Co. Ltd's Application* (1946) 63 RPC 97. Adapted to the relative ground for refusal in Article 8(1)(b) of the CTMR or Article 4(1)(b) of the Directive, it requires the tribunal to assess likelihood of confusion against the backdrop of notional, future use of both marks.

Neither Jacob J's staged approach to nor his test for likelihood of confusion accord with the apparent intentions of the CTMR or the Directive. As to the staged approach, Recital 7 of the Preamble to the CTMR states:

> Whereas an interpretation should be given of the concept of similarity *in relation to* the likelihood of confusion. (emphasis added)

Recital 10 of the Preamble to the Directive is in almost identical terms:

Whereas it is indispensable to give an interpretation of the concept of similarity *in relation to* the likelihood of confusion. (emphasis added)

Furthermore, both recitals set out the same list of factors to be taken into account when assessing likelihood of confusion as follows:

(a) the recognition of the trade mark on the market;
(b) the association which can be made with the used or registered sign;
(c) the degree of similarity between the trade mark and the sign; and
(d) the degree of similarity between the goods or services identified.

Jacob J acknowledged in *British Sugar* that at least his staged approach to likelihood of confusion prevents a greater degree of protection being given to highly distinctive marks. By contrast, both the CTMR and the Directive seem to envisage a sliding scale of protection depending on the strength of the mark. In *JUICY FRUIT* [1984] NJ 71 the Benelux Court of Justice ruled that it was appropriate to make a link between the distinctiveness of a mark and its scope of protection because a sign will be less likely to evoke an association in the minds of the public with a mark that has less distinctive power and vice versa.

Informal sources indicate that OHIM will not follow the precedents set by Jacob J in applying Article 8(1)(b) of the CTMR. Instead it will follow the broader approach advocated by the Regulation.

The German Supreme Court (Bundesgerichtshof) has referred for a preliminary ruling by the European Court of Justice the question of whether the strength of the earlier trade mark has an impact on the assessment of similarity (*Canon KK* v *Pathé Communications Corporation* (case C-39/97) [1997] OJ C 94/11).

Earlier registered trade marks — identical or similar marks and dissimilar goods or services — Article 8(5)
The proprietor of an earlier trade mark may also oppose the registration of a CTM applied for where it is identical or similar to the earlier trade mark and is to be registered for goods or services which are dissimilar to those for which the earlier trade mark is registered, provided that the earlier trade mark has a reputation in the EC and use of the mark applied for, without due cause, would take unfair advantage of or be detrimental to the distinctive character or repute of the earlier trade mark (Article 8(5) CTMR).

'Earlier trade mark' for the purposes of Article 8(5) means registered earlier CTMs or registered earlier national trade marks (contrast the use of the words 'earlier trade mark is protected' in Article 8(1)). Well known marks do not receive the protection of Article 8(5) of the CTMR unless they are registered as CTMs or as national trade marks in Member States. This conflicts with the obligation under TRIPs Article 16(3) to extend the protection of well known marks under Article 6*bis* of the Paris Convention to cover use or registration of a later mark in relation to dissimilar goods or services. The term 'national trade mark' is used elsewhere in the Regulation to include an international registration having effect in a Member State (see Article 34 of the CTMR). The proprietor of such an international registration is therefore thought to be entitled to bring an opposition based on Article 8(5).

Article 8(5) makes no mention of confusion. Like its counterpart Article 9(1)(c) of the CTMR (infringement for use in relation to dissimilar goods or services), Article 8(5) is said to have been included in the final version of the CTMR at the instigation of the Benelux delegation (reliance is placed on the account of the negotiations in H. R. Furstner and M. C. Geuze, 'Scope of protection of the trade mark in the Benelux countries and EEC Harmonisation' [1988] BIE 215, reprinted in (1989) ECTA Newsletter No. 15, p. 10). As such, it can be seen as complementing the protection offered by the 'likelihood of association' criterion (interpreted in the Benelux sense) in Article 8(1). Viewed as a package, Article 8(1) and (5) would then protect an earlier trade mark against dilution by registration of a later mark for competing *or* non-competing goods or services and *irrespective* of likelihood of confusion (contrast the position under the Federal Trademark Dilution Act 1995, under which dilution is actionable regardless of (a) competition between the trade mark owner and other parties and (b) likelihood of confusion, but a dilution claim is probably unavailable in opposition and cancellation proceedings).

Article 8(5) specifies that registration of a CTM must be refused if use of it would 'take unfair advantage of, or be detrimental to, the distinctive character or the repute of the earlier trade mark'. These words seem to encompass at least the two main recognised forms of dilution, namely, dilution by blurring and dilution by tarnishment. With dilution by blurring, the distinctiveness of the earlier trade mark is eroded due to use in relation to the applicant's goods or services. Dilution by tarnishment occurs where the earlier trade mark is linked to products of an unsavoury quality or is portrayed in an unwholesome context.

Examples of dilution by blurring in the present context of use in relation to dissimilar goods or services include, from the Benelux case law, DUNHILL for tobacco products, leather goods and stationery against CHRISTOPHER DUNHILL for glasses [1982] BIE 42 and APPLE for computers against APPLE for advertising and promotional services [1986] BIE 152. Hypothetical examples often given to illustrate blurring under American Federal and State dilution laws are DUPONT shoes, BUICK aspirin and KODAK pianos.

Dilution by tarnishment is neatly illustrated by the Benelux Court of Justice's decision in *CLAERYN/KLAREIN* (1976) 7 IIC 420 where the owner of CLAERYN Dutch gin was able to restrain the use of KLAREIN for household cleanser.

Other forms of potentially diluting use may fall within the ambit of Article 8(5) of the CTMR. For example, in the American Second Circuit decision in *Deere & Co.* v *MTD Products Inc.* (1994) 41 F 3d 39 the trade mark owner was able to restrain the showing of a television commercial which portrayed its 'leaping deer', usually depicted in two-dimensional 'static' profile, as a small animated animal running away from the defendant's tractor.

It was noted above that Article 8(5) of the CTMR does not require confusion as a condition for refusing registration. The English High Court has on two occasions indicated that, in its view, confusion *is* a prerequisite to protection under the equivalent infringement criteria in Section 10(3) of the Trade Marks Act 1994 (in similar terms to Article 9(1)(c) of the CTMR). In *BASF plc* v *CEP (UK) plc* (26 October 1995, unreported), Knox J thought that it was impossible to show either the taking of unfair advantage, or any detriment to the distinctive character or the repute of the plaintiff's trade mark if there was no risk of relevant confusion. Knox J's approach was cited with approval by Crystal QC (sitting as a deputy High Court judge) in *Baywatch Production Co. Inc.* v *The Home Video Channel* [1997] FSR 22, where he explained that the need for likelihood of confusion arose out of the requirement for similarity of marks in s. 10(3).

With respect, it is suggested that such restrictive interpretations are unwarranted and unjustified by the wording or the intentions of Community or national provisions corresponding to Article 8(5) of the CTMR (Articles 4(3) and (4)(a) and 5(2) of the Directive).

In order to succeed in an opposition under Article 8(5) of the CTMR the owner of a CTM must show that his mark has reputation within the Community, and the owner of a national trade mark must show that his mark has reputation in a Member State. However, it is unclear what level of reputation will be required. The American courts have tended to give dilution protection to famous marks only and this is now an express requirement of the Federal Trademark Dilution Act 1995 (prescribed factors to be taken into account in determining whether a mark is famous include: the degree of inherent or acquired distinctiveness of the mark; the duration, extent and geographical areas of use of the mark; the duration and extent of publicity and advertising of the mark; the channels of trade for goods or services sold under the mark; recognition of the mark in the plaintiff's and the defendant's trading circles; and the degree of use by third parties of the same or similar marks). By contrast, the Benelux courts have protected marks which are not of repute against dilution.

It has been suggested that the requirement for reputation in Article 8(5) of the CTMR imposes a lower threshold than 'well known' in Article 6*bis* of the Paris Convention: the former meaning 'known' and the latter meaning 'generally known' (C. Gielen and B. Strowel, 'The Benelux Trademark Act: a guide to trademark law in Europe (1996) 86 TMR 543). However, informal sources suggest that OHIM may equate 'of repute' to 'well known'.

The final requirement under Article 8(5) of the CTMR is that use of the trade mark applied for must be without due cause. In the *CLAERYN* case the Benelux Court of Justice construed the phrase to mean 'necessity'. However, the English High Court case of *Barclays Bank plc* v *RBS Advanta* [1996] RPC 307 on comparative advertising suggests that use which takes unfair advantage of, or is detrimental to the distinctive character or the repute of the trade mark is *ipso facto* without due cause.

Proprietor's trade mark applied for by an agent — Article 8(3)
Article 8(3) of the CTMR reflects Article 6*septies* of the Paris Convention in entitling the proprietor of a trade mark to oppose an application for CTM registration in the name of an agent or representative, unless the agent or representative can justify his action. For the purposes of Article 8(3), it is immaterial where in the world the rights of proprietorship reside.

Unregistered trade marks — Article 8(4)
The final category of prior rights upon which opposition to CTM registration may be based comprises unregistered trade marks and other signs used in the course of trade of more than mere local significance. The rights in such a mark or sign must

have been acquired before the date of filing or the date of priority of the CTM applied for. Furthermore the law of the relevant Member State must confer upon the owner of the earlier unregistered trade mark or earlier sign used in the course of trade the right to prohibit use of the CTM in question. In the context of United Kingdom law, this means that the owner of the prior right must be in a position to succeed in a passing-off action. Guidance is awaited from OHIM on the meaning of the phrase 'of more than mere local significance'.

Copyright and designs
Although Article 8 of the CTMR, unlike its counterpart Article 4(4) of the Directive, makes no reference to a prior copyright or design being treated as a relative ground for refusal, the existence of such a prior right is a ground of invalidity under Article 52(2) of the CTMR.

Chapter Three
Obtaining Registration of a Community Trade Mark 2:
Registration Procedure

Introduction

The official date from which applications for Community trade marks (CTM) could be filed was 1 April 1996 (Decision No. CA-95-19 of the Administrative Board of OHIM of 11 July 1995, OHIM OJ 1/95, p. 13, made under Article 143(3) CTMR). This was also the date on which OHIM opened its doors to the public.

Transitional provisions allowed for the filing and the provisional examination of CTM applications as from 1 January 1996 (Article 143(4) CTMR, Article 2 IR). But such transitional applications could bear a filing date of no earlier than 1 April 1996, no final decision could be taken on provisional examination before 1 April 1996 and priority for transitional CTM applications could only be claimed from 1 October 1995, that is, six months prior to 1 April 1996 (claiming priority for a CTM application is discussed below). Transitional CTM applications were not searched against each other by OHIM although searches by national offices could be carried out (see below).

OHIM expected to receive 15,000 CTM applications in 1996. By 1 April 1996 it had received 21,000 CTM applications and by the middle of August 1996 a total of about 30,000 applications (letter from the President of OHIM, 14 August 1996). OHIM statistics for November 1996 showed that it would receive between 36,000 and 40,000 CTM applications for the year 1996, with the highest number of applications coming from the United States of America (33 per cent), Germany (18 per cent), the United Kingdom (13 per cent), Spain (6 per cent), Italy (5 per cent), Japan (3 per cent) and France (3 per cent). In fact, 43,000 CTM applications were filed in 1996. By 15 April 1997 the total number of CTM applications received by OHIM had risen to 49,678 and France (4 per cent) had overtaken Japan (3 per cent) in the highest number of application stakes. Throughout 1997 OHIM has been receiving about 500 CTM applications per week, which means that by the end of 1997, a total of around 69,000 CTM applications will have been filed.

This overwhelming interest in the CTM coupled with OHIM's stated goal of operating an essentially paperless trade mark management system (EUROMARC) has resulted in significant delays in the timings of the registration procedure as set out in the CTMR and in the IR. Those timings contemplate the ideal of completion of the registration procedure, assuming no opposition, within nine months from filing. The reality is that, again assuming no opposition, a CTM registration can currently be expected to take approximately two years to process. As this chapter progresses through the various steps in the registration procedure ideal and currently realistic timings will be indicated wherever possible. A diagrammatic representation of the steps from the filing of a CTM application to the registration of a CTM is found at appendix 9.

Making an application for CTM registration

Where does the applicant file a CTM application? (Article 25 CTMR)
An application for CTM registration must be filed either at OHIM or at the trade marks office of a Member State or at the Benelux Trade Mark Office (Article 25(1) CTMR). The national or Benelux office must 'take all steps' to forward the application to OHIM within two weeks of filing (Article 25(2) CTMR). In such a case the application will be deemed to have been received by OHIM on the date of receipt by the national or by the Benelux office. Applications made via the national route which are not received by OHIM within one month are deemed to be withdrawn (Article 25(3) CTMR).

How is the application acknowledged? (Rule 5 IR)
Whether the application is received directly or through a national or the Benelux office, OHIM will mark each page of all the documents making up the application with the date of receipt and its file number and issue a receipt on form 101 which will enclose a copy of the application as filed. Where the application has not been received directly, the receipt will state the date of receipt by OHIM (Rule 5(1) and (3) IR, OHIM Examination Guidelines, Guideline 3.1, OHIM OJ 9/96, p. 1324). The filing receipt must be issued by OHIM to the applicant or his representative 'without delay'. The issue of filing receipts and the assignment of file numbers have been spasmodic but are currently taking around two weeks from filing.

Where the application is first filed with a national or the Benelux office, that office is under a similar obligation to acknowledge receipt 'without delay' to the applicant or his representative. The receipt must indicate the nature and the number of the documents making up the application and the date of receipt by the national or Benelux office (Rule 5(2) IR).

A national or the Benelux office may charge an administrative fee for receiving and forwarding a CTM application (Article 25(2) CTMR). The United Kingdom Patent Office charges a handling fee of £15 and dispatches CTM applications to OHIM by courier (for further details see *The Trade Mark Journal, Application for a Community Trade Mark, Explanatory Notes*, 20 December 1995).

All CTM applications are scanned into the OHIM database and are available on CD-ROM for searching (at a cost of ECU 5,000 for 1997 — Decision No. EX-96-9 of the President of OHIM of 25 October 1996 laying down the charges to be paid for the data concerning Community trade mark applications for 1997, OHIM OJ 12/96, p. 1711).

In what language may a CTM application be filed? (Article 115 CTMR)
An application for CTM registration may be filed in any of the 11 languages of the European Community (Spanish, Danish, German, Greek, English, French,

Italian, Dutch, Portuguese, Finnish, Swedish) (Article 115(1) CTMR). The language selected by the applicant is the language of the application proceedings (the 'first language') (Article 115(4) CTMR).

The applicant must additionally specify a second language which must be one of the five languages of OHIM (Spanish, German, English, French, Italian) and which must be different from the first language (Article 115(2) and (3) CTMR). The second language must be selected even when the first language is one of the languages of OHIM. The second language will be used by OHIM in communicating with the applicant or his representative when the first language is not one of the five languages of OHIM (Article 115(4) CTMR). The second language is also the language, or one of the languages, available for opposition and cancellation proceedings (Article 115(6) CTMR; see below and chapter 5).

Where an application is not filed in a language of the Office, OHIM will arrange for it to be translated into the applicant's second language (Article 115(3) CTMR). The applicant will be given the opportunity to comment on such translation within two months of the translation being submitted to him (on a 128 communication). If no comments are forthcoming within this period or the examiner considers any proposed changes to be inappropriate, the translation proposed by OHIM stands and the applicant will be notified accordingly (by means of a 129 notice) (OHIM Examination Guidelines, Guideline 3.11.1, OHIM OJ 9/96, p. 1327).

Statistics compiled by OHIM in April 1997 show that English is by far the most popular first language of deposit (43 per cent of total applications), followed by German (21 per cent of total applications) and Dutch (12 per cent of total applications). The most popular second language of deposit is English (52 per cent of total applications), followed by French (29 per cent of total applications) and Spanish (9 per cent of total applications).

In what form must a CTM application be made? (Rule 83 IR)

OHIM produces an official application form (pursuant to Rule 83(1)(a) IR) which can be obtained (and copied) free of charge from OHIM or from trade marks offices of Member States including the Benelux Trade Mark Office. A copy of the paper version of the application form (with accompanying notes) is in appendix 5. An electronic version of the application form on 3.5 inch diskette is also available, but it is not yet possible to communicate electronically with OHIM. Alternatively the applicant or his representative may use a self-generated form with the same content and format.

How is the application form communicated by the applicant? (Rules 79–82 IR)

The application form may be submitted direct to OHIM by post, by hand delivery, by fax, by telex or by telegram or, in future, by electronic mail (Rule 79 IR). Although fax is the means of communication presently preferred by OHIM, early delays in the CTM system have been caused through incomplete fax transmissions, losses of faxes and double or triple entries of application data resulting from receipt of both fax and confirmation copies.

CTM applications made to OHIM via the United Kingdom Patent Office may be posted, hand delivered or faxed to the UK Patent Office in Newport. Alternatively they may be delivered by hand to the UK Patent Office, London.

A hard-copy application form may be completed in handwriting.

The application form must be signed by the applicant or his representative (Rule 79(a) IR). An application which is submitted by fax is considered to be signed provided that the fax copy received by OHIM contains a reproduction of the signature on the original (Rule 80(3) IR). Where the application is submitted by telex or by telegram, the indication of the name of the sender is deemed equivalent to the signature (Rule 81(3)). There is a similar rule for the deemed signing of an electronic application form (Rule 82(3) IR).

Obtaining a filing date

Minimum requirements for a CTM application (Article 26(1) CTMR)
In order to obtain a filing date, the application must contain:

(a)   a request for registration of the mark as a CTM;
(b)   information identifying the applicant;
(c)   a list of goods and services for which the mark is to be registered; and
(d)   a representation of the trade mark.

Request for registration   The OHIM Examination Guidelines advise that this is presumed from use of the OHIM application form for registration of a CTM (Guideline 3.3.1, OHIM OJ 9/96, p. 1325).

Information identifying the applicant   Rule 1(1)(b) of the IR requires full details of the applicant to be given in the application (see below). However, all that is needed for a filing date is that the application makes clear who the applicant is.

List of goods and services   The filing date is not dependent on the proper classification of the list of goods and services. The minimum requirement is for *a list*. Difficulties have occurred over specifications for 'all goods/services in Class X'. OHIM originally regarded such a specification as a failure to *list* goods or services. But in response to practitioner concern, OHIM now substitutes a list of the headings of goods or services appearing in the relevant Nice Class (see below) so that a filing date can be accorded.

Representation of the trade mark   The rules regarding representation of a trade mark are set out in chapter 2 (see 'Capable of graphic representation'). It will be remembered that anything other than a word mark (including a letter and numeral mark) must be reproduced on a separate sheet of A4 paper. The date of filing is not prejudiced by failure to fulfil the detailed requirements for reproduction in Rule 3 of the IR. A filing date can be accorded even if a clearer representation of the mark is subsequently required (OHIM Examination Guidelines, Guideline 3.3.1, OHIM OJ 9/96, p. 1325). Nevertheless, applicants or their representatives must bear in mind that there is very limited scope for amending the representation of a trade mark after the filing of a CTM application (Article 44(2) CTMR discussed below).

According a filing date and notifying any deficiencies (Articles 27 and 36(1)–(3) CTMR, Rule 9(1) and (2) IR)
Provided the above minimum requirements are met and the basic fee for the application (see below) has been paid within one month of the filing of the

application with OHIM or with a national or the Benelux trade marks office, OHIM will notify the applicant or his representative that the application has been accorded the date of receipt of the application as the date of filing (by means of a 127 notification) (Article 27 CTMR). The date of filing of a CTM application is important for determining entitlement to prior rights for the purposes of the relative grounds for refusal under Article 8 of the CTMR and under national laws of Member States.

If the application fails to comply with the minimum requirements and/or the basic fee for the application has not been paid by the due date, the applicant or his representative will be informed on a 104 notification that the application cannot be accorded a filing date and that he has two months (non-extendible) from the date of the notification within which to correct any deficiency (Article 36(1)(a) and (2) CTMR, Rule 9(1) and (2) IR). The date of filing will then be the date on which all the deficiencies are remedied (the applicant or his representative will be notified of this date on a 126 notification). If deficiencies are not remedied within the two-month period, the application is deemed abandoned and any fee paid is returned (Article 36(3) CTMR, Rule 9(2) IR). The applicant or his representative will be told that the application file has been closed by means of a 105 notification.

The ideal time for according a filing date is within two weeks from the filing of a CTM application (in cases where the application fee is paid at the same time as filing). The current average time for the granting of a filing date is around two months from filing. (Initially the granting of a filing date could have been delayed up to eight months from filing.) This puts the onus on the applicant or his representative to ensure that an application is in correct order when filed. The date of filing might otherwise be delayed for several months.

Once a filing date has been given the application is subject to the search procedure (see below).

Examination for formalities and classification

Having examined for the filing date, OHIM will then examine for formalities and classification, including that class fees have been paid (Articles 36(1)(b) and (c) and 37 CTMR, Rules 9(3) and 10 IR).

In order to manage the initial wave of CTM applications, OHIM introduced a 'pre-classification' step into the registration procedure. 'Pre-classification' involves the preliminary checking of a CTM application to ensure that goods and services are properly classified before the application is sent to national offices for searching (national offices search against marks in classes of goods and services; and see below). OHIM eventually intends to undertake full classification before commencement of the search procedure.

Entitlement (Article 37 CTMR, Rule 10 IR, OHIM Examination Guidelines, Guideline 3.4, OHIM OJ 9/96, p. 1325)
The applicant must be eligible to be the proprietor of a CTM pursuant to Article 5 of the CTMR (Article 37(1) CTMR). The conditions of Article 5 of the CTMR are listed and explained in chapter 2. If the applicant appears ineligible to be the proprietor of a CTM, OHIM will invite him on a 102 notice within a period of two months from receipt of the notice to withdraw the application or submit observa-

tions (Article 37(2) CTMR, Rule 10 IR). The Legal Department of OHIM may need to consider whether the applicant's country of origin needs to be added to the reciprocity list, in which case the period for reply by the applicant will be extended. If the applicant does not withdraw the application or submit observations sufficient to overcome the objections within the time period specified, the application will be refused using a 103 letter (Rule 10 IR). The OHIM Examination Guidelines state:

> In practical terms the applicant's observations will need to establish that the initial view of the examiner was incorrect. (Guideline 3.4.2)

The refusal or rejection of an application for the registration of a CTM is a decision of the examiner which can be appealed against directly (Article 57(1) CTMR and see chapter 8).

Applicant's details (Article 36(1)(b), (2) and (4) CTMR, Rule 9(3)(a) and (4) IR, OHIM Examination Guidelines, Guideline 3.5, OHIM OJ 9/96, pp. 1325–6)
Rule 1(1)(b) of the IR requires the applicant to state in the application his name, address and nationality and the State in which he is domiciled or has his seat or establishment. Names of natural persons must be indicated by the person's family name and given name. Names of legal entities must be given in full, although their official designation may be abbreviated (for example, Ltd, plc, SA). The law of the State governing the legal entity must also be given.

If the applicant gives more than one address, the first address is deemed to be the applicant's address for service unless otherwise indicated by the applicant.

Telephone and fax numbers, an e-mail address and so on may be provided or requested by OHIM but their absence on the application form does not constitute a formal deficiency.

Any deficiency in compliance with the compulsory elements of Rule 1(1)(b) must be remedied by the applicant within two months of receipt of notification by OHIM (on a 106 notice), otherwise the application will be rejected (Article 36(1)(b), (2) and (4) CTMR, Rule 9(3)(a) and (4) IR). The two-month period may be extended by OHIM at the request of the applicant or his representative, provided the request is received before expiry of the two-month period and an extension is 'appropriate under the circumstances' (Rule 71(1) IR).

Where the applicant has been issued by OHIM with an identification number it is sufficient for the applicant to state on the application form his name and that number.

Representatives (Article 36(1)(b), (2) and (4) CTMR, Rule 9(3)(a) and (4) IR, OHIM Examination Guidelines, Guideline 3.6, OHIM OJ 9/96, p. 1326)
It has already been stated in chapter 2 that non-Community applicants must appoint a qualified representative to act for them in all proceedings before OHIM other than the filing of a CTM application (Article 88(2) CTMR). Community applicants may choose to represent themselves or to act through a qualified representative (Article 88(1) and (3) CTMR). Chapter 2 additionally describes who may act as a representative (Articles 89 and 88(3) CTMR) and the need for a representative to file a general or specific authorisation to act (Rule 76 IR).

Under Rule 1(1)(e) of the IR a representative must supply in the application his name and business address in accordance with Rule 1(1)(b) of the IR described above. Where the representative has an OHIM identity number, his name and ID number will suffice.

If the applicant has failed to appoint a representative and/or the representative has failed to file an authorisation and/or the name and business address of the representative (or ID number) have been incorrectly notified, the applicant or his representative will be invited by a 106 notice to remedy such irregularities within two months of receipt of the notice (Article 36(1)(b) and (2) CTMR, Rule 9(3)(a) IR). If the irregularities are not remedied within this time period the application will be refused (Article 36(4) CTMR, Rule 9(4) IR). The two-month period is extendible by OHIM as described above (Rule 71(1) IR).

Representation of the trade mark (Article 36(1)(b), (2) and (4) CTMR, Rule 9(3)(a) and (4) IR, OHIM Examination Guidelines, Guideline 3.7, OHIM OJ 9/96, p. 1326)
The representation of the trade mark must comply with the requirements of Rule 3 of the IR (Rule 1(1)(d) IR). The application of Rule 3 of the IR to word marks, device marks, three-dimensional marks, colour marks, sound marks and smell marks is described in chapter 2. If the representation of the trade mark is deficient in respects which do not affect the filing date (see above) the applicant will be given by means of a 106 notice two months from receipt of the notice within which to supply a further reproduction (Article 36(1)(b) and (2) CTMR, Rule 9(3)(a) IR). If the deficiencies are not corrected within this period or any extended period granted by OHIM (in accordance with Rule 71(1) IR, see above) the application will be refused (Article 36(4) CTMR, Rule 9(4) IR).

Other formalities (Article 36(1)(b), (2), (4), (6) and (7) CTMR, Rule 9(3)(a), (4), (6)–(8) IR, OHIM Examination Guidelines, Guideline 3.8–3.10, OHIM OJ, pp. 1326–7)
The application is also examined to ensure that the following have been provided as appropriate (Article 36(1)(b) CTMR, Rule 9(3)(a) IR):

(a)   a declaration claiming the priority of a previous application under Article 30 of the CTMR stating the date on and the country in or for which the previous application was filed (Rule 1(1)(f) IR);

(b)   a declaration claiming exhibition priority under Article 33 of the CTMR stating the name of the exhibition and the date of the first display of the goods or services (Rule 1(1)(g) IR);

(c)   a declaration claiming the seniority of one or more registrations under Article 34 of the CTMR stating the Member State in or for which the earlier mark is registered, the number of and the date from which the relevant registration was effective and the goods or services for which it is registered and for which seniority is claimed (Rule 1(1)(h) IR);

(d)   an indication of the first and second languages of the application (Article 115 CTMR); and

(e)   the signature of the applicant or his representative (Rule 79 IR).

The claiming of priority, exhibition priority and seniority for a CTM application are dealt with under separate headings below. For each, a declaration in proper form must be provided in the CTM application form or within two months of filing. This two-month period is non-extendible. When the CTM registration procedure is operating according to a normal timetable the formalities check can be expected to be carried out within two months of filing. However, in view of the delays at the time of writing the applicant cannot rely upon the examiner to point out in time any deficiency in or absence of a declaration of priority, exhibition priority or seniority. The applicant must ensure that any such claim is in order otherwise the relevant right claimed for the CTM application will be lost (Article 36(6) and (7) CTMR, Rule 9(6) and (7) IR). If this is the case the applicant will be sent a 125 notification informing him of:

(a)   the loss of the relevant right; and
(b)   the right within two months of receipt of the notification to request a decision of OHIM against which an appeal can be made (Rule 54 IR).

If there is a formal deficiency in the application concerning the indication of languages and/or signature the applicant will be informed by a 106 notice. The applicant has two months from receipt of the notice (extendible under Rule 71(1) IR, see above) within which to remedy the deficiency otherwise the application will be refused (Article 36(2) and (4) CTMR, Rule 9(3)(a) and (4) IR).

Classification (Article 36(1)(b), (2) and (4) CTMR, Rule 9(3)(a) and (4) IR, OHIM Examination Guidelines, Guideline 4, OHIM OJ 9/96, pp. 1327–8)
The list of goods and services in the application must be classified according to the most recent version of the Nice classification (see chapter 1) (Article 28 CTMR, Rule 2(1) IR; see also Article 9(1) Trademark Law Treaty 1994). The list must be worded in such a way as to indicate clearly the nature of the goods and services and to allow each item to be classified 'preferably' in only one class of the Nice classification (Rule 2(2) IR, OHIM Examination Guideline 4.1). The goods and services must be grouped in the appropriate Nice classes, each group must be preceded with the relevant Nice class number and the list must be presented in the Nice classification order (Rule 2(3) IR).

OHIM will accept specifications which use the terms of the Nice class headings (but not Class 42 'services not included in other classes') or the Alphabetical List. A specification for 'all goods/services in Class X' is unacceptable. OHIM will substitute the headings of the relevant class.

Where a product cannot be classified according to the List of Classes or the Alphabetical List, OHIM will apply the following criteria (OHIM Examination Guideline 4.3):

Goods
(a)   Finished products are classified, in principle, according to their function or purpose: if that criterion is not provided for in the List of Classes, finished products are classified by analogy with other comparable finished products contained in the Alphabetical List. If none is found, other subsidiary criteria such as the material of which the goods are made or the mode of operation should be applied.
(b)   Finished products which are multipurpose composite objects, for instance clocks incorporating radios, may at the request of the applicant be

classified in all the classes that correspond to each of their functions or intended purposes. If those criteria are not provided in the List of Classes, then other criteria indicated in (a) should be applied.

(c)   Raw materials, unworked or semi-worked, are classified, in principle, according to the material of which they consist.

(d)   Goods intended to form part of another product are, in principle, classified in the same class as that product only in cases where the same type of goods cannot normally be used for another purpose. In all other cases point (a) applies.

(e)   Where goods, whether finished or not, are classified according to the material of which they are made and where they are made of different materials, such goods are in principle classified according to the material which predominates.

(f)   Cases adapted to the product they are intended to contain (e.g. violin cases) are classified, in principle, in the same classes as the product.

Services

(g)   Services are classified, in principle, according to the branches of activity specified in the headings of the service classes and their explanatory notes or, otherwise, by analogy with other comparable services contained in the Alphabetical List.

(h)   Rental services are classified, in principle, in the same classes as the service provided by means of the rented object (e.g. rental of telephones is Class 38).

(i)   Services that cannot be classified according to the above criteria are classified, in principle, in Class 42.

Any proposed changes to the specification of goods and services will be discussed by OHIM with the applicant or his representative informally over the telephone wherever possible. The list of goods and services cannot be extended (Article 44(2) CTMR). But a rearrangement of goods or services which extends the number of classes is not an extension of the list. The OHIM Examination Guidelines give the example of an application for beer, wine and tobacco in Class 33 which should be corrected to Class 32 beer; Class 33 wine; Class 34 tobacco (Guideline 4.5).

If the proposed amendments to the list are agreed, OHIM will invite the applicant or his representative to apply to amend the list within two months of the receipt of a 108 notice (Article 36(1)(b) and (2) CTMR, Rule 9(3)(a) IR). If such an application is not made within the two-month period the application is refused (Article 36(4) CTMR, Rule 9(4) IR). In the event of disagreement, the 108 notice will inform the applicant or his representative that unless the application is amended as specified within two months of receipt of the notice it will be refused. The two-month period from receipt of a 108 notice is extendible (Rule 71(1) IR).

Class fees (Article 36(1)(c), (2) and (5) CTMR, Rule 9(3)(b) and (5) IR, OHIM Examination Guidelines, Guideline 3.10, OHIM OJ 9/96, p. 1327)
OHIM will check to ensure that the relevant class fees have been paid in respect of the application in accordance with Article 26(2) of the CTMR, Rule 4(b) of the

IR and Article 2(2) of the FR (see below) (Article 36(1)(c) CTMR, Rule 9(3)(b) IR). The number of classes covered by the original application may have changed following classification.

If the outstanding class fees are not paid within two months (extendible under Rule 71(1) IR, see above) of receipt of a request by OHIM, the application is deemed to have been withdrawn unless it is clear which class or classes the amount paid is intended to cover. In the absence of such information, the OHIM examiner will take the classes into account in the order of classification. The application will be deemed to have been withdrawn for any class in respect of which the full fee has not been paid (Article 36(2) and (5) CTMR, Rule 9(3)(b) and (5) IR).

Classification of figurative elements (OHIM Examination Guidelines, Guideline 4.7, OHIM OJ 9/96, p. 1328)
As part of the search procedure, OHIM will classify all applications which contain elements which are not letters or numbers according to the Vienna Classification system.

Priority

Right of priority (Article 29 CTMR)
Article 29 of the CTMR incorporates into the CTM system a right of priority pursuant to Article 4 of the Paris Convention as extended by TRIPs Article 2(1) (Convention priority). Thus, an applicant for a CTM, or his successors in title, may claim the priority of a previous trade mark application filed by him in the following circumstances:

(a)   the previous application was filed in a State party to the Paris Convention or to the Agreement establishing the WTO or which accords to a national trade mark application filed in that State an equivalent right of priority based on a filing made at OHIM;

(b)   the previous application was the first application filed in the countries in (a) for the trade mark in respect of the goods and/or services for which priority is claimed in the CTM application;

(c)   the first filing is a regular national filing (determined by the law of the country concerned) which means that it must be possible from the documents filed to determine the date when the application was made. The outcome of the first application is irrelevant;

(d)   the CTM application is for the same trade mark in respect of goods or services which are identical with or contained within the first application;

(e)   the CTM application is filed no later than six months from the date of filing of the first application;

(f)   a subsequent application which is filed in the same country as the first application for the same trade mark in respect of the same goods or services is treated as the first filing provided that the first filing has been withdrawn, abandoned or refused, has not been published and has not served as a basis for claiming priority before the date of filing of the subsequent application. A claim of priority cannot thereafter be based on the previous application.

Effect of a right of priority (Article 31 CTMR)
The effect of a valid claim of priority for a CTM application is that the date of priority (that is, the date of filing of the first application) counts as the date of filing of the CTM application for the purposes of determining entitlement to prior rights under Article 8 of the CTMR and the equivalent grounds for relative refusal of registration under the laws of Member States.

Partial priority (Article 29(1) CTMR, OHIM Examination Guidelines, Guideline 5.1, OHIM OJ 9/96, p. 1328)
Article 29(1) of the CTMR states that in order to make a valid claim of priority the goods or services in the CTM application must be 'identical with or contained within' the goods or services in the first application. The words 'contained within' clearly permit partial priority claiming where the specification of the first application is wider than the specification of the CTM. For example, priority for a CTM application for clothing can be claimed from a first application for clothing and shoes. However, the use of the word 'identical' in Article 29(1) leads to speculation over whether priority can validly be claimed where the CTM specification is wider than the specification of the first application: clothing and shoes (CTM) from clothing (first application).

OHIM's view is that partial priority claiming is possible in either situation (OHIM Examination Guideline 5.1):

Applicants may claim priority for part of the goods and services covered by the application for a Community trade mark or for part of the goods and services of the previous application.

Where the CTM application is for a wider specification of goods or services than the first application, priority can only be claimed in respect of those goods and services which overlap.

Multiple priorities (Rule 6 IR, OHIM Examination Guidelines, Guideline 5.1, OHIM OJ 9/96, p. 1328)
Although not expressly stated in the CTMR, Rule 6 of the IR makes clear that it is possible to claim priority for a CTM application from more than one previous application for the same trade mark in Convention countries or in countries with which the European Community has reciprocal trade mark arrangements (see also OHIM Examination Guideline 5.1). The OHIM application form contains a box for checking where multiple priorities are claimed and directs the applicant to supply the required indications for additional priorities on an attachment to the form.

How is priority claimed for a CTM application? (Article 30 CTMR, Rule 1(1)(f) and 6 IR, OHIM Examination Guidelines, Guideline 5.1, OHIM OJ 9/96, p. 1328)
Priority can be claimed for a CTM application either in the application or within two months of the date of filing of the application (Article 30 CTMR, Rule 6(1) and (2) IR).

Rule 1(1)(f) of the IR states that the required indications for making a valid priority claim in the application are:

(a)   a declaration claiming priority;
(b)   the date on which the previous application was filed; and

(c)   the country in or for which the previous application was filed.

The OHIM application form contains a section for supplying these required indications (page 5, boxes 72–80). If priority is not claimed for all the goods and services of the first filing, the applicant is also required to list the goods and services of the first filing for which priority is claimed.

Where priority is claimed subsequent to the application exactly the same indications must be supplied by the applicant (Rule 6(2) IR). There is presently no official form for making a subsequent claim of priority. (The applicant may use page 5 of the CTM application form and attach a covering letter explaining that the present application is a subsequent priority claim and giving the file number of the CTM application to which it relates.) The claim may be filed either in the language of the registration proceedings (first language) or in the second language specified in the application (Rule 95(a) IR). The two-month period for making a subsequent claim of priority is non-extendible (see 'Examination for formalities' above).

Filing evidence in support of a priority claim (Article 30 CTMR, Rule 6 IR, OHIM Examination Guidelines, Guideline 5.1, OHIM OJ 9/96, p. 1328)
Within three months of the date of filing or within three months of the date of receipt by OHIM of a subsequent claim of priority, the applicant must provide OHIM with the file number of the previous application and an exact copy of the previous application from the authority which received it stating the date of filing of the previous application (Article 30 CTMR, Rule 6(1) and (2) IR). The copy supplied need not be a certified copy (Decision No. EX-96-3 of the President of OHIM of 5 March 1996, OHIM OJ 4/96, p. 395 made pursuant to Rule 6(4) IR). The three-month period is extendible and the applicant will be issued by OHIM with a reminder to supply the required documentation within a stated period (Rule 9(3)(c) IR).

The documentation may be presented in any language of the Community (Rule 96(2) IR) but OHIM may require the applicant to supply within three months a translation of a previous application into one of the languages of the Office where applicable (using a 119 request) (Article 30 CTMR, Rule 6(3) IR) . The period for supplying such a translation can be extended for a further three months at the request of the applicant provided good reasons are given (Rule 71(1) IR).

Irregularities in a priority claim (Article 36(1)(b) and (6) CTMR, Rule 9(3)(a) and (c) and (6) IR)
If the applicant has not complied with the formal requirements within the non-extendible two-month period or the required documentation has not been supplied within the three-month period as extended, the priority claim is lost for the CTM application. OHIM will inform the applicant of the loss of priority and his right (under Rule 54(2) IR) within two months to request a decision of OHIM which can then be appealed.

Substantive examination of the priority claim (OHIM Examination Guidelines, Guideline 5.1, OHIM OJ 9/96, p. 1328)
The priority claim will be examined against the substantive requirements for claiming priority: that is, the trade mark in the previous application and the CTM

application is the same, there is an overlap of the goods and services and the proprietor in each case is the same. OHIM Examination Guideline 5.1 states:

> The examiner will object only if there is a clear discrepancy in any of these respects.

Where the previous application has been transferred to the applicant for the CTM it is thought that OHIM will require to see proof that the change has been recorded in the relevant national register.

Exhibition priority

Article 33(1) of the CTMR entitles an applicant to claim exhibition priority where the CTM application is filed within six months of the display of goods or services under the mark at an exhibition recognised for this purpose under the terms of the Convention on International Exhibitions 1928. OHIM keeps a list of officially recognised international exhibitions. The date of display is the date of priority of the CTM application and governs which rights take precedence in the event of opposition or cancellation proceedings. Article 33(3) of the CTMR makes clear that an exhibition priority granted to a previous national application cannot extend the right of Convention priority granted by Article 29 of the CTMR.

Exhibition priority can be claimed by the applicant either in the CTM application or within two months of the date of filing of the application (Rules 1(1)(g) and 7 IR). In either case the applicant must furnish OHIM with:

(a) a declaration claiming exhibition priority;
(b) the name of the exhibition; and
(c) the date of the first display of the goods or services.

Partial exhibition priority claiming would appear to be acceptable under the wording of Article 33(1). The two-month period for supplying the required indications is non-extendible.

Within three months from the date of filing of the application or the receipt by OHIM of a subsequent declaration of exhibition priority, the applicant must file with OHIM a certificate issued at the exhibition by the responsible authority (Rule 7 IR). This certificate must state that the mark was in fact used for the goods or services, the opening date of the exhibition and, where the first public use did not coincide with the opening date of the exhibition, the date of first public use. The certificate must be accompanied by an identification of the actual use of the mark, duly certified by the authority.

Rule 96(2) of the IR indicates that the above documents should be filed in one of the languages of the Community and that, if this is not the language of the registration proceedings (first language), the applicant may be required to supply a translation of the certificate into the first language or into a language of OHIM. OHIM Examination Guideline 5.2 (OHIM OJ 9/96, p. 1328) states rather differently:

> If . . . the documents above are not in one of the languages of the European Community the examiner will issue a 120 [notice] giving the applicant two

months within which to file a translation into the language of the application or a language of the Office.

If the required indications for making a valid claim of exhibition priority are not filed within the non-extendible two-month period or the relevant documents are not filed within the three-month period or such extended period as OHIM may specify (Article 36(1)(b) and (2) CTMR, Rule 9(3)(a) and (c) IR), the right to exhibition priority is lost (Article 36(6) CTMR, Rule 9(6) IR). The applicant will be notified (on a 125 notification) of the loss of exhibition priority and of his right within two months to request a decision of OHIM against which an appeal can be lodged (Rule 54 IR).

Seniority

Seniority is a mechanism which allows a trade mark owner to consolidate his existing trade mark registrations in Member States under the 'umbrella' of a CTM registration. Seniority can be claimed for a CTM application (Article 34 CTMR) or for a CTM registration (Article 35 CTMR).

Where seniority is claimed for a CTM application this must be done either in the application or within two months of the date of filing of the application (Rule 8(2) IR). Seniority may be claimed for a CTM registration at any time during the life of the CTM registration.

The effect of seniority is that if and when the existing registrations are abandoned, the rights of the proprietor are deemed to continue in the Member States concerned through proper maintenance of the CTM (Articles 34(2) and 35(2) CTMR). The advantage of seniority to the trade mark owner is, therefore, a significant saving in renewal fees and other administrative costs.

The concept of seniority is new to European trade mark law and has provoked much interest and debate. For those reasons a separate chapter — chapter 4 — has been devoted to its detailed coverage.

Search

Search by national offices (Article 39(2)–(4) CTMR, OHIM Examination Guidelines, Guideline 7.1, OHIM OJ 9/96, p. 1329)
Once the CTM application has been accorded a filing date, and provided the goods and services in the application are properly classified, a copy of the application is sent by OHIM to the trade marks offices of Member States (including the Benelux Trade Mark Office) which have notified their intention to search their national registers against CTM applications (all of the Member States bar France, Germany and Italy) (Article 39(2) CTMR). The date on which OHIM sends a copy of the application to national offices is noted on the application file. This can be within three to four weeks of the according of a filing date. But given the backlog of applications at the time of writing, a more reasonable expectation for 'pre-classification' and dispatch to national offices is six to eight weeks.

Within three months from the date on which it received the CTM application, the national (or Benelux) office must send a search report to OHIM either citing earlier national (or regional) trade marks or trade mark applications discovered which may form the basis of opposition under Article 8 of the CTMR or stating that the search was clear (Article 39(3) CTMR). Because of the unexpected number of CTM applications, doubts have been expressed over whether national offices can process OHIM search requests in time. The writer's own experience is that national search reports have been sent to OHIM well within the three-month period.

By April 1997 OHIM had sent over 6,000 CTM applications to national offices for searching and national search reports for around one half of these had been received.

National search reports are sent by OHIM to the CTM applicant but not to the owner of any conflicting national (or regional) trade mark or trade mark application (see below). The minutes of the meeting at which the CTMR was adopted contain the following statement:

> The Council and the Commission consider that, in the framework of the procedure provided for in Article 39(6) [see below], the central industrial property offices of the Member States are free to inform the proprietors of any earlier national trade marks or national trade mark applications cited in the national search report of the publication of the Community trade mark application. (Joint statements by the Council and the Commission of the European Communities entered in the minutes of the Council meeting, at which the Regulation on the Community Trade Mark is adopted on 20 December 1993, OHIM OJ 5/96 613)

The United Kingdom Trade Marks Registry does not inform the owner of any conflicting United Kingdom trade mark or trade mark application cited in its search report of the publication of the CTM application.

National offices receive a fee of ECU 25 for each search report provided pursuant to Article 39 of the CTMR (Decision No. CB-95-11 of the Budget Committee of OHIM concerning the amounts to be paid for national offices' search reports, OHIM OJ 1/95, p. 14 made pursuant to Article 39(4) CTMR).

Search by OHIM (Article 39(1) CTMR, OHIM Examination Guidelines, Guidelines 7.2–7.5, OHIM OJ 9/96, pp. 1329–1330)
In the meantime, and after the application has been examined for formalities (see above), OHIM will make a search of CTM registrations and CTM applications and compile a similar search report (Article 39(1) CTMR). CTM applications received between 1 January and 31 March 1996 are not the subject of a search by OHIM. OHIM expects to commence Community searches against CTM applications filed after 1 April 1996 in 1998.

The width of the Community search is to identify earlier CTMs (that is, CTM applications or CTM registrations with an earlier date of filing or an earlier date of priority than the CTM application searched) with which there is a possible conflict under Article 8(1) of the CTMR (see chapter 2). Therefore the search is for:

(a)   an identical CTM registered or applied for in respect of identical goods or services (Article 8(1)(a) CTMR); and/or
(b)   an identical CTM registered or applied for in respect of similar goods or services where there is a likelihood of confusion including a likelihood of association (Article 8(1)(b) CTMR); and/or

(c)   a similar CTM registered or applied for in respect of identical or similar goods or services where there is a likelihood of confusion including a likelihood of association (Article 8(1)(b) CTMR).

As the OHIM Examination Guidelines observe, the OHIM search cannot be comprehensive (Guideline 7.2):

> The search strategy of the Office is not a complete evaluation of possible conflict between various rights and the results will not bind Opposition or Cancellation Divisions.

In particular, OHIM does not undertake a search for possible conflict under Article 8(5) of the CTMR (see chapter 2):

> The Office will not be able to assess at this point whether 'the [earlier] trade mark has a reputation in the Community' or 'the use without due cause of the trade mark applied for would take unfair advantage of, or be detrimental to, the distinctive character or the repute of the earlier trade mark'. (OHIM Examination Guideline 7.2)

OHIM's search strategy for possible conflict under Article 8(1)(a) of the CTMR is limited to the classes of goods or services covered by the application. It is clear that the smallest difference in either the trade marks or the goods or services will lead to a finding of non-identity and a nil search result. However, differences in the size of trade marks are ignored as are differences in the use of lower-case and capital letters.

In looking for possible conflict under Article 8(1)(b) of the CTMR, OHIM first considers whether there is any similarity in trade marks and/or goods or services (OHIM Examination Guideline 7.4.1). Nice classes are not determinative of similarity of goods or services (Rule 2(4) IR) and classes are therefore cross-searched. An overlap between goods or services in an application and in an earlier trade mark will obviously result in a citation in the search report. OHIM promises to introduce a computerised search strategy for identifying possible conflict under Article 8(1)(b) of the CTMR.

When comparing marks, OHIM recognises that a word mark may have a similar impact on the public as a figurative mark. The example is given of the words 'red star' and a star coloured red. Account is taken of the impression on the public of a mark *as a whole* rather than as a collection of individual elements. Similar considerations apply to the comparison of marks by United Kingdom tribunals.

The OHIM Examination Guidelines make the point that the search report is designed to indicate cases where there exists a likelihood of confusion on the part of the public; including the likelihood of association between the trade marks (Examination Guideline 7.5). Concerning likelihood of association the Guidelines state:

> In order to deal with the issue of association the report will have to assess whether, taking one trade mark and the goods or services which it covers, the ordinary user of such goods or services would consider that the other trade mark identifies the same or a related undertaking. (Examination Guideline 7.5)

This suggests that OHIM, like the English High Court in *Wagamama Ltd* v *City Centre Restaurants plc* [1995] FSR 713, interprets the 'likelihood of association' criterion in Article 8(1)(b) of the CTMR as *including* origin confusion and origin association but *excluding* non-origin association in the Benelux sense (see also the opinion of Advocate-General Jacobs in *Sabel BV* v *Puma AG* (case C-251/95) 29 April 1997 and the discussion in chapter 2).

Nevertheless, the Examination Guidelines indicate a composite approach by OHIM to the identification of possible conflict in cases of similarity. That is, the similarity of trade marks and/or goods or services is assessed in the context of likelihood of association as required by Recital 7 of the Preamble to the CTMR. This contrasts with the three-stage test put forward by Jacob J in *British Sugar plc* v *James Robertson & Sons Ltd* [1996] RPC 281 for undertaking the equivalent exercise under the relative grounds for refusal in s. 5(2) of the United Kingdom Trade Marks Act 1994 namely:

(a)   consider whether the goods or services in the application and in the earlier trade mark are similar; only if yes

(b)   consider whether the trade marks are similar; only if yes

(c)   there is a likelihood of confusion including a likelihood of association.

The implications of these two different approaches are discussed in chapter 2.

Communication of the search reports to the applicant (Article 39(5) CTMR, OHIM Examination Guidelines, Guideline 7.6, OHIM OJ 9/96, p. 1330)

The Community and national (or Benelux) search reports are transmitted by OHIM to the applicant 'without delay' after the expiry of the three-month period allowed for national (or the Benelux) offices to respond (Article 39(5) CTMR). (If all the searches are completed before the end of the three-month period they may be dispatched to the applicant earlier.) The search reports are transmitted under cover of a 109 letter. The application file is noted with the date of issue of the search reports to the applicant.

To date the quality and usefulness of national search reports have been variable.

It must be remembered that OHIM does not examine a CTM application for the relative grounds for refusal of registration. These grounds must be raised on opposition (or invalidation) if at all.

Examination on absolute grounds

When is examination as to absolute grounds undertaken ? (Article 38 CTMR, Rule 11 IR)

The CTM application must be examined by OHIM for compliance with Article 7 of the CTMR (Article 38(1) CTMR, Rule 11 IR). The absolute grounds for refusal of registration were described in chapter 2. Ideally the examination as to absolute grounds for refusal should be undertaken contemporaneously with search. Realistically it is requiring at least an additional two months.

Wide specifications and intent to use

The CTMR contains no absolute bar to registration where a CTM is applied for in bad faith. By contrast s. 3(6) of the United Kingdom Trade Marks Act 1994 (adopted under optional Article 3(2)(d) of the Directive) provides:

A trade mark shall not be registered if or to the extent that the application is made in bad faith.

Additionally s. 32(3) of the 1994 Act requires an applicant to state in the application that the trade mark is being used for the goods or services or that he has a bona fide intention that it should be so used. There is no such requirement in the CTMR.

If a United Kingdom trade marks examiner suspects that the applicant has no intention of using the trade mark for *all* the goods or services claimed, he will raise an objection under s. 3(6) of the 1994 Act. It is then up to the applicant to justify the width of his specification (*Trade Marks Registry Work Manual*, ch. 5, 5.10–5.12 and ch. 6, 19.1–19.3). In *Mercury Communications Ltd* v *Mercury Interactive (UK) Ltd* [1995] FSR 850, which concerned an application under the United Kingdom Trade Marks Act 1938, Laddie J commented in relation to a specification of goods covering computer software that such wide specifications 'may not be possible under the 1994 Act' (see also *Road Tech Computer Systems Ltd* v *Unison Software (UK) Ltd* [1996] FSR 805 discussed in chapter 5).

OHIM has no equivalent means of controlling wide specifications at application stage. CTM applications advertised in the *Community Trade Marks Bulletin* display a tendency on the part of applicants to broad claiming (see, for example, Application No. 000000498 for computer hardware, computer software and computer firmware).

Article 51(1)(b) of the CTMR states that a CTM registration may be invalidated where the applicant was acting in bad faith when he filed the application. Furthermore a CTM registration may be revoked for non-use in connection with goods or services, though not within five years of registration (Articles 15(1) and 50(1)(a) of the CTMR). But such grounds for invalidity or revocation can only be raised on application to OHIM or by way of counterclaim to an infringement action (invalidity and revocation are discussed in chapter 5).

What if an objection as to absolute grounds is raised? (Article 38(1) and (3) CTMR, Rule 11(1) and (3) IR, OHIM Examination Guidelines, Guidelines 8.1.1, 8.1.2, 8.1.5 and 8.1.6, OHIM OJ 9/96, p. 1330)
In drawing up a report on the possible absolute grounds for refusal, OHIM examines the CTM application separately against each of the grounds listed in Article 7(1) of the CTMR even though there may be an element of overlap (Article 38(1) CTMR, Rule 11(1) IR).

Before any formal objection is raised, OHIM first discusses the nature of the possible absolute ground for refusal with the applicant or his representative over the telephone. If the objection is informally maintained, OHIM issues the applicant or his representative with a formal notice of the objection on form 110. This lists separately the grounds in Article 7(1) of the CTMR which are thought by OHIM to apply to the CTM application. It also invites the applicant or his representative to withdraw or amend the application or to submit observations within two months of receipt of the notice, failing which the application will be refused (Article 38(3) CTMR, Rule 11(1) IR). The two-month period is extendible at the request of the applicant or his representative (Rule 71(1) IR, see above).

As described in chapter 2, objections raised against a CTM application on the absolute grounds for refusal in Article 7(1)(b)–(d) of the CTMR (marks which are devoid of any distinctive character, descriptive or generic) may be overcome by evidence of use (Article 7(3) CTMR). No formal time period seems to have been set by OHIM for the filing of such evidence of use.

If no response is received within the time specified by OHIM, or if the response received does not remove the absolute grounds for refusal, OHIM will issue the applicant or his representative with a 123 communication refusing the application in whole or in part and giving the grounds for doing so (Article 38(1) CTMR, Rule 11(3) IR). The refusal is a decision of OHIM which can be appealed against (Article 57(1) CTMR and see chapter 7).

Proceedings relating to the examination of a CTM application on absolute grounds are carried out in writing. Although there is provision in Article 75(1) of the CTMR for the applicant or his representative to request an oral hearing this will only be granted 'if OHIM considers it expedient'. OHIM interprets 'expediency' as 'absolute necessity' (Guidelines concerning proceedings before OHIM, Part A — General Provisions, Guideline 3, OHIM OJ 12/96, p. 1798). Telephone conversations do not constitute oral proceedings.

Disclaimers (Article 38(2) CTMR, Rule 11(2) and (3) IR, OHIM Examination Guidelines, Guideline 8.13, OHIM OJ 9/96, p. 1332)
OHIM may require the applicant, as a condition of registration, to disclaim any exclusive right to an element of his trade mark where (Article 38(2) CTMR):

(a)   the element is non-distinctive; and
(b)   the inclusion of the element in the trade mark could give rise to doubts as to the scope of protection of the trade mark.

OHIM's power to impose compulsory disclaimers on registration of a CTM contrasts with the system of voluntary disclaimers only introduced into United Kingdom trade marks law by s. 13(1) of the Trade Marks Act 1994.

The Examination Guidelines indicate that OHIM will exercise this power discriminatingly (Guideline 8.13.1):

Examiners should not have recourse to this provision automatically when the mark contains elements that are not distinctive. Typical elements which designate the kind, quality, quantity, value or geographical origin of goods or services need not be disclaimed. Similarly, ordinary words which would be common to many marks (the, of, etc.) or other non-distinctive matter (borders, commonplace shapes of containers, etc.) do not need to be disclaimed.

Where a trade mark consists of a combination of elements each of which in themselves is clearly not distinctive there is no need for a disclaimer of the separate elements. For example, if a periodical had as its trade mark 'Alicante Local and International News', the individual elements within it would not need to be disclaimed.

Any proposed disclaimer is discussed informally by OHIM with the applicant or his representative over the telephone. The informal discussions may include whether a restriction of the goods or services in the application is a viable alternative to disclaimer.

If OHIM decides that a disclaimer is necessary, the applicant or his representative will be notified on form 111 (Rule 11(2) IR). The notification will identify the element to be disclaimed, set out the reasons for the disclaimer and give the applicant or his representative two months from receipt of the notification within which:

(a)   to submit a statement of why the disclaimer is not necessary; or
(b)   to withdraw the application; or
(c)   to agree to the disclaimer.

The two-month period is extendible (Rule 71(1) IR).

If the applicant's statement fails to overcome the ground for refusal of registration or if the applicant refuses to disclaim, OHIM will refuse the application in whole or in part (Rule 11(3) IR). The applicant will be notified of this decision on form 112.

On the other hand if OHIM decides that the application is acceptable the applicant will be so informed by a 124 notification.

An applicant is not advised to enter a disclaimer *voluntarily* in the application. The disclaimer will stay even though OHIM considers it unnecessary (OHIM Examination Guideline 8.13.4).

Publication of the CTM application

When and where is a CTM application published? (Articles 39(6) and 40(1) CTMR) Provided the CTM application fulfils all the conditions required for acceptance, it is published in the *Community Trade Marks Bulletin* (Article 40(1) CTMR). However, publication cannot take place any earlier than one month after the Community and national search reports have been transmitted to the applicant (Article 39(6) CTMR). This is to give the applicant time to consider whether to proceed with the application in the face of possible opposition by the owner of any earlier trade mark revealed by the searches. A similar 'cooling-off' period is afforded to the applicant if opposition is lodged after publication (see below).

OHIM notifies the publication of the CTM application to the owners of the prior Community rights revealed by its search (Article 39(6) CTMR). OHIM does not notify the publication of the CTM application to the owners of the earlier national trade mark registrations and applications revealed by the national search reports.

National search reports are very brief and do not cover Germany, France and Italy (normally three of the European Community countries that are more commercially important to applicants). Applicants and their representatives must decide whether to pursue fuller independent enquiries or simply to wait for publication and the opposition period. The latter may prove the most cost-effective method of proceeding especially in view of the ability to convert a CTM application into national trade mark applications in Member States where conflicting rights do not exist (see chapter 4).

Although the technical preparation of an application for publication is ideally achieved by OHIM within the one-month consideration period, a gap of several months (to allow also for examination on absolute grounds) must realistically be expected on the part of applicants and their representatives.

Content and format of publications in the Community Trade Marks Bulletin (Rule 12 IR, OHIM Examination Guidelines, Guideline 9.2, OHIM OJ 9/96, p. 1332)
The content of the publication of CTM applications is governed by Rule 12 of the IR. The order of arrangement of these items in the *Bulletin* is different with each item being preceded by a number code in brackets as shown below. Lists of goods and services and other appropriate items (for example, the description of a mark) are published in the 11 languages of the Community (Article 116(1) CTMR) in the order: Spanish, Danish, German, Greek, English, French, Italian, Dutch, Portuguese, Finnish and Swedish. The reproduction of a trade mark is published in colour where colour is claimed.

The layout of publishable items in the *Bulletin* is as follows:

(210)   Application Number
(220)   Date of filing
(442)   Date of publication of the application
(541)   Reproduction of the mark where it is represented in standard characters
(546)   Reproduction of the mark where it is represented in non-standard characters
(554)   Three-dimensional mark
(556)   Sound mark
(571)   Description of the mark
(591)   Description of colours claimed
(531)   Vienna Classification of figurative elements in the mark
(526)   Disclaimer
(551)   Collective mark
(731)   Name and address of applicant
(740)   Name and address of representative
(270)   Indication of first (1) and second (2) language of the application
(511)   List of goods and services classified according to Nice Classification
(300)   Country, date and number of priority application
(340)   Partial priority (not included after *Bulletin* 24/97)
(350)   Seniority: Country, (a) number of registration, (b) date of registration, (c) filing date, (d) priority date
(360)   Partial seniority (not included after *Bulletin* 24/97)

OHIM ceased to publish indications of partial priority and seniority claims in the latter part of October 1997 (Communication No. 1/97 of the President of OHIM of 17 June 1997 concerning examinations of seniority claims, OHIM OJ 9/97, pp. 751–7).

Rule 12 of the IR further requires the publication of an application to contain where appropriate details of exhibition priority and a statement of acquired distinctiveness under Article 7(3) of the CTMR (Rule 12(g) and (i) IR respectively). The numbers and positioning of these items in a publication are not yet known.

The first issue of the *Bulletin* came out in early March 1997 with a publication date of 10 March 1997. This contained 85 of the CTM applications received by OHIM at the beginning of 1996, including such familiar marks as AIPPI, INTA, ECTA, MARS, SNICKERS and INTEL. Subsequent issues of the *Bulletin* have been published monthly and, more recently, weekly. Issues 1–22/97 of the *Bulletin* related to CTM applications only. The first CTM registrations were published in *Bulletin* 23/97 of 13 October 1997 (four in total: AIPPI — CTM Registration No. 00000001; INTA — CTM Registration No. 00000005; MAGISTER device — CTM Registration No. 00000003; and ECTA — CTM Registration No. 00000002). *Bulletin* issues after 23/97 are divided into two parts: Part A relating to CTM applications and Part B containing other details such as registrations, amendments and cancellations.

The date of publication of a CTM application is the date that appears on the cover of the relevant issue of the *Bulletin* and is set at approximately two weeks after release in order to facilitate the distribution of the *Bulletin* in Member States. That date, known as the 'official date of publication', determines the opposition period. As from *Bulletin* 6/97 the date of publication of a CTM application is indicated in each advertised application against the number code (442).

The quality of translations of CTM applications (provided by the Translation Centre for the Bodies of the European Union in Luxembourg) for publication in early issues of the *Bulletin* was sometimes lacking. According to Article 116(3) of the CTMR:

> In cases of doubt, the text in the language of the Office in which the application for the Community trade mark was filed shall be authentic. If the application was filed in an official language of the European Community other than one of the languages of the Office, the text in the second language indicated by the applicant shall be authentic.

OHIM checks the translation of a CTM application into the second language indicated by the applicant, where this will be authoritative, before publication of the application.

Correction of mistakes and errors in a publication (Rule 14 IR)
A mistake or error attributable to OHIM in the publication of a CTM application can be corrected by OHIM of its own motion or at the request of the CTM applicant (Rule 14(1) IR). A request for correction must contain (Rule 14(2) IR):

(a)   the file number of the application;
(b)   the name and address of the applicant;
(c)   the name and address of any representative;
(d)   an indication of the element to be corrected and that element in its corrected version;
(e)   where the correction relates to the representation of the CTM, a correct representation of the mark.

No fee is payable for the correction.

Any deficiency in the request is notified by OHIM to the applicant and must be remedied within the time limit specified (extendible, Rule 71(1)) otherwise the request will be rejected (Rule 14(2) IR).

Corrections made under Rule 14 of the IR are published in the *Community Trade Marks Bulletin* (Rule 14(3) IR). Where such corrections concern the list of goods or services or the representation of the mark they are subject to the opposition procedure (see below).

Opposition

Opposition proceedings in respect of the registration of CTMs are governed by Articles 42 and 43 of the CTMR, Rules 15 to 22 of the IR and Article 2(5) of the FR. Guidelines relating to the opposition procedure ('OHIM Opposition Proceedings Guidelines') were adopted by Decision of the President of OHIM No. EX-97-3 of 31 July 1997 and are to be published in the October issue of the OHIM *Official Journal* (OHIM OJ 10/97). Guidelines relating to the substantive issues of opposition are not expected to issue from OHIM until at least 1998 (although it is hoped that a first draft will be circulated to interested parties for comment before the end of 1997).

A schematic representation of the opposition procedure is in appendix 10. An overall estimate of the length of straightforward opposition proceedings not involving an oral hearing is 12 months.

Oppositions are being filed against around 30% of the CTM applications which have been published so far. OHIM had expected the figure to be 20%. It is feared that this underestimate in the number of oppositions will exacerbate the current delays in the application process.

When may opposition against registration of a CTM be brought? (Article 42(1) and (3) CTMR, Rule 18(1) IR, Article 2(5) FR)
Notice of opposition to the registration of a CTM must be given within a period of three months following the date of publication of the CTM application in the *Community Trade Marks Bulletin.*

The date of publication of the CTM application is the date appearing on the cover of the relevant issue of the *Bulletin* (for example, the date of publication of CTM applications contained in *Bulletin* 1/97 is 10 March 1997) and as from *Bulletin* 6/97 also against number code (442) in each publication of a CTM application. Calculation of the three-month period starts on the day following the date of publication (Rule 70(2) IR). Expiry of the three-month period is on the day in the third month with the same number as the day of publication (for example, the opposition period for applications published in *Bulletin* 1/97 expired on 10 June 1997). Where publication is on the last day of the month or where the third month has no day with the same number as the day of publication, the opposition period expires on the last day of the third month (Rule 70(4) IR).

A fee of ECU 350 is payable for lodging notice of opposition (Article 2(5) FR). The opposition fee must be paid to OHIM within the opposition period, otherwise the opposition is deemed not to have been entered (Article 42(3) CTMR, Rule 18(1) IR).

The three-month period for the giving of notice of opposition and for payment of the opposition fee is non-extendible. Further the *restitutio in integrum* procedure (see chapter 8) is inapplicable to the opposition period including payment of the opposition fee (Article 78(5) CTMR).

On what grounds may opposition be made and by whom? (Article 42(1) CTMR)
The registration of a CTM may only be opposed on the relative grounds for refusal of registration in Article 8 of the CTMR (see chapter 2). By contrast registration of a United Kingdom trade mark can be opposed on relative and/or absolute grounds for refusal of registration (s. 38(2) Trade Marks Act 1994).

Any person may oppose the registration of a United Kingdom trade mark (s. 38(2) Trade Marks Act 1994). However, *locus standi* to oppose the registration of a CTM is limited to the following persons (Article 42(1) CTMR):

(a)   for Article 8(1) and (5) of the CTMR (protection against registration of an identical or similar CTM for identical, similar or dissimilar goods or services) the proprietor of an earlier trade mark as defined in Article 8(2) of the CTMR (an earlier Community, national, Benelux or international registration or application which matures to registration or a well known trade mark in a Member State) or a licensee authorised by the proprietor to enter opposition (but the proprietor or licensee of a well known trade mark cannot ground an opposition on Article 8(5) of the CTMR (to prevent registration of an identical or similar CTM for dissimilar goods or services) unless the well known trade mark is registered as a CTM or as a national trade mark in a Member State or in the Benelux: see chapter 2;

(b)   for Article 8(3) of the CTMR (application for the registration of a CTM unjustifiably filed in the name of an agent without the proprietor's consent) the proprietor of the trade mark;

(c)   for Article 8(4) of the CTMR (protection for an earlier unregistered trade mark or other sign used in the course of trade of more than mere local significance where the law of the relevant Member State would prevent use of a later CTM) the proprietor of an earlier unregistered trade mark or an earlier sign or a person authorised by the relevant national law to exercise rights in the unregistered trade mark or sign.

Where is notice of opposition filed? (Article 42(1) and (3) CTMR, Rule 83 IR, OHIM Opposition Proceedings Guidelines, ch. 1, 1.1 and 1.2)

An opposition to an application for the registration of a CTM may be made only to OHIM.

There is no provision in the regulatory texts for filing notices of opposition elsewhere than at OHIM, in contrast to CTM applications which can be filed either at OHIM or at the trade mark offices of Member States or at the Benelux Trade Mark Office (Article 25(1) CTMR).

All oppositions must be expressed in writing and signed (Article 42(3) CTMR, Rule 79 IR). Opponents should use the official form for filing notice of opposition available free of charge from OHIM or from national offices of Member States (including the Benelux Trade Marks Office). The official form may be freely photocopied. Alternatively opponents may use forms of a similar structure or format, such as computer-generated forms (Rule 83(1)(b), (5) and (6) IR). A copy of the OHIM notice of opposition form (with accompanying notes) is at appendix 6.

Notices of opposition may be submitted to OHIM by fax or, in future, by electronic mail (OHIM's preferred methods of filing), by post or by hand delivery (Rule 79 IR). A faxed notice of opposition is deemed to have been duly signed provided the signature appears on the fax copy (Rule 80(3) IR).

A receipt on letter 201 is issued by OHIM to the opponent or his representative stating the date when the notice of opposition was received by the Office and the number allocated to the opposition (OHIM Opposition Proceedings Guidelines, ch. 1, 1.2).

What is the language of opposition proceedings? (Article 115(5)–(7) CTMR, Rule 17(1) and (3) IR, OHIM Opposition Proceedings Guidelines, ch. 1, 3.1)
Notice of opposition may be filed in any of the languages of OHIM (Spanish, German, English, French, Italian) (Article 115(5) CTMR). A notice of opposition filed in one of the languages of the Community which is not one of the languages of OHIM is inadmissible. This inadmissibility must be remedied before the expiry of the opposition period (OHIM Opposition Proceedings Guidelines, ch. 1, 3.1).

If the language chosen by the opponent coincides with either the first or the second language of the CTM application, that language becomes the language of the opposition proceedings (Article 115(6) CTMR).

If the opposition is filed in a language of OHIM which is not one of the two languages of the CTM application, the opponent must supply OHIM with a translation of the notice within one month from the expiry of the opposition period (non-extendible). The translation must be into either the first language of the CTM application, provided this is one of the languages of OHIM, or into the second language. The language of the translation becomes the language of the opposition proceedings (Article 115(6) CTMR, Rule 17(1) IR).

Alternatively, the parties may agree that opposition proceedings are to be conducted in a different official language of the European Community (Article 115(7) CTMR). Such an agreement must be notified to OHIM either by the applicant or by the opponent before the date of commencement of the opposition proceedings (see below). The opponent must file, where necessary, a translation of the notice within a period of one month from the date of commencement of the opposition proceedings (non-extendible) (Rule 17(3) IR). Because of the timetable for opposition this may result in double translation costs for the opponent.

What must the notice of opposition contain? (Rule 15 IR)
The contents of a notice of opposition are governed by Rule 15 of the IR. Opposition may be based on one or more earlier marks as defined in Article 8(2) of the CTMR and/or on one or more earlier rights as defined by Article 8(4) of the CTMR (Rule 15(1) IR).

The required indications for a valid notice of opposition are grouped under four headings as listed below (Rule 15(2) IR).

(a) *Details of the contested CTM application:*

   (i)   the file number of the contested CTM application;
   (ii)   the goods or services in the CTM application against which opposition is entered; and
   (iii)   the name of the CTM applicant.

(b) *Details of the earlier mark or the earlier right on which opposition is based:*

   (i)   whether opposition is based on an earlier mark (registration or application) (for Article 8(1) CTMR); an earlier registered mark with reputation (for Article 8(5) CTMR); an earlier well known mark (for Article 8(1) CTMR); an earlier unregistered mark (for Article 8(4) CTMR); an earlier sign used in the course of trade (for Article 8(4) CTMR); or a mark filed by an agent (for Article 8(3) of the CTMR);

(ii)   where opposition is based on an earlier mark — whether the earlier mark is a Community, national, Benelux or international mark; the Member State(s) (including the Benelux) in or for which the national, Benelux or international mark is registered or applied for; a representation of the earlier mark; the file number or the registration number and the filing date and any priority date of the earlier mark (the official notice of opposition form further requests the registration date of the earlier mark where appropriate); and the goods and/or services on which opposition is based;

(iii)   where opposition is based on an earlier registered mark with reputation — the details in (ii) above; whether the earlier mark has reputation in the Community or in a Member State; the Member State(s) in which the mark has reputation (as appropriate); and the goods and/or services for which the earlier mark is registered and in respect of which reputation is claimed;

(iv)   where opposition is based on an earlier well known mark — the Member State(s) in which the earlier mark is well known; a representation of the well known mark; and the goods and/or services in respect of which the mark is well known and on which opposition is based;

(v)   where opposition is based on an earlier unregistered mark — the Member State(s) in which the earlier unregistered mark is protected; a representation of the earlier unregistered mark; and the goods and/or services for which the earlier unregistered mark is protected and on which opposition is based;

(vi)   where opposition is based on an earlier sign used in the course of trade — the Member State in which the earlier sign is protected; a representation of the earlier sign; and the goods and/or services for which the earlier sign is protected and on which opposition is based;

(vii)   where opposition is based on a mark filed by an agent — the country or countries in which the opponent is proprietor of the mark (note that the country need not be a Member State); and a representation of the mark.

(c)   *Details of the opponent and any representative:*

(i)   the name and address of the opponent (or identification number);

(ii)   whether the opponent is the proprietor of the earlier mark or the earlier right, or a licensee authorised to enter opposition based on the earlier mark, or a person authorised under national law to enter opposition based on the earlier right (where the opponent is the assignee of a CTM who has not yet been registered as the new proprietor, this must be stated in the notice of opposition together with the date on which the application for registration of the assignment was received by or sent to OHIM);

(iii)   the name and address of any representative (or identification number) and an indication of authorisation to act.

(d)   *Statement of grounds on which opposition is based.*   That is, opposition is based on an earlier mark or on a well known mark and the criteria of Article 8(1) of the CTMR are satisfied; opposition is based on an earlier registered mark with reputation and the criteria of Article 8(5) of the CTMR are satisfied; opposition is based on an earlier right and the criteria of Article 8(4) of the CTMR are satisfied; or opposition is based on a mark filed by an agent and the criteria of Article 8(3) of the CTMR are satisfied.

(e) *Language of opposition.* The official notice of opposition form also requires the opponent or his representative to enter the language of the opposition which must be one of the languages of OHIM (see above).

Opposition based on more than one earlier mark and/or earlier right Where the opposition to a CTM application is based on more than one earlier mark and/or earlier right separate copies of pp. 4 and 5 of the official notice of opposition form must be completed giving the required details for each earlier mark and/or earlier right.

However, there appears to be no reason why a single copy of pp. 4 and 5 of the form should not be used to present alternative arguments based on the same earlier mark, for example, that opposition is based on an earlier mark and the criteria of Article 8(1) of the CTMR are satisfied or, in the alternative, that opposition is based on an earlier mark which has reputation and the criteria of Article 8(5) of the CTMR are satisfied.

Facts, evidence and arguments presented in support of the opposition (Rule 16 IR)
Rule 16(1) of the IR provides that a notice of opposition may contain particulars of the facts, evidence and arguments presented in support of the opposition and be accompanied by the relevant supporting documentation.

Rule 16(2) of the IR urges the opponent in slightly stronger terms (repeated in the notes accompanying the official notice of opposition form and in the OHIM Opposition Proceedings Guidelines, ch. 2, 1.6) to file with the notice of opposition, as appropriate:

(a) a copy of the registration or application for the earlier national or international mark (there seems to be no requirement that this should be a certified copy; evidence of an earlier CTM need not be supplied);
(b) evidence of reputation of the mark;
(c) evidence of the mark being well known; and/or
(d) evidence of the existence and protection of the earlier unregistered mark or sign.

Nevertheless Rule 16(3) of the IR makes clear that supporting facts, evidence and arguments may be filed subsequent to the filing of notice of opposition or within such period after commencement of the opposition proceedings (see below) as OHIM may specify. That period is two months from the receipt of a request by OHIM to submit the further information (OHIM Opposition Proceedings Guidelines, chapter 1, para. 2). An extension of the period may be granted by OHIM subject to the agreement of the applicant (Rule 71(2) IR).

Although not expressly mentioned, Rule 16(3) of the IR presumably also applies to evidence of entitlement to bring opposition (for example, certificate of registration of assignment of earlier mark, authorisation of licensee to enter opposition). The official form advises opponents to include such evidence with the notice of opposition where appropriate and available.

Language of facts, evidence and arguments (Rules 96 and 17(2) IR)   Particulars of facts, evidence and arguments presented in support of the opposition may be filed either in the language of the proceedings chosen, or in one of the languages of OHIM (Rule 96(1) IR). If such evidence is not filed in the language of the opposition proceedings, a translation into that language must be filed with OHIM within one month from expiry of the opposition period or within such period after commencement of the opposition proceedings specified by OHIM as mentioned above (Rule 17(2) IR).

Supporting documents may be filed in any official language of the Community. OHIM may require a translation of such documents into the language of the opposition proceedings or into a language of OHIM of the opponent's choice within a specified period (Rule 96(2) IR).

Examination of the notice of opposition for admissibility (Rule 18 IR)
The notice of opposition is examined by OHIM for admissibility prior to any communication to the applicant. Failure to comply with the admissibility conditions renders an opposition liable to be rejected by OHIM.

Causes of inadmissibility that cannot be remedied outside the three-month opposition period (Rule 18(1) IR, OHIM Opposition Proceedings Guidelines, ch. 2, 1.1–1.6)   Certain deficiencies render a notice of opposition inadmissible if they are not remedied before expiry of the three-month opposition period (non-extendible) (Rule 18(1) IR). These deficiencies are:

(a)   failure to comply with Article 42 of the CTMR;
(b)   failure clearly to identify the CTM application against which opposition is entered; and
(c)   failure clearly to identify the earlier mark or the earlier right on the basis of which opposition is being entered.

(a)   *Failure to comply with Article 42 of the CTMR.* A notice of opposition is inadmissible if it is entered outside the opposition period of three months from the date of publication of the CTM application in the *Community Trade Marks Bulletin* (see above) or if it is not in writing. A notice of opposition received by OHIM after publication of the relevant issue of the *Bulletin* but before the official date of publication of the CTM application is deemed to have been filed on that latter date. An opposition which is received before publication of the relevant issue of the *Bulletin* is treated as a simple mail. If a fee has been paid it is returned to the sender.

A notice of opposition is also inadmissible if it does not disclose an entitlement on the part of the opponent to enter opposition under Article 42(1) of the CTMR by supplying the indications required by Rule 15(2)(c) of the IR (see above).

Article 42(3) of the CTMR provides that a notice of opposition must contain a statement of grounds. It is sufficient at this stage merely to indicate the grounds upon which opposition is brought. Reasons and arguments can be supplied subsequently (see below) although the OHIM Opposition Proceedings Guidelines urge applicants to provide these with the notice of opposition (ch. 2, 1.6).

(b)   *Failure clearly to identify the CTM application against which opposition is entered.* Rule 15(2)(a) of the IR requires the opponent to state the file number of the contested CTM application and the name of the CTM applicant (see above). Failure to supply this indication before expiry of the opposition period will cause the notice of opposition to be inadmissible unless OHIM has other means of identifying the contested application.

Rule 15(2)(a) of the IR also requires the opponent to specify the extent of the opposition, that is, the goods and services in the CTM application against which opposition is entered. If opposition is entered against all the goods and services in the CTM application, a statement to that effect suffices. Otherwise the relevant goods or services must be specifically listed.

OHIM will accept an opposition whose extent is indicated by reference to the numbers of classes in the CTM application. In such a case, OHIM will treat the opposition as extending to all the goods or services in the application which are included in that class or classes.

Where the opposition fails to indicate its extent, OHIM will deem the opposition to extend to all the goods and services in the CTM application.

The opponent is always advised specifically to list the relevant goods and services. If the opposition is later partially withdrawn, liability for the applicant's costs may be incurred (Article 81(3) CTMR).

(c) *Failure clearly to identify the earlier mark or the earlier right.* The notice of opposition will be inadmissible if the indications required by Rule 15(2)(b) of the IR (see above) are not supplied by the opponent before expiry of the opposition period. This includes the goods or services in the earlier trade mark or earlier sign upon which opposition is based. Where the opposition is based on an earlier trade mark (an earlier registration or application for registration) within the meaning of Article 8(2) of the CTMR (with the exception of well known marks) the comments in (b) above on the method of specifying the extent of the opposition apply. Where the opposition is based on an earlier well known mark, a national unregistered trade mark or a national sign used in the course of trade, OHIM requires the relevant goods and services to be listed specifically.

Causes of inadmissibility that can be remedied after the opposition period (Rule 18(2) IR, OHIM Opposition Proceedings Guidelines, ch. 2, 2.1 and 2.2) Other deficiencies in the notice of opposition can be remedied within a period of two months from the receipt by the opponent or his representative of notification (on letter 206) of the deficiencies by OHIM (Rule 18(2) IR). The two-month period is non-extendible. These deficiencies chiefly relate to the formal aspects of the notice of opposition and in particular to:

(a) the requirement for representation in proceedings before OHIM (see chapter 2);

(b) the contents of the notice of opposition which may be sufficient for the purposes of Rule 18(1) of the IR but may not contain all the indications required by Rule 15 of the IR; and

(c) the signature by the applicant or his representative of the notice of opposition.

Failure to satisfy the admissibility requirements (Rule 18(3) IR, OHIM Opposition Proceedings Guidelines, ch. 2, 3) If the opponent fails to satisfy the admissibility requirements, either within the opposition period or within the two-month period set by OHIM (as appropriate), the notice of opposition is rejected by OHIM. The opponent is notified of OHIM's decision to reject the notice of opposition and of his right to appeal against that decision (the OHIM Opposition Proceedings Guidelines provide no standard letter for this notification but doubtless one will be devised).

There is no provision for the refund of the opposition fee where the notice of opposition has been rejected by OHIM as inadmissible. The CTM applicant is informed by OHIM (on letter 205) of a notice of opposition which has been rejected as inadmissible for information purposes.

Failure to pay the opposition fee (Rule 18(1) IR)   The notice of opposition will also be ineffective if the opposition fee of ECU 350 is not paid within the opposition period (non-extendible). However, in such a case the opposition is deemed not to have been entered and the opponent will be notified accordingly (by letter 203). OHIM is under no obligation to examine an opposition which is deemed not to have been entered due to non-payment of the opposition fee.

If the opposition fee is paid after expiry of the opposition period it is refunded by OHIM to the opponent.

Commencement of opposition proceedings (Rule 19 IR, OHIM Opposition Proceedings Guidelines, ch. 3, 1.1 and 1.2)
Provided the notice of opposition is in order, it is communicated by OHIM to the applicant or his representative under cover of letter 209 (together with any additional documents filed in support of the opposition, see above) (Rule 19(1) IR). The applicant is informed in the communication that:

(a)   opposition proceedings are deemed to commence two months after receipt of the communication; and

(b)   observations in response to the notice of opposition must be filed within such further period as OHIM may specify. This further period is in principle one month, which means that the time limit for filing observations in response by the applicant is three months (OHIM Opposition Proceedings Guidelines, ch. 3, 1.1) (extendible provided the opponent agrees, Rule 71(2) IR).

The opponent is also informed of the date of commencement of the opposition proceedings (by letter 210).

During the two-month 'cooling-off' period the applicant may unilaterally decide to withdraw his CTM application or to restrict the application to goods and services against which the opposition is not directed (Rule 19(1) IR). In either case no liability in costs to the opponent is incurred. The opponent is notified of the withdrawal or the restriction of the application (on letter 214) and is refunded the opposition fee (Rule 19(3) IR).

Alternatively the parties may reach a negotiated settlement. However, unless the settlement results in withdrawal of the CTM application or restriction of the application to goods and services against which opposition is not directed, there is no provision for a refund of the opposition fee. In other words, if the notice of opposition is withdrawn, the opposition fee is lost. The apportionment of any costs of the settlement is for the parties to determine. OHIM has no power to intervene as the opposition proceedings have not formally commenced.

In order to facilitate negotiations OHIM may extend the two-month 'cooling-off' period on one or more occasions. The request for extension must be presented to OHIM before expiry of the period and jointly by the applicant and the opponent (Rule 19(2) IR). The request for extension may be in the form of a 'brief statement' (OHIM Opposition Proceedings Guidelines, ch. 3, 1.2). Where the 'cooling-off' period is extended, the time for the applicant's observations is one month from the (extended) date of the commencement of the opposition proceedings (the parties will be informed by OHIM on letter 212a/b that the 'cooling-off' period has been extended to a stated date).

No provision is made in the IR for operating the 'cooling-off' period in the case of multiple oppositions (see below). In order properly to appraise his position the CTM applicant needs to know the number, nature and extent of possible oppositions. Ideally this means that OHIM should not communicate any notice of opposition to the applicant until the period for remedying deficiencies in all notices of opposition received within the opposition period expires. An alternative would be for OHIM to communicate oppositions to the applicant as and when they are found admissible, while reserving the date of commencement of the opposition proceedings until two months after receipt of communication of the last.

The compromise arrived at by OHIM in the Opposition Proceedings Guidelines (ch. 3, 1.1) is that no opposition is sent to the applicant before the end of the three-month opposition period. At the end of the opposition period the applicant is sent all those oppositions which have been found by OHIM to be admissible. The 'cooling-off' periods for most multiple oppositions will therefore run contemporaneously and in no case will opposition proceedings commence until at least five months have expired from the publication date of the CTM application. However, the applicant may receive at a later date oppositions with deficiencies which can be remedied outside the opposition period. Such oppositions are communicated by OHIM to the applicant as and when they are deemed admissible and may result in concurrent 'cooling-off' periods and different dates for the commencement of opposition proceedings against the same CTM application.

'Within the technical means available' OHIM communicates to the applicant information on oppositions where the admissibility has not yet been determined at the end of the opposition period.

Examination of the opposition (Article 43 CTMR, Rules 20 and 22 IR, OHIM Opposition Proceedings Guidelines, ch. 3)

General comment Opposition proceedings are governed by the 'adversarial principle' (Article 43(1) CTMR). Essentially this means that the parties to an opposition have the right to reply to all information lodged by the other side and to all communications and requests for clarification issued by OHIM. While the adversarial principle is commendable it means that some oppositions may be procedurally complex and long drawn out.

The general rule is that oppositions are determined on the basis of written proceedings. Although the parties to opposition proceedings may request oral proceedings, the decision to hold an oral hearing depends on whether OHIM considers it 'expedient' (Article 75(1) CTMR). It is understood that OHIM will only contemplate oral proceedings in cases of genuine need (OHIM Opposition Proceedings Guidelines, ch. 4, para. 4).

OHIM must decide opposition proceedings according to the information provided by the parties and the relief sought (Article 74(1) CTMR). Other de facto considerations are irrelevant. OHIM may disregard information provided by the parties outside the time limits specified (Article 74(2) CTMR).

Applicant's observations on the notice of opposition   Within three months of the date of communication of the notice of opposition, the applicant must file with OHIM his observations in response (Rule 20(1) IR). This period can be extended by OHIM subject to the agreement of the opponent (Rule 71(2) IR).

Where the two-month 'cooling-off' period has been extended but has not resulted in settlement the applicant must submit his observations to OHIM within one month of the (extended) date of the commencement of the opposition proceedings (OHIM Opposition Proceedings Guidelines, ch. 3, 1.1).

Furthermore, where OHIM has specified a time period after the date of commencement of the opposition proceedings for the opponent to file facts, evidence and arguments in support of his opposition, the period for the applicant's observations runs from the date on which the applicant receives the information supplementing the opposition (see below). This allows the applicant to submit his observations only once on the notice of opposition as a whole.

The applicant's observations are communicated by OHIM (on letter 227) 'without delay' to the opponent who is invited to reply within two months of receipt of the observations (Rule 20(4) IR, OHIM Opposition Proceedings Guidelines, ch. 3, 2.4). The two-month period is extendible provided the applicant agrees (Rule 71(2) IR).

If the applicant files no observations in response to the notice of opposition OHIM may decide the opposition based on the evidence before it (Rule 20(3) IR).

Facts, evidence and arguments in support of the opposition   Where the opponent has not submitted facts, evidence and arguments in support of the opposition OHIM sends a request on letter 215 inviting the opponent to submit his further information within two months from receipt of the request (Rule 20(2) IR, OHIM Opposition Proceedings Guidelines, ch. 1, 2 and ch. 3, 1.3). The two-month period is extendible by OHIM provided the applicant agrees to the extension (Rule 71(2) IR).

OHIM sends a copy of the request to the applicant. The applicant is informed (on letter 216) that he may submit his observations on the notice of opposition and the furnished facts, evidence and arguments at the same time, within the term that will be set in the notification of the items filed by the opponent.

The opponent's evidence filed in support of the opposition is copied by OHIM to the applicant 'without delay' (under cover of letter 217). The applicant is given an exact date for his response to the opposition which will be two months from receipt of OHIM's communication (extendible if the opponent agrees, Rule 71(2) IR) (Rule 20(2) IR, OHIM Opposition Proceedings Guidelines, ch. 3, 1.3 and 2.1).

If the opponent submits no supporting evidence, OHIM rules on the opposition on the basis of the evidence before it and the reply of the applicant.

Calling on the opponent to furnish proof of use   Apparently at any time during the opposition proceedings, the applicant can call upon the opponent to file evidence of use of the earlier trade mark upon which opposition is based (Article 43(2) and (3) CTMR).

The applicant's request may be made:

(a)   in respect of an earlier Community, national or international trade mark;

(b)   to prove use of the earlier trade mark during the period of five years preceding the date of publication of the contested CTM application; and

(c)   provided the earlier Community, national or international trade mark has at that date been registered for at least five years.

In response, the opponent will need to show:

(a)   genuine use of the earlier trade mark in the Community or in the Member State in or for which it is registered;

(b)   use of it in respect of the goods or services in the earlier trade mark upon which opposition is based; or

(c)   proper reasons for non-use.

Although neither the CTMR nor the IR specify the stage of the opposition proceedings when the applicant's request for proof of use may be made, OHIM recommends that the applicant enters this request as early as possible in the proceedings, preferably with his initial observations. OHIM suggests that a request submitted late in the proceedings, after the parties have had the opportunity to file all their observations and there is enough information on file to reach a decision, might be rejected as being contrary to the general principles of adversarial procedure (OHIM Opposition Proceedings Guidelines, ch. 3, 2.2, citing Articles 79 and 74(2) CTMR).

Provided the applicant's request is admissible it is communicated by OHIM to the opponent (on letter 228). The opponent is given two months from the receipt of the communication to furnish proof of use or to show proper reasons for non-use (Rule 22(1) IR, OHIM Opposition Proceedings Guidelines, ch. 1, 2). This two-month period may be extended by OHIM provided the applicant agrees (Rule 71(2) IR). Particulars of use should indicate the place, time, extent and nature of use of the opponent's trade mark for the goods and services in respect of which it is registered and on which opposition is based. Exhibits should in principle be confined to supporting documents and items such as packages, labels, price lists, catalogues, invoices, photographs, newspaper advertisements and written expert or witness statements (Rule 22(2) and (3) IR). OHIM recommends that two copies of bulky documents be provided in order to facilitate their communication to the applicant (OHIM Opposition Proceedings Guidelines, ch. 3, 2.2). OHIM may require the opponent to provide a translation of a proof of use not submitted in the language of opposition proceedings into that language (Rule 22(4) IR).

If the opponent fails to furnish proof of use or to show proper reasons for non-use within the specified time period, OHIM will reject the opposition (Article 43(2) CTMR, Rule 22(1) IR). Where the opponent can adduce proof of use or show reasons for non-use in respect of some only of the goods or services for which the earlier trade mark is registered, the opposition proceeds on the assumption that the mark is registered only in respect of those goods or services (Article 43(2) CTMR).

Withdrawal or restriction of the application for registration   During the opposition proceedings the applicant may decide to withdraw his CTM application or restrict it to the goods and services against which the opposition is not directed (Article 44(1) CTMR). A withdrawal or restriction cannot be cancelled. Both are published in the *Community Trade Marks Bulletin*.

There are no formal requirements for the withdrawal of a CTM application. OHIM advises that the withdrawal should be notified in writing and state the number of the application and the name and address of the applicant or his representative (OHIM Opposition Proceedings Guidelines, ch. 3, 2.3.1). The withdrawal will then be communicated to the opponent (on letter 244a) and the applicant will be notified by OHIM of his right to request conversion of his CTM application into national trade mark applications in Member States including the Benelux (Article 108(1) CTMR, see chapter 4).

There can be no refund of the opposition fee where the application is withdrawn after the commencement of opposition proceedings. Furthermore, since the applicant is the party terminating the opposition proceedings, he must bear the fees and costs incurred by the opposing party in the course of the proceedings (Article 81(3) CTMR, see below). OHIM may decide a different apportionment of costs for reasons of equity (Article 81(2) CTMR).

Alternatively the applicant may decide to restrict the list of goods and services in the contested CTM application. A request for restriction of the list of goods and services must be filed with OHIM and must contain (Rule 13 IR):

(a)   the file number of the CTM application;

(b)   the name and address of the applicant and any representative; and

(c)   a clear indication of the goods or services for which the application is withdrawn or for which it is maintained.

The restriction is communicated by OHIM to the opponent or his representative (on letter 232). The opponent must inform OHIM within two months of receipt of the communication (extendible if the applicant agrees, Rule 71(2) IR) whether he maintains the opposition and, if so, against which of the remaining goods and services (Rule 20(5) IR). Obviously the opponent cannot extend the list of goods and services against which opposition was originally entered. If the opponent does not reply within the time specified, OHIM deems the opposition to be maintained (OHIM Opposition Proceedings Guidelines, ch. 3, 2.3.2).

If the opposition is maintained, the applicant is invited by OHIM to submit further observations where necessary (on letter 233).

Where the opposition is not maintained, it may be withdrawn by the opponent. Alternatively the opposition becomes groundless and does not proceed to judgment. In either case the applicant bears the opponent's costs (unless equity dictates otherwise) because the restriction of the application led to the termination of the proceedings (Article 81(3) CTMR, OHIM Opposition Proceedings Guidelines, ch. 3, 2.3.2.2). The restriction is published in the *Community Trade Marks Bulletin* (Article 44(1) CTMR) and OHIM informs the applicant of the possibility of converting the CTM application into a national trade mark application in a Member State (including the Benelux) for the goods and services withdrawn (Article 108(1) CTMR).

Friendly settlement   Article 43(4) of the CTMR empowers OHIM to invite the parties to make a friendly settlement. The power is discretionary and will only be exercised by OHIM if a settlement between the parties seems desirable on the particular facts of the case or if there is reason to believe that the proceedings can be brought to an early end by settlement, for example, if one party indicates a desire to negotiate. OHIM has expressed a willingness to act as mediator provided the parties bear the costs (OHIM Opposition Proceedings Guidelines, ch. 4, 3). OHIM may suspend the opposition proceedings in order to facilitate a friendly settlement (Rule 20(6) IR).

Where settlement negotiations result in either a withdrawal of the CTM application or of the opposition, the parties may wish to include an apportionment of costs in their agreement. The usual rule is that the costs of the other party are to be borne by the party withdrawing the application or the opposition (Article 81(3) CTMR). Alternatively the parties may simply ask OHIM to rule that the opposition will not proceed to judgment because of their agreement. In this case the apportionment of costs is at the discretion of OHIM unless the parties have agreed otherwise (Article 81(4) CTMR).

Decision on the opposition   There is no indication in the CTMR or in the IR when opposition proceedings must be deemed to be 'closed'. OHIM is free to determine the number of exchanges between the parties required in any particular case (Article 43(1) CTMR).

When OHIM has received, within the time limits specified, all the observations of the parties and, where necessary, evidence of use of the earlier trade mark, it gives a ruling on the opposition. If the examination of the opposition file reveals that Article 8 of the CTMR prevents the registration of the CTM in respect of some or all of the goods or services applied for, the application must be refused in respect of those goods or services. Otherwise, the opposition must be rejected (Article 43(5) CTMR).

The ruling on the opposition is given by a panel of the Opposition Division comprising three members, at least one of whom must be legally qualified (Article 127 CTMR). The panel's decision must be in writing, must state the reasons on which it is based and must be signed by the panel members (Article 73 CTMR, Rules 52(1) and 55(1) IR). The decision must also notify the parties of their right to file at OHIM written notice of appeal within two months of the date of notification of the decision (Articles 57–9 CTMR, Rule 52(2) IR and see chapter 8). The decision is communicated to the parties (Rule 61 IR) and, if it concerns refusal of the CTM application, is published in the *Community Trade Marks Bulletin* on the decision becoming final (Article 43(6) CTMR).

Oral proceedings   The general rule is that opposition proceedings are normally conducted in writing. Nevertheless the parties may at any time request an oral hearing and such proceedings may be instigated by OHIM if it considers them expedient (Article 75(1) CTMR). OHIM will hold oral proceedings only 'in cases of genuine need' (OHIM Opposition Proceedings Guidelines, chapter 4, 4). Oral proceedings before the Opposition Division are not open to the public (Article 75(2) CTMR).

OHIM may not summon the parties to an oral hearing on less than one month's notice unless the parties agree otherwise (Rule 56(1) IR) . The summons must draw the parties' attention to the points which in OHIM's opinion need to be discussed in order to arrive at a decision (Rule 56(2) IR). The failure of either party to appear at the oral hearing does not prevent those proceedings from continuing (Rule 56(3) IR).

Minutes are drawn up for oral proceedings and are signed by the person who drew them up and by the person who conducted the oral proceedings. The minutes contain the essentials of the oral proceedings and relevant statements made by the parties and are submitted to the latter for approval. If a party fails to approve the minutes his objections are noted and are referred to in the decision on the opposition. The parties may obtain a transcript of the recording of an oral proceeding at their own cost (Rule 60 IR).

Similar provision is made in the IR for the taking of oral evidence of witnesses or experts under Article 76 of the CTMR (Rules 57 and 60 IR). OHIM may require a deposit against costs from a party requesting such evidence to be taken (Rule 59(1) IR).

Costs of the opposition   The basic rule is that costs follow the event. The losing party bears the fees and costs of the winning party (Article 81(1) CTMR). Fees and costs are limited to those actually incurred by the winning party which are essential to the opposition proceedings (Rule 94(6) and (7) IR). Costs may include travel and subsistence and the remuneration of an agent, adviser or advocate within the limits of the scales set for each category of costs by Rule 94(7) of the IR.

However, where either party wins on some points but loses on others OHIM may decide a different apportionment of costs between the parties. The same is true 'if reasons of equity so dictate' (Article 81(2) CTMR).

Apportionment of costs is dealt with by the Opposition Division in its decision on the opposition (see above). The Opposition Division must take note of any costs settlement concluded by the parties before it (Article 81(5) CTMR).

The parties may request that a decision on the amount of costs be taken by the registry of the Opposition Division (Article 81(6) CTMR). The amount of costs so determined can be reviewed by a decision of the Opposition Division provided this is requested by the parties within one month of the date of notification of the award of costs by the registry (Rule 94(4) IR).

Multiple oppositions (Rule 21 IR, OHIM Opposition Proceedings Guidelines, ch. 4, 1.2 and 2)
Where several oppositions are filed against the same CTM application (a likely event under the CTM system) OHIM has the choice of three ways of proceeding:

(a)   It may examine each of the oppositions in separate proceedings.
(b)   It may combine the oppositions into one set of proceedings (Rule 21(1) IR). Oppositions may be combined where several oppositions, each in a separate class, are entered in respect of an application filed in several classes or where several

oppositions against the same application are entered by legally independent but related undertakings (OHIM Opposition Proceedings Guidelines, ch. 4, 2). The parties are informed of the combination and the proceedings are dealt with in the same way as a single opposition. The proceedings may subsequently be individualised if OHIM thinks fit.

(c)   OHIM may examine one or several of the oppositions and suspend the others (Rule 21(2) IR).

This third option has caused consternation among trade mark owners and their representatives. There are no clear criteria for deciding which oppositions will be examined and which oppositions will be suspended. Although Rule 21(2) of the IR states that the option becomes available to OHIM only when an initial examination of one or more oppositions reveals that the CTM application has little chance of succeeding (or 'is very likely to be rejected' — OHIM Opposition Proceedings Guidelines, ch. 4, 1.2), the outcome of a suspension is that the opposition is deemed to have been disposed of once a final decision has been taken to reject the CTM application.

All trade mark owners have the same interest in having their oppositions examined by OHIM, in particular, because of the possibility of conversion of a CTM application into national applications in Member States (including the Benelux). Say, for example, that a CTM application is finally rejected because of an opposition based on a United Kingdom trade mark. An opposition based on an Italian trade mark is consequently deemed to have been disposed of. The CTM applicant may request conversion of his CTM application into an Italian trade mark application which the owner of the Italian opposition mark would then need to challenge. The owner of the United Kingdom opposition mark is in a much better position. Conversion of the CTM application into a United Kingdom trade mark application is impossible since the opposition based on the United Kingdom mark has already been decided by OHIM (Article 108(2)(b) CTMR).

Furthermore, the opponent whose suspended opposition is deemed to have been disposed of is only entitled to a 50 per cent refund of the opposition fee (Rule 21(4) IR). Apportionment of costs is on the basis that the opposition has not proceeded to judgment and is, therefore, at the discretion of OHIM (Rule 21(3) IR).

Suspension where opposition is based on an application for trade mark registration (Rule 20(6) IR, OHIM Opposition Proceedings Guidelines, ch. 4, 1.1)
Opposition may be entered against a CTM application on the basis of an application for trade mark registration within the meaning of Article 8(2)(b) of the CTMR (see above). In such a case OHIM may decide to suspend the opposition proceedings until a final decision has been taken on that application for registration. Suspension may only take place after the date of commencement of opposition proceedings. But, if appropriate, an order for suspension is likely to be made soon after that date.

Observations

Observations by third parties (Article 41 CTMR)
After publication of a CTM application any natural or legal person or trade association may submit to OHIM observations explaining on which grounds in

Article 7 of the CTMR (the absolute grounds for refusal of registration, see chapter 2), in particular, the trade mark should be refused registration ex officio (contrast the United Kingdom position where observations may be made on absolute and relative grounds for refusal under s. 38(3) of the Trade Marks Act 1994). Third-party observations must be in writing and are communicated to the applicant for comment (on a 113 notice). Any such comments are copied by OHIM to the third party (by means of a 114 notice). Third-party observers do not, however, become party to the registration proceedings.

Unlike oppositions there is no time limit for the making of observations. They can be made at any time in between publication of the CTM application and registration of the CTM. Observations may lead to the re-examination by OHIM of a CTM application for entitlement and/or on absolute grounds. Where a CTM application is refused on either basis after publication, the decision that it has been refused must be published in the *Community Trade Marks Bulletin*.

Re-examination by OHIM of the CTM application may in turn lead to the suspension of opposition proceedings (Rule 20(6) IR). If following re-examination OHIM refuses the CTM application, opposition proceedings are discontinued. However, neither the CTMR nor the IR seems to have foreseen the possibility of reimbursement of the opposition fee and costs in this situation. OHIM has stated that the opposition will be regarded as a case not proceeding to judgment so that costs are at its discretion unless otherwise decided by the parties (Article 81(4) CTMR, OHIM Opposition Proceedings Guidelines, ch. 3, 4.2.4.2).

Trade mark practitioners have regretted that the IR fails to provide for the making of observations. The OHIM Opposition Proceedings Guidelines add little to Article 41 of the CTMR.

Registration

Registration of the CTM (Article 45 CTMR, Rules 23 and 84(2) IR)
Once the opposition period has expired with no opposition being entered or any opposition filed has been successfully overcome by the applicant, the trade mark is entered in the Register of Community trade marks (Article 45 CTMR).

Payment of the registration fee (see below) is a precondition to registration (Article 45 CTMR, Rule 23(1) IR). This must be paid by the applicant to OHIM within two months from the receipt of OHIM's request for payment (Rule 23(2) IR). If the applicant fails to pay the registration fee within this period, OHIM sends a reminder. The applicant then has a further two months from the receipt of the reminder to pay the registration fee plus an additional late payment fee (Rule 23(3) IR).

On receipt of the registration fee and any late payment fee the following details are recorded in the CTM Register (Rules 23(4) and 84(2) IR):

(a)   the date of filing of the CTM application;
(b)   the file number of the CTM application;
(c)   the date of publication of the CTM application;
(d)   the name and address of the applicant;
(e)   the name and address of the applicant's representative;
(f)   the reproduction of the mark and any description of the mark;

(g) the list of goods and services;
(h) details of any claim of priority;
(i)   details of any claim of exhibition priority;
(j)   details of any seniority claim;
(k) any statement of distinctiveness acquired through use;
(l)   any disclaimer;
(m) the first and second languages of the CTM application; and
(n) the date of registration of the CTM and the registration number.

The registration is then published in the *Community Trade Marks Bulletin*. The proprietor's right to sue for infringement of a CTM runs from the date of publication of the CTM registration (Article 9(3) CTMR and see chapter 6).

If the registration fee and any additional late payment fee are not paid within the time periods specified, the CTM application is deemed to have been withdrawn (Article 45 CTMR). Any registration fee paid in respect of a CTM application which does not proceed to registration is refunded by OHIM to the applicant (Rule 23(6) IR).

Registration certificate (Rule 24 IR)
Following registration, OHIM issues the proprietor with a certificate of registration containing the details mentioned above and a statement to the effect that those details have been entered in the CTM Register. The proprietor may obtain certified and uncertified copies of the registration certificate from OHIM on payment of a fee of ECU 30 or 10 per copy respectively (Article 2(28) FR).

Duration of registration (Article 46 CTMR)
The initial registration of a CTM lasts for a period of 10 years *from the date of filing of the application*. Thereafter it can be renewed for further periods of 10 years (see chapter 5).

Fees

Application and registration fees (Article 2(1), (2), (7), (8) and (11) FR)
The basic fee for the filing of a CTM application is ECU 975. A class fee of ECU 200 is payable in respect of each class of goods and services in the CTM application exceeding three.

The basic fee for the registration of a CTM is ECU 1,100. A class fee of ECU 200 is payable in respect of each class of goods and services in the registration exceeding three. The additional fee for late payment of the registration fee is 25 per cent of the belated fee up to a maximum of ECU 750.

Place and methods of payment (Articles 5–10 FR)
Fees must be paid direct to OHIM. They may be paid (Article 5(1) FR):

(a) by payment or transfer to a bank account held by the Office;
(b) by delivery or remittance of cheques made payable to the Office; or
(c) in cash.

Fees may also be paid by deduction from a current account opened at OHIM (Article 5(2) FR). The conditions for opening current accounts at OHIM are set out in Decision No. EX-96-1 of the President of OHIM of 11 January 1996 (OHIM OJ 1/96, p. 49) as amended by Decision No. EX-96-7 of the President of OHIM of 30 July 1996 (OHIM OJ, p. 1455).

Payments made by methods (a) or (b) above or by deduction from an OHIM current account must be made in ECUs (Article 6(1) FR). Payments in cash may only be made in Spanish pesetas and at the premises of OHIM (Article 6(2) FR).

A time limit for payment is not considered to have been met until the full amount of the fee has been paid (Article 9(1) FR). Wherever possible, OHIM will remind the person making the payment that amounts remain outstanding and small outstanding balances may be overlooked (Article 9(2) FR). However, Communication No. 6/96 of the President of OHIM of 8 August 1996 concerning the payment of fees by cheque (OHIM OJ 9/96, p. 1275) makes clear that a shortfall in the amount of fees paid by cheque due to the deduction of bank handling charges will not be overlooked by OHIM after 30 September 1996. A part payment of a fee is refunded to the person making payment after the time limit has expired (Article 9(1) IR). Overpayments are also refunded unless OHIM considers the sum insignificant (Article 10(1) FR).

Every payment must indicate the name of the person making the payment, his address or reference number and the necessary information to enable OHIM to establish both the nature of the payment and the file or trade mark to which it relates. Thus, for example, payment of the registration fee should be accompanied by the description 'registration fee' and the file number allocated to the application for which registration is requested (Article 7(1) IR). If the purpose of a payment is unclear the person making the payment is given one month to remedy the situation, failing which the payment is deemed not to have been made and is refunded (Article 7(2) FR).

The rules governing the date on which payment is deemed to have been made to OHIM are set out in Article 8 of the FR (and see Guidelines concerning proceedings before OHIM, Section 3, OHIM OJ 12/96, p. 1801).

Other matters relating to the registration procedure

Inspection of files (Article 84 CTMR, Rules 88–90 IR)
Any person may inspect the files relating to a *published* CTM application and the resulting CTM registration (Article 84(3) CTMR). A request for inspection must be made to OHIM and the inspection fee of ECU 30 paid (Rule 89(1) IR, Article 2(27) FR). Inspection takes place at the premises of OHIM (Rule 89(3) IR). Inspection may also take place by the issue of copies of documents on file (Rule 89(4) IR). The fee for uncertified copy documents is ECU 10 per copy and for certified copy documents ECU 30 per copy plus ECU 1 for each page exceeding 10 (Rule 89(4) IR, Article 2(28) FR).

A CTM application which has not been published can only be inspected if (Article 84(1) and (2) CTMR):

(a)   the CTM applicant consents to the inspection; or
(b)   the party seeking inspection has been threatened by the applicant with infringement proceedings once the CTM is registered.

The request for inspection must be supported by evidence of one of the above circumstances (Rule 89(2) IR).

Certain documents may be withheld from inspection as follows (Article 84(4) CTMR, Rule 88 IR):

(a)   documents relating to exclusion or objection pursuant to Article 132 of the CTMR (examiners or members of Divisions or the Boards of Appeal);

(b)   draft decisions and opinions; and

(c)   'parts of the file which the party concerned showed a special interest in keeping confidential before the application for inspection of the files was made, unless inspection of such part of the file is justified by overriding legitimate interests of the party seeking inspection'.

The provisions for inspection of the files are of obvious assistance to those wishing to oppose a CTM application or to challenge the resulting registration. The other side of the coin is that arguments submitted to OHIM by the applicant to overcome objections may be used by a third party in subsequent proceedings for infringement, revocation or invalidity. Applicants filing evidence of use of trade marks in support of a CTM application (for example, sales figures, advertising expenditure) must consider whether any information supplied to OHIM is to be treated as confidential.

OHIM's policy on the handling of requests for confidentiality is unknown. If it is as strict as the policy applied by the United Kingdom Trade Marks Registry (*Trade Marks Registry Work Manual*, ch. 6, 32.1–32.3) applicants and their representatives may need to devise ways of disguising commercially sensitive information (for example, by providing 'not less than' figures for sales).

Withdrawal, restriction and amendment of the application (Article 44 CTMR, Rule 13 IR)

The applicant may at any time withdraw his CTM application or restrict the list of goods and services in the application. If the application has already been published the withdrawal or restriction is also published (Article 44(1) CTMR). The procedure to be followed on withdrawal or restriction is described above under 'Examination of the opposition'.

In other respects, a CTM application can be amended only by correcting the name and address of the applicant, errors of wording or of copying or obvious mistakes 'provided that such correction does not substantially change the trade mark or extend the list of goods or services' (Article 44(2) CTMR). Regarding the interpretation of 'obvious mistakes':

The Council and the Commission consider that the words 'obvious mistakes' should be understood as meaning mistakes which obviously require correction, in the sense that nothing else would have been intended than what is offered as the correction (Joint statements by the Council and the Commission of the European Communities entered in the minutes of the Council meeting, at which the Regulation on the Community Trade Mark is adopted on 20 December 1993, OHIM OJ 5/96, p. 613).

If an amendment affects the representation of the trade mark or the list of goods or services and is made after publication of the application, the CTM application is published as amended. The opposition procedure applies to the republication (Rule 13(4) IR).

The procedure on amendment is governed by Rule 13 of the IR. The application for amendment must contain (Rule 13(1) IR):

(a)   the file number of the CTM application;

(b)   the name and address of the applicant;

(c)   the name and address of the applicant's representative;

(d)   an indication of the element of the application to be amended and that element in its amended version;

(e)   where the amendment affects the representation of the mark, an amended reproduction of the mark.

No official form for applying to amend a CTM application is available at the time of writing (pursuant to Rule 83(1) IR). A fee of ECU 200 is payable in respect of an amendment which relates to the representation of the trade mark (Article 140(2) CTMR, Article 2(6) FR). Otherwise no fee is payable in respect of an application to amend.

An application to amend is not deemed to have been filed unless the fee, if any, is paid in full (Rule 13(2) IR). Any other deficiencies in the application to amend must be remedied within the time period specified by OHIM (Rule 13(3) IR) (extendible, Rule 71(1) IR).

The procedure in Rule 13 may be used *mutatis mutandis* for applications to correct the name or address of a representative. No fee is payable in respect of such an application (Rule 13(6) IR).

Alteration of a CTM (Article 48 CTMR, Rule 25 IR)

The basic rule is that a CTM cannot be altered at any time during its lifetime (Article 48(1) CTMR).

The one exception to this rule is where the CTM includes the name and address of the proprietor. This may be altered at the request of the proprietor provided the alteration 'does not substantially affect the identity of the trade mark as originally registered' (Article 48(2) CTMR). The altered representation of the CTM must be published in the *Community Trade Marks Bulletin* and may be opposed within a period of three months from the date of publication (Article 48(3) CTMR). The normal procedure applies to such an opposition (Rule 25(4) IR).

An application for the alteration of a CTM must contain (Rule 25(1) IR):

(a)   the registration number of the CTM;

(b)   the name and address of the CTM proprietor;

(c)   the name and address of the proprietor's representative;

(d)   an indication of the element in the mark to be altered and that element in its amended version; and

(e)   an amended reproduction of the CTM.

Again, no official form for applying to alter a CTM is available at the time of writing (pursuant to Rule 83(1)(c) IR). A fee of ECU 200 appears to be payable in respect of the alteration (Article 140(2) CTMR), although this is not entirely clear from Article 2(6) of the FR.

An application to alter a CTM is not deemed to have been filed unless the fee is paid to OHIM in full (Rule 25(2) IR). Any other deficiency in the application must be remedied within the time limit specified by OHIM (Rule 25(3) IR) (extendible, Rule 71(1) IR).

Review of the filing and search procedures (Articles 25(4) and 39(7) CTMR)
Article 25(4) of the CTMR charges the Commission of the EC with the task of reporting in 2004 on the operation of the system for filing CTM applications. The report is to be accompanied by proposals for modifying that system, if any.

Under Article 39(7) of the CTMR the Commission is also to report to the Council in 2001 on the operation of the system of searching a CTM application, including the payments made to trade mark offices of Member States. The report is to contain proposals for updating the system to take account of new searching techniques.

Chapter Four
Features of the Community Trade Mark System

(The 'Seniority' section of this chapter is based on and in part excerpted from a chapter written by Ruth Annand and Luis-Alfonso Durán of Durán-Corretjer, Barcelona, Spain for *The Community Trade Mark*, published by the International Trademark Association, New York, United States of America.)

Introduction

The aim of this chapter is to describe and evaluate three features of the Community trade mark (CTM) system:

(a)   seniority;
(b)   conversion; and
(c)   the coexistence of national trade marks in Member States alongside a CTM.

Each of these features contributes to the attractiveness of the CTM system, in particular, for the commercial user. To date, seniority has prompted the most concern and debate.

Seniority

What is seniority?
Seniority is not defined in the CTM legislation. Instead seniority is described according to its requirements and its effects.

Defined according to its requirements, seniority consists of:

(a)   a declaration;
(b)   made by the applicant for or the proprietor of a CTM;
(c)   claiming for the CTM the seniority of an earlier national, Benelux or international trade mark registration;
(d)   in respect of the EC Member State in or for which the earlier trade mark is registered;
(e)   to the extent that the marks, the goods and services and the proprietors are the same.

If accepted by OHIM, particulars of a seniority claim are published in the *Community Trade Marks Bulletin* and entered in the Register of CTMs.

Defined according to its effect, seniority means that if and when the earlier trade mark is surrendered or is allowed to lapse, the rights enjoyed by the earlier mark are deemed to continue in respect of the EC Member State in or for which it was registered provided the CTM is kept in force. Seniority lapses if the earlier trade mark is invalidated or revoked, or is surrendered prior to the registration of the CTM.

Thus the advantage of seniority for the CTM owner (at least on paper) is that parallel registrations in EC Member States can be consolidated under the 'roof' of a single registration (the CTM) without any loss of trade mark rights and with a consequent saving in renewal costs. Furthermore, seniority is largely a matter for national law.

Seniority and priority It is important to distinguish between seniority and priority, both of which may be claimed for a CTM.

Priority enables a CTM application to benefit from the earlier filing date of the Paris Convention or World Trade Organisation application from which priority is claimed and is relevant for determining prior rights to the mark (see chapter 3).

By contrast seniority does not affect the CTM itself but is a mechanism for centralising trade mark holdings in EC Member States in a single trade mark (the CTM) without forfeiting local rights.

The legal basis for seniority
The legal basis for seniority is Articles 34 and 35 of the CTMR. Article 34 sets out the substantive requirements for claiming seniority for a CTM application. It then goes on to prescribe the effect of seniority and its lapse. Article 35 makes like provision for claiming seniority for a CTM registration, as to effect and lapse by reference back to Article 34. Article 34 is implemented by Rules 1(1)(h) and 8 of the IR: Article 35 is implemented by Rule 28 of the IR.

Article 14 of the Directive states that the laws of Member States must provide for declaratory actions for revocation or invalidation with regard to national or international trade marks which have been abandoned subsequent to the acceptance by OHIM of a seniority claim for a CTM.

The Examination Guidelines give some insight into how seniority claims will be examined by OHIM (OHIM OJ 9/96, pp. 1324–46; see also Communication No. 1/97 of the President of OHIM of 17 June 1997, OHIM OJ 9/97, pp. 751–7). Decision No. EX-96-3 of 5 March 1996 (OHIM OJ 4/96, pp. 395–7) and Communication No. 3/96 of 22 March 1996 (OHIM OJ 5/96, pp. 595–601) of the President of OHIM concern the filing of evidence in support of, inter alia, a seniority claim.

When and how may seniority be claimed?

When may seniority be claimed? (Articles 34 and 35 CTMR, Rule 8(2) IR)
Seniority may be claimed for a CTM application (Article 34 CTMR) or for a CTM registration (Article 35 CTMR). Where seniority is claimed for a CTM application this may be done either in the application or within two months (non-extendible)

of the filing date of the application (Rule 8(2) IR). A seniority claim for a CTM registration may be made at any time after the CTM is registered.

Fees   No fee needs to be paid when claiming seniority regardless of whether this is done at the time of filing the application, or within two months of the filing date of the application (although, of course, the CTM application fees must be paid, see chapter 3), or after registration of the CTM.

Claiming seniority at the time of filing the CTM application (Article 34(1) CTMR, Rules 1(1)(h) and 8(1) IR, OHIM Examination Guidelines, Guideline 6.1, OHIM OJ 9/96, p. 1329)
According to Rule 1(1)(h) of the IR the required indications for making a valid claim of seniority in the CTM application are:

(a)   a declaration claiming seniority;
(b)   the Member State in or for which the earlier trade mark is registered;
(c)   the date from which the earlier registration was effective;
(d)   the number of the earlier registration; and
(e)   the goods and services for which the earlier trade mark is registered.

The official CTM application form obtainable from OHIM or national offices (see chapter 3 and appendix 5) contains a section for supplying these required indications (page 6, boxes 81 to 89). The seniority claim will be in the same language as the CTM application. A CTM application may be filed in any of the official languages of the EC although a second language, which must be one of the languages of OHIM (Spanish, German, English, French and Italian) must always be given (Article 115 CTMR and see chapter 3).

A declaration claiming seniority   The necessary declaration is effected by checking box 81 on the form. Seniority may be claimed from an earlier national registration in an EC Member State (including the Benelux) or from an international registration under the Madrid Agreement or the Protocol to the Madrid Agreement which has effect in an EC Member State (see chapter 10). The applicant is required to state on the application form (at box 82) whether seniority is claimed from an earlier national or Benelux registration or from an earlier international registration. Seniority may be claimed from one or more of such earlier registrations (Rule 8(1) IR). Where multiple seniorities are claimed the applicant must tick box 89 and supply the required indications for the additional seniorities on attachments to the form.

The Member State in or for which the earlier trade mark is registered   The name of the relevant Member State may be written in full or represented by the standard two-letter code (box 83).

The date from which the earlier registration was effective   There is some confusion surrounding this required indication in Rule 1(1)(h) of the IR. It is unclear whether the 'effective date' of the earlier registration means the priority date (if any), the filing date or the date of actual registration, or for an international registration the date when the period for notifying refusal of protection expires (Article 5, Madrid Agreement and Madrid Protocol — 12 months under the Agreement and 18 months under the Protocol) or the international mark becomes protected in the designated Contracting Party, if earlier (the international registration of trade marks under the Madrid System is described in chapter 10).

As explained below, one of the substantive requirements for claiming seniority under Article 34 of the CTMR is that the earlier mark is *registered* before the filing date of the CTM application. This requirement has led A. von Mühlendahl to conclude ('Seniority in Community Trade Mark Law', ECTA Special Newsletter No. 30, May 1996) that the only indication which OHIM is entitled to require as the 'effective date' under Rule 1(1)(h) of the IR is the date of *actual* registration of the earlier trade mark. For an international trade mark this must be the date of the international registration because of the difficulties involved in OHIM determining when an international mark becomes protected in a designated EC Member State (see below).

On the other hand it is also a substantive requirement under Article 34 of the CTMR that a seniority claim be supported by an *earlier* registration: that is, the filing date or the priority date of the national trade mark (for an international trade mark, the date of international registration or the priority date, or the filing date or priority date of a national registration which the international registration is deemed to replace under Article 4*bis* of the Madrid Agreement or the Madrid Protocol, see chapter 10) must be earlier than the filing date or the priority date of the CTM application.

The standard CTM application form asks the applicant to state the registration date or the international registration date of the earlier trade mark (box 84/85). This suggests that the date of actual registration must be inserted for a national or Benelux trade mark and the date of international registration for an international trade mark. However, the notes on the OHIM CTM application form state in relation to p. 6 — 'Seniority':

[T]he relevant date must be indicated. This is always the date from which the earlier registration was effective as an earlier mark. This will generally be the *filing date, or any priority date* claimed for the earlier registration, and *not the registration date* where that date is different from the filing date. Where the earlier registration is an international registration pursuant to the Madrid Agreement or the Protocol to the Madrid Agreement, the international registration date (or *any priority* claimed for the international registration) should be indicated. (emphasis added)

In view of this apparent confusion applicants are advised to supply the priority date (if any), the filing date and the actual registration date where seniority is claimed from an earlier national or Benelux trade mark: the priority date (if any) and the international registration date where seniority is claimed from an earlier international trade mark. For an international registration it may also be necessary to supply the priority date (if any) and the filing date of a national registration which the international registration has replaced (see chapter 10). Likewise for a Benelux registration where rights have been claimed under the earlier laws of the Benelux countries. It would assist applicants if the standard CTM application form and accompanying notes could be amended to elicit this information more clearly.

The number of the earlier registration   This requirement is self-explanatory. The filing number should also be supplied where it is different from the registration number.

The goods and services for which the mark is registered   The list of goods and services to be entered in the application form depends on whether seniority is claimed for all or only part of the goods and/or services for which the earlier mark is registered.

Where seniority is claimed for all the goods and/or services in the earlier trade mark the list need not be stated. The applicant simply checks box 86 on the form: the goods and/or services for which seniority is claimed will appear from the copy of the earlier registration.

Where the applicant claims partial seniority, the relevant goods and/or services in the earlier registration must be stated in the application (box 87) grouped in the appropriate Nice classes and listed in ascending class order. The statement of goods and/or services may be in either the language of the application proceedings (the first language) or in the language in which they are written in the earlier registration (see notes on the OHIM application form).

The above practice is at variance with Rule 1(1)(h) of the IR, which simply requires the goods and services in the earlier mark to be stated. It has been adopted by OHIM to facilitate the claiming of partial seniority (see below).

Because of difficulties experienced by applicants in defining identical goods and services for partial seniority claims (especially where the CTM application and the earlier registration are in different languages), OHIM recently decided to accept broad or unspecific claims such as 'seniority is claimed for all the goods and services which are found in the earlier mark to the extent that they are also found in the application' (Communication No. 1/97 of the President of OHIM of 17 June 1997, OHIM OJ 9/97, pp. 751–7).

Supporting evidence   Where a seniority claim is made in the CTM application there is a period of three months from the filing date (or such further period as OHIM may specify) for submitting evidence in support (see below).

Claiming seniority within two months from the filing date of the CTM application (Rule 8(2) IR, OHIM Examination Guidelines, Guideline 6.2, OHIM OJ 9/96, p. 1329)
It is also possible to claim seniority for a CTM application for a period of two months after the filing date (non-extendible). Within that period a declaration must be filed with OHIM containing the indications described above. At the time of writing there is no standard form for making a subsequent claim of seniority. The applicant may employ page 6 of the official CTM application form and attach a covering letter stating that the present application is a subsequent claim for seniority and identifying the CTM application to which it relates. The subsequent claim may be filed either in the language of the application proceedings (the first language) or in the second language specified by the CTM applicant (Rule 95(a) IR).

Evidence in support must be submitted to OHIM within three months of the date of receipt by OHIM of the subsequent seniority claim (or such further period as OHIM may specify).

Claiming seniority after the registration of the CTM (Article 35(1) CTMR, Rule 28(1) IR)
A seniority claim made after the registration of a CTM must be filed directly at OHIM. It cannot be made via national offices of Member States or the Benelux Trade Mark Office, in contrast to a seniority claim made in the application for a CTM (see chapter 3).

A standard form for post-registration seniority applications is promised but not available at the time of writing (again the applicant may adapt page 6 of the standard CTM application to make the claim). The application must contain the same indications as described above for claiming seniority for a CTM application together with the following additional indications:

(a)   the registration number of the CTM;
(b)   the name and address of the CTM proprietor; and
(c)   details of any appointed representative.

The first two additional indications enable OHIM to identify the file to which the seniority application relates. Non-EC applicants must appoint a representative in all proceedings before OHIM other than the filing of a CTM application (Article 88(2) CTMR and see chapter 2).

A post-CTM-registration seniority application may be filed in any of the languages of OHIM (Rule 95(b) IR). The language chosen by the applicant becomes the language of the proceedings relating to the seniority application. The list of goods and/or services may be presented in the same language as the seniority application or in the language which appears on the national registration certificate.

Evidence in support of the claim must be submitted at the same time as the application for seniority (or within such further period as OHIM may specify, Rule 28(2) IR and see below).

Substantive requirements for claiming seniority

The trade mark from which seniority is claimed must be 'earlier' than the CTM (Articles 34(1) and 35(1) CTMR)
A seniority claim must be supported by an 'earlier' registration. This means that the filing date or the priority date (if any) of the trade mark from which seniority is claimed must be earlier than the filing date or the priority date (if any) of the CTM.

'Earlier' means prior in time and not the same date. Hence it is not possible to claim simultaneously priority and seniority from the same national trade mark.

No advantage would be gained in any event. Priority grants to a CTM, for the purposes of determining which of several conflicting rights is earlier, an earlier date (the priority date) than the filing date. Seniority does not grant any priority date to the CTM. It merely enables the proprietor of a CTM to surrender or allow to lapse the national trade mark from which seniority is claimed.

If it was possible to claim simultaneously priority and seniority from the same national trade mark the result would be the same date for the CTM and the abandoned national trade mark for the purposes of determining the order of prior rights *in the Member State concerned* — with nothing achieved.

In such a situation the applicant for a CTM must choose between:

(a)   securing a priority date for the CTM which can then be used in opposition or cancellation proceedings against a later conflicting application or registration for a CTM or for a national trade mark in EC Member States; and

(b)   the ability through seniority to abandon the national trade mark while preserving the rights in that mark in or for the Member State of registration.

It is obviously impossible to claim seniority from trade marks which have a filing date, or where priority is claimed a priority date, after the CTM. But again no advantage would be served in being able to do this. Even if the CTM is lost the trade mark owner can convert the CTM into national applications in EC Member States retaining for this purpose the filing date or the priority date of the CTM (see below).

The trade mark from which seniority is claimed must be 'registered' (Articles 34(1) and 35(1) CTMR, OHIM Examination Guidelines, Guideline 6.3, OHIM OJ 9/96, p. 1329)

Seniority can only be claimed from *registered* trade marks. The earlier trade mark must be registered at the time when the seniority claim is made.

When seniority is claimed under Article 34 of the CTMR, the registration requirement must be fulfilled at the date of the filing of the CTM application. This is true even where a subsequent seniority claim is made within two months after the filing date of the CTM application.

If the earlier trade mark is not registered by the filing date of the CTM application, seniority must instead be claimed under Article 35 of the CTMR. The applicant must wait until both the CTM and the earlier trade mark are registered before filing the seniority claim.

The date of registration of a national trade mark must be determined by the law of the place of registration.

No Member State within the Community operates a deposit system for the registration of trade marks. All EC Member States (including the Benelux) conduct some sort of examination and a time period always elapses in between filing and registration. Thus, even for those Member States (for example, the United Kingdom) in which, after actual registration, exclusive rights are backdated to the date of filing, the date of *actual* registration is the appropriate date for controlling when seniority can be claimed from a national trade mark.

This means that the applicant must wait until the national mark is actually entered on the register before claiming seniority from that national mark for the CTM. The date of actual registration may be several months (if not one or two years) after the date of filing of the national mark. OHIM will accept as determinative the registration date appearing on the national registration certificate even though for some Member States this may not be the date of actual registration (for example, former United Kingdom practice was to show the registration date (filing date) on the certificate of registration and not the date of actual registration). An objection will only be raised if it is evident to OHIM from the circumstances that the national mark has not actually been registered at the time of the CTM application.

The position is less clear in those Member States (for example, Germany) which provide for post-registration oppositions. The official view is that the controlling date is still the date of actual registration and that a seniority claim can be presented even though opposition proceedings are pending against the national trade mark. Apparently, post-registration opposition proceedings are to be assimilated to invalidity proceedings and may cause seniority to be lost under Article 34(3) or Article 35(2) of the CTMR.

For international trade marks OHIM regards the date of the international registration as decisive (notes on the OHIM application form, section 6).

The date of international registration is the date on which the international application from which it resulted was received by the office of origin, provided that the application is received by the International Bureau of WIPO within a period of two months from this date. Where the international application is received by the International Bureau more than two months after the application was received by the office of origin, the international registration will bear the date on which the application was actually received by the International Bureau (Article 3(4) of the Madrid Agreement and the Madrid Protocol and Rule 15 of the Common Regulations; there is an equivalent rule governing the date of a subsequent designation under Rule 24(6) of the Common Regulations).

Nevertheless, once an international registration has been accorded a registration date, it must undergo in each country designated for protection the same procedure as a national filing (Article 4 of the Madrid Agreement and the Madrid Protocol). This means that in countries which provide for examination and/or opposition the international trade mark may be refused protection. The period allowed for national offices to notify the International Bureau of any such refusal of protection is 12 months under the Madrid Agreement and 18 months under the Madrid Protocol (Article 5 of the Madrid Agreement and the Madrid Protocol).

OHIM considers it impracticable to ascertain when an international trade mark becomes protected in an EC Member State, which is why it will accept a seniority claim in respect of an international trade mark as from the date of the international registration. As for post-registration oppositions (see above), OHIM argues that the refusal of national protection to an international trade mark is equivalent to revocation or invalidation of a national trade mark (that is, loss of seniority under Article 34(3) or Article 35(2) of the CTMR).

One problem with the above approach is that it discriminates against the owners of national trade marks, who must wait until their trade marks are actually entered on the national register before making a seniority claim. Furthermore, international registration is not available to a trade mark owner whose trade mark office is the office of origin.

It is suggested that the more appropriate rule is that an international trade mark is deemed to be registered for the purposes of claiming seniority for a CTM at the expiration of the 12 or 18-month period for notifying refusal, or when the international trade mark becomes protected in the EC Member State, whichever is the earlier (see, for example, Article 12(1) of the United Kingdom Trade Marks (International Registration) Order 1996, SI 1996/714).

There must be 'triple identity' (Articles 34(1) and 35(1) CTMR)
Because seniority preserves the effect of a national or international registration

once it is surrendered or is allowed to lapse in or for an EC Member State, there is a requirement that the earlier registration from which seniority is claimed must be identical to the CTM. The need for identity extends to the proprietor, the mark and the goods or services of the CTM and the earlier registration. Hence the requirement is often referred to as the 'triple identity' rule (see generally A. von Mühlendahl, 'Seniority in Community trade mark law' ECTA Special Newsletter No. 30, May 1996).

The proprietor of the CTM and the earlier registration must be the same (Articles 34(1) and 35(1) CTMR, OHIM Examination Guidelines, Guidelines 6.3 and 6.5, OHIM OJ 9/96, p. 1329)
The first limb of the triple identity rule is that the applicant for or the proprietor of the CTM must also be the proprietor of the earlier trade mark. Discrepancies may be objected to by OHIM as described below.

Change of address A change of address does not affect the identity of ownership or the seniority claim.

Different version of the same name For a natural person, one or more different given names will be tolerated. Similarly when a legal person is permitted to use different indications to describe its legal nature, such as 'Ltd' and 'AG' for a Swiss corporation or 'SA' and 'NV' for a Belgian corporation, the identity of ownership is unaffected.

A satisfactory explanation is normally sufficient to overcome any query raised by OHIM concerning the use of a different version of the same name (that is, further documentary evidence is not required).

Some applicants, especially from the Asian region, use their English company name for filing trade mark applications in Europe. However, some European countries do not allow use of the English translation of the company name but require the use of the company name in the language of the applicant's country. Thus, for example, the Japanese company X may own a United Kingdom trade mark registration in the name of X Kabushiki Kaisha (because the United Kingdom Patent Office formerly did not permit use of the English translation) but may apply for a CTM, claiming seniority from the United Kingdom trade mark registration, in the name of X Co. Ltd (the English translation of the Japanese company name).

Again, identity of ownership is unaffected and it is suggested that the above practice should be followed by OHIM.

Change of name Examples might include a change in the family name following marriage or a change of name by a company.

Identity of ownership remains in these cases. Nevertheless, because OHIM requires such changes to have been recorded in the national or international register and to appear on the registration certificate, a seniority claim may be delayed. A notable exception to this rule is where a United Kingdom company changes from 'Ltd' to 'plc'.

Change of legal identity If there has been a change in the legal identity of the owner (for example, when a partnership is subsequently incorporated) identity of ownership is no longer fulfilled. The change to the new legal identity must be recorded in the national or international register before the seniority claim can proceed. (Recordal of an assignment of an international trade mark raises a similar problem to that identified above in connection with the international registration date. Change of ownership is entered on the international register and then notified to designated Contracting Parties, who may declare that the assignment is ineffective in their territory; see chapter 10.)

Change of ownership   OHIM will not accept a seniority claim unless the proprietor appearing on the registration certificate for the earlier trade mark is the same as the applicant for or the proprietor of the CTM. Any assignment of the earlier trade mark to the applicant for seniority must, therefore, have been recorded in the national or international register.

Members of the same group of companies   There is no identity of ownership where the earlier trade mark from which seniority is claimed stands in the name of an associated or subsidiary company. The earlier trade mark must be assigned to and registered in the name of the applicant for or the proprietor of the CTM before the seniority claim may proceed. Trade mark owners may need to consider the fiscal implications of such an assignment.

Multiple owners   Where the earlier trade mark from which seniority is claimed is in multiple ownership, *all* the multiple owners must be the applicants for or the proprietors of the CTM.

Time for satisfying identity of ownership   When seniority is claimed for a CTM application the 'same owner' requirement must be met at the time of filing the CTM application (even where the claim is made subsequently within two months of the date of filing of the CTM application).

The earlier trade mark and the CTM must be the same (Articles 34(1) and 35(1) CTMR, OHIM Examination Guidelines, Guidelines 6.3 and 6.4, OHIM OJ 9/96, p. 1329)
Under the second limb of the triple identity rule, the earlier trade mark from which seniority is claimed must be the same as the mark which is the subject of the CTM application or registration.

Word marks   Bearing in mind the various publication and registration practices of national offices, differences in the use of typefaces and/or capital letters or lower case will be ignored by OHIM. However, any difference in the number, content or arrangement of letters, numerals or other typographical signs (for example, the use of hyphenation or accentuation in one mark but not in the other) will be objected to. (An exception to this rule is the use of quotation marks provided these do not form part of the trade mark.)

Figurative marks   These must be exactly the same. No variations are allowed save in the size of the representations and provided the proportions of the earlier mark are the same as for the CTM.

Colour marks   The colours clamed for the earlier trade mark and the CTM must be the same. Where the colours claimed are different, the identity requirement is not met.

The earlier trade mark may not have been published or registered by the national office in colour. This will not affect the seniority claim, provided that the written description or other indications on the registration evidence submitted by the applicant make clear that the colour or colours of the earlier trade mark are the same as for the CTM.

Three-dimensional marks   The test is whether the marks look the same. Such comparison is necessarily based on the two-dimensional graphic representation of the three-dimensional mark. Any difference in office practices relating to the graphic representation of three-dimensional marks is disregarded for the purposes of comparison. Seniority for a three-dimensional CTM cannot be claimed from a two-dimensional earlier trade mark and vice versa.

Sound and smell marks   OHIM has yet to formulate its approach to the manner of graphic representation of sound signs. In the meantime seniority claims for sound marks will be accepted only if the graphic representation of the earlier trade mark is the same as for the CTM. OHIM's policy on smell marks, whether as to seniority, registrability or otherwise, is unknown.

Disclaimers and limitations   Trade mark office practices have changed over the years and differ between Member States and between Member States and OHIM. This is also true of requirements for written descriptions of marks, particulars of colour claims and so on.

A seniority claim will not fail because the CTM application or registration does not contain the same additional elements as the earlier trade mark. However, the additional elements may be taken into account in assessing the identity of the marks.

Compulsory elements   Some EC Member States used to insist that in certain circumstances the applicant for trade mark registration state their name or place of establishment under the trade mark. It was never the intention of the applicant that these compulsory elements should form part of the trade mark. Such marks still exist. It would be consistent with the policy outlined above if seniority claims from these earlier marks were accepted by OHIM despite the non-appearance of the compulsory elements in the CTM.

The goods or services in the CTM and the earlier registration must be the same; partial seniority (Articles 34(1) and 35(1) CTMR, Rule 28(1)(e) IR, OHIM Examination Guidelines, Guideline 6.3, OHIM OJ 9/96, p. 1329)
Under the third limb of the triple identity rule, the goods and services in the earlier registration must be the same as those for which seniority is claimed in the CTM application or registration.

As a matter of policy, OHIM has interpreted Articles 34 and 35 of the CTMR as permitting partial seniority claims where:

(a) the CTM application or registration contains a broader specification of goods and services than the earlier registration; and

(b) the earlier registration contains a broader specification of goods and services than the CTM application or registration.

Article 34 of the CTMR speaks of 'goods or services which are identical with *or contained within* those for which the earlier trade mark has been registered'. It clearly permits a partial seniority claim for a CTM application in situation (b) described above. Article 35 CTMR refers only to 'identical goods or services' and arguably precludes partial seniority claiming for a CTM registration in either situations (a) or (b).

However, a closer reading of Article 34 and 35 of the CTMR, reveals that whereas Articles 34 is referring to the goods and services of the CTM, which must be identical to or contained within those for which the earlier trade mark is registered, Article 35 refers to the goods and services in the earlier registration, which must be identical to the goods and services of the CTM.

One possible interpretation which might reconcile the wording of these two articles and OHIM's policy position is as follows:

(a) Where seniority is claimed at the time of filing or within two months of the filing date (Article 34 CTMR), the goods and services in the CTM application must be identical to or contained in the earlier registration. 'Identical' does not mean that all the goods and services in the CTM application must be the same as in the earlier registration, only that the goods and services for which seniority is claimed must be identical. Accordingly, the CTM application may extend to additional goods and services, but seniority cannot be claimed in respect of these additional goods and services. Equally, partial seniority is allowed where the earlier registration has a broader specification of goods and services than the CTM application, but again seniority cannot be claimed from these additional goods and services because they do not also appear in the CTM. The latter is confirmed by the words 'contained within' in Article 34 of the CTMR (but these words could be regarded as superfluous).

(b) Where seniority is claimed after registration of the CTM (Article 35 CTMR), the goods and services in the earlier registration must be identical to those in the CTM registration. Again 'identical' does not mean 'all': the applicant is not prevented from claiming seniority in respect of some only of the goods and services in the earlier registration; nor is it fatal to the seniority claim that the CTM is registered for goods and services which are additional to those included in the earlier registration. This interpretation of Article 35 CTMR is thought to be supported by Rule 28(1)(e) of the IR which states that a post-CTM-registration seniority claim must contain, inter alia: 'an indication of the goods and services in respect of which seniority is claimed' (contrast the requirement under Rule 1(1)(h) or Rule 8(2) of the IR to state 'the goods and services for which the [earlier] mark is registered', when seniority is claimed under Article 34 CTMR).

The consequences of a partial seniority claim for a narrower list of goods and services than in the earlier registration must not be overlooked. If the earlier trade mark is surrendered or is allowed to lapse, the rights of the proprietor are deemed to continue in the Member State concerned *only* in respect of the goods or services from which seniority was claimed and not the full list of goods and services in the earlier registration.

A valid seniority claim is not dependent on formal classification. The issue is whether the relevant goods and services in the earlier registration are also in the CTM application or registration, regardless of the Class into which they were put by the national office.

Documents to support a seniority claim

Certified copies and 'accurate photocopies' (Rules 8(1), (2) and (4) and 28(1)(f) and (4) IR, Decision No. EX-96-3 of 5 March 1996, OHIM OJ 4/96, pp. 395–7, OHIM Examination Guidelines, Guideline 6.1, OHIM OJ 9/96, p. 1329)
The applicant for seniority must submit to OHIM 'a copy of the relevant registration':

(a)   where seniority is claimed in the CTM application, within three months of the filing date (Rule 8(1) IR);

(b)   where seniority is claimed within two months of the filing date of the CTM application, within three months of receipt by OHIM of the declaration of seniority (Rule 8(2) IR);

(c)   where seniority is claimed after registration of the CTM, at the same time as the declaration of seniority (Rule 28(1) IR).

Time is not of the essence for the filing of supporting documentation (see below).

The 'copy' must document the current status of the earlier registration from which seniority is claimed. This will normally be the copy registration certificate but it may also be necessary to file a copy of any renewal certificate and/or certificate of assignment.

The applicant may submit original documents, certified copies of original documents or 'accurate photocopies' of original documents. This latter possibility was introduced in one of the first decisions of the President of OHIM — Decision No. EX-96-3 of 5 March 1996 (OHIM OJ 4/96, pp. 395–7) made under Rules 8(4) and 28(4) of the IR. Communication No. 3/96 of 22 March 1996 of the President of OHIM (OHIM OJ 5/96, pp. 595–601) explains the reasons for that decision:

Submitting 'original documents' would require the applicant to relinquish documents which he may need to prove ownership. Requesting current certified copies of registrations is an expensive and time-consuming effort. In view of this situation and given the fact that an accurate photocopy of an original document contains the same information as the original document, it was determined . . . that the applicant, instead of submitting original documents, may present an accurate photocopy of such document.

If the applicant chooses to submit a photocopy of an original document, the photocopy must be accompanied by a statement of the applicant or his representative that the information contained in the photocopy corresponds to the current status of the earlier registration (Article 2(2), Decision No. EX-96-3). The only exception to this rule is where the photocopy is of an original document which is dated no later than six months before the date when the photocopy is submitted to OHIM. The statement may be made either on the photocopy itself or in an accompanying letter and must be signed. Where, or to the extent that, an original document is in colour the photocopy must also be in colour.

The representative referred to in Article 2(2) of Decision No. EX-96-3 is the person appointed to represent the applicant in proceedings before OHIM, even though the applicant's local representative might be better placed to vouch for the current status of the earlier trade mark.

OHIM's decision to allow photocopy evidence of seniority may be queried on grounds of legal certainty. A requirement for certified copies provides a fail-safe mechanism for checking the validity of seniority claims. In cases where mere photocopies are supplied, the onus is on competitors wishing to challenge the CTM application or registration to verify such claims.

Three points may be made:

(a)   It is questioned whether the President of OHIM had power under Rules 8(4) and 28(4) of the IR to allow 'accurate photocopies' instead of copies 'certified by the competent authority to be an exact copy of the relevant registration' as stipulated by Rules 8(1) and 28(1)(f) of the IR. The power to allow lesser evidence of seniority is subject to the information being available from 'other sources'. Is the applicant or his representative an appropriate 'other source' of authenticity?

(b)   The decision may facilitate spurious claims of seniority. There appears to be no sanction against submitting incorrect details of seniority apart from losing the claim of seniority once the inaccuracies are discovered. An applicant in bad faith could submit a false claim of seniority in order to avoid an opposition. Once the opposition period had expired, the applicant could withdraw the seniority claim or the applicant could correct the situation after registration of the CTM by deleting, amending or submitting a new seniority claim.

(c)   There is presently no obligation on Member States or WIPO to maintain files of abandoned registrations or designations for protection which have formed the basis of seniority claims. The only obligation is on OHIM to inform national offices of accepted seniority claims (Rules 8(3) and 28(3) IR). This may cause problems of proof where, inter alia:

(i)   the earlier right effect of the abandoned trade mark is relied upon in opposition or cancellation proceedings brought by the CTM owner;
(ii)   the earlier right effect of the abandoned trade mark is relied upon in cancellation proceedings brought against the CTM;
(iii)   cancellation of the abandoned earlier trade mark is sought *a posteriori* before the national tribunal;
(iv)   the CTM owner seeks to enforce infringement rights in the abandoned earlier trade mark before the national court;
(v)   the owner wishes to convert a lost CTM into national applications in Member States in effect 'reviving' any abandoned earlier registrations.

One possible solution is that OHIM and national tribunals should accept the evidence available from the CTM register and the files of the CTM registration, but the system is obviously deficient where all that is on file is photocopies. National offices, in particular, may refuse to recognise rights in earlier registrations which they did not certify and which no longer appear on their files.

Obliging Member States and WIPO to maintain files of abandoned trade marks from which seniority has been claimed has cost implications, which must ultimately be borne by the trade mark owner. A measure intended to save costs seems more likely to multiply them. It could be argued that Decision No. EX-96-3 is in need of urgent reconsideration.

Languages (Rule 96(2) IR)
The evidence to support a seniority claim may be submitted in any of the 11 official languages of the Community. OHIM may require a translation into the language of proceedings or into any of the five languages of OHIM.

Examination of the seniority claim

The seniority claim is examined for formalities and also for compliance with the substantive requirements of seniority.

Formal requirements (Rules 9(3)(d) and (7) and 28(2) IR, OHIM Examination Guidelines, Guidelines 3.8, 3.9 and 6.2, OHIM OJ 9/96, pp. 1326–7 and 1329)
The claim is checked first to ensure that it contains the required indications, namely, the Member State in or for which the earlier trade mark is registered, the number of the earlier registration, the date from which the earlier registration was effective and the goods and services for which the earlier trade mark is registered and for which seniority is claimed (see above).

Where seniority is claimed for a CTM application, the required indications must be supplied either in the application itself or within two months of the filing date (Rule 8(2) IR). The two-month period is non-extendible. When OHIM is operating according to a normal timetable the examiner will notify any formal deficiencies in the seniority claim to the applicant (on a 106 notice) so that they may be remedied within the two-month period. However, with the number of applications awaiting examination at the time of writing it is unlikely that OHIM will examine seniority claims within two months of the filing date The onus is therefore on applicants to ensure that seniority claims are formally correct.

The supporting documentation must be filed within three months of the filing date when seniority has been claimed in the CTM application or within three months from the date when the subsequent seniority claim was received by OHIM (Rule 8(1) and (2) IR). The three-month period is extendible and the applicant will be issued with a 121 reminder to supply the required documentation within a stated period (Rule 9(3) IR) (the period may be further extended at the request of the applicant if OHIM deems it 'appropriate', Rule 71(1) IR).

If the applicant has not complied with the formal requirements within the non-extendible two-month period, or the required documentation has not been supplied within the three-month period as extended, the seniority claim is lost for the CTM application (Rule 9(7) IR). The applicant will be sent a 125 notification informing him of:

(a)   the loss of seniority; and

(b)   the right within two months of receipt of the notification to request a decision of OHIM against which an appeal can be made (Rule 54 IR).

Where seniority is claimed for a CTM registration, the required indications and documentation must be supplied at the time of filing the declaration (Rule 28(1) IR). If the claim is deficient in any respect, the applicant will be invited to remedy the defects within a stated period (generally two months, extendible under Rule 71(1) IR). If the deficiencies are not remedied within the time limit set, the seniority claim is rejected (Rule 28(2) IR). Such a rejection is a decision of OHIM against which an appeal can be made.

Substantive requirements (Rules 9 and 28 IR)

Once the formal examination is complete, the claim is examined against the substantive requirements for seniority, namely, the existence of an earlier registration with 'triple identity' to the CTM. If no discrepancies are found, or if any objection is successfully overcome, the applicant and the relevant national office are informed (Rules 8(3) and 28(3) IR).

For seniority claims which OHIM finds unjustified, the procedure differs according to whether the claim is for a CTM application or registration. A finding that a seniority claim for a CTM application is unjustified results in the loss of rights procedure described above. Such a finding in respect of a CTM registration results in rejection of the seniority claim, which can be appealed directly.

A seniority claim may be refused or rejected in whole or in part.

Registration and publication (Rules 12, 23, 84 and 85 IR)

Details of an accepted seniority claim for a CTM application are published with the application in the *Community Trade Marks Bulletin* against number code 350 (Rule 12(1)(h) IR and see chapter 3). Assuming the CTM application proceeds to registration, the particulars of the seniority claim are entered in the Register (Rule 84(2)(j) IR) and published in the *Bulletin* together with the registration (Rule 23(5) IR). Particulars of an accepted seniority claim for a CTM registration are entered in the Register (Rule 84(3)(f) IR) and published in the *Bulletin* (Rule 85(2) IR).

Tactical considerations of refusal

Where seniority is refused for a CTM application, it may be tactically advantageous to withdraw the seniority claim rather than to request a decision from OHIM and eventually to appeal that decision. Requesting a decision and appealing will inevitably delay the CTM application. If the seniority claim is abandoned before registration, there is nothing to prevent a fresh claim for seniority under Article 35 of the CTMR after the CTM is registered. However, once a decision has been taken to refuse a seniority claim for a CTM application, it would be difficult to argue that the same claim should be allowed for the CTM registration, unless in the meantime the circumstances (for example, as to proprietor) had changed.

Changes after the seniority claim

After a seniority claim has been accepted by OHIM changes may occur in respect of the CTM, the earlier registration, or the seniority claim itself. Some of these changes will result in seniority being lost; others will bring the advantages of seniority into effect.

Changes in the CTM

The following changes in relation to a CTM application or registration possess the common characteristic that they may break the triple identity rule and cause seniority to be lost.

Breaking the same owner rule: assignments (Articles 17(1) and 24 CTMR) A CTM may be transferred with or without the goodwill of the business in which it is used and for some or all of the goods or services for which it is registered (Articles 17(1) and 24 CTMR and see chapter 8).

When a CTM application or a CTM registration is transferred while the earlier trade mark from which seniority is claimed remains registered, the earlier trade mark must be transferred to the new CTM owner, otherwise seniority is lost.

When the CTM transfer takes place after the earlier registration has been abandoned, the position is unclear. One suggestion is that the CTM transfer must take with it the seniority effect. Member States are not obliged to provide for assignment of the continued rights in an abandoned national trade mark from which seniority has been claimed. Furthermore, such an assignment to a third party who is not the CTM owner would be a meaningless exercise. Seniority (that is, the continued rights effect) is lost since the triple identity rule has been broken and the earlier national registration no longer remains.

Nevertheless, it may be advisable for the parties to a post-abandonment CTM transfer to state that the assignment includes continued rights in the earlier abandoned trade mark. This will facilitate any subsequent enforcement of the earlier rights in the national court or conversion of the CTM into national trade mark applications enjoying the benefit of seniority rights.

Breaking the same mark rule: amendments and disclaimers (Articles 44(2), 48(2) and 38(2) CTMR) The CTMR confers only limited power to amend a CTM while the application is pending or to alter a CTM during the period of registration or on renewal (Articles 44(2) and 48(2) CTMR and see chapter 3). Basically a CTM cannot be amended or altered unless it contains the name and address of the proprietor and a change to that name or address does not 'substantially change' (amendment) or does not 'substantially affect the identity of' (alteration) the CTM. The issue for present purposes is whether an allowable amendment or alteration to a CTM breaks the triple identity rule, which requires *identity* (and not substantial identity) between the CTM and the earlier trade mark from which seniority is claimed. (This is not the same issue as whether name changes break the same owner limb of the triple identity rule.)

Since it is acknowledged by OHIM that slight differences in a mark (not resulting from different office practices) lead to non-fulfilment of the same mark rule (see above), the safest course of action to preserve seniority is to amend or alter the earlier trade mark at the same time as the CTM. This, of course, becomes impossible after the earlier trade mark has been abandoned and creates an uncertainty within the system.

Disclaimers are compulsory under the CTM system (Article 38(2) CTMR and see chapter 3). They limit the scope of protection of a CTM and as indicated earlier in this chapter must be taken into account when deciding whether a seniority claim is affected. Where the disclaimer concerns the representation of the mark, it would seem that the triple identity rule is broken and that seniority is lost. However, it is suggested that the preservation or loss of seniority rights depends on the reason for imposition of the disclaimer as follows:

(a) The need for the disclaimer may arise out of the CTMR. This would be the case where, for example, the mark is descriptive in one Member State but not in the Member State in or for which the earlier registration was effected. The absence of the disclaimer on the earlier trade mark should not break the triple identity rule and should not affect the continuation effect of seniority in that Member State once the earlier registration is surrendered or is allowed to lapse. If the CTM is later converted into national applications, the law of the Member State in which conversion is requested should govern whether a disclaimer needs compulsorily or voluntarily to be imposed.

(b) The need for a disclaimer on the CTM may address a problem in the mark which is not specific to a particular Member State. Here it is appropriate that seniority is lost if the disclaimer is not (or cannot be) made in the earlier registration.

Breaking the same goods and services rule: restriction of the list (Articles 44(1) and 49(1) CTMR) The list of goods and services in a CTM may be restricted while the application is pending (Article 44(1) CTMR and see chapter 3) or after registration through surrender (Article 49(1) CTMR and see chapter 5).

As regards restriction of the goods and services in the CTM, it must be remembered that partial seniority is permitted. Thus, seniority will remain in respect of those goods and services which remain common to the CTM and the earlier registration.

Irrespective of whether the restriction is made before or after the abandonment of the earlier registration, seniority will be lost for those goods and/or services which have been deleted for the CTM but are included in the earlier registration. Further, if conversion of the CTM into national applications is requested subsequent to the restriction, seniority rights cannot be enjoyed in respect of the goods and/or services which have been eliminated from the CTM.

Changes in the earlier trade mark
Any change in the earlier national or international trade mark which breaks the triple identity rule will destroy seniority as described in the preceding section. Accordingly, nothing further will be said concerning the effect on seniority of assignment, amendment or alteration, disclaimer or restriction of the earlier mark, except to draw attention to the wider powers in some Member States to allow amendment to a mark. Such an amendment to the earlier trade mark will definitely result in seniority being lost.

Instead this section will discuss how seniority is affected by surrender, non-renewal, revocation and invalidation of the earlier trade mark.

Surrender (Articles 34(2) and (3) and 35(2) CTMR) One of the benefits of seniority is that if the earlier trade mark is surrendered the proprietor is deemed to continue to have the same rights as he would have had if the earlier trade mark had continued to be registered (Articles 34(2) and 35(2) CTMR).

Where seniority is claimed for a CTM application the earlier trade mark must not be surrendered prior to registration of the CTM (Article 34(3) CTMR). If the earlier trade mark is surrendered before the CTM is registered, not only is seniority lost but also the earlier right.

Where seniority is claimed for a CTM registration, the earlier trade mark should not be surrendered before the acceptance by OHIM of the seniority claim.

Non-renewal (Articles 34(2) and 35(2) CTMR)   A further benefit of seniority is that the proprietor may allow an earlier trade mark to lapse and continue to have the same rights as he would have had if the earlier trade mark had continued to be registered.

The earlier trade mark may be allowed to lapse before the CTM has been registered but not before the seniority claim has been accepted by OHIM.

Revocation and invalidity (Articles 34(3) and 35(2) CTMR)   Where the earlier trade mark is revoked or declared invalid in national proceedings, the right to seniority is lost. As explained below, such cancellation proceedings may take place before or after the earlier trade mark is surrendered or is allowed to lapse.

One question frequently asked is: must local user requirements continue to be satisfied post-abandonment of an earlier trade mark, or is use in another Member State sufficient to keep seniority alive? (Use in one Member State only maintains the validity of a CTM under Article 15 CTMR, see chapter 5.) The answer is that there is a continued need to comply with local user requirements, otherwise the earlier trade mark is liable to be revoked *a posteriori* under national law and seniority will be lost.

Suppose, for example, a CTM claims seniority from earlier registrations in the United Kingdom and Spain which are subsequently abandoned. The CTM is used by the proprietor in Spain but genuine use of the CTM in the United Kingdom is interrupted for a continuous period of five years for reasons related to the proprietor's business. The proprietor's use in Spain suffices to protect the CTM from challenge on grounds of non-use. However, the deemed continuation of rights in the United Kingdom mark is vulnerable to attack for non-use in *a posteriori* revocation proceedings before the United Kingdom tribunals. If the United Kingdom registration is revoked *a posteriori*, seniority is lost for the CTM in respect of the United Kingdom but not, of course, for Spain.

Amendment or withdrawal of the seniority link   The final way in which seniority may be lost is through withdrawal or amendment of the seniority claim. This may occur, for example, when a seniority claim has been made erroneously.

There is no provision in the CTMR or the IR for amending or withdrawing a seniority claim, although Rule 84(3)(r) of the IR provides for an entry to be made in the Register when seniority is cancelled.

It is understood that OHIM intends to follow either the amendment (Article 44 CTMR and Rule 13 IR) or the alteration (Article 48 CTMR and Rule 25 IR) procedure *mutatis mutandis* for this purpose.

Impact of seniority in the CTM system

A threefold impact (Articles 34(2) and 35(2) CTMR)
Article 34(2) of the CTMR provides that:

> Seniority shall have *the sole effect* under this Regulation that, where the proprietor of the Community trade mark surrenders the earlier trade mark or allows it to lapse, he shall be deemed to continue to have the same rights as he would have had if the earlier trade mark had continued to be registered. (emphasis added)

The provision applies whether seniority has been claimed for a CTM application or a CTM registration (Article 35(2) CTMR).

Although Article 34(2) speaks of a 'sole effect', the impact of seniority in the CTM system is threefold:

(a) Even after abandonment, the national or international trade mark from which seniority is claimed remains an 'earlier trade mark' for the purposes of Article 8 of the CTMR (relative grounds for refusal). This is the 'sole effect' mentioned in Article 34(2) and undoubtedly the most important to the trade mark owner.

(b) Where seniority is claimed for a CTM application, publication gives 'notice' to would-be opposers that earlier rights belonging to the CTM applicant exist in one or more Member States. This by-product of a seniority claim can act as a valuable deterrent to possible oppositions.

(c) Where a CTM application or registration is lost, the trade mark owner has the opportunity under Article 108 of the CTMR to convert his CTM into national trade mark applications in Member States which carry with them seniority rights. The interrelation of seniority and conversion is explored further below.

Seniority has no infringement effect under the CTMR. Exclusive rights in a CTM run from the date of publication of the CTM registration, although damages may be recovered for infringements occurring in between the date of publication of a CTM application and the date of publication of its registration (Article 9(3) CTMR).

Impact of seniority in national laws

As mentioned in the introduction to seniority, its major impact is in national laws.

Conversion of Community trade marks into national trade mark applications (Article 108(1) and (3) CTMR, Rule 44(1)(d) IR)
When a CTM application is withdrawn, refused or abandoned or a CTM registration is surrendered, allowed to lapse, revoked or declared invalid, the applicant for or the proprietor of the CTM may request that his CTM application or registration be converted into one or more national trade mark applications (Article 108(1) CTMR and see below). If seniority was validly claimed for the CTM application or registration, the national trade mark application enjoys the rights of the earlier

national or international trade mark in the Member State concerned (Article 108(3) CTMR).

In order to maintain the seniority right, the applicant will need to check that the triple identity rule is satisfied at the time the request for conversion is filed. To summarise: the new national trade mark application will enjoy the seniority claimed for the CTM application or registration provided that the CTM applicant or proprietor requesting conversion is the same as the owner of the earlier trade mark, the marks are identical and there is some overlap in the goods or services covered by the CTM and the new trade mark application and the earlier trade mark (see 'Substantive requirements for claiming seniority' above).

While the earlier trade mark continues to be registered, it is unlikely that the CTM applicant or proprietor will request conversion in that Member State for the same goods or services. The conversion effect of seniority becomes significant only after the earlier trade mark has been surrendered or allowed to lapse. The following examples may assist with the sometimes complex situations which can arise out of the triple identity rule in respect of the list of goods or services of the new trade mark application.

The situation is simple when the goods and/or services in the CTM application or registration are exactly the same as those in the earlier trade mark. Assume that the goods in the CTM are 'clothing' and that the goods in the earlier trade mark are 'clothing'. The new trade mark application will be for 'clothing' and will enjoy seniority in respect of those goods.

Assume now that the goods in the CTM were contained within those of the earlier trade mark. Thus, the goods in the CTM are 'clothing' and in the earlier trade mark 'clothing and shoes'. The new trade mark application covers and enjoys seniority only for 'clothing'. There is no protection for 'shoes'.

Finally, assume that the goods of the earlier trade mark were contained within those of the CTM. Thus, the goods in the CTM are 'clothing and shoes' but in the earlier trade mark 'clothing'. The new trade mark application enjoys seniority in respect of 'clothing'. 'Shoes' are protected by the new trade mark application but only from the filing date (or the priority date, if any) of the CTM.

The deemed continuation of rights in abandoned earlier trade marks and the adaptation of national trade mark laws (Article 34(2) CTMR, Article 14 Directive)
Article 34(2) prescribes the effect of seniority under the CTMR. It is left to Member States to provide for the effect of seniority in national laws.

Seniority continues the effect of abandoned earlier national and international trade marks. Such concept is unfamiliar to the trade mark laws of most Member States, which traditionally provide for registered trade marks. However, unless the continuation effect of abandoned earlier trade marks is incorporated into Member States' laws, this major benefit of seniority in the CTM system is frustrated.

The main areas in which national laws need adaptation to accommodate the continuation of rights in abandoned earlier trade marks which are the basis of seniority claims are:

(a)   the relative grounds for refusal;
(b)   infringement;
(c)   cancellation; and

(d)   dealings (assignment, licensing, etc.).

Article 14 of the Directive obliges Member States to legislate in one of these areas, namely, cancellation. Member States must provide for declaratory actions of revocation or invalidation in respect of trade marks which have been abandoned subsequent to acceptance of a seniority claim. It may be the case that a competitor wishing to challenge a CTM must first initiate proceedings to cancel the abandoned earlier trade mark upon which seniority is based. This is a matter for the national tribunal concerned and not for OHIM.

The possibility of, for example, a national action for infringement of an abandoned trade mark raises evidential issues of proof as discussed above ('Documents to support a seniority claim'). It is probable that the offices of Member States will eventually need to maintain records of registrations which have been abandoned subsequent to acceptance of seniority claims. A suggestion is that a proportion of renewal fees collected by OHIM might be paid to national offices towards the costs of keeping such records.

Links between OHIM and national offices (Rules 8(3) and 28(3) IR, OHIM Examination Guidelines, Guideline 6.7, OHIM OJ 9/96, p. 1329)
The formal mechanisms for cooperation between OHIM and national offices over seniority are minimal (there appear to be no formal mechanisms for cooperation with the International Bureau of WIPO over seniority). Rules 8 and 28 of the IR merely oblige OHIM to communicate an accepted seniority claim to the national office(s) concerned. There is no obligation on national offices to inform OHIM of changes in the earlier trade mark which may affect the seniority claim, or vice versa regarding changes in the CTM.

Article 86 of the CTMR states a general principle of administrative cooperation between OHIM and the tribunals of Member States. Liaison meetings are held regularly in Alicante between OHIM and experts from national offices (OHIM OJ 7-8/96, p. 1087). Further links over issues relating to seniority might, therefore, reasonably be expected to follow.

Conversion

What is conversion?
Conversion builds a safety net for trade mark owners into the CTM system. One of the consequences of unitary character is that it may be impossible to obtain or to maintain a CTM because, for example, there exists a prior right in one or several Member States. Equally it may be possible to register the same trade mark validly in one or more other Member States. Articles 108 to 110 of the CTMR and Rules 44 to 47 of the IR enable the proprietor of a CTM application or registration to request its conversion into a national trade mark application in one or more Member States or in the Benelux either where the CTM application is withdrawn or refused or where the CTM ceases to have effect.

Conditions for conversion to apply (Article 108(1) and (2) CTMR)
The option to convert only applies when and to the extent that (Article 108(1) CTMR):

(a) a CTM application is refused, withdrawn or deemed to be withdrawn; or
(b) a CTM ceases to have effect.

According to a statement entered in the minutes of the meeting at which the CTMR was adopted (OHIM OJ 5/96, p. 623) the latter situation will cover: failure to renew (Article 47 CTMR); voluntary surrender in whole or in part (Article 49 CTMR); and revocation and a declaration of invalidity (Article 54 CTMR).

The option to convert is *not* available to the applicant for or the proprietor of a CTM where (Article 108(2) CTMR):

(a) the CTM has been revoked for non-use, unless the mark has been used in the Member State for which conversion is requested; or
(b) grounds for the refusal of the CTM application or for the revocation or invalidity of the CTM exist in the Member State for which conversion is requested. An important consequence of this provision (noted in chapter 3) is that it prevents the owner of an application which has been successfully opposed on the basis of a prior right from seeking protection as a national mark rather than as a CTM thus necessitating a further opposition in the national office by the owner of the prior right.

The first limb of Article 108(2) CTMR is puzzling when contrasted with the widely held view that use of a CTM in *one* Member State suffices to fend off attack on the grounds of non-use:

The Council and the Commission consider that use which is genuine within the meaning of Article 15 [CTMR] in one country constitutes genuine use in the Community. (Joint statements by the Council and the Commission of the European Communities entered in the minutes of the Council meeting, at which the Regulation on the Community Trade Mark is adopted on 20 December 1993, OHIM OJ 5/96, p. 615)

The full text of Article 108(2)(a) of the CTMR states:

Conversion shall not take place:
(a) where the rights of the proprietor of the Community trade mark have been revoked on the grounds of non-use, unless in the Member State for which conversion is requested the Community trade mark has been put to use which would be considered to be genuine use under the laws of that Member State.

In view of the coequal use requirements in the Regulation and the Directive, it seems inconceivable that differing standards of 'genuine use' are contemplated by Article 108(2)(a) of the CTMR as capable of existing at Community and national levels. Article 108(2)(a) of the CTMR therefore casts doubt on the statement quoted above.

Effect of conversion (Articles 108(3) and 32 CTMR)
The advantage to the trade mark owner of the ability to convert is that the filing date of the CTM is maintained. The national trade mark application resulting from

the conversion of the application or the CTM enjoys, in the Member State in which it is filed, the same filing date or the same priority date as that application or CTM. The national trade mark application also enjoys any seniority claimed for the CTM application or registration from an earlier trade mark of the Member State concerned (see above).

Request for conversion (Articles 108(4)–(7) and 109(1) and (2) CTMR, Rule 44(1)(j) IR)
A request for conversion must be filed with OHIM:

(a)   where the CTM application is deemed to be withdrawn or is refused by a decision of OHIM which has become final, within three months of receipt of the communication by OHIM informing the applicant of his right to apply for conversion (Article 108(4) CTMR);

(b)   where the CTM has been revoked or invalidated by a decision of OHIM which has become final or where the surrender of the CTM has been registered, within three months of receipt of the communication by OHIM informing the proprietor of his right to request conversion (Article 108(4) CTMR);

(c)   where the CTM application is withdrawn or the CTM lapses through non-renewal, within three months from the date on which the CTM application was withdrawn or within three months from the last day on which the CTM registration could be renewed (basically six months after the end of the month in which the CTM expires, Article 47(3) CTMR) (Article 108(5) CTMR as amended by Rule 44(1)(j) IR);

(d)   where the CTM is cancelled by a national court, within three months of that decision becoming final (Article 108(6) CTMR).

No extension of these periods is permitted. If the request for conversion is not filed with OHIM in due time the effect of conversion is lost (Article 108(7) CTMR).

A request for conversion must be filed with OHIM (Article 109(1) CTMR). It cannot be routed through a national office. All requests for conversion are published in the *Community Trade Marks Bulletin* unless they relate to a CTM application which has not itself been published (Article 109(2) CTMR, Rule 46 IR).

Contents of the request for conversion (Article 109(1) CTMR and Rule 44(1) IR)
A standard form for requesting conversion is not available at the time of writing. An application for conversion must contain the indications required by Rule 44(1) of the IR namely:

(a)   The name and address of the applicant for conversion.
(b)   The name and address of any appointed representative.
(c)   The file number of the CTM application or the registration number of the CTM.
(d)   The date of filing of the CTM application or the CTM and where applicable details of any claim to priority, exhibition priority or seniority.
(e)   A representation of the CTM applied for or registered.
(f)   The Member State or Member States (including the Benelux) for which conversion is requested.

(g)   The goods or services for which conversion is requested. A list of goods and services need not be supplied where the application for conversion relates to all the goods and services in the CTM application or registration. Where conversion is requested in more than one Member State and the list of goods and services is not the same for all Member States, the respective goods and services for each Member State must be stated.

(h)   Where conversion is requested pursuant to Article 108(4) of the CTMR, an indication to that effect.

(i)   Where conversion is requested pursuant to Article 108(5) of the CTMR following withdrawal of the CTM application, an indication to that effect and the date on which the CTM application was withdrawn.

(j)   Where conversion is requested pursuant to Article 108(5) of the CTMR following non-renewal of the CTM, an indication to that effect and the date of expiry of the registration.

(k)   Where conversion is requested pursuant to Article 108(6) of the CTMR, an indication to that effect, the date on which the decision of the national court became final and a copy of that decision, which may be filed in the language of the decision (Rule 44(2) IR).

Conversion fee (Article 109(1) CTMR, Rule 45(2) IR, Article 2(20) FR)
A fee of ECU 200 is payable in respect of an application for conversion (regardless of the number of Member States for which conversion is requested). The fee must be paid within the relevant three-month period (non-extendible) otherwise the application for conversion is deemed not to have been filed.

Examination of the application for conversion (Article 109(3) CTMR, Rule 45 IR)
The application is examined for compliance with the formal requirements, including payment of the conversion fee, and the conditions for requesting conversion apply.

OHIM must reject a request for conversion filed outside the relevant three-month period (Rule 45(1) IR). The request must at least specify the Member State or State in which conversion is desired and be accompanied by the conversion fee in order to be validly filed (Article 109(1) CTMR, Rule 45(2) IR).

Any other formal deficiency in the application for conversion (for example, a failure to supply a representation of the mark in accordance with Rule 44(1)(e) IR) will be notified by OHIM to the applicant. If the deficiency is not remedied within the time period allowed by the notification (extendible pursuant to rule 71(1) IR) the application for conversion is rejected (Rule 45(3) IR).

The application is examined by OHIM to ensure that the substantive requirements of Article 108(1) of the CTMR are complied with. These are that conversion may be requested by the applicant to the extent that his CTM application has been refused or withdrawn or that his CTM has ceased to have effect. If the substantive requirements are not complied with the application is rejected (Rule 45(1) IR).

Transmission to national offices (Articles 109(3) and 110 CTMR, Rule 47 IR)
Provided it is in order, the application is sent by OHIM 'without delay' to those national offices which the applicant has specified for conversion. OHIM notifies the applicant of the date of transmission (Rule 47 IR).

The national office also examines the request for admissibility pursuant to Article 108 of the CTMR (Article 110(1) CTMR). OHIM must assist in this exercise, if asked to do so, by supplying the national office with 'information enabling that office to decide as to the admissibility of the request' (Article 109(3) CTMR). Such information might relate, for example, to the existence of prior rights.

Thereafter the request for conversion is treated as a national trade mark application and its fate is decided according to national law. However, it cannot be subjected to formal requirements of national law which are additional to those required by the CTMR other than (Article 110(3) CTMR):

(a)   the payment of the national application fee;
(b)   the provision of a translation of the conversion application into the language of the country;
(c)   the indication of a local address for service; and/or
(d)   the filing of additional representations of the mark.

A converted application is subjected to the full application fee in the United Kingdom.

Coexistence of national trade marks and CTMs

An infrequently discussed and perhaps little appreciated advantage of the CTM system is the ability for earlier national rights and earlier CTMs to exist alongside a later CTM. This is made possible by Articles 106 and 107 of the CTMR, which are nicknamed the 'Emmental cheese' provisions because they permit a hole to subsist in the unitary character of the CTM — an area where the CTM cannot be used. By preserving the right to invoke national or Community law to prevent use of a later CTM in one or more EC Member States, the earlier right owner is afforded an effective alternative to opposing the later CTM on application or seeking its cancellation on registration. Further in cases of actual conflict settlement is facilitated, although the parties must bear in mind the competition law implications of any delimitation agreement they enter into pursuant to settlement negotiations and also their ability (or inability) subsequently to control the importation of each other's trade-marked products (see chapters 9 and 7 respectively).

It must be remembered in discussion of Articles 106 and 107 that a CTM is widely believed to be capable of being maintained through use in *one* Member State only of the Community.

Article 106 CTMR — earlier rights

Article 106 CTMR applies to 'earlier rights within the meaning of Article 8 or Article 52(2) [CTMR] in relation to use of a later Community trade mark' (Article 106(1) CTMR). This will cover:

(a)   earlier CTMs or national, Benelux or international trade marks (registrations or applications for registration) to which the criteria of Article 8(1) or Article 8(5) apply;

(b)   well known trade marks to which the criteria of Article 8(1) or Article 8(5) apply;

(c)   the rights of the owner of a mark which has been registered as a CTM unjustifiably and without authority by an agent within the meaning of Article 8(3);

(d)   unregistered national trade marks or other national signs used in the course of trade of more than mere local significance to which the conditions of Article 8(4) apply; and

(e)   rights to a name, rights to personal portrayal, copyrights or industrial property rights to which the conditions of Article 52(2) apply.

Provided national or Community law so permits (whether by civil, administrative or criminal proceedings), the owner of any of the above earlier rights may bring an action before a national or Community tribunal as appropriate to prevent use of the later CTM in the relevant Member State. Protection is in certain cases achieved through the fiction that the later CTM is a national trade mark (Article 106(2) CTMR). Some examples may assist appreciation of the workings of Article 106 of the CTMR:

(a)   A is the owner of a trade mark registered in France. A can oppose or apply to cancel a later conflicting CTM. Alternatively A can object to the use of the CTM in France by bringing an infringement action under French law before a French court.

(b)   B is the owner of an unregistered trade mark in the United Kingdom. B can oppose or apply to cancel a later conflicting CTM. Alternatively B can bring an action in passing-off before a United Kingdom court to prevent use in the United Kingdom.

(c)   C is the Spanish owner of a trade mark which is registered as a CTM by his agent unjustifiably and without authority. C can oppose or apply to cancel the CTM. Alternatively C can rely on Article 11 of the CTMR to prohibit use of the CTM in Spain, provided Spanish law would allow C to prohibit use of a Spanish trade mark in equivalent circumstances (that is, for this purpose the CTM is deemed to be a national trade mark). Jurisdiction at C's option would seem to lie either with a Spanish court or with a CTM court of appropriate forum (Articles 92 and 93 CTMR and see chapter 7).

(d)   D is the owner of a CTM which he uses in Finland and Sweden. D can oppose or apply to cancel a later conflicting CTM. Alternatively D can rely on the infringement provisions in Article 9 of the CTMR to prevent use of the later CTM in Finland and Sweden. Again the later CTM is treated as a national mark for this purpose. Jurisdiction would lie with the Finnish and Swedish courts or a CTM court determined according to the rules of proper forum (Articles 92 and 93 CTMR).

(e)   E is the owner of a trade mark which is well known in the United Kingdom. E can oppose or apply to cancel a later conflicting CTM. Alternatively E can bring an action before the United Kingdom courts under s. 56 of the Trade Marks Act 1994 to restrain use of the CTM in the United Kingdom.

(f)   F is the owner of copyright in Germany. F cannot oppose but can apply to cancel a later conflicting CTM. Alternatively F can bring an infringement action before the German courts under German copyright law to prevent use of the CTM in Germany.

The defence of acquiescence applies to the enforcement of earlier rights under Article 106 of the CTMR (Article 106(1) and see chapters 5 and 7) if the earlier right owner has known of the use of the later CTM in the Member State concerned for five successive years. If acquiescence is made out, the right to prohibit use of the later CTM in that Member State is lost unless the later CTM was applied for in bad faith. Knowledge on the part of the earlier right owner of the registration of the later CTM or of the use of the later CTM in other countries is insufficient to raise the defence. The defence of acquiescence does not apply to the earlier rights in Article 8(3) of the CTMR (CTM registered by an agent) or in Article 52(2) CTMR (right to a name, right of personal portrayal, copyright, industrial property right).

Article 107 — prior rights applicable to particular localities
The 'Emmental cheese' exception to the unitary principle also extends to prior exclusive rights obtained in a particular locality of a Member State. Whether exclusive rights in a particular locality can be acquired is a matter for national law. Owners of these rights may not oppose the registration or apply for a declaration of invalidity of a CTM. But they may successfully object to use of the CTM in the particular locality in which the prior right exists (Article 107(1) CTMR).

The right to oppose use of a CTM under Article 107(1) ceases to apply if the prior right owner knowingly acquiesces in the use of the CTM in his locality for a period of five successive years, unless the CTM was applied for in bad faith (Article 107(2) CTMR). Even where the defence of acquiescence is present, the owner of the CTM is not entitled to oppose use of the prior right.

Simultaneous or successive actions based on a CTM and a national trade mark (Article 105 CTMR)
It can be envisaged that the same proprietor may wish to bring an infringement action to prevent use of a later CTM in one Member State on the basis of an earlier CTM and in another Member State on the basis of an earlier national trade mark. The reason may be, for example, that the goods or services in each mark are not the same. In such a case the rules for the bringing of civil actions on the basis of more than one trade mark contained in Article 105 of the CTMR may need to be considered. These rules are discussed at chapter 7.

Chapter Five
Maintaining and Losing a Community Trade Mark

Introduction

Although they may differ in detailed application, the basic rules of maintenance in the CTM system are the same as for most other trade mark jurisdictions. A CTM is capable of indefinite duration provided it is:

(a)   renewed;
(b)   used; and
(c)   used in accordance with the legislative texts.

Renewal of a CTM

When must a CTM be renewed? (Article 46 CTMR)
A CTM is registered for an initial period of 10 years from the date of filing of the application. The registration must be renewed at the end of the initial 10-year period and thereafter every 10 years (Article 46 CTMR). The 10-year initial registration and renewal periods facilitate the linking of the CTM and Madrid systems through EC membership of the Madrid Protocol (see chapter 10).

Renewal of a CTM is governed by Article 47 of the CTMR, Rules 29 and 30 of the IR and Article 2(12), (13) and (16) of the FR.

Notice of renewal (Article 47(2) CTMR, Rule 29 IR)
At least six months before expiry of the registration, OHIM must send notice of renewal to the proprietor of the CTM and any person having a registered right, including a licence, in respect of the CTM. Failure on the part of OHIM to send notice of renewal neither involves the responsibility of OHIM nor affects the expiry of the registration. However, it may be a valid reason for invoking the *restitutio in integrum* (re-establishment of rights) procedure under Article 78 of the CTMR in favour of a proprietor who has failed to renew the CTM registration in time (see below and chapter 8).

Request for renewal (Article 47(1), (3)–(5) CTMR)
A request for renewal may be made by the proprietor of the CTM or by any person authorised by him (or by a representative of either) (Article 47(1) CTMR). The

request for renewal must be submitted within the period of six months ending on the last day of the month in which the registration expires and must be accompanied by payment of the renewal fees. Failing this, renewal may be requested and the fees paid within a further period of six months from the last day of the month in which the CTM expires. An additional fee is payable in respect of late renewal (Article 47(3) CTMR).

A CTM may be renewed for part only of the goods or services for which it is registered (Article 47(4) CTMR).

Renewal takes effect from the day following the date on which the existing registration expires (Article 47(5) CTMR). Renewals are entered in the CTM Register (Article 47(5)) and are published in Part B of the *Community Trade Marks Bulletin* (Rule 85(2) IR).

Filing the request for renewal (Rule 30(1) IR)

A request for renewal must be filed directly with OHIM. There is no provision for renewing a CTM through trade mark offices of Member States as there is for making an application for a CTM (Article 25(1) CTMR).

The request must be filed in one of the languages of OHIM (Spanish, German, English, French, Italian) (Rule 95(b) IR). An official form will be made available before the first CTM registrations are due for renewal (Rule 83(1)(f) IR) but does not exist at the time of writing.

The IR provides that an application for renewal must contain the following information (Rule 30(1)):

(a) where the application is made by the CTM proprietor, his name and address;

(b) where the application is made by a person authorised to do so by the proprietor of the CTM, the name and address of that person and evidence that he is authorised to file the application;

(c) details of any representative appointed by the applicant;

(d) the registration number of the CTM to be renewed;

(e) an indication that renewal is requested for all the goods and services in the registration or only part of those goods and services. Where part renewal is required this must be shown by listing in Nice classification order either the classes of the goods and services for which renewal is requested or the classes of the goods and services for which renewal is not requested. Goods or services must be grouped under the appropriate Nice class with each group being preceded by the class number.

An application for renewal must be signed by the applicant or his representative and may be submitted by post, by hand delivery, by fax or in the future by e-mail (Rules 79–82 IR).

Fees on renewal (Rule 30(2) IR, Article 2(12), (13) and (16) FR)

The fees payable on renewal are:

(a) the basic renewal fee of ECU 2,500, which will cover renewal of a CTM in up to three classes;

(b)   class fees of ECU 500 for each class of goods and services exceeding three;

(c)   an additional fee of 25 per cent of the above subject to a maximum of ECU 1,500 for late payment of the renewal fees or late submission of the request for renewal.

Fees must be paid direct to OHIM. Methods of payment are as described in the penultimate section of chapter 3.

Deficiencies in an application to renew (Rule 30(3) and (4) IR)

Any deficiencies (for example, failure to provide the registration number or failure to pay the correct renewal fees) in an application to renew which is filed before the end of the month when the CTM expires or in the further six-month grace period allowed for late renewal are notified by OHIM to the applicant or his representative. Where the applicant is a person authorised to request renewal, the proprietor is also notified of the deficiencies (Rule 30(3) IR). Such deficiencies must be remedied before expiry of the late renewal period (Rule 30(4) IR).

Cancellation from the CTM Register (Rule 30(4)–(6) IR)

OHIM will determine that a registration has expired where (Rule 30(4) IR):

(a)   a request for renewal is not submitted by the end of the month in which the CTM expires or by the end of the further six-month grace period allowed for late renewals; or

(b)   the renewal fees and any additional late payment fee are not paid by the end of the periods mentioned in (a) above; or

(c)   any deficiencies in the renewal application are not remedied within the periods mentioned in (a) above.

OHIM will notify expiry and the right to appeal against the determination within two months of the date of the notification (Rule 52(2) IR and see chapter 8) to the CTM proprietor and, where appropriate, the applicant for renewal and any person recorded in the Register as having rights in the CTM (Rule 30(4) IR). When that determination becomes final, the CTM is removed from the Register with effect from the day on which the existing registration expired (Rule 30(5) IR). A record of the determination is entered in the Register (Rule 84(3) IR) and published in Part B of the *Community Trade Marks Bulletin* (Rule 85(2) IR).

A determination of expiry will not be made where the only irregularity is insufficiency of renewal fees. If the applicant has not made clear the class or classes of goods and services in the CTM to be renewed, OHIM will apply the fees received in the order of classification (Rule 30(4) IR).

Any renewal fees paid in respect of a CTM which is not renewed are refunded by OHIM to the payer (Rule 30(6) IR).

There is no equivalent in the CTMR or IR to the public interest provision in s. 6(3) of the United Kingdom Trade Marks Act 1994. Section 6(3) states that an expired national, international (UK) or Community trade mark shall continue to be taken into account for the purpose of determining the registrability of later marks in or for the United Kingdom during the 12 months following expiry, unless the Registrar is satisfied that there has been no bona fide use of the trade mark (presumably in the United Kingdom) during the two years immediately preceding expiry.

Restoration to the Register of an expired CTM (Article 78 CTMR)

Restoration to the Register of a CTM which has been removed for non-submission of a request for renewal or for non-payment of renewal fees is possible under the *restitutio in integrum* (re-establishment of rights) procedure in Article 78 of the CTMR.

An application for restoration of a CTM must be made to OHIM within six months from expiry of the grace period allowed for late renewal (that is, within one year from the last day of the month in which the CTM expired) *and* within two months of removal of the cause for non-observance of the time limits for renewal (Article 78(2) CTMR). The omitted act, that is, the submission of the request for renewal and/or the payment of the renewal fee and any additional late payment fee, must be completed within this period. The application must be in writing, state the grounds and facts upon which it is based and be accompanied by a re-establishment of rights fee of ECU 200 (Article 78(3) CTMR, Article 2(19) FR).

Restoration of a CTM will be granted provided the applicant exercised 'all due care required by the circumstances' to meet the time limits for renewal of the CTM specified in Article 47(3) CTMR (Article 78(1) CTMR). The condition is the same as for restoration of patents under Article 122(1) of the European Patent Convention 1973 and involves similar principles to restoration of patents under s. 28(3) of the United Kingdom Patents Act 1977 (where the patentee must have taken 'reasonable care' to ensure timely payment of renewal fees). Cases decided under these provisions may shed light on the application of Article 78 of the CTMR in the context presently under consideration.

In *Ling's Patent* [1981] RPC 85 the United Kingdom Patents Court held that it was reasonable for an individual patentee to rely on the Patent Office renewal notice (which was not received) rather than to set up a reminder system of his own. By contrast, in *Re Proweco BV* (decision J 12/84) EPO OJ 4/1985, pp. 108–12, the European Patent Office Legal Board of Appeal noted with regard to the absence of the EPO renewal reminder that the patentee had not exercised due care in relying on third parties outside his control to intercept his mail.

The illness of an individual patentee was accepted as a ground for restoration in the United Kingdom case of *Mead's Patent* [1980] RPC 146. However, while stating that less strict standards may apply to the duty of care of a sole representative as opposed to an association of representatives, the EPO Legal Board of Appeal refused to grant restoration because of the illness of a sole representative in *Re Marron Blanco* (decision J 41/92) EPO OJ 3/95, pp. 93–100. The representative should have sought cover during her illness, for example, from a colleague or a professional organisation.

In *Textron's Patent* [1989] RPC 441 the United Kingdom House of Lords granted restoration of a patent which had lapsed due to the inexplicable failure of a legal assistant to follow her principal's clear instructions about renewal.

A patentee's financial circumstances at the time of renewal can be a ground for restoration of a patent under both the European and the United Kingdom patent systems (*Radakovic, Svätopluk/Re-establishment of rights* (decision J 22/88) [1990] EPOR 495; *Ament's Application* [1994] RPC 647).

Restoration to the Register of a CTM which has been removed following non-renewal is published in Part B of the *Community Trade Marks Bulletin* (Rule 85(2) IR).

Protection of third party rights on restoration of a CTM (Article 78(6) and (7) CTMR)

Article 78(6) of the CTMR provides for the protection of the rights of third parties where a person, in good faith, has used in the course of trade a sign which is identical or similar to a CTM in relation to identical or similar goods or services in the period between cancellation of the CTM from the Register and publication of the restoration of the CTM in the *Community Trade Marks Bulletin*. Such a person may bring third-party proceedings to oppose the grant of restoration of the CTM within two months of the publication of the restoration in the *Bulletin* (Article 78(7) CTMR).

Lack of good faith in this context may include knowledge of the circumstances preventing timely renewal of the CTM, for example, the financial difficulties of the proprietor. It may also include knowledge of the continued use of the CTM, although where such use is in other Member States the third party may attribute the use to national registrations or other national rights.

Use of a CTM

The CTM use requirement (Article 15(1) CTMR)

In accordance with internationally recognised standards (see TRIPs Articles 15(3) and 19(1)), the CTM system only protects CTMs which are in use. The basic requirement is that the CTM proprietor must be able to prove *genuine use* in the Community within any continuous period of five years after registration or *proper reasons for non-use*. If the proprietor is unable to prove either, then the CTM may no longer be enforced and is liable to revocation on application by a third party. Thus Article 15(1) of the CTMR provides that:

> If, within a period of five years following registration, the proprietor has not put the Community trade mark to genuine use in the Community in connection with the goods or services in respect of which it is registered, or if such use has been suspended during an uninterrupted period of five years, the Community trade mark shall be subject to the sanctions provided for in this Regulation, unless there are proper reasons for non-use.

Article 10(1) of the Directive imposes a similar use requirement for national trade marks in the harmonised trade mark laws of Member States. Although implicit in United Kingdom trade marks law, this use requirement is not stated as such in the Trade Marks Act 1994.

Genuine use of the CTM (Article 15(1)–(3) CTMR)

Commercial use versus token use   The CTM must be put to genuine use in the Community. The original Draft CTMR specified 'serious use' (Article 13 Draft CTMR, COM (80) 635 final of 19 November 1980, reprinted in Bull EC suppl.

5/80), which indicates that Article 15(1) of the CTMR fixes a lesser standard. Indeed the *Oxford English Reference Dictionary* (1995) defines 'genuine' as 'properly so called; not sham'.

The words 'genuine use' in the harmonised non-use grounds for revocation under the United Kingdom Trade Marks Act 1994 (s. 46(1)(a) and (b)) are thought to encapsulate a similar standard to 'bona fide use' under the Trade Marks Act 1938 (s. 26; United Kingdom Government White Paper, *Reform of Trade Marks Law* (Cm 1203, 1990), para. 4.29). This was set as substantial and genuine use judged by ordinary commercial standards, such standards being considered in relation to the trade concerned.

Thus in *Imperial Group Ltd* v *Philip Morris & Co. Ltd* [1982] FSR 72 and *CONCORD Trade Mark* [1987] FSR 209 fake and insubstantial launches of existing makes of cigarettes under 'ghost' marks were insufficient to fend off attacks on the grounds of non-use. Similarly in *ORIENT EXPRESS Trade Mark* [1996] RPC 25 the supply of clothing to a friend of the president of the registered proprietors did not show use in the ordinary course of trade and was insufficient to rebut the prima facie case of non-use. However, provided there was an intention to derive trading profit and trading goodwill from marketing goods or services under the trade mark, the fact that use was initiated in order successfully to sue a competitor for infringement was irrelevant (*Electrolux Ltd* v *Electrix Ltd* (1954) 71 RPC 23).

The conclusion that 'genuine use' under Article 15(1) of the CTMR excludes token use would be consistent with the trade mark laws of other Member States. For example, in the Benelux case of *Switch International Hi-Fi Ltd* v *Swatch AG* [1995] BIE 96, a few deliveries of SWATCH telephones were held to be token sales designed to enhance the ownership rights in the SWATCH trade mark for telephones and not commercial sales within the Benelux sufficient to prevent cancellation of the registration.

The conclusion is further supported by *Levin* v *Staatssecretaris van Justitie* (case 53/81) [1982] ECR 1035, where the Court of Justice of the European Communities, on being asked to explain the notion of 'worker' in the context of Article 48 of the Treaty, stated that the rules relating to the freedom of workers within the Community covered: 'only the pursuit of *effective and genuine* activities, *to the exclusion of activities on such a small scale as to be regarded as purely marginal and ancillary*' and 'guarantee only the freedom of movement of persons who *pursue or are desirous of pursuing an economic activity*'. (emphasis added)

Pre-launch preparations   Depending on their nature and extent, it is suggested that preparations for placing goods or services on the market in the Community may constitute genuine use of a CTM even though no actual sales have resulted (this seems to borne out by the wording of the corresponding non-use ground for revocation in Article 50(1)(a) CTMR, see below).

In the United Kingdom case of *HERMES Trade Mark* [1982] RPC 425 the registered proprietors had sufficiently used the mark in relation to watches by placing orders with their component suppliers and by the preparation of price lists (see also *REVUE Trade Mark* [1979] RPC 27 — advertisements and orders to suppliers constituted sufficient use of REVUE for binoculars; and *ARLITE Trade Mark* [1995] RPC 504 — the mailing of promotional literature and the solicitation of orders amounted to sufficient use of ARLITE for building panels). By contrast, the Austrian trade mark JOHANN STRAUSS registered for spirits and liqueurs was cancelled for non-use despite such preparatory activities as designing, ordering and delivering labels and correspondence with manufacturers (Supreme Patent and Trademark Board, 31 May 1995 (Om 2/95, Nm 35/91)).

Genuine use in connection with the registered goods or services   Article 15(1) of the CTMR states that the proprietor must put the CTM to genuine use in connection with the goods or services for which it is registered. An immediate question is — what types of uses count for this purpose? Which in turn prompts the question — what functions of a trade mark does the CTMR recognise? The problem is best illustrated by case law from the Member States.

In *KODIAK Trade Mark* [1990] FSR 49 the KODAK trade mark was registered in the United Kingdom for clothing. Kodak Ltd used the mark on T-shirts to promote sales of its photographic goods. This was held not to be use of the trade mark to indicate the origin of the T-shirts and the KODAK registration for clothing was cancelled. Similar reasoning was applied to deny registration in the United Kingdom of three ELVIS trade marks for toiletries in *Re Trade Mark Applications by Elvis Presley Inc.* [1997] RPC 543 (Laddie J). ELVIS was too well known as the name of the famous singer to be capable of indicating the trade origin of the goods for which registration was sought. (This case has repercussions for the United Kingdom character merchandising industry which are paralleled in passing-off by the case of *Nice and Safe Attitude Ltd* v *Flook* [1997] FSR 14.)

In Sweden, a successful non-use attack was launched by Payless ShoeSource Inc. against the trade mark PAYLESS registered for footwear, clothing and headgear. The trade mark had been used on T-shirts to promote the registered proprietor's Sko-Uno stores campaign event. PAYLESS was also used on the labels of sales stock and appeared on signs during the Sko-Uno twice yearly sales. It was held that the trade mark had not been used in a trade mark sense and should be cancelled (Svea Court of Appeals, Case No. T 979/95, 6 May 1997).

Although Recital 7 of the Preamble to the CTMR mentions only the origin function of a CTM, the words 'in particular' suggest that other interests of the CTM proprietor may be capable of protection:

> Whereas the protection afforded by a Community trade mark, the function of which is *in particular* to guarantee the trade mark *as an indication of origin.* (emphasis added)

This proposition is borne out by the inclusion of protection against dilution of a CTM in Articles 8(5) and 9(1)(c) of the CTMR (see chapters 2 and 6 respectively).

In *Bristol-Myers-Squibb* v *Paranova A/S* (cases C-427, 429 and 436/93) [1996] ECR I-3457; *Eurim-Pharm Arzneimittel GmbH* v *Beiersdorf AG* (cases C-71 and 72/94) [1996] ECR I-3603; and *MPA Pharma GmbH* v *Rhône-Poulenc Pharma GmbH* [1996] ECR I-3671 (see chapter 7) the Court of Justice of the European Communities recognised the right of a trade mark owner to oppose defective, poor quality or untidy repackaging of his products which might damage the reputation of the trade mark.

The opinion of Advocate-General Jacobs in *Parfums Christian Dior SA* v *Evora BV* (case C-337/95) 29 April 1997, recommends that a trade mark owner should also have the right to oppose the use of his mark by a reseller in advertising, where such advertising is liable to damage significantly the reputation of the trade mark and of its owner. With luxury goods like perfumes, the damage may consist of damage to the luxurious image of the goods.

Both the *Bristol-Myers-Squibb* repackaging cases and Advocate-General Jacob's opinion in *Dior* arguably recognise the wider advertising function of a trade mark, that is, the trade mark as a 'carrier' of goodwill. But both concern the limits of the exhaustion of rights doctrine under Article 13 of the CTMR, Article 7 of the Directive and Articles 30 to 36 of the EC Treaty.

When it comes to defining the extent of protection of a CTM under the CTMR (or of a national trade mark under the Directive), the prior case law of the Court of Justice of the European Communities (see, for example *Deutsche Renault AG* v *Audi AG* (case C-317/91) [1993] ECR I-6227 and *IHT Internationale Heiztechnik GmbH* v *Ideal-Standard GmbH* (case C-9/93) [1994] ECR I-2789 discussed in chapter 7) and the opinion of Advocate-General Jacobs in *Sabel BV* v *Puma AG* (case C-251/95) 29 April 1997, indicate that the trade mark owner's rights on opposition, invalidation and infringement will be limited by the origin function of a trade mark (except possibly where the trade mark has reputation and the later sign is applied for or used in relation to dissimilar products). Since the requirement for use of a CTM in Article 15(1) of the CTMR (and use of a national trade mark in Article 10 of the Directive) is inextricably linked to the rights of the trade mark owner on opposition, invalidity and infringement, it is probable that satisfaction of that requirement will similarly be limited to uses which fulfil the origin function of a trade mark. Thus the *KODIAK*, *ELVIS* and *PAYLESS* decisions mentioned above may be characteristic of future decisions on similar facts at Community level.

Specific qualifying uses   Article 15(2) of the CTMR follows Article 10(2) of the Directive in providing that use for the purposes of Article 15(1) of the CTMR includes:

> (a)   use of the CTM in a form differing in elements which do not alter the distinctive character of the mark in the form in which it was registered;
> (b)   affixing of the CTM to goods or to the packaging thereof in the Community solely for export purposes.

Paragraph (a) implements Article 5C(2) of the Paris Convention. Case law on a similar provision in the United Kingdom Trade Marks Act 1938 (s. 30(1)) may assist in illustrating its possible operation. In *HUGGARS Trade Mark* [1979] FSR 310 the proprietor's use of HUGGERS was not accepted as use of the registered trade mark HUGGARS. This was because HUGGARS was meaningless whereas HUGGERS was descriptive of the registered goods — clothing. By contrast in *PELICAN Trade Mark* [1978] RPC 424 substitution of the letter 'K' for the letter 'C' in the trade mark (in script form) was not an alteration affecting its distinctive character. In *Seaforth Maritine Ltd's Trade Mark* [1993] RPC 72 the representation of a device trade mark was changed from black and white to pure white on a black background. The visual impressions created by the original and altered trade marks were different. The altered form was therefore unacceptable as proof of use of the original.

In *ELLE TradeMark* [1997] FSR 529, decided under s. 46(2) of the United Kingdom Trade Marks Act 1994 (implementing Article 10(2) of the Directive), use of ELLE in capital letters and in a special typeface did not constitute use of the registered trade mark 'elle' in lower case enclosed in a circle with a female gender symbol off the bottom right of the circle.

Paragraph (b) means that a CTM can be maintained even though goods manufactured in the Community are intended solely for export to third countries (see COM (84) 470 final of 31 July 1984, Amended Proposal for a Council Regulation (EEC) on the Community Trade Mark). Article 15(2)(b) of the CTMR does not mention use of a CTM in connection with *services* to be provided outside the Community. For example, in *Le Lido SA v Nationale Stichting tot Exploitatie van Casinospelen in Nederland* [1994] IER 28 the Benelux mark LE LIDO for entertainment services was sufficiently used in the Benelux by travel agents offering reservations under the mark with the proprietor's consent for the LE LIDO show in Paris. Use of a CTM in the Community for export trade in services might be covered by the general wording of Article 15(1) of the CTMR.

Genuine use in one Member State   One of the claimed advantages of the CTM is that it needs use in one Member State only in order to remain valid. This advantage is not expressly stated in the CTMR although it is noted that Article 15(1) requires use in the Community, not use in one or more Member States of the Community (hence the possibility in Article 15(2)(b) CTMR that a CTM can be used solely for export trade). The advantage is, however, confirmed by the minutes of the Council meeting at which the CTMR was adopted:

> Re Article 15
> The Council and the Commission consider that use which is genuine within the meaning of Article 15 in one country constitutes genuine use in the Community. (Joint statements by the Council and the Commission of the European Communities entered in the minutes of the Council meeting, at which the Regulation on the Community Trade Mark is adopted on 20 December 1993, OHIM OJ 5/96, p. 615)

In chapter 4 attention was drawn, during the discussion of conversion, to Article 108(2)(a) of the CTMR. In stating that conversion of a CTM cannot take place where the CTM has been revoked for non-use 'unless in the Member State in which conversion is requested the CTM has been put to use which would be considered to be genuine use under the laws of that Member State' doubt is cast on the so-called rule that a CTM is not invalidated by being used solely in one Member State. On the other hand the 'rule' is consistent with Articles 106 and 107 of the CTMR allowing for the coexistence of CTMs and national rights (see chapter 4).

Use with consent   Article 15(3) of the CTMR follows Article 10(3) of the Directive in stating that:

> Use of the Community trade mark *with the consent of the proprietor* shall be deemed to constitute use by the proprietor. (emphasis added)

This recognises that the proprietor is not obliged to use the CTM himself but may invoke the use made of the CTM by third parties and in particular (where the proprietor is a company) by other members of the group of companies concerned (Explanatory Memorandum to the Draft CTMR, COM (80) 635 final of 19 November 1980, reprinted in Bull EC suppl. 5/80). Use is not discounted in the absence of a formal licence. Moreover where use is by a licensee it is irrelevant for this purpose that the licence has not been recorded in the Register of Community Trade Marks and so cannot be pleaded in accordance with Article 23(1) of the CTMR to defeat third parties (see chapter 9).

Although not expressly stated in the CTMR, there is a danger that *uncontrolled* use of a CTM by a third party with consent or by a licensee (whether registered or not) will not count as genuine use of the proprietor under Article 15 of the CTMR. The danger is increased if (as seems increasingly likely) primary emphasis is placed in the CTM system on the guarantee of origin function of a CTM. In *JOB Trade Mark* [1993] FSR 118 a United Kingdom trade mark was found to be open to attack on grounds of non-use, even though the licence had been recorded as a registered user agreement under the 1938 Act (and therefore contained quality control provisions), because the lack of control *in fact* meant that the arrangement amounted to little more than a bare licence.

Article 19(2) of TRIPs makes the point explicitly:

When subject to the control of its owner, use of a trademark by another person shall be recognised as use of the trademark for the purpose of maintaining the registration. (emphasis added)

When does the requirement for use begin?   Article 15(1) of the CTMR states that a CTM must be put to genuine use in the Community within a period of five years *following registration*. Article 46 of the CTMR states that the initial duration of a CTM registration is 10 years *from the date of filing of the application*. Article 9(3) of the CTMR specifies that infringement rights in a CTM run *from the date of publication of registration of the trade mark*. It is thus unclear when the initial five year use period for a CTM begins.

Article 10(1) of the Directive states that a national trade mark must be put to genuine use in the Member State within a period of five years *following the date of completion of the registration procedure*. In the United Kingdom the relevant date is understood to be the date when the mark is actually entered on the Register (meaning that s. 46(1)(a) Trade Marks Act 1994 makes no change to the previous law as interpreted in *BON MATIN Trade Mark* [1989] RPC 537). However, the minutes of the Council meeting on the Directive state:

Re Article 10(1)
The Council and the Commission consider that Member States may decide that the date of publication of the completion of the registration procedure marks the beginning of the five year period. (Joint statements by the Council and the Commission of the European Communities entered in the minutes of the Council meeting, on the first Council Directive approximating the laws of Member States on trade marks adopted on 21 December 1988, OHIM OJ 5/96, p. 607)

Since the purpose of the publication of registration of a CTM is to inform third parties of the proprietor's rights in the CTM and not to complete the registration procedure, it is suggested that the five-year use period following registration in Article 15(1) of the CTMR should commence on the date when the CTM is registered in the Register of Community trade marks. That date is itself entered in the Register (Rule 84(2)(o) IR) and is shown on the CTM certificate of registration (Rule 24(1) IR).

Proper reasons for non-use (Article 15(1) CTMR)
It is a defence to an allegation of non-user if proper reasons exist for the non-use. 'Proper reasons' are not defined in the CTMR but should at least include:

Circumstances arising independently of the will of the owner of the trademark which constitute an obstacle to the use of the trademark, such as import restrictions on or other government requirements for goods or services protected by the trademark. (TRIPs Article 19(1) and see the original Draft CTMR, Article 13(2))

The phrase 'proper reasons for non-use' in the new grounds for revocation of a United Kingdom trade mark in s. 46 of the Trade Marks Act 1994 (implementing Articles 10(1) and 12(1) of the Directive) was considered by the Registry in *INVERMONT Trade Mark* [1997] RPC 125. The Registry noted that 'proper reasons' imposes a more liberal standard than 'special circumstances in the trade' in the equivalent grounds for revocation under the former Act. This more liberal standard might now include disruptive situations affecting the proprietor's business alone and 'proper' must be interpreted in a business sense to mean: apt, acceptable, reasonable, justifiable in the circumstances. In *INVERMONT Trade Mark* the proprietor's reasons were unreasonable. They were that it takes a long time to develop and launch a new product in the field of alcoholic beverages but these were considered by the Registry to be normal and routine difficulties faced by the drinks trade generally.

In contrast to normal delays found in the marketing function, the Registry in *INVERMONT* thought that normal delays occasioned by some unavoidable regulatory requirement, such as the approval of a medicine, might form an acceptable reason for non-use. The Explanatory Memorandum to the Draft CTMR also cites marketing approval for pharmaceuticals as a possible 'proper' reason for non-use (COM (80) 635 final of 19 November 1980, reprinted in Bull EC suppl. 5/80). However the Benelux case of *De Demeulemeester and Grünenthahl GmbH* v *Bristol-Myers Squibb Co.* [1994] IER 29 suggests that pharmaceutical companies are aware of how long it takes to test and obtain marketing approval for drugs and should time their applications for trade mark registration accordingly.

Sanctions for no genuine use or no proper reasons for non-use
The sanctions for failure to comply with Article 15(1) of the CTMR are:

(a)   The CTM proprietor may be called upon to prove genuine use or proper reasons for non-use in opposition brought by him before OHIM under Article 42 of the CTMR. If the proprietor is unable to show either then the opposition is rejected (Article 43(2) CTMR, Rule 22 IR).

(b)   The CTM proprietor may be called upon to prove genuine use or proper reasons for non-use in invalidation proceedings brought by him before OHIM under Article 52(1) of the CTMR. If the proprietor is unable to show either then the application for a declaration for invalidity is rejected (Article 56(2) CTMR, Rule 40(5) IR).

(c)   The CTM may be revoked for lack of use pursuant to a counterclaim to infringement (Article 50(1) CTMR).

(d)   A defendant may plead non-use of the CTM as a defence to infringement (Article 95(3) CTMR).

(e)   The CTM may be revoked for lack of use pursuant to an application by a third party to OHIM (Article 50(1) CTMR).

(f)   Conversion may not be available where the CTM is revoked on grounds of non-use (Article 108(2)(a) CTMR).

Any of these sanctions may, of course, be applied to the CTM wholly or in part.

Opposition and conversion are dealt with in chapters 3 and 4 respectively. The remaining sanctions for non-use are discussed below and in chapter 7.

Revocation of a CTM

The grounds for revocation of a CTM are set out in Article 50(1) of the CTMR and, bar the last, are the same as the grounds for revocation of a national trade mark in Member States under Article 12 of the Directive.

A CTM can be revoked on application to OHIM or on the basis of a counterclaim in infringement proceedings. In addition, the claim that the CTM in suit could be revoked for non-use can be pleaded by the defendant as a defence to infringement (Article 95(3) CTMR).

Article 95 of the CTMR instructs the Community trade mark courts to treat a CTM as valid unless its validity is put in issue by the defendant with a counterclaim for revocation or for a declaration of invalidity. There is no equivalent provision regarding cancellation proceedings before OHIM. While it is incontrovertible that generally speaking the onus of proof in revocation proceedings should lie with the challenger, this is not the case for revocation on the ground of non-use where the challenger would be required to prove a negative. In recognition of this difficulty s. 100 of the United Kingdom Trade Marks Act 1994 provides that:

> If in any civil proceedings under this Act a question arises as to the use to which a registered trade mark has been put, it is for the proprietor to show what use has been made of it.

The CTMR makes clear that in opposition and invalidity proceedings before OHIM based on an earlier CTM or an earlier national trade mark, the owner of the earlier mark may be called upon for proof of use. But there is no similar obligation imposed in the CTMR on the proprietor of a CTM which is challenged on the ground of non-use (unless this is implicit in Article 15(1), see above). The conclusion therefore seems to be that the onus of proof in all cancellation proceedings, including revocation for non-use and whether before OHIM or a CTM court, is on the person challenging the CTM.

Non-use (Article 50(1)(a) CTMR)
Article 50(1)(a) of the CTMR is the corollary of Article 15(1) of the CTMR discussed above. If it is shown that within a continuous period of five years the CTM has not been put to genuine use in the Community for the registered goods or services then the CTM must be revoked unless the CTM proprietor can adduce proper reasons for non-use. The terms 'genuine use' and 'proper reasons for non-use' and the start period for use of a CTM have been explored in connection with Article 15(1). It is noted that a younger than five-year-old CTM cannot be revoked under Article 50(1)(a) of the CTMR on the ground that it was applied for with no intention to use, although such a CTM may be capable of being invalidated under Article 51(1)(b) of the CTMR 'where the applicant was acting in bad faith when he filed the application for the trade mark' (see below).

A CTM may not be revoked if, during the interval between the expiry of the five-year period and the filing of the application or counterclaim, genuine use of the CTM has started or has been resumed. Such commencement or resumption of genuine use of the CTM is, however, disregarded in the three-month period preceding the filing of the application or counterclaim, where preparations for the commencement or resumption of use were made by the CTM proprietor only after he had become aware that the application or counterclaim might be filed. This three-month period of disregard facilitates negotiations between the CTM proprietor and the challenger.

Generic use (Article 50(1)(b) CTMR)
The second ground on which a CTM can be revoked is:

> if, in consequence of acts or the inactivity of the proprietor, the trade mark has become the common name in the trade for a product or service in respect of which it is registered.

A CTM is only liable to revocation on this ground if members of the trade (in contrast to members of the public) use it to signify the name of the registered product rather than the brand of that product. Examples of trade marks which have become generic in this way include ASPIRIN, ESCALATOR, CORN FLAKES and VASELINE.

As is the case with the corresponding absolute ground for refusal of registration in Article 7(1)(d) of the CTMR, generic trade use in any part of the Community spells the death of a CTM. Although there is no like provision in Article 50 to Article 7(2) of the CTMR (see chapter 2), the latter is a consequence of the unitary principle of CTMs and is confirmed by Article 108(2)(b) of the CTMR (see chapter 4).

Generic use by the trade of the CTM must be 'in consequence of acts or inactivity of the proprietor'. The words quoted both limit the scope of Article 50(1)(b) of the CTMR and serve as a useful reminder that the genericisation of a trade mark often occurs because the proprietor himself uses the trade mark as the ordinary name of the registered product or permits widespread infringement. For example, in the Benelux case of *Nederlandse Dermolin Maatschappij Nederland BV* v *Beaphar BV* [1995] IER 13 the trade mark owner contributed to the genericisation of his heart shape trade mark for yeast tablets by allowing other suppliers to produce heart-shaped yeast tablets bearing their own names without reference to the trade mark owner.

Some companies, particularly in America (for example, Xerox Corporation and 3M), run aggressive and quite clever advertising campaigns designed to prevent their trade marks from becoming generic (M. Donovan, *Remarks*, May 1997, International Trademark Association). Other companies publish in-house books or other educational tools on proper trade mark usage (for example, Levi Strauss & Co.). But preventative actions need not extend to quite these lengths.

What is required on the part of the CTM proprietor is that he controls the way in which his CTM used. This is achieved by ensuring that employees, licensees and product retailers observe the following rules (which may be communicated through a pamphlet or brochure) in publicity and promotional materials, in advertising, on labels, in business documents and in all correspondence including internal memoranda:

(a)   A CTM should be emphasised as compared with the surrounding text to show that it is a trade mark and not a descriptive term. The CTM should be capitalised or placed in inverted commas — SCHMACKOS — 'Intel'.

(b)   A CTM is a proper adjective and should always be followed by the generic term it modifies — TOBLERONE chocolate. A CTM should not be used as a noun — 'Pentiums' instead of PENTIUM microprocessors, nor as a verb — 'to Xerox' instead of 'to copy'.

(c)   A prominent indication, for example, by the use of an asterisk, should be given in each piece of printed material that the mark is the registered Community trade mark of X Company.

The symbol ® is traditionally used to signify proprietary rights in a registered trade mark. The practice of placing ® after the mark is expected to continue in relation to a CTM — INTA® — even though the symbol itself has no legal significance in the CTM system.

If use of the CTM is licensed or otherwise authorised there should also be a notice stating that the CTM is being used under licence from or with the authority of the registered proprietor, X Co.

(d)   A company or trade name should be used to identify the overall business of a company or person. A CTM is associated with the products or services of that company or person. For example, Pizza Express plc is the name of the overall restaurant business in which PIZZA EXPRESS pizzas are sold.

(e)   Any use by any other company or person of the same or a similar trade mark or any other misuse of the CTM (particularly in trade catalogues, directories, dictionaries) in any part of the Community should be reported to the CTM proprietor immediately so that appropriate action may be taken. Small rewards like T-shirts or mugs can act as incentives to the prompt delivery of such information.

The CTM proprietor is also advised to maintain a watch on CTM applications and on national trade mark applications in Member States for possible trespassers on his trade mark. The opposition, invalidation and infringement criteria in the CTMR enable the CTM proprietor to control many of the misuses which might ultimately lead to genericisation of his CTM, namely, use of the same or a similar mark for the same or similar goods or services (see chapters 2 and 6 and below).

In addition Article 10 of the CTMR gives the CTM proprietor the valuable right to control the generic use of his CTM in dictionaries, encyclopaedias and similar reference works:

> If the reproduction of a Community trade mark in a dictionary, encyclopaedia or similar reference work gives the impression that it constitutes the generic name of the goods or services for which the trade mark is registered, the publisher of the work shall, at the request of the proprietor of the Community trade mark, ensure that the reproduction of the trade mark at the latest in the next edition of the publication is accompanied by an indication that it is a registered trade mark.

Misuse as a generic term (or less frequently in parody) by the media can be troublesome to the owner of a successful brand. It is entirely unclear whether such misuses of a CTM are covered by the infringement criteria of Article 9(1) of the CTMR (see chapter 6). Further misuse is often prevented by correspondence. Ultimately, if the CTMR fails to provide a remedy, any resulting harm to the CTM cannot be said to be in consequence of the inactivity of the CTM proprietor.

Misleading use (Article 50(1)(c) CTMR)
The third ground for revocation of a CTM is:

> if, in consequence of the use made of it by the proprietor of the trade mark or with his consent in respect of the goods or services for which it is registered, the trade mark is liable to mislead the public, particularly as to the nature, quality or geographical origin of those goods or services.

A CTM is liable to be revoked if it becomes misleading through use in any part of the Community. The difficulties presented to the CTM owner by this ground are illustrated by the COTONELLE case decided by the Court of Justice of the European Communities in November 1996 (*Fratelli Graffione SNC* v *Fransa* (case C-313/94) [1996] ECR I-6039).

The COTONELLE trade mark was revoked in Italy due to its misleading use for toilet paper and disposable handkerchiefs not containing cotton. Similar attempts to revoke the trade mark in France and Spain failed. The question then arose whether imports of these goods lawfully marketed in France where the COTONELLE trade mark was valid could be prohibited in Italy.

The CTM system accepts that in some situations the same trade mark can mislead consumers in one Member State but not those in another Member State (see, for example, Article 108(2)(b) CTMR). The practical solution for the CTM proprietor is to convert his revoked CTM into national trade mark registrations in those Member States where the trade mark is not considered to be misleading (see chapter 4). The parallel importation of products under the mark can then be prevented in the Member States for which the mark is invalid under national consumer protection laws (but not unfair competition laws) subject to the principle of proportionality in Community law (see the ruling of the Court of Justice in *Fratelli Graffione SNC* v *Fransa*).

A CTM proprietor must not himself render the CTM misleading nor must he allow an authorised user to do so. If the CTM suggests that goods originate, say, in Spain, the CTM must not be used by the proprietor in connection with goods originating from France (*TONINO Trade Mark* [1973] RPC 568, United Kingdom). Similarly if the CTM signifies a certain quality of knives it must not be used by a licensee in connection with a different quality of knives (*K. SABATIER Trade Mark* [1993] RPC 97, United Kingdom). Licences and other authorised user agreements must clearly define the licensed goods or services and must contain effective quality control provisions which are exercised in fact. Where a licensee breaches a term in his licensing contract governing duration, form of use, scope of goods or services, the territory of use or the quality of the licensed goods or services, the CTM proprietor may sue the licensee for infringement (Article 22(2) CTMR).

The need to control authorised use of a CTM, not only to prevent the CTM from becoming deceptive but also to prevent its genericisation and to ensure that its use amounts to genuine use, is an important reason why it is preferable for the CTM owner to enter into formal licensing arrangements over his mark even though such formalities are strictly unnecessary under the CTMR.

An assignment can also render a CTM misleading. In particular, Article 17(1) of the CTMR states that a CTM may be assigned independently of the goodwill of the business in which it is used and an assignment may be partial as to the registered goods or services. Either type of assignment may cause deception, for example, the assignment of the same CTM to different assignees in respect of similar products. Article 17(4) provides some assistance to the parties by investing OHIM with the power to refuse the registration of obviously misleading CTM assignments:

> Where it is clear from the transfer documents that because of the transfer the Community trade mark is likely to mislead the public concerning the nature, quality or geographical origin of the goods or services in respect of which it is registered, the Office shall not register the transfer unless the successor agrees to limit registration of the Community trade mark to goods or services in respect of which it is not likely to mislead.

Dealings with a CTM are dealt with in chapter 9.

In contrast to the previous ground, Article 50(1)(c) of the CTMR does not refer to the 'inactivity of the proprietor'. This leaves open the question of whether a CTM can be revoked under Article 50(1)(c) on the basis that use of the CTM in the face of infringements has rendered the mark misleading (see the Australian case of *New South Wales Dairy Corporation* v *Murray Goldburn Co-operative Co.* [1991] RPC 144).

Proprietorship (Article 50(1)(d))
The fourth and final ground on which a CTM can be revoked is:

> if the proprietor of the trade mark no longer satisfies the conditions laid down by Article 5.

Article 5 of the CTMR specifies who is entitled to own a CTM and these conditions must be satisfied not only at the time of application for a CTM but also throughout the lifetime of a CTM. The conditions for entitlement in Article 5 of the CTMR are discussed in chapter 2.

Extent and effect of revocation (Articles 50(2) and 54(1) and (3) CTMR)
A CTM may be revoked for all or only some of the goods or services in respect of which it is registered (Article 50(2) CTMR).

The effect of revocation is that the proprietor's rights in the CTM cease as from the date of the application for revocation or the counterclaim, to the extent that the CTM has been revoked. However, an earlier date may be fixed at the request of one of the parties, which will be the date when one of the grounds for revocation occurred (Article 54(1) CTMR). For example, if the non-use has been over a period of eight years then the date may be set at the expiry of five years from when use of the CTM ceased. The effective date of revocation can be important where the proprietor is suing for infringement of the CTM and claiming damages for past infringements (see the United Kingdom case of *Second Sight Ltd* v *Novell UK Ltd* [1995] RPC 423).

The retroactive effect of revocation will not affect any decision on infringement which has become final and has been enforced prior to the revocation decision (Article 54(3)(a) CTMR). Nor will it affect any contract concluded prior to the date of the revocation decision in so far as the contract has been performed before that decision. However, sums paid under the contract may be reclaimed on grounds of equity (Article 54(3)(b) CTMR). These exceptions to the retroactive effect of revocation are subject to the application of national provisions in Member States relating to negligence, lack of good faith or unjust enrichment (Article 54(3) CTMR).

Invalidity of a CTM

A CTM may be declared invalid on absolute and/or on relative grounds. The absolute grounds for invalidity are set out in Article 51 of the CTMR; the relative grounds for invalidity in Article 52 of the CTMR. Either set of grounds may be raised in an application to OHIM or on the basis of a counterclaim in infringement proceedings. In addition a defendant may plead that the CTM could be declared invalid on account of an earlier right belonging to the defendant in his defence to infringement proceedings (Article 95(3) CTMR).

The onus of proof in invalidity proceedings is on the challenger to the CTM (Article 95(1) CTMR and see above).

The grounds for invalidity of a CTM are similar to the grounds for invalidity of a national trade mark in Member States set out in Articles 3 and 4 of the Directive.

In contrast to revocation, invalidity deals with circumstances existing at the time of registration of the CTM.

Absolute grounds for invalidity (Article 51(1) and (2) CTMR)
A CTM is liable to be declared invalid if it was registered in breach of Article 5 or Article 7 of the CTMR (Article 51(1)(a) CTMR). Article 5 relates to persons who can be proprietors of CTMs and Article 7 sets out the absolute grounds for refusal of a CTM. Articles 5 and 7 of the CTMR are discussed in chapter 2. A third party cannot raise the absolute grounds for refusal of a CTM in opposition proceedings. This must be done either in an application to have the CTM declared invalid or by making observations pursuant to Article 41 of the CTMR (see chapter 3).

Article 51(2) of the CTMR states that even if a CTM was registered in breach of Article 7(1)(b), (c) or (d) of the CTMR (trade mark devoid of any distinctive character, descriptive or generic) it may not be declared invalid if as a result of the use which has been made of it, it has acquired *after registration* a distinctive character in relation to the goods or services for which it is registered.

A CTM is also liable to be declared invalid 'where the applicant was acting in bad faith when he filed the application for the trade mark' (Article 51(1)(b) CTMR). No indication is given in the CTMR as to the meaning of 'bad faith' in this ground.

In *Road Tech Computer Systems Ltd* v *Unison Software (UK) Ltd* [1966] FSR 805 the English High Court was asked to consider, in the context of an application for summary judgment on infringement, the meaning of the equivalent ground for invalidity in ss. 47(1) and 3(6) of the Trade Marks Act 1994 (implementing Article 3(2)(d) of the Directive). The plaintiff's ROADRUNNER trade mark was registered in class 9 for computer software and programs. It was used by the plaintiff on applications software for the transport industry. The defendant claimed that the registration was invalid due to the plaintiff's lack of intention at the time of application to use the trade mark across the width of the specification. Argument centred on whether 'bad faith' required dishonesty (which was not alleged) on the part of the applicant or the lesser standard of insincerity or artificiality — 'the lack of a real or genuine intention or purpose'.

Robert Walker J dismissed the linguistic evidence as tenuous and contradictory. It was unhelpful in construing the Directive which did not define 'bad faith'. The judge sympathised with the view that wide claiming was impermissible under the Trade Marks Act 1994 (see *Mercury Communications Ltd* v *Mercury Interactive (UK) Ltd* [1995] FSR 850). However, had this been the trial of the action, he would have referred the question to the Court of Justice of the European Communities for a preliminary ruling. The application for summary judgment was dismissed.

In *Ben & Jerry's Homemade Inc.* v *Mayfair Projects Ltd* [1995] IER 39 the defendant's Benelux registration for BEN & JERRY'S was held to have been applied for in bad faith. The defendant had been aware of the American company's use of the trade mark outside the Benelux and of their expanding ice cream business. The defendant was stockpiling trade marks with the intention of selling them on.

The OHIM brochure describes applying for a CTM in bad faith as 'unfair practices involving lack of good faith on the part of the applicant at the time of filing'.

Relative grounds for invalidity (Article 52(1)–(4) CTMR)
A CTM may be declared invalid on relative grounds where there existed at the time of the application for the CTM:

(a)   an earlier trade mark as referred to in Article 8(2) of the CTMR and the marks are identical and the goods or services are identical (Article 52(1)(a) CTMR);

(b)   an earlier trade mark as referred to in Article 8(2) of the CTMR where, because the marks are identical or similar and the goods or services are identical or similar, there exists a likelihood of confusion on the part of the public in the territory in which the earlier trade mark is protected: the likelihood of confusion includes the likelihood of association with the earlier trade mark (Article 52(1)(a) CTMR);

(c)   an earlier trade mark as referred to in Article 8(2) of the CTMR and the marks are identical or similar but the goods or services are dissimilar and the earlier trade mark has a reputation in the territory for which it is registered and the use of the later trade mark without due cause would take unfair advantage of or be detrimental to the distinctive character or the repute of the trade mark (Article 52(1)(a) CTMR);

(d)   an unregistered trade mark or other sign which is used in the course of trade and is of more than mere local significance and the rights to that mark or sign were acquired prior to the rights to the CTM and that mark or sign confers on its proprietor the right to prohibit the use of the subsequent trade mark (Article 52(1)(c) CTMR);

(e)   any other earlier right protected by national law against use of the CTM, in particular, a right to a name, a right of personal portrayal, a copyright or an industrial property right (Article 52(2) CTMR).

An 'earlier trade mark' for the purposes of (a) to (c) above means (Article 8(2) CTMR):

(i)   a CTM, a national trade mark in a Member State, a Benelux trade mark or an international trade mark having effect in a Member State with a filing date or a priority date which is earlier than the filing date or the priority date of the CTM;

(ii)   an application for any of the trade marks in (i) which matures to registration;

(iii)   a trade mark which is 'well known' within the meaning of Article 6*bis* of the Paris Convention (see chapter 2) at the filing date or the priority date of the CTM. Note that to constitute a relative ground in (c) the well known trade mark must be registered as a CTM or as a national trade mark in a Member State or in the Benelux (Article 8(5) CTMR).

The relevant reputation for (c) is: for an earlier CTM, reputation in the Community; and for a national trade mark including a Benelux trade mark and an international trade mark having effect in a Member State, reputation in the Member State concerned (Article 8(5) CTMR).

The substantive criteria for invalidity in (a) to (d) above, for example, the meaning of 'likelihood of association', are discussed in chapter 2 in relation to the corresponding relative grounds for refusal of a CTM in Article 8 of the CTMR (Article 8(1)(a), 8(1)(b), 8(5) and 8(4) respectively). Opposition proceedings cannot be brought on the basis of an earlier right mentioned in (e) above, for example, a copyright. Ground (e) is unique to invalidity proceedings.

The final relative ground on which a CTM may be declared invalid is where the CTM is registered in the name of an agent or representative of the 'proprietor' of the trade mark without the proprietor's consent unless the agent or the representative can justify his action (Article 52(1)(b) CTMR). This ground for invalidity corresponds to the relative ground for refusal in Article 8(3) of the CTMR. The country of location of proprietorship rights in the trade mark is irrelevant.

A CTM may not be declared invalid where the proprietor of an earlier right referred to above has expressly consented to the registration of the CTM before the submission of the application for a declaration of invalidity or the counterclaim (Article 52(3) CTMR). Furthermore, where the owner of one or more of the earlier rights has previously applied for a declaration of invalidity or made a counter-claim in infringement proceedings he may not submit a new application or counterclaim on the basis of another right which he could have invoked in support of his first application or counterclaim (Article 52(4) CTMR).

Extent and effect of invalidity (Articles 51(3), 52(5) and 54(2) and (3) CTMR)
Where the ground for invalidity exists in respect of only some of the goods or services then the trade mark shall be declared invalid as regards those goods or services only (Articles 51(3) and 52(5) CTMR).

A CTM which is declared invalid is deemed not to have had any effect under the CTMR from the outset to the extent that the trade mark has been declared invalid (Article 54(2) CTMR).

The exceptions to the retroactive effect of a declaration of invalidity are the same as those which apply to a backdated revocation, subject again to national defences of negligence, lack of good faith and unjust enrichment (Article 54(3) CTMR, see above).

Acquiescence (Article 53 CTMR)
A plea of acquiescence may be raised against a claim for invalidity on relative grounds (Article 53(1) and (2) CTMR). What is required is:

(a)　acquiescence on the part of the earlier right owner;
(b)　for a period of five successive years;
(c)　in the use of the later CTM;
(d)　where the earlier right is a CTM, in the Community, or where the earlier right is a national, Benelux, international or well known trade mark or an unregistered trade mark or other sign used in the course of trade of more than mere local significance, in the Member State concerned;
(e)　while being aware of such use.

The plea is not available where the earlier right falls within Article 52(2) of the CTMR (a right to a name, a right of personal portrayal, a copyright or an industrial property right) nor where an agent or representative registers a CTM without his principal's authority.

Acquiescence on the part of the earlier right owner must be 'for a period of five successive years'. The United Kingdom chose to implement the same wording in Article 9 of the Directive (the counterpart of Article 53 CTMR) with the phrase 'for a continuous period of five years' (s. 48(1) Trade Marks Act 1994). It is suggested that the latter phrase better reflects in the English language the intention behind the time requirement in Article 53 of the CTMR.

The earlier right owner must have acquiesced in the use of the later CTM while being aware of such use. Knowledge of the registration of the CTM alone is insufficient. The requisite standard of knowledge of use seems to be actual knowledge rather than any type of constructive knowledge attributable to the earlier right owner by virtue of his negligence. (Support for a standard of actual knowledge can be ιgained from the Directive. In explaining acquiescence under Article 9, Recital 11 of the Preamble to the Directive speaks of the use of the later trade mark being 'knowingly tolerated' by the owner of the earlier right. The Preamble to the CTMR does not mention Article 53.)

The effect of acquiescence under Article 53 of the CTMR is that the earlier right owner is no longer entitled to seek a declaration of invalidity of the later CTM based on his earlier right. This forfeiture of entitlement extends only to those goods or services in respect of which the later CTM is used. Any remaining goods or services in the later CTM may be declared invalid because of the earlier right.

A further effect of acquiescence under Article 53 of the CTMR is that the earlier right owner cannot oppose the use of the later CTM for the goods or services in respect of which it is so used. Conversely the later CTM owner cannot oppose the use of the earlier right even though that right can no longer be invoked against the later CTM (Article 53(3) CTMR). Thus the net effect of Article 53 is the coexistence of the earlier right and the later CTM in the CTM system.

Nothing in Article 53 of the CTMR prevents either party from attacking the other party's trade mark on the grounds for absolute invalidity or for revocation at Community or national level as appropriate.

Even if a plea of acquiescence on the part of the earlier right owner is made out under Article 53 of the CTMR, it will have no effect if 'the *registration* of the later Community trade mark was *applied for* in bad faith'. The words quoted may be compared to those used in Article 51(1)(b) of the CTMR which provides an absolute ground for invalidity of a CTM 'where the applicant was acting in bad faith when he *filed the application* for the trade mark'.

'Bad faith' is not defined by the CTMR. Its possible meaning in Article 51(1)(b) of the CTMR is explored above. Additional uncertainties in the present context include:

(a)   Is bad faith in the registration of a later CTM restricted to the conduct of the applicant in relation to the earlier right or does it cover that applicant's conduct in general?

(b)   Must bad faith be assessed at the time of filing the application or at any time up to the registration of the later CTM? The latter would include the applicant's conduct on opposition.

Acquiescence under Article 53 of the CTMR is discussed also in connection with defences to infringement of a CTM in chapter 7.

Article 53 of the CTMR is the result of a compromise arrived at over the original proposal that after a certain period a CTM should become incontestable vis-à-vis all proprietors of prior rights even where they had no knowledge of the existence of the trade mark (Explanatory Memorandum to the Draft CTMR, COM (80) 635 final of 19 November 1980, reprinted in Bull EC suppl. 5/80).

Proceedings in OHIM in relation to revocation and invalidity

Revocation and invalidity proceedings before OHIM are governed by Articles 55 and 56 of the CTMR, Rules 37 to 40 of the IR and Article 2(17) of the FR.

Guidelines relating to such proceedings are expected to issue from OHIM sometime in the future (OHIM OJ 12/96, p. 1782). Time limits to be specified by OHIM are, in principle, two months (Guidelines relating to general provisions on proceedings before the Office, Section 1, para. 2, OHIM OJ 12/96, p. 1790).

Who may file an application for revocation or for a declaration of invalidity at OHIM? (Article 55(1) and (3) CTMR)
Any natural or legal person or any trade association which has the capacity to sue or to be sued in its own name may apply to OHIM for revocation or for a declaration of invalidity on absolute grounds (Article 55(1)(a) CTMR).

However, an application for a declaration of invalidity on relative grounds may be submitted to OHIM only by the following persons:

(a)   the proprietor of an earlier registration or application for a CTM, a national trade mark in a Member State, a Benelux trade mark or an international trade mark having effect in a Member State, or the proprietor of an earlier trade mark which is well known in a Member State, and any authorised licensee of that proprietor (Article 55(1)(b) CTMR);

(b)   the proprietor of the trade mark where an agent or a representative registers a CTM unjustifiably without his principal's authority (Article 55(1)(b) CTMR);

(c)   the proprietor of an earlier unregistered trade mark or other sign used in the course of trade of more than mere local significance and any person authorised by national law to prohibit the use of the later CTM on the basis of those rights (Article 55(1)(b) CTMR);

(d)   the owner of a right to a name, a right to personal portrayal, a copyright or an industrial property right and any person authorised by national law to prohibit use of the later CTM on the basis of those rights (Article 55(1)(c) CTMR).

In contrast there appear to be no such restrictions on who may bring a counterclaim for a declaration of invalidity on relative grounds before the CTM courts (Article 96 CTMR). Restricted *locus standi* for such proceedings before OHIM is achieved in Article 55(1) by reference back to Article 42(1) of the CTMR, to which are added the owners of Article 52(2) rights (as in (d) above). Article 42(1) specifies who is entitled to bring opposition proceedings on the relative grounds for refusal of registration in Article 8 of the CTMR (see chapter 3). There is no reference back to Article 42(1) nor any mention of the owners of Article 52(2) rights in Article 96 of the CTMR which governs the admissibility and hearing of counterclaims.

Where the defendant to a counterclaim for a declaration of invalidity of the CTM based on an earlier right wishes to put the earlier right owner to proof of use (Article 96(5) CTMR and see below) the earlier right owner must be joined as a party to the action unless already named as plaintiff. Counterclaims for revocation and for a declaration of invalidity are dealt with in chapter 7.

No application for revocation or for a declaration of invalidity is admissible by OHIM if an application relating to the same subject matter and cause of action and involving the same parties has been adjudicated on by a court in a Member State and has acquired the authority of a final decision (Article 55(3) CTMR).

Where must the application for revocation or for a declaration of invalidity be filed? (Article 55(1) and (2) CTMR)

An application for revocation or for a declaration of invalidity must be submitted direct to OHIM (Article 55(1) CTMR). There is no facility for filing such an application through national trade mark offices of Member States as there is for making a CTM application (Article 25(1) CTMR).

An application for revocation or for a declaration of invalidity must be filed in a written reasoned statement and must be signed (Article 55(2) CTMR, Rule 79 IR). Rule 83(1)(g) of the IR states that OHIM shall make available a form for the application but none exists at the time of writing.

The application may be submitted to OHIM by fax or, in future, by electronic mail (OHIM's preferred methods of filing), by post or by hand delivery (Rule 79 IR). A faxed application is deemed to have been duly signed provided the signature appears on the fax copy (Rule 80(3) IR).

No provision is made in the legislative texts for OHIM to acknowledge receipt of the application to the applicant or his representative. It is probable that this omission will be remedied in the Guidelines as it was for opposition (see OHIM Opposition Proceedings Guidelines, Chapter 1, 1.2).

What is the language of revocation and invalidity proceedings? (Article 115(5)–(7) CTMR, Rule 38 IR)

An application for revocation or for a declaration of invalidity must be filed in one of the languages of OHIM (Spanish, German, English, French, Italian) (Article 115(5) CTMR). If the language of the application is either the first or the second language in which the application for the CTM was filed then that language becomes the language of the revocation or invalidity proceedings (Article 115(6) CTMR). Otherwise the applicant must supply a translation of the application either into the first language of the CTM application, provided that is a language of OHIM, or into the second language within one month of the filing of his application (Rule 38(1) IR). The language chosen by the applicant for the translation then becomes the language of the revocation or invalidity proceedings (Article 115(6) CTMR).

The applicant and the proprietor of the CTM may agree a different language for the revocation or invalidity proceedings, but this must be one of the official languages of the European Communities (Article 115(7) CTMR). Such an agreement must be notified by one of the parties to OHIM within two months of the receipt by the CTM proprietor of the OHIM communication informing him of the application. Where the application was not filed in that language, the applicant must supply OHIM with a translation of the application into that language within one month of the expiry of the two-month period mentioned above (Rule 38(3) IR).

As on opposition (see chapter 3) it seems that double translation costs may be incurred by the applicant where the parties decide upon a different language of proceedings because of the different time periods involved.

What must the application for revocation or for a declaration of invalidity contain? (Rule 37 IR)

An application to OHIM for revocation or for a declaration of invalidity must contain the following indications (Rule 37 IR):

(a) *Details of the contested CTM registration:*

(i)   the registration number of the contested CTM registration;
(ii)   the name and address of the CTM proprietor; and
(iii)   the goods and services in the CTM in respect of which revocation or a declaration of invalidity is sought.

(b) *Details of the grounds of revocation or invalidity:*

(i)   in the case of an application for revocation or for a declaration of invalidity on absolute grounds, a statement of the grounds on which the application is based;
(ii)   in the case of an application for a declaration of invalidity on relative grounds, particulars of the right on which the application is based and if necessary particulars showing that the applicant is entitled to adduce the earlier right as grounds for invalidity (where the earlier right is a right to a name, a right of personal portrayal, a copyright or an industrial property right, the applicant must give particulars showing that he is the proprietor of the right or that he is entitled under the relevant national law to lay claim to such a right); and
(iii)   an indication of the facts, evidence and arguments presented in support of these grounds.

(c) *Details of the applicant:*

(i)   the name and address of the applicant;
(ii)   the name and address of any representative appointed by the applicant.

Evidence in support of the application for revocation or for a declaration of invalidity (Rules 37 and 38(2) IR)
Rule 37 of the IR requires an application for revocation or for a declaration of invalidity to contain 'an indication' of the facts, evidence and arguments presented in support of the application. In contrast to opposition (Rule 20(2) IR, see chapter 3) the IR makes no provision for the filing of evidence in support of the application *after* the application has been communicated to the CTM proprietor. This means that the applicant's evidence must be filed together with the application or within the time period allowed by OHIM for the remedying of any deficiencies in the application. If the evidence is not submitted before the expiry of such period then the application will be deemed inadmissible (Rule 39(1) IR).

Evidence in support of the application may be filed in any of the languages of OHIM or in a different language of the Community where that language has been designated by the parties as the language of proceedings (Rule 96(1) IR). Where the evidence is not filed in the language of the proceedings the applicant must supply a translation of the evidence into that language within two months of the filing of such evidence (Rule 38(2) IR). Again there is the possibility that the applicant may have to incur double translation costs where a different language of proceedings is agreed between the parties during the two-month period following the communication of the application to the CTM proprietor (see above).

Exhibited documents may be filed in any official language of the Community. OHIM may require the documentation to be translated into the language of proceedings within a specified period (Rule 96(2) IR).

Fee for an application for revocation or for a declaration of invalidity (Article 55(2) CTMR, Rule 39(2) and (3) IR, Article 2(17) FR)
The fee for applying to OHIM for revocation or for a declaration of invalidity is ECU 700 (Article 2(17) FR). The fee should accompany the application at the time of filing. Place and methods of payment of OHIM fees are discussed at the end of chapter 3.

An application for revocation or for a declaration of invalidity is deemed not to have been filed unless the fee has been paid (Article 55(2) CTMR). The applicant will be informed by OHIM of any non-payment or shortfall in payment of fees and given a time within which to remedy the deficiency (extendible, Rule 71(1) IR). Any fees paid after the expiry of the period specified are refunded to the applicant (Rule 39(2) IR).

Since the effect of failure to pay the required fee in full is that the application for revocation or for a declaration of invalidity is deemed not to have been filed, OHIM does not have to examine the application. The applicant is notified by OHIM that the application is deemed not to have been filed for non-payment of due fees (Rule 39(3) IR).

Admissibility of the application for revocation or for a declaration of invalidity (Rule 39(1) and (3) IR)
The application for revocation or for a declaration of invalidity is examined by OHIM for compliance with Article 55 of the CTMR (entitlement to file the application), Rule 37 of the IR (content of the application) and other relevant provisions of the CTMR and the IR (for example, appointment of a representative and signature). The applicant is notified by OHIM of any deficiencies in the application and is invited to remedy them by a specified date (extendible, Rule 71(1) IR). If the deficiencies are not remedied by the expiry of the time limit then the application is rejected (Rule 39(1) IR). OHIM notifies the applicant of the rejection of the application and informs the applicant of his right to appeal against that decision within two months of the date of the notification (Rule 52 IR).

There is no provision in the IR for informing the proprietor of the CTM of an application for revocation or for a declaration of invalidity which has been rejected as inadmissible or is deemed not to have been filed for non-payment of fees. Such a procedure may be introduced in the Guidelines as it was for opposition (see OHIM Opposition Proceedings Guidelines, Chapter 2, para. 3).

Examination of the application for revocation or for a declaration of invalidity (Article 56 CTMR, Rule 40 IR)
Assuming the applicant has complied with the admissibility requirements, OHIM will communicate the application for revocation or for a declaration of invalidity to the CTM proprietor (or his representative) and invite him to file his observations within a specified period of time (extendible if the applicant agrees, Rule 71(2) IR) (Rule 40(1) IR).

If the proprietor does not file any observations, OHIM may decide the case on the basis of the applicant's evidence (Rule 40(2) IR).

Any observations filed by the CTM proprietor are communicated to the applicant. The applicant may be invited to reply to the observations within a specified time limit (extendible if the CTM proprietor agrees, Rule 71(2) IR) if OHIM considers that a reply is necessary (Rule 40(3) IR).

Proof of use in invalidity proceedings based on an earlier CTM or an earlier national or international trade mark registered or having effect in a Member State or the Benelux (Article 56(2) and (3) CTMR, Rule 40(4) and (5) IR)

The proprietor of the CTM that is subject to invalidity proceedings based on an earlier CTM may request that the proprietor of the earlier CTM proves that his trade mark has been put to genuine use in the Community in the five years prior to the date of filing of the application for declaration of invalidity, provided the earlier CTM has been registered at that date for five years or longer. Where, at the date of the publication of the CTM application, the earlier CTM had been registered for five years or longer, the proprietor of the earlier CTM must additionally prove that his trade mark had been put to genuine use in the Community in the five years prior to that publication date. If use is proved only in respect of some of the goods or services in the earlier CTM then it is deemed to be registered only for those goods or services for the purposes of the application for the declaration of invalidity (Article 56(2) CTMR).

The same request may be made where the applicant for a declaration of invalidity is relying upon an earlier national or international trade mark registered or having effect in a Member State or the Benelux. In that case the applicant must prove genuine use of the earlier trade mark in the Member State concerned (Article 56(3) CTMR).

If the applicant does not provide proof of use or give proper reasons for non-use, OHIM rejects the application for the declaration of invalidity (Rule 40(5) IR).

The request for proof of use may be made by the CTM proprietor at any time during the invalidity proceedings. The most appropriate time for making the request is when the CTM proprietor files his observations on the application. A request submitted late in the invalidity proceedings, after the parties have had an opportunity to file all their observations and there is enough information on file to reach a decision, might be rejected as being contrary to general principles of adversarial procedure (Articles 79 and 74(2) CTMR).

Assuming the request for proof of use is admissible it is communicated by OHIM to the applicant or his representative. The applicant is allowed a specified time within which to furnish proof of use or to give proper reasons for non-use. The time period is extendible provided the CTM proprietor agrees (Rule 71(2) IR). The rules governing the indications and evidence for furnishing proof of use are the same as on opposition (see chapter 3). A proof of use may be filed in any language of the Community but OHIM may require a translation of it into the language of the proceedings (Rule 40(5) IR).

Friendly settlement (Article 56(4) CTMR)

OHIM may invite the parties to revocation or invalidity proceedings to enter into a friendly settlement (Article 56(4) CTMR). By analogy with opposition, it is probable that such an invitation will be extended only where settlement is desirable on the particular facts of the case or where one of the parties indicates a wish to negotiate (see chapter 3). In contrast to opposition (Rule 20(6) IR) there is no provision for suspending the proceedings in order to accommodate settlement negotiations. The forthcoming Guidelines might be expected to apply Rule 20(6) of the IR *mutatis mutandis*.

Where the outcome of settlement negotiations is either the withdrawal of the application for revocation or for a declaration of invalidity or the surrender or non-renewal of the CTM the parties are advised to consider the inclusion of an apportionment of costs in their agreement (see below).

Decision on the revocation or invalidity (Article 56(1), (5) and (6) CTMR, Rule 40(4) IR)
OHIM may invite the parties as often as necessary to file observations within set time limits either on communications from the other party or on communications issued by OHIM (Article 56(1) CTMR). All such communications and observations must be copied by OHIM to the parties concerned (Rule 40(4) IR).

When OHIM has received, within the time limits specified, all the observations of the parties and, where necessary, evidence of use of the earlier trade mark, it will give a ruling on the application.

Revocation and invalidity are usually decided by OHIM on the basis of written submissions. Oral proceedings may be held by OHIM on its own volition or following a request by one of the parties (Article 75(1) CTMR). However, oral proceedings will only be permitted by OHIM if it considers them absolutely necessary (General provisions for proceedings before the Office, Section 2, para. 3, OHIM OJ 12/96, p. 1798). The conduct of oral proceedings is described in connection with opposition in chapter 3.

The ruling on the revocation or the invalidity is given by a panel of the Cancellation Division comprising three members at least one of whom must be legally qualified (Article 129 CTMR). The panel's decision must be in writing, must state the reasons on which it is based and must be signed by the three members (Article 73 CTMR, Rules 52(1) and 55(1) IR). The decision must also notify the parties of their right to file at OHIM written notice of appeal within two months of the date of notification of the decision (Articles 57 to 59 CTMR, Rule 52(2) IR and see chapter 8).

If the examination of the case reveals that the CTM should not be or should not have been registered for some or all of the goods or services, it must be revoked or declared invalid in respect of those goods or services. Otherwise the application for revocation or for a declaration of invalidity must be rejected (Article 56(5) CTMR).

The decision of the Cancellation Division is communicated to the parties (Rule 61(1) IR) and, if it concerns the revocation or invalidation of the CTM, entered in the Register of CTMs on becoming final (Article 56(6) CTMR). If appropriate, the CTM proprietor will be informed of his right to convert the CTM into national trade mark applications in Member States (see chapter 4).

Costs of the revocation of invalidity proceedings (Article 81 CTMR, Rule 94 IR)
The losing party in revocation and invalidity proceedings bears the fees and costs of the winning party (Article 81(1) CTMR). The fees and costs are limited to those actually incurred by the winning party which are essential to the revocation or invalidity proceedings (Rule 94(6) and (7) IR). Costs may include travel and subsistence and the remuneration of an agent, adviser or advocate limited on an official scale (Rule 94(7) IR).

A different apportionment of costs may be decided by OHIM where each party wins on some points but loses on others or for reasons of equity (Article 81(2) CTMR).

If the proceedings are terminated either by the withdrawal of the application or by the surrender or the non-renewal of the CTM, the party so terminating must bear the fees and costs of the other party (Article 81(3) CTMR). Where the case does not proceed to judgment, for example, at the request of the parties following settlement, costs are at the discretion of OHIM (Article 81(4) CTMR). The parties may agree their own apportionment of costs following settlement (Article 81(5) CTMR).

The *apportionment* of costs is dealt with by the Cancellation Decision either in their decision on the application or in a decision on costs (Rule 94(1) and (2) IR). The parties may request that a decision on the *amount* of costs be taken by the registry of the Cancellation Division. The amount of costs so determined can be reviewed by a decision of the Cancellation Division provided this is requested by the parties within one month of the date of the notification of the award of costs by the registry (Article 81(6) CTMR, Rule 94(4) IR).

Multiple applications for revocation and for a declaration of invalidity (Rule 41 IR)

Where a number of applications for revocation or for a declaration of invalidity have been filed against the same CTM, OHIM may:

(a)   examine each of the applications in separate proceedings;

(b)   consolidate the applications into one set of proceedings, for example, where several applications against the same CTM are filed by legally independent but related undertakings (the applications may subsequently be unconsolidated); or

(c)   examine one or several of the applications and suspend the others. The remaining applicants are informed of relevant decisions taken during those proceedings which are continued. But once a decision revoking or invalidating the CTM becomes final, the remaining applications are deemed to have been disposed of and one half of the application fees are refunded to the applicants. Since all applicants have the same interest in having their cases decided, in particular, because of the possibility of conversion of the CTM into national trade mark applications in Member States, it is of some consolation to know that this method of proceeding may only be chosen in clear-cut cases of cancellation.

The same options are open to OHIM in dealing with multiple oppositions (Rule 21 IR) and are discussed further in chapter 3.

Surrender of a CTM

The surrender of a CTM is provided for in Article 49 of the CTMR and Rule 36 of the IR. It may be effected at any time during the lifetime of the CTM and no fee is payable.

Extent of surrender of a CTM (Article 49(1) CTMR)

A CTM may be surrendered in respect of some or all of the goods or services for which it is registered (Article 49(1) CTMR).

The most likely reason for a CTM proprietor wishing to surrender his trade mark will be a potential conflict with third-party rights. Rather than enter into or continue with cancellation proceedings the CTM proprietor agrees to surrender the CTM in whole or in part.

How is surrender of a CTM effected? (Article 49(2) CTMR, Rule 36 IR)
The surrender of a CTM is effected by the CTM proprietor making a written signed declaration of surrender to OHIM (Article 49(2) CTMR, Rule 79 IR).

There is no express provision for the production by OHIM of an official form for surrender (Rule 83(1) IR) and none is available at the time of writing.

Nevertheless, Rule 36(1) of the IR states that a declaration of surrender must contain the following information:

(a)   the registration number of the CTM;
(b)   the name and address of the CTM proprietor;
(c)   the name and address of any representative appointed by the CTM proprietor; and
(d)   where surrender is declared only for some of the goods and services in the CTM, the goods and services for which surrender is declared or the goods and services for which the CTM is to remain registered.

The surrender is not effective until it is entered in the Register of CTMs (Article 49(2) CTMR).

Third-party rights (Article 49(3) CTMR, Rule 36(2) IR)
The surrender of a CTM may only be entered on the Register of CTMs with the agreement of the proprietor of a right entered in the Register. A distinction is drawn between a registered licensee and the holder of any other registered right, for example, a person to whom the CTM has been given as security under Article 19(1) of the CTMR (Article 49(3) CTMR).

In the case of the latter, the proprietor of the CTM must produce to OHIM a written declaration of consent to the surrender signed by the proprietor of the registered right or his representative (Rule 36(2) IR).

By contrast, the CTM proprietor needs only to satisfy OHIM that he has informed a registered licensee of his intention to surrender the CTM and the surrender will automatically be registered by OHIM three months later (Article 49(3) CTMR, Rule 36(2) IR). Alternatively, the surrender can be registered before the three-month period has elapsed if the CTM proprietor can produce to OHIM proof of the registered licensee's consent to the surrender (Rule 36(2) IR). To conclude, therefore:

(a)   a licensee has no right under the CTMR to object to the surrender of the CTM;
(b)   a licensee must be registered to be informed under the CTMR of an intended surrender of the CTM; and
(c)   the parties to a licence might wish to cover surrender of the CTM in their agreement.

Examination of the declaration of surrender (Rule 36(3) IR)
The declaration of surrender is examined by OHIM for compliance with Article 49 of the CTMR, Rule 36(1) and (2) of the IR and other relevant provisions of the

CTMR and the IR (for example, the appointment of a representative and the filing of general or specific authorisations covering the surrender). Any deficiencies are communicated by OHIM to the CTM proprietor or his representative. If the deficiencies are not remedied within the period of time specified by OHIM in that communication (extendible, Rule 71(1) IR), OHIM will reject the entry of the surrender in the Register (Rule 36(3) IR).

Once the surrender is entered in the Register it is published in Part B of the *Community Trade Marks Bulletin* (Rule 85(2) IR).

Corrections to the CTM Register

Correction of mistakes and errors (Rule 27 IR)
A mistake or error in the registration of a CTM or the publication of the registration which is attributable to OHIM may be corrected by OHIM of its own volition or at the request of the proprietor (Rule 27(1) IR). A request for correction made by the proprietor must contain the following information (Rule 27(2) IR):

(a)   the registration number of the CTM;
(b)   the name and address of the registered proprietor;
(c)   an indication of the correction; and
(d)   the name and address of any representative.

No fee is payable.

Any deficiencies in the request will be notified by OHIM to the proprietor or his representative and must be remedied within a specified time limit (extendible, Rule 71(1) IR). Corrections are published in Part B of the *Community Trade Marks Bulletin* (Rule 27(3) IR).

Change of name or address (Rule 26 IR)
A change of the name and address of the CTM proprietor which neither amounts to an alteration of the CTM (see chapter 3) nor is the result of a transfer of the CTM may be entered in the Register of CTMs at the request of the proprietor (Rule 26(1) IR). The request must contain (Rule 26(2) IR):

(a)   the registration number of the CTM;
(b)   the name and address of the CTM proprietor as presently entered on the Register;
(c)   the name and address of the CTM proprietor as amended;
(d)   the name and address of any representative appointed.

No fee is payable. A single request may cover the change in the name and address in respect of two or more CTM registrations of the same proprietor (Rule 26(4) IR).

Any deficiency in the request is notified to the CTM proprietor or his representative. If the deficiency is not remedied within the period of time specified by OHIM (extendible, Rule 71(1) IR) the request will be rejected by OHIM (Rule 26(5) IR).

The above also applies to the notification of a change in the name and address of an appointed representative or in the name and address of a CTM applicant or his representative. In the case of the latter, the change is recorded in the CTM application file (Rule 26(6) and (7) IR).

Chapter Six
Infringement 1: Rights in A Community Trade Mark

Introduction

In relation to the infringement of a Community trade mark (CTM), this chapter will concentrate solely on the rights conferred on its owner by a CTM registration. For the sake of convenience, three related matters are left to the next chapter, namely, limitations placed on those rights by the CTMR, arguments which may be raised by a defendant to an infringement action by way of a counterclaim for revocation or declaration of invalidity, and questions of jurisdiction over and procedure relating to CTM infringement actions.

Rights conferred by a CTM

Applicable law (Article 14 CTMR)
The wording of Article 9 of the CTMR follows closely that of Article 5 of the Directive in spelling out the scope of the CTM right. Article 14 makes clear that the effects of a CTM registration are to be governed solely by the terms of the CTMR, although the procedural details of infringement are to be determined by national law, as explained in the next chapter. This means that while the CTMR delegates the handling of infringement actions to the courts of Member States, when deciding whether a CTM registration has been infringed they are to have regard only to the terms of the CTMR and must therefore avoid incorporating domestic notions of infringement. No doubt this will prove a fertile source of references to the Court of Justice of the European Communities for guidance on the meaning of the CTMR, just as the Directive has already prompted requests from national courts for preliminary rulings on *its* meaning. In the long term, the preliminary rulings mechanism found in Article 177 of the Treaty of Rome will have the effect of bringing together the substantive rules on trade mark infringement within both national and Community systems. It would be unthinkable if identical wording were to be ascribed different meanings under national law (based on the Directive) and under the CTMR.

Infringement of a CTM (Article 9 CTMR)
Article 9 of the CTMR declares that a CTM shall confer on the proprietor exclusive rights therein, entitling him to prevent all third parties not having his consent from

using in the course of trade any sign which is identical or similar to the CTM in relation to the same, similar or dissimilar goods or services, subject to certain requirements. The wording of Article 9(1) of the CTMR therefore covers three principal categories of infringement:

Use of an identical sign for identical goods or services (Article 9(1)(a) CTMR) Under Article 9(1)(a) of the CTMR, the proprietor of a CTM can prevent the use of any sign which is identical with the CTM in relation to goods or services which are identical with those for which the CTM is registered. Liability for this type of infringement is strict, as there is no need to prove a likelihood of confusion.

Use of an identical or similar sign on identical or similar goods or services (Article 9(1)(b) CTMR) The language of Article 9(1)(b) of the CTMR is not particularly clear but reference may be had to the less condensed wording in the Commission's 1984 draft of the CTMR to ascertain its meaning (such wording being adopted for the sake of clarity in s. 10(2) of the United Kingdom Trade Marks Act 1994). Whichever version is considered, however, the following 10 permutations can be ascertained:

(a)   where the CTM is registered in respect of goods, it will be infringed by the use in the course of trade of:

   (i)   an identical sign in relation to similar goods;
   (ii)   an identical sign in relation to similar services;
   (iii)   a similar sign in relation to identical goods;
   (iv)   a similar sign in relation to similar goods;
   (v)   a similar sign in relation to similar services.

(b)   where the CTM is registered in respect of services, it will be infringed by the use in trade of:

   (i)   an identical sign in relation to similar services;
   (ii)   an identical sign in relation to similar goods;
   (iii)   a similar sign in relation to identical services;
   (iv)   a similar sign in relation to similar services;
   (v)   a similar sign in relation to similar goods.

In each case, however, there must exist a likelihood of confusion on the part of the public. Article 9(1)(b) of the CTMR goes on to say that 'likelihood of confusion includes a likelihood of association *between* the sign and the trade mark'. This should be compared with the wording of s. 10(2) of the United Kingdom Trade Marks Act 1994 which, although supposedly based on the identical wording in Article 5(1) of the Directive, uses the somewhat more restrictive language, 'which includes the likelihood of association *with* the trade mark'. As explained below, it is unclear whether this subtle grammatical difference will prove to be significant when the phrase 'likelihood of association' falls to be interpreted.

Use of an identical or similar sign on dissimilar goods or services (Article 9(1)(c) CTMR)   Article 9(1)(c) of the CTMR provides that the registered proprietor of a CTM can prevent the use in the course of trade of an identical or similar sign in relation to dissimilar goods or services provided the CTM has a reputation within the Community and the use of such sign without due cause takes unfair advantage of, or is detrimental to, the distinctive character or repute of the CTM. Those familiar with trade mark law will recognise this as the doctrine of dilution which has been part of the Benelux law of trade marks since 1971. It is also found in the trade mark law of roughly half of the individual states in the USA, and has recently been introduced into the federal law of trade marks as a result of the new USA Federal Trademark Dilution Act of 1995.

It should be noted that the words of Article 5(2) of the Directive and of Article 9(1)(c) of the CTMR do not require any likelihood of confusion as an element of the dilution action. As was pointed out by Advocate-General Jacobs in his recent opinion in *Sabel BV* v *Puma AG* (case C-251/95) 29 April 1997, albeit commenting on the similar form of wording found in Article 4 of the Directive (relative grounds for refusal), the omission is deliberate, as the Directive and CTMR provide different criteria for the dilution action than for the 'classical' form of trade mark infringement. However, the absence of any requirement of confusion has already proved difficult for the United Kingdom courts to accept (see below).

Likely interpretation of the CTMR

A number of questions can be raised concerning the interpretation of key words and phrases in Article 9(1) of the CTMR. This is a matter ultimately for the Court of Justice to determine, but some guidance (both positive and negative) may be gleaned from current national law. Taking the concepts in the order in which they appear in the Article:

'In the course of trade'
This phrase (which also appears in Article 5(1) of the Directive) is not defined anywhere in the CTMR. It could be taken to mean simply that trade mark infringement has to be a commercial activity. Support for this can be found in the original 1964 proposal for a CTM which spoke of 'use in commerce'.

United Kingdom trade mark practitioners will, however, call to mind the decision in *M. Ravok (Weatherwear) Ltd* v *National Trade Press Ltd* (1955) 72 RPC 110, in which it was held that use of the plaintiff's trade mark in a trade directory was not 'use in the course of trade', because the defendants had not used the mark in the course of trade *in the registered goods*, their own business being the publication of directories. Obviously, at the time of the *Ravok* decision, the trade mark right in United Kingdom law was limited to the goods of the registration. Nevertheless, it might be argued that there is still a requirement under the new law that the defendant must be trading in the goods or services in relation to which the plaintiff alleges the sign has been misused. The *Ravok* defence was, however, never conclusively established under the former law of the United Kingdom (see *Ind Coope Ltd* v *Paine & Co. Ltd* [1983] RPC 326 and *Rolls-Royce Motors Ltd* v *Dodd* [1981] FSR 517) and it may be questioned whether it has any place in the new pan-European regime.

Article 5(1) of the Directive and Article 9 of the CTMR both state that 'the proprietor shall be entitled to prevent *all* third parties not having his consent from using in the course of trade . . .' thus suggesting that the trade mark owner is not limited to suing only those who trade in the relevant goods or services.

Further, Article 10 of the CTMR gives the CTM proprietor the right to object to the generic use of the mark in reference works. There is no parallel entitlement in the Directive, although the original version contained such a provision. The Commission's comments accompanying the 1980 draft of the Directive and CTMR stated that the right to object under what is now Article 10 of the CTMR should be viewed as 'supplementary' to the basic CTM right. The significance of Article 10 lies in the fact that the specific right of correction which it confers is considered by the Commission as the most effective remedy in the circumstances. This implies that correction is available in addition to other forms of relief and from this it could be deduced that use of the same or similar sign in any commercial medium will infringe, subject to available defences.

Alternatively, it could be argued that 'use in the course of trade' requires the defendant to have made use of the sign in a trade mark sense, that is, to indicate the origin of the defendant's goods or services, a concept frequently found in decisions of United Kingdom courts under the Trade Marks Act 1938 as amended (see in particular *Mars (GB) Ltd* v *Cadbury Ltd* [1987] RPC 387 and *Mothercare (UK) Ltd* v *Penguin Books Ltd* [1988] RPC 113, confirming *Aristoc Ltd* v *Rysta Ltd* [1945] AC 68 at 85 and *Bismag Ltd* v *Amblins (Chemists) Ltd* [1940] Ch 667). This begs the question whether 'use in a trade mark sense' under the new law refers only to the function of a trade mark as an indicator of origin or whether any of the other functions of a trade mark, particularly the advertising function, can be considered. Reference to Recital 7 of the CTMR shows that the Council and Commission regard the principal function of the trade mark as an indicator of origin. By contrast, the definition of 'trade mark' in Article 4 of the CTMR points to the product differentiation function, whilst the recognition of the dilution action in Article 9(1)(c) of the CTMR suggests acceptance of the advertising function. Such discussion may, however, turn out to be otiose if the interpretation given to the word 'sign' by Jacob J in *British Sugar plc* v *James Robertson & Sons Ltd* [1996] RPC 281 (explained next) were to be adopted by the Court of Justice.

'Sign'

In *British Sugar plc* v *James Robertson & Sons Ltd* [1996] RPC 281, Jacob J commented that the word 'sign' as it appears in Article 5 of the Directive and Article 9 of the CTMR was not to be subjected to the gloss that there had to be 'use in a trade mark sense', as the wording of s. 9 of the United Kingdom Trade Marks Act 1994 ('by the use of the trade mark') might be thought to require. Such wording appears neither in the Directive nor in the CTMR. It is merely necessary, according to Jacob J, for the court to see whether the sign is being used in the course of trade and then consider whether the defendant's conduct falls within one of the three categories of infringement, as explained above.

This approach should be contrasted with that of *Bravado Merchandising Ltd* v *Mainstream Publishing Ltd* [1996] FSR 205, where the Court of Session found itself constrained by counsel's concession (relying on *Hansard*) that the 1994 Act requires there to be use in a trade mark sense. Such concession was felt by Jacob

J in *British Sugar* to be misconceived in light of the fact that the wording of the Directive, not the intentions of the United Kingdom Parliament, must be conclusive. Lest it be thought that this would give the trade mark owner the ability to object to a wide range of activities not normally thought of as amounting to trade mark infringement, Jacob J pointed out that such an interpretation was matched by the defence of descriptive use found in Article 6 of the Directive and Article 12 of the CTMR, explained in the next chapter. It should be noted, however, that Rattee J in *Trebor Bassett Ltd* v *Football Association* [1997] FSR 211 avoided the point entirely by stating that in the light of the facts (explained below) he considered it unnecessary and inappropriate to adopt the views of Jacob J on whether use of a sign had to be 'trade mark use'.

'In relation to'

This phrase appears in Article 9(1)(a) and (c) of the CTMR. It is not defined in the CTMR although some guidance can be found in Article 9(2) of the CTMR, which declares that the following, inter alia, may be prohibited under Article 9(1), namely, affixing the sign to goods or packaging, offering the goods, putting them on the market or stocking them for such purposes or offering or supplying services thereunder, importing or exporting goods under that sign, or using the sign on business papers and in advertising. The list is not exhaustive.

The reference to 'stocking' goods under the sign overcomes the difficulty encountered in the pre-harmonisation United Kingdom decision of *AUTODROME Trade Mark* [1969] RPC 564. Here it was held that naming a car showroom AUTODROME did not infringe the registration of the word as a trade mark for cars as it was not 'in relation to' such goods. The clarification that using the sign as the name of retail premises will amount to CTM infringement has its corollary in statement 2 by the Council and Commission in the Minutes of the Council Meeting at which the CTMR was adopted (see OHIM OJ 5/96, p. 613). The statement is to the effect that there cannot be a registration for 'retail services'. Such an argument had previously been used (unsuccessfully) in the United Kingdom in an attempt to overcome the limitation of the *AUTODROME* case: see *Re Dee Corporation plc* [1990] RPC 159.

Article 9(2) of the CTMR, however, does not explain the degree of proximity required between the sign which is alleged to infringe and the product, particularly where the registered trade mark consists of a known word which can be used descriptively in everyday language. Such language might form the text of a label which is 'affixed' to the goods or be found in any form of commercial publication, such as leaflets, newspaper articles or books (assuming that these qualify as 'business papers' or 'advertising'). Alternatively, the alleged infringing sign might appear on the side of a lorry carrying another trader's goods, be a company name or (to give an extreme example) be included in the script of a television or radio programme.

In decisions which pre-date the CTMR, the Benelux Court of Justice has held that the use by the defendant of a company name which is identical to the registered mark can, in the appropriate circumstances be 'use in relation' to goods and services (*OMNISPORT* [1989] NJ 300, [1989] 6 EIPR D-99). And the Irish High Court has held that use of a cigarette mark as part of an anti-smoking campaign was 'in relation to' cigarettes (*Gallaher (Dublin) Ltd* v *Health Education Bureau* [1982] FSR 464).

As regards United Kingdom law, in *Bravado Merchandising Ltd* v *Mainstream Publishing Ltd* [1996] FSR 205 a distinction was drawn between the product itself and something used 'in relation to it'. The example given was that of using a descriptive trade mark (*in casu*, the phrase WET WET WET as the name of a pop group) in the text of a book and its use in the book's title. The former would not be 'use in relation to' the book whereas the latter would be, because the trade mark would be 'affixed' to the outside of the goods. Such an interpretation accords with the pre-harmonisation decisions in *News Group Newspapers Ltd* v *Rocket Record Co. Ltd* [1981] FSR 89 and *Games Workshop Ltd* v *Transworld Publishing Ltd* [1993] FSR 705, concerned respectively with the title of a sound recording and the title of a series of books.

By contrast, Jacob J in *British Sugar plc* v *James Robertson & Sons Ltd* [1996] RPC 281 thought that such use of a descriptive word trade mark in the title of the book was not use 'in relation to' the book but was simply referring to the subject matter of the book and accordingly fell within the descriptive use defence found in s. 11(2) of the United Kingdom Trade Marks Act 1994 (equivalent to Article 12 of the CTMR). Such interpretation of 'in relation to' appears to come dangerously close to saying that there must be use in a trade mark sense as stipulated by the now-rejected decision of the Court of Appeal in *Mothercare (UK) Ltd* v *Penguin Books Ltd* [1988] RPC 113. It places too much emphasis on the descriptive use defence found in Article 12 of the CTMR at the expense of spelling out the exact scope of the trade mark right. It also contradicts the learned judge's own statement that the presence of the word 'sign' obviates the need for there to be trade mark use.

The *British Sugar* comment, however, appears to coincide with that of the Benelux Court of Justice in *JAKOBS/JACOBS* [1982] NJ 624, where use of the alleged infringing sign on a lorry carrying a competitors' similarly trade-marked coffee was held not to be 'in relation to' such goods.

A final illustration comes from the observations of Rattee J in *Trebor Bassett Ltd* v *Football Association* [1997] FSR 211, where he held that the depiction (on collectable insert cards in packs of candy sticks) of English footballers wearing the England 'three lions' logo (which was the defendant's registered trade mark) was not use of the sign 'in respect of' (sic) the cards.

It is apparent from these contradictory views that guidance from the European Court of Justice is urgently needed on the meaning of 'in relation to' and whether it imports some requirement of trade mark use into Article 9 of the CTMR.

'Identical sign'

It seems that for an infringement action to fall within Article 9(1)(a) of the CTMR, the sign and the trade mark must correspond in all respects. If there is any difference between them, then the action must be decided under Article 9(1)(b) of the CTMR. Support for this view can be found in the United Kingdom decision of *Origins Natural Resources Inc.* v *Origin Clothing Ltd* [1995] FSR 281, where Jacob J was of the opinion that the difference of one letter between the registered trade mark and the alleged infringing sign took the matter outside the scope of s. 10(1) of the United Kingdom Trade Marks Act 1994.

However, in the case of a word mark (and also by parity of reasoning a mark consisting of letters and/or numerals whether or not in conjunction with a word), because what is entered on the register is merely a graphic representation of the mark, it is irrelevant that the defendant uses a different typeface for the infringing sign (*Bravado Merchandising Ltd* v *Mainstream Publishing Ltd* [1996] FSR 205, relying on *Morny Ltd's Trade Marks* (1951) 68 RPC 131). (For a similar decision under Benelux law, see *MICHELIN/MICHELS* [1996] NJ 34, Benelux Court of Justice.)

Likewise, there will be infringement by use of an identical sign if the mark is surrounded by non-trade-mark matter (decided in the context of s. 10(2)(a) of the Trade Marks Act 1994, the equivalent of Article 9(1)(b) of the CTMR, rather than s. 10(1), the equivalent of Article 9(1)(a) of the CTMR, by Jacob J in *British Sugar plc* v *James Robertson & Sons Ltd* [1996] RPC 281). And, by inference from the decision in *Road Tech Computer Systems Ltd* v *Unison Software (UK) Ltd* [1996] FSR 805, the addition of a hyphen between the two elements of a word mark will not take the case outside Article 9(1)(a) of the CTMR.

'Identical goods or services'
As the wording of Article 9(1)(a) of the CTMR makes clear, 'identical goods' means the goods or services for which the CTM is actually registered. Nevertheless, the facts of *British Sugar plc* v *James Robertson & Sons Ltd* [1996] RPC 281 illustrate that determining whether an infringer's product falls within the trade mark owner's statement of goods and services may not be an easy matter, especially if (as in this case) the former is capable of more than one use.

As regards multiple use products (like that of the defendants in *British Sugar*, which could be used both as a jam-like spread and a dessert topping), Jacob J suggested that regard should be had to the use which accounted for the largest proportion of the volume of sales; if need be, consideration should also be given to the views of those in the trade, particularly the suppliers of the product to the end-user.

Where the trade mark owner's statement of goods and services is drawn widely, then according to *British Sugar*, regard should be had to the Arrangement of Nice for the International Classification of Goods and Services 1957, as amended, to determine into which class the defendant's principal use falls.

'Similarity'
It is frequently pointed out that Article 5 of the Directive and Article 9 of the CTMR contain concepts found in Article 13A of the Uniform Benelux Trademarks Law of 1971. This is confirmed by statement 5 by the Council and Commission in the minutes of the Council of Ministers attached to the Directive and statement 6 by the Council and Commission in the minutes of the Council of Ministers attached to the CTMR, OHIM OJ 5/96, p. 609 and p. 613 respectively. For a detailed account of the background to these statements see H.R. Furstner and M.C. Geuze, 'Scope of protection of the trade mark in the Benelux countries and EEC harmonisation' [1988] BIE 215, reprinted in (1989) ECTA Newsletter No. 15, p. 10. Doubt has, however, been cast on the value of the minutes by the opinion of Advocate-General Jacobs in *Sabel BV* v *Puma AG* (case C-251/95) 29 April 1997 (see chapter 1).

It will be remembered that likelihood of confusion is the criterion for assessing similarity under Article 9(1)(b) of the CTMR, and that reference to Recital 10 to the Directive and Recital 7 to the CTMR indicates that a flexible, factual test is to be applied, the outcome of which will vary from case to case. Both Recitals state that the assessment of likelihood of confusion depends on numerous elements, in particular:

(a) the recognition of the trade mark on the market;
(b) the association which can be made with the used or registered sign;
(c) the degree of similarity between the goods and services; and
(d) the degree of similarity between the trade mark and the sign.

The approach taken by the Directive and the CTMR towards likelihood of confusion reflects the interpretation by the Benelux Court of Justice of the concept of 'similarity' embodied in the infringement criteria of Article 13A of the Uniform Benelux Trademarks Law 1971.

In the leading case of *UNION/UNION SOLEURE* (case A 82/5) [1984] NJ 72, the Benelux Court decided that:

> ... there is similarity between a trade mark and a sign when, taking into account the particular circumstances of the case, such as the distinctive power of the trade mark, the trade mark and the sign, each looked at as a whole and in relation to one another, demonstrate such auditive, visual or conceptual resemblance, that associations between sign and trade mark are evoked merely on the basis of this resemblance.

The case-by-case technique shows some affinity with the protection of unregistered trade marks under the United Kingdom law of passing off, but should be contrasted with the mechanistic approach to trade mark infringement in the United Kingdom under both the 1938 Act and (regrettably) the 1994 Act. The emphasis placed by the Recitals on the recognition of the strength of the trade mark on the market and the association which can be made with it means that the nature of the registered mark and the extent and manner of the previous use which has been made of it will be highly relevant. Thus an inherently distinctive mark (such as an invented word) will enjoy better protection than will a descriptive mark (as to the sliding scale of distinctiveness of marks, see the comments of the Benelux Court of Justice in the *JUICY FRUIT* case [1984] NJ 71, [1983] EIPR D-81). Equally, the owner of a mark which has been the subject of prolonged use or an extensive advertising campaign will be able to sue a wider class of infringers than will the owner of a less-used registration. For United Kingdom passing-off cases which illustrate these points (although admittedly they are not on all fours with Article 9(1)(b)) see *Eastman Photographic Materials Co. Ltd* v *John Griffiths Cycle Corporation Ltd* (1898) 15 RPC 105 and *Lego System A/S* v *Lego M. Lemelstrich Ltd* [1983] FSR 155.

Such flexibility should be compared with the sterile exercise conducted in United Kingdom cases decided under both the 1938 Act, as amended, and the 1994 Act, in which only the notional, future use of the registered mark is compared with the actual use made of the alleged infringing sign by the defendant.

In *Origins Natural Resources Inc.* v *Origin Clothing Ltd* [1995] FSR 281, Jacob J stated that s. 10(2) of the 1994 Act (equivalent to Article 9(1)(b) of the CTMR) required the court to assume that the mark of the plaintiff is to be used in a normal and fair manner in relation to the goods for which it has been registered and then to assess the likelihood of confusion in relation to the way in which the defendant has used its mark. In *British Sugar plc v James Robertson & Sons Ltd* [1996] RPC 281 the same judge confirmed that this was the correct approach under s. 10(2), except in so far as the wording of the section demands that the test be modified to incorporate the word 'sign' in place of the word 'mark'. Terminology apart, this is the same analysis as was applied under the 1938 Act (see *Portakabin Ltd* v *Powerblast Ltd* [1990] RPC 471, echoing the test applied in opposition proceedings under the old Act in *Smith Hayden & Co. Ltd's Application* (1946) 63 RPC 97), and takes no account of the strength of nor manner of use of the plaintiff's mark.

A further difference can be highlighted between the Benelux approach in *UNION SOLEURE* and the assessment of infringement in United Kingdom cases. Benelux law requires that the question of likelihood of confusion be considered as a matter of general, even paramount, concern, within which context the court should assess whether the goods or services are similar and whether the mark and the alleged infringing sign are similar. Contrast this with the way in which s. 10(2) of the United Kingdom Trade Marks Act 1994 has been applied. In *British Sugar plc v James Robertson & Sons Ltd* [1996] RPC 281, the formula set out by Jacob J requires the court to determine the question of similarity of marks and similarity of goods *before* considering the likelihood of confusion. Yet, ironically, the wording of Recital 10 to the Directive is given as authority for the proposition that questions of similarity are independent of the question of likelihood of confusion. It is worth restating the relevant wording from Recital 7 to the CTMR:

> whereas an interpretation should be given to the concept of similarity in relation to the likelihood of confusion; whereas the likelihood of confusion, the appreciation of which depends on numerous elements and, in particular, on . . . the degree of similarity between the trade mark and the sign and between the goods or services identified.

to make the point that what is required is an overall assessment of similarity under Article 9(1)(b) of the CTMR (and equally, Article 5(1) of the Directive).

It accordingly remains to be seen whether OHIM, when hearing oppositions on relative grounds under Article 8 of the CTMR, and CTM courts, when hearing infringement actions under Article 9 of the CTMR, elevate likelihood of confusion to a dominant requirement (as arguably the wording of the relevant Recitals would suggest) or relegate it to the position of an afterthought to be dealt with once it has been decided that there is similarity of both marks and products. Some guidance may be expected when the Court of Justice delivers its preliminary ruling in *Canon KK v Pathé Communications Corporation* (case C-39/97) [1997] OJ C 94/11, a reference from the Bundesgerichtshof. The German court has asked whether the strength of the earlier mark has an impact on the decision whether goods or services are similar, even if customers attribute the goods or services to different commercial origins. Unfortunately, the case is unlikely to be decided before 1999.

'Likelihood of confusion'
The classical notion of trade mark infringement is an inevitable corollary of the orthodox view of the function of a trade mark, namely, to indicate to the consumer

that the goods or services come from a particular (albeit anonymous) commercial source. Accordingly, there will be source confusion and hence trade mark infringement where, as a result of the defendant's conduct, the consumer purchases a product thinking it comes from source A when in fact it comes from source B.

Recital 7 to the CTMR states that indication of origin is, in particular, the function of a CTM, the words 'in particular' implying that other functions are to be recognised. This wording, together with the wording of Article 9(1)(b), of the CTMR must be considered as indicating a change of mind on the part of the Council and Commission, as the original drafts of both the CTMR and Directive stated that there would only be infringement where there was a 'serious risk of confusion' (a phrase found in German trade mark law).

The transformation of the criterion for trade mark infringement from 'serious risk of confusion' to 'likelihood of confusion [including] likelihood of association' therefore points to the trade mark infringement action encompassing more than classical source confusion. Nevertheless, it has to be admitted that the wording of both the CTMR and Directive is unclear. The wider notion, likelihood of association, is mentioned as a sub-category of the narrower concept, likelihood of confusion. The question which will ultimately have to be determined by the European Court of Justice is which of the two concepts is the dominant one. Will likelihood of association only be considered where it occurs within the narrower confines of likelihood of confusion? Or has the addition of likelihood of association as a criterion for infringement completely recast the law of trade marks as it has traditionally been understood? If the Court accepts the advice of Advocate-General Jacobs in *Sabel BV* v *Puma AG* (case C-251/95) 29 April 1997 (and it must be remembered that it is not obliged to do so), it will opt for the former interpretation.

As regards confusion, it is arguable that the trade mark proprietor may take steps to prevent not only direct confusion of the type outlined above, but indirect or association confusion where, although the mark and the sign as such will not be confused, the consumer would assume on the basis of their resemblance, or, where they are identical, because of the resemblance of their respective products, that there is some sort of organisational or economic relationship between undertakings concerned (such relationship including licensing, franchising or some other sort of sponsorship). This notion of indirect confusion, which is part of German trade mark law, has received judicial recognition by the Court of Justice of the European Communities in *Deutsche Renault AG* v *Audi AG* (case C-317/91) [1993] ECR I-6227, where it was stated that the specific subject matter of the trade mark right extends equally to risk of confusion in this broader sense.

It goes without saying that *direct* confusion is part of United Kingdom law, applying even to the situation where the customer believes that the alleged infringer's goods are associated with the proprietor's goods or services, for example, that they are an extension of the range of goods made by the proprietor, as there is still confusion as to source (see *Ravenhead Brick Co. Ltd* v *Ruabon Brick and Terra Cotta Co. Ltd* (1937) 54 RPC 341 cited with approval in *Wagamama Ltd* v *City Centre Restaurants plc* [1995] FSR 713). Whether the new United Kingdom trade mark law will recognise indirect confusion as supporting a trade mark infringement action is not yet clear. Cases decided under the 1938 Act where indirect confusion was recognised were all brought under s. 4(1)(b), where the gist of the action was 'importing a reference' (see, for example, *British*

Northrop Ltd v *Texteam Blackburn Ltd* [1974] RPC 57; *News Group Newspapers Ltd* v *Rocket Record Co. Ltd* [1981] FSR 89). In the context of passing-off, there are occasional instances of indirect confusion (see, for example, *Morny Ltd* v *Ball and Rogers (1975) Ltd* [1978] FSR 91). Nevertheless, United Kingdom courts have tended to cling to classical source confusion and have experienced difficulty in accepting that the public would be misled by a misrepresentation to the effect that the defendant's goods were licensed or approved by the plaintiff even where the goods or services in question were similar (although see *Annabel's (Berkeley Square) Ltd* v *Schock* [1972] RPC 838; and *Mirage Studios* v *Counter-Feat Clothing Co. Ltd* [1991] FSR 145). The situation where there is alleged to be passing-off by suggesting approval or sponsorship of *dissimilar* goods or services has proved even more problematic, as explained below.

'Likelihood of association'

In the extract from the judgment in *UNION/UNION SOLEURE* (case A82/5) [1984] NJ 72 given above, likelihood of association was explained as occurring where the consumer (subconsciously) calls to mind the registered mark when seeing the alleged infringing sign. An example of such a mental link being made is the case of *MONOPOLY/ANTI-MONOPOLY* [1978] BIE 39 and 43, a Dutch Supreme Court decision concerning use for similar products (board games). The second game was of a totally anti-capitalistic nature and it was highly improbable that any person would think that the two games originated from the same company. Nevertheless the court ruled that there was infringement: the public when seeing or hearing ANTI-MONOPOLY would think of MONOPOLY, therefore the danger of association was made out. In other words, it was not necessary to prove that the public were *confused*. The mere fact that the public on perceiving the sign make a mental link ('association') between the sign and the trade mark is enough to reach a finding of similarity.

The reaction of the United Kingdom courts to the phrase 'likelihood of association' has been less than receptive. The chance to discuss it arose in the case of *Wagamama Ltd* v *City Centre Restaurants plc* [1995] FSR 713, which ultimately (and fortunately) resulted in success for the plaintiff on the basis of classical source confusion. Nevertheless, the opportunity was taken to argue that use of the name RAJAMAMA in relation to an Indian-themed restaurant would cause the public to think of the name WAGAMAMA which was registered for restaurant services and used in respect of a Japanese-style noodle bar. Laddie J had to decide whether s. 10(2) of the Trade Marks Act 1994 (which, as already noted, is grammatically yet subtly different from the wording of the Directive and the CTMR) meant that 'likelihood of association' was simply a subspecies of 'likelihood of confusion', in which case it added nothing to the scope of trade mark infringement, or whether it was broader, thereby introducing non-origin confusion. He concluded, applying domestic canons of interpretation, that 'likelihood of association' was included within the notion of 'likelihood of confusion'. Turning to the alternative European interpretation route, he rejected three arguments advanced by the plaintiffs in support of their contention that the Benelux view of 'likelihood of association' should be adopted. First, he dismissed the attempt by the plaintiffs to introduce as evidence statement 5 by the Council and Commission in the minutes of the Council of Ministers attached to the Directive on the ground that it was not permissible to refer to such minutes, Council meetings being confidential (though this point has since been met by the publication of the minutes in OHIM OJ 5/96, p. 609). He next dismissed the argument that it was 'popular belief' that the Directive reflected Benelux law as 'unveriable rumours', despite the view expressed by the Brussels Court of Appeal in the *ALWAYS/REGINA* case [1993] IER 4, 112 that the Benelux Uniform Trademark Law 1971 was in conformity with the Directive. Finally, he rejected the argument that, for the sake of comity, British courts should pay attention to the decisions of trade mark courts in other Member States:

> It would not be right for an English court to follow the route adopted by the courts of another Member State if it is firmly of a different view simply because the other court expressed a view first. The scope of European legislation is too important to be decided on a first past the post basis.

Having said that, Laddie J approached the question of interpretation from first principles and concluded that the indication of origin function must govern the scope of the trade mark right, so that the rights of the proprietor against alleged infringers was limited to 'classic infringement'.

> If the broader scope were to be adopted, the Directive and our Act would be creating a new type of monopoly not related to the proprietor's trade but in the trade mark itself. Such a monopoly could be likened to a quasi-copyright in the mark. However, unlike copyright, there would be no fixed duration for the right and it would be a true monopoly effective against copyist and non-copyist alike. I can see nothing in the terms of the Directive (or our Act), or in any secondary material which I could legitimately take into account, which would lead me to assume that this was its objective.

Laddie J's remarks in the *WAGAMAMA* case have been both criticised and applauded in British academic writing. At the time it was a matter of regret that he did not refer the question of the meaning of 'likelihood of association' in Article 5(1) of the Directive to the Court of Justice of the European Communities. However, this has been done, in the context of Article 4(1) of the Directive, by the German Bundesgerichtshof in *Sabel BV* v *Puma AG* (case C-251/95) [1995] OJ C 248/6. The tenor of Advocate-General Jacobs's opinion, delivered on 29 April 1997, has been to agree with the approach of Laddie J in *WAGAMAMA*, that is, that likelihood of association is to be regarded as a subspecies of likelihood of confusion. Calling the plaintiff's trade mark to mind will not be sufficient for liability unless there exists a serious risk of origin confusion.

'Similar marks'
Regardless of whether the issue of similarity between the mark and the sign is to be considered in isolation or as part of the wider question of likelihood of confusion, a difficulty which presents itself to the potential plaintiff is that the comparison of word marks is essentially one of language (for an example of how the average German consumer would treat two known words in the English language see *DRAGON/RACOON* (case 26 W (pat) 230/94) [1996] GRUR 414, Bundespatentgericht). What therefore appears to be a sign dissimilar to the

registered mark in English may be held to be similar by a court in Germany (or for that matter by a court in Spain or Finland). This raises the possibility that a CTM proprietor may succeed against a particular defendant in one Member State but not another, a factor to be considered when choosing jurisdiction under Article 93 of the CTMR (see the next chapter).

Be that as it may, it would seem that there is a certain degree of congruence between the existing case law of the Member States as to the test to be applied in comparing a registered mark with the alleged infringing sign. As Advocate-General Jacobs pointed out in his opinion in *Sabel BV v Puma AG* (case C-251/95) 29 April 1997, the primary consideration throughout all the Member States of the EC would appear to be the overall impression created by the mark.

The basic principles applied by the Benelux courts are that first, the mark as registered is compared to the sign as used, although the court may take into account unregistered elements of the mark in appropriate cases (*DROSTE/TJOKLAT* [1991] NJ 148, decision of the Dutch Hoge Raad). The comparison must be between the mark and the sign as a whole, avoiding detailed analysis. Because the public will only see the sign fleetingly, the court will not consider detailed differences, preferring to pay more attention to similarities (*UNION SOLEURE* [1984] NJ 72; *CAMPARI/LONGONI* [1983] NJ 204). In the case of labels, similarity between the graphic elements of the mark and the sign will often predominate over differences in the words (*DROSTE/TJOKLAT*). Finally, as the *UNION SOLEURE* case itself makes clear, similarity of any one of the visual, phonetic or conceptual effects of the mark will suffice. Conceptual similarity was found to exist in *SAFARI/KENIA* [1991] RDI 284.

In Germany, the Bundesgerichtshof in its referral of *Sabel BV v Puma AG* (case C-251/95) [1995] OJ C 248/6 to the Court of Justice (admittedly in the context of Article 4(1)(b) of the Directive) has set out its thinking in relation to conflicts between marks which are predominantly pictorial (see Ullmann, 'Reconciling trade mark decisions of national courts and the European Court of Justice' (1996) 27 IIC 791). The court is to focus on the overall impression made by the trade mark as registered and the sign, so that in the case of a composite mark it is not open to one party to argue that particular emphasis is to be given to an individual element in the mark or sign. Nevertheless, as a question of fact, a particular element in a composite sign may be significant enough to characterise the sign as a whole. As in the Benelux, the greater the distinctive character of the earlier mark, because of its originality or as a result of its commercial prominence, the greater the risk of confusion, but where a mark is not particularly distinctive, minor differences between the mark and the later sign are sufficient to rule out such risk. Advocate-General Jacobs in his opinion does not appear to dissent from this approach.

Under United Kingdom law, the guiding principle for deciding whether there is similarity between a registered mark and the alleged infringing sign is that set out by Parker J in *Pianotist Co.'s Application, PIANOLA Trade Mark* (1906) 23 RPC 774 at 777:

You must take the two words. You must judge them, both by their look and by their sound. You must consider the nature and kind of customer who would be likely to buy those goods. In fact you must consider all the surrounding circumstances.

Following on from that, several sub-rules applicable both to opposition and infringement proceedings can be stated, as follows:

(a)   The idea of the mark is the prime consideration, so that, as in the Benelux, conceptual similarity is conclusive. In *Broadhead's Application* (1950) 67 RPC 209, ALKA-VESCENT was considered to convey the same information as ALKA-SELTZER.

(b)   A letter-by-letter comparison should be avoided, rather marks should be compared as a whole to assess their overall impact on the consumer. In *William Bailey (Birmingham) Ltd's Application* (1935) 52 RPC 136 EREKTIKO was refused registration because it was too close to ERECTOR; by contrast in *POL-RAMA Trade Mark* [1977] RPC 581 POL-RAMA was allowed despite the prior registration of POLAROID for identical goods.

(c)   Subject to the principle of overall comparison, the first syllable is the most important because of the tendency to slur the final syllable of a word in speech, so that BULER was too close to BULOVER (*BULER Trade Mark* [1966] RPC 141) but TRIPCASTROID was not too close to CASTROL (*London Lubricants (1920) Ltd's Application* (1925) 42 RPC 264).

(d)   An aural as well as a visual comparison should be made of the marks, so that in the case of words which have little or no meaning, phonetic similarity is given considerable weight (*Electrolux Ltd v Electrix Ltd* (1954) 71 RPC 23). Regard should be had to how the goods are to be ordered, as the risk of mispronunciation is greater if goods are to be ordered over the telephone. There is less similarity if the goods are expensive and likely to be bought after negotiations between buyer and seller. Hence in *LANCER Trade Mark* [1987] RPC 303 it was held that there was no risk of confusion between LANCER and LANCIA for cars because of the way in which the goods were sold.

(e)   The court should always be guided by the 'doctrine of imperfect recollection'. The potential customer, in whose shoes the court is to stand rather than rely on its own specialist knowledge, will rarely be comparing the two marks side by side. He or she will probably remember only one brand name and that fleetingly and imperfectly. Further, allowance is to be made for careless pronunciation by both customer and supplier.

'Similar goods'

Under United Kingdom law (established primarily in the context of oppositions under s. 12(1) of the 1938 Act, as amended) the test for whether goods were of the same description was that laid down in *Jellinek's Application, PANDA Trade Mark* (1946) 63 RPC 59, where Romer J stated that the matters to be taken into account were the nature and composition of the goods; the respective uses to which they are put; and the trade channels through which they may be sold.

This test has now been adopted in relation to the question of similarity of goods under s. 10(2) of the Act of 1994 (based on Article 5(1) of the Directive, equivalent to Article 9(1)(b) of the CTMR), but modified to take account of changing trading conditions, by Jacob J in *British Sugar plc v James Robertson & Sons Ltd* [1996] RPC 281 at 296–7.

Jacob J, having decided that the phrase 'similar goods' was analogous to 'goods of the same description' found in s. 12(1) of the 1938 Act, took as a starting point the statement of goods for which the mark is registered and observed that it would be illogical if a mark with a narrow statement of goods obtained a wide scope of protection through an incautious interpretation of 'similarity'. He then restated the factors to be taken into account as follows:

(a)   the respective uses of the goods or services;
(b)   the respective users of the goods or services;
(c)   the physical nature of the goods or acts of services;
(d)   the respective trade channels through which the goods or services reach the market;
(e)   in the case of self-serve consumer items, where, in practice, they are respectively found, or likely to be found, in supermarkets and, in particular, whether they are, or are likely to be, found on the same or different shelves;
(f)   the extent to which the goods or services are competitive, taking into account how those in the trade (including market research companies) classify such goods.

His conclusion was that the goods in question (dessert toppings and flavoured spreads) were not similar as they were not in 'direct competition': consumers would find them in different parts of the supermarket and market researchers viewed them as falling within different sectors.

With due respect, to require that the plaintiff's and defendant's goods be in 'direct competition' would make s. 10(2) (and consequently Article 9(1)(b) of the CTMR) almost meaningless in so far as these provisions seek to give protection beyond the scope of the statement of goods or services. Such interpretation gives the trade mark proprietor no wider scope than was enjoyed under the 1938 Act. Further, it encourages applicants to seek initial protection for a wide range of products, which is contrary to the policy of trade mark law. Finally, (and this is a domestic point) if s. 10(2) (and indeed s. 5(2)) are to be viewed as similar to s. 12(1) of the 1938 Act, the requirement that the parties' goods must be in competition flies in the face of a century of United Kingdom case law, where the use of the same or similar mark on non-competing goods has been enjoined in opposition proceedings. To argue that such proceedings protect the public interest whilst infringement proceedings protect only the trade mark owner's right is flying in the face of the deliberate structure of both the Directive and the CTMR in making the relative grounds for refusal and the infringement provisions as mirror images of each other.

Dilution

Origins of dilution
The doctrine of dilution encapsulated in Article 9(1)(c) of the CTMR (and the non-mandatory Article 5(2) of the Directive, adopted by all the Member States with the exception of Austria) owes much to Frank Schechter's seminal article 'The rational basis of trademark protection' (1927) 40 Harv L Rev 813. In this, he described dilution as 'the gradual whittling away or dispersion of the identity and hold upon the public mind of the mark or name by its use upon non-competing goods' and stressed that likelihood of confusion was not a prerequisite of liability.

Types of dilution

The harm which trade mark dilution seeks to prevent is twofold, namely, unauthorised acts which blur the distinctiveness of the mark into non-distinctiveness, and those which tarnish the mark's reputation by using it in a disparaging or embarrassing context. Classic examples of dilution by 'blurring' from cases in the USA include DUPONT for shoes, BUICK for aspirin tablets, KODAK for pianos and SCHLITZ for varnish. The following have been held to be infringement under Benelux dilution law: DUNHILL for glasses (*Dunhill* v *Christopher Dunhill* [1982] BIE 42, District Court, the Hague) and APPLE for advertising services (Court of Appeal, Amsterdam, [1986] BIE 152).

Examples (again from the USA) of the destruction of the positive associations a mark has come to convey to the public by its being linked to inferior products or being used in an unwholesome or unsavoury manner include a poster saying 'Enjoy Cocaine' in a script and colour identical to that of COCA-COLA; a cartoon showing the Pillsbury doughboy/doughgirl characters engaging in sexual intercourse; and the sale of a 'joke' fake AMERICAN EXPRESS card which contained a condom and the phrase NEVER LEAVE HOME WITHOUT IT. Closer to home, in the leading Benelux Court of Justice decision of *CLAERYN/KLAREIN* (1976) 7 IIC 420, the owner of CLAERYN Dutch gin was able to prevent Colgate using KLAREIN for liquid cleanser: both marks had an identical pronunciation in the Dutch language and consumers would not wish to be reminded of a cleaning agent whilst drinking a glass of good Dutch gin.

Dilution, though, may comprise another type of harm not covered by Article 9(1)(c) of the CTMR (nor by Article 5(2) of the Directive). Use of an identical or similar sign for competing goods or services can lead to genericisation of a mark and its 'death' (see chapter 5). However, because the defendant's goods are similar, the plaintiff will be required to show likelihood of confusion in order to succeed in an infringement action under Article 9(1)(b) of the CTMR. If, as seems likely, the meaning of this phrase is limited to source confusion, the plaintiff may not succeed if the public merely 'call to mind' the registered trade mark, yet the mark itself will have been weakened. A plaintiff in such a situation will be better off arguing that the goods are not similar so as to get the advantage of Article 9(1)(c) of the CTMR, where source confusion need not be proved. It would indeed be ironic if protection against use on competing goods or services were weaker than protection against use on non-competing goods or services under Article 9(1)(c) of the CTMR. Only if likelihood of confusion is given the broad interpretation accorded to it in Benelux law will the CTM owner receive effective protection against dilution by use of the mark on similar goods.

Another type of harm (though one which could be considered to be a lesser form of tarnishment) is poking fun at the registered mark (for an example see the recent US Court of Appeals for the Second Circuit decision in *Deere and Co.* v *MTD Products Inc.* (1994) 41 F 3d 39, 32 USPQ 2d 1936, which also involved dilution in relation to competing goods).

Requirements for dilution (Article 9(1)(c) CTMR)

Reputation   In order to succeed in an action for infringement under Article 9(1)(c), the plaintiff must prove firstly that its mark has *reputation* in the

Community. This is somewhat further down the scale than the USA requirement that the mark be 'famous' and the Paris Convention concept of the 'well known' mark. Conversely, such requirement was not part of the Benelux Uniform Trademark Law 1971, although it is generally recognised that there is a greater likelihood of success under Benelux law if the mark has acquired a reputation. There is no requirement that the mark be *used* in the Community (although if the user requirements in Article 15 of the CTMR are not met, the mark will be liable to revocation). It is unclear whether, by analogy with statement 10 by the Council and Commission in the minutes of the Council of Ministers attached to the CTMR, OHIM OJ 5/96, p. 615, which is to the effect that use in one Member State suffices for the requirements of Article 15 of the CTMR, reputation in just one Member State will suffice for Article 9(1)(c) of the CTMR.

It is a matter for speculation, therefore, what type of Community marks with reputation will be protected against dilution under Article 9(1)(c) of the CTMR. As stated above, the practice under American state dilution laws has been to protect only 'famous' marks, for example, MARLBORO, COCA-COLA, NES-CAFÉ, BUICK, TIFFANY'S and PAMPERS. The new Federal Trademark Dilution Act of 1995, prompted by the International Trademark Association model code, contains a non-exclusive list of factors to be taken into account. It is by no means inconceivable that such criteria will not be adopted in due course by CTM courts. The list includes:

(a)   the degree of inherent or acquired distinctiveness of the mark;
(b)   the duration and extent of use of the mark in connection with the goods or services with which the mark is used;
(c)   the duration and extent of advertising and publicity of the mark;
(d)   the geographical extent of the trading area in which the mark is used;
(e)   the channels of trade for the goods or services with which the mark is used;
(f)   the degree of recognition of the mark in the trade areas and channels of trade used by the mark's owner; and
(g)   the nature and extent of use of the same or similar sign by third parties.

Absence of due cause   Secondly, the defendant will only infringe under Article 9(1)(c) of the CTMR if its use is without 'due cause'. 'Due cause' is not defined by the CTMR and will need to be determined by the courts on a case-by-case basis. The words 'due cause' in Article 13A(2) of the Uniform Benelux Trademarks Law 1971 have been interpreted narrowly (*CLAERYN/KLAREIN* (1976) 7 IIC 420). There must be 'necessity' for the defendant's use, for example, in connection with accessories or spare parts, or the defendant must have a prior right to use the sign.

No confusion   Finally, it was noted above that likelihood of confusion is not necessary to a finding of infringement under Article 9(1)(c) of the CTMR. United Kingdom case law decided under s. 10(3) of the 1994 Act (which is based on Article 5(2) of the Directive) shows an uncanny tendency to follow the earlier example set by US judges interpreting state anti-dilution laws, by dismissing claims for trade mark dilution unless supported by clear evidence of consumer confusion (see *BASF plc* v *CEP (UK) plc* (26 October 1995, unreported); and *Baywatch Production Co. Inc.* v *The Home Video Channel* [1997] FSR 22).

Examination of the relevant wording, whether in the Directive or CTMR will show that confusion is not a prerequisite for liability, as confirmed by Advocate-General Jacobs in his opinion in *Sabel BV* v *Puma AG* (case C-251/95) 29 April 1997.

Categories of infringing acts

Article 9(2) of the CTMR contains (as does Article 5 of the Directive) a non-exhaustive list of the types of activity which may amount to infringement of a CTM, namely:

(a)   affixing the sign to goods or packaging;
(b)   offering or exposing goods for sale, putting them on the market, stocking them for those purposes under the sign, offering to supply services under the sign;
(c)   importing or exporting goods under the sign; and
(d)   using the sign on business papers or advertising.

Mention has already been made of the overriding requirements that this conduct must amount to 'use of the sign', which use itself must be 'in the course of trade' and 'in relation to' goods and services; and of cases decided under national law concerning the degree of proximity between the alleged infringing sign and the product.

The potential difficulties inherent in determining the exact scope of this wording can be illustrated yet again by reference to *Trebor Bassett Ltd* v *Football Association* [1997] FSR 211, where the act of reproducing the defendant's trade mark in photographs of football players on collectable insert cards was held not to amount to 'affixing' the sign to the cards, nor putting the cards on the market under the sign.

There is no equivalent in the CTMR of the acts of contributory infringement proscribed by s. 10(5) of the United Kingdom Trade Marks Act 1994.

Comparative advertising

In statement 7 by the Council and Commission in the minutes of the Council of Ministers attached to the CTMR, OHIM OJ 5/96, p. 615, it is declared that reference to advertising in Article 9(2)(d) of the CTMR ('using the sign on business papers or in advertising') does not cover the use of a CTM in comparative advertising. The statement should be contrasted with statement 6 in the minutes relating to the Directive (ibid., p. 609), where it is declared that 'The Council and the Commission consider that the prohibition on using the sign in advertising does not affect the national provisions concerning the possibility of using or not using a trade mark in comparative advertising'. The contradiction between the two statements therefore raises the intriguing possibility that whilst a nationally registered mark may, depending on the provisions of national law, be infringed by comparative advertising, a CTM cannot.

It must be stressed, however, that the attitude of Member States towards comparative advertising varies considerably, so that in the Benelux such practice may be regarded as 'other use' pursuant to Article 13A2 of the Uniform Benelux Trademark Law 1971, whereas under the United Kingdom Trade Marks Act 1994,

s. 10(6), it is not trade mark infringement unless contrary to 'honest practices in industrial or commercial matters'. For how s. 10(6) has been subjected to an objective interpretation, thereby encouraging the use of comparative advertising, see *Barclays Bank plc* v *RBS Advanta* [1996] RPC 307; *Vodafone Group plc* v *Orange Personal Communications Services Ltd* [1997] FSR 34; and *British Telecommunications plc* v *AT & T Communications (UK) Ltd* (18 December 1996, unreported).

Other Member States use the law of unfair competition to control comparative advertising.

Two further observations may be made concerning comparative advertising. First, it is arguable that in relation to both a Community and national trade mark, comparative advertising could be viewed as falling within the doctrine of exhaustion of rights (Article 13 of the CTMR, Article 7 of the Directive) discussed in the following chapter, in so far as the alleged infringing sign is being used 'in relation to goods which have been put on the market in the Community under that trade mark by the proprietor or with his consent', though the point remains to be judicially determined.

Secondly, the right of the proprietor of a nationally registered trade mark has been clarified by Directive 97/55/EC of 6 October 1997, [1997] OJ L 290/18 which amends the earlier misleading advertising Directive so as to include comparative advertising. Contrary to the culture of current United Kingdom law which allows such advertising unless it is contrary to 'honest practices in industrial and commercial matters', the Directive permits comparative advertising only when certain conditions are met, namely (Article 1):

(a)   the advertisement must not be misleading;

(b)   it must compare goods or services meeting the same needs or intended for the same purpose;

(c)   it must objectively compare one or more essential, verifiable and representative features of the goods and services, including price;

(d)   it must not create confusion in the market place between the advertiser and a competitor, or between their marks, goods or services;

(e)   it must not discredit or denigrate the marks, goods or services, personal qualities or circumstances of a competitor;

(f)   it must not take unfair advantage of the reputation of the trade mark.

Recitals 13 to 15 of the Comparative Advertising Directive cross-refer to the First Trade Marks Directive, but state that making use of another's trade mark does not breach the exclusive use referred to in Article 5 of the Trade Marks Directive in cases which comply with the conditions in the later Directive.

Dictionaries

Mention has already been made of Article 10 of the CTMR, which gives the proprietor of the CTM the right to control the way in which the trade mark appears in dictionaries, encyclopaedias and other reference works so as to ensure that it does not become generic, though such right does not extend to periodical publications. The specific remedy granted by the Article is the right to insist that the next edition of the work carries an indication that what has been reproduced is a registered trade mark.

Registration by agent

Under Article 11 of the CTMR, registration of a CTM by an agent or representative of the proprietor without the latter's authorisation, entitles the proprietor to oppose use of the mark by the agent. This reproduces substantially the text of Article 6*septies* of the Paris Convention and is matched by the text of Article 8(3) of the CTMR discussed in chapter 3.

Chapter Seven
Infringement 2:
Limitations, Counterclaims and Jurisdiction

Introduction

This chapter is concerned with matters ancillary to the infringement of a Community trade mark (CTM). It therefore considers:

(a)   limitations which are placed by the CTMR on the rights of the trade mark owner (which operate primarily, but not exclusively, as defences to infringement);

(b)   the ability of the defendant to a CTM infringement action to counterclaim that the mark should be revoked or declared invalid;

(c)   where the CTM right is to be enforced; and

(d)   the role of the Court of Justice of the European Communities in giving guidance to Community trade mark courts (CTM courts) by way of a preliminary ruling under Article 177 of the Treaty of Rome.

Limitations placed on the CTM

The principal defences to the infringement of a CTM are set out in Article 12 of the CTMR. The CTM right is, however, equally vulnerable to a plea of acquiescence under Article 53 of the CTMR (which is not a defence, but rather operates to prevent the CTM being enforced). There are also special savings for prior rights under Articles 106 and 107 of the CTMR, which likewise have the same effect of stopping the enforcement of the CTM in a particular Member State or locality and there is the limited defence 'as to the merits' found in Article 95(3) of the CTMR. Because of its importance, the defence of exhaustion of rights found in Article 13 of the CTMR is dealt with separately below.

Use of own name and address (Article 12(a) CTMR)
Article 12(a) of the CTMR (which is identical in its wording to Article 6(1)(a) of the Directive) states that a CTM shall not entitle the proprietor to prohibit a third party from using in the course of trade his own name and address.

The scope of this defence must be interpreted in the light of statement 7 by the Council and Commission in the minutes of the Council Meeting at which the

Directive was adopted and statement 8 by the Council and Commission in the minutes of the Council Meeting at which the CTMR was adopted (see OHIM OJ 5/96, p. 609 and p. 615 respectively). Both statements are to the effect that the words 'his own name and address' are applicable only to natural persons.

The defence in Article 12(a) of the CTMR would therefore appear to protect sole traders and no one else. It clearly will not extend to legal persons as defined in Article 3 of the CTMR, which definition, as noted in chapter 2, covers not just companies but other non-legal entities which are recognised under the applicable national law as legal persons (Explanatory Memorandum to the Draft CTMR, COM (80) 635 final of 19 November 1980). This is a significant change for those familiar with the pre-harmonisation law of the United Kingdom. The defence formerly found in s. 8(a) of the Trade Marks Act 1938, although containing the word 'person', was readily applied to companies (*Baume & Co. Ltd* v *A.H. Moore Ltd* [1957] RPC 459, [1958] RPC 226; *Parker-Knoll Ltd* v *Knoll International Ltd* [1962] RPC 243). Further, s. 8(a) referred to the defendant's 'predecessor in business', which is not to be found in Article 12(a) of the CTMR.

Chapter 2 has already noted the difficulty faced by United Kingdom partnerships and unincorporated bodies in meeting the definition of 'legal person' in Article 3 of the CTMR. Article 12(a) of the CTMR presents yet another problem. It could be argued that use of the partners' own names as the name of the partnership (for example, 'Smith & Jones, Solicitors' where the partners are called Smith and Jones) would fall within the scope of the defence, but were the partnership to adopt a name which bore no relation to the partners' individual names (for example, 'Legal Eagles') then this would appear to be outside the intended scope of Article 12(a) of the CTMR, as the partnership name could hardly be described as that of a 'natural person'.

The practical message behind the Article 12(a) defence is clear. Anyone contemplating forming an organisation which amounts to a legal personality within Article 3 of the CTMR would be foolish to choose a name for that undertaking without first consulting the Register of CTMs (or indeed national registers, in view of the wording in Article 6 of the Directive). Use of the name in connection with the supply of goods or services within the Community (and in particular, use of that name on wholesale or retail premises or on business papers and in advertising — Article 9(2) of the CTMR) may well amount to trade mark infringement. Equally, a company incorporated in another jurisdiction which imports goods into the Community should consider how its goods are labelled (that is, whether they bear that company's own trade marks or just its corporate name) as use of the corporate name would not secure the benefit of Article 12(a) of the CTMR (cf. the facts in the United Kingdom decision of *Mercury Communications Ltd* v *Mercury Interactive (UK) Ltd* [1995] FSR 850 explained below).

One matter which remains to be determined under Article 12(a) of the CTMR is the precise meaning of the word 'name'. As Laddie J pointed out in the *Mercury* case, an individual may be christened one name but be known by variants of this name or even by an adopted name. He was minded (without deciding the point) to interpret s. 8(a) of the United Kingdom Trade Marks Act 1938 as covering the name by which an individual is known rather than the name which they officially bear. Only the Court of Justice will be able to determine this point in the context of the CTMR.

The defence in Article 12(a) of the CTMR is subject to the proviso that such use must be in accordance with honest practices in industrial or commercial matters. This is explained below.

Descriptive use of the CTM (Article 12(b) CTMR)

Article 12(b) of the CTMR (again having identical wording to Article 6(1)(b) of the Directive) states that a CTM shall not entitle the proprietor to prohibit a third party from using in the course of trade 'indications concerning the kind, quality, quantity, intended purpose, value, geographical origin, the time of production of the goods or of rendering of the service, or other characteristics of the goods or service'. To give examples, the manufacturer of soft drinks may wish to tell potential consumers that they contain a certain type of artificial sweetener, or the makers of fashion garments may wish to indicate that they contain a particular brand of textile. In each case this is permissible under Article 12(b) of the CTMR as long as the conditions in its proviso (explained below) are observed.

The difficulty which is likely to arise with the interpretation of Article 12(b) of the CTMR is the corollary to the problematic scope of Article 9 of the CTMR, discussed in chapter 6. It will be recalled that one of the key issues in Article 9 of the CTMR is the extent to which 'use in a trade mark sense' is a prerequisite for liability. If (as argued in *British Sugar plc* v *James Robertson & Sons Ltd* [1996] RPC 281 in the context of post-harmonisation United Kingdom law) all that Article 9 of the CTMR requires is that there be use 'in the course of trade' of an infringing 'sign', then there is no requirement for trade mark use. The result is that the defence of descriptive use has too much of a role to play in striking a balance between the interests of the trade mark proprietor and those of other traders. If, however, the thinking in *Bravado Merchandising Ltd* v *Mainstream Publishing Ltd* [1996] FSR 205 is followed, the phrase 'in relation to' found in Article 9(1)(a) and (c) of the CTMR will be crucial in helping to differentiate between infringement and descriptive use, albeit at the expense of importing a requirement of trade mark use.

Use of the CTM to indicate the intended purpose of the goods or services (Article 12(c) CTMR)

Article 12(c) of the CTMR (in like manner to Article 6(1)(c) of the Directive) provides that a CTM shall not entitle the proprietor to prohibit a third party from using in the course of trade the trade mark where it is necessary to indicate the intended purpose of a product of service, in particular as accessories or spare parts. The defence is likely to be most relevant for those manufacturing replacement parts for consumer 'white goods' (such as washing machines and vacuum cleaners) and motor vehicles (subject, of course, to design right constraints) but again needs to be read in the light of the proviso, explained next.

Proviso to Article 12 of the CTMR

The proviso to Article 12 of the CTMR (found also as a proviso to Article 6(1) of the Directive) is to the effect that the third party's use must be 'in accordance with honest practices in industrial and commercial matters'.

Origins of the phrase The wording of the proviso can be traced to Article 10*bis*(2) of the Paris Convention where it is given as the definition of unfair competition. It may be noted in passing that Article 10*bis*(1) imposes the obligation on countries of the Union to assure effective protection against unfair competition and Article 10*bis*(3) gives three specific but non-exhaustive illustrations of what amounts to unfair competition. Of interest in the present context are Article 10*bis*(3)(1) ('acts of such a nature as to create confusion by any means whatever with the establishment, the goods, or the industrial or commercial activities of a competitor') and Article 10*bis*(3)(3) ('indications or allegations the use of which in the course of trade is liable to mislead the public as to the nature, the manufacturing process, the characteristics, the suitability for their purpose, or the quantity of the goods'). The proviso to Article 12 of the CTMR therefore appears to state that conduct falling within paragraphs (a), (b) and (c) will not be acceptable if it amounts to unfair competition of the type delineated. Nevertheless, and despite its origins, the proviso will still fall to be construed by the European Court of Justice as a specific qualification to the three defences to an action for the infringement of a CTM, rather than as a provision on unfair competition per se.

Subjective or objective   One further but important matter to be resolved by the Court of Justice is whether the proviso to Article 12 of the CTMR imports a subjective or objective standard.

United Kingdom lawyers may be tempted to have recourse to case law decided under the pre-harmonisation defences to domestic trade mark infringement found in the Trade Marks Act 1938. The defences in ss. 8(a), 8(b) and 4(3)(b) appear at first glance to equate to those found in Article 12(a), (b) and (c) of the CTMR. In like manner to the proviso to Article 12 of the CTMR, each defence was qualified by the phrase 'bona fide', although those found in ss. 8(b) and 4(3)(b) additionally required that the defendant's conduct in using the plaintiff's mark must not amount to 'importing a reference'.

However, such temptation must be resisted. The old United Kingdom defences were given inconsistent judicial treatment. That found in s. 8(a) (use of own name and address) was held to impose a requirement of *subjective* honesty. In *Mercury Communications Ltd* v *Mercury Interactive (UK) Ltd* [1995] FSR 850, Laddie J went so far as to say that:

> when a trader innocently uses his own name . . . he does not need to look over his shoulder to make sure that a registered trade mark is not in the way, unless, of course, he has been warned in advance.

Yet cases decided under s. 8(b) (descriptive use) appear to have given 'bona fide' an objective meaning. In both *Newton Chambers & Co. Ltd* v *Neptune Waterproof Paper Co. Ltd* (1935) 52 RPC 399 and *British Northrop Ltd* v *Texteam Blackburn Ltd* [1974] RPC 57, although the descriptive use of the plaintiff's mark in relation to the defendant's goods was not subjectively *dishonest*, the court found in each case that the defendant's conduct went beyond the bounds of what was considered commercially acceptable behaviour in that it amounted to an unfair exploitation of the reputation of the trade mark. The *Northrop* case, by analogy, can also be considered as authority that an objective test applied also under s. 4(3)(b) (spare parts). (For another example of the inconsistency of treatment accorded to the phrase 'bona fide' in pre-harmonisation United Kingdom law, see the discussion of bad faith in relation to *acquiescence*, below.)

It is to be hoped that the Court of Justice is influenced by the reasoning of Laddie J in the post-harmonisation United Kingdom decision of *Barclays Bank plc v RBS Advanta* [1996] RPC 307. Here, the phrase 'honest practices in industrial and commercial matters' formed the first part of the proviso to s. 10(6) of the United Kingdom Trade Marks Act 1994, which in essence permits comparative advertising unless the terms of the proviso are breached (the second part of the proviso to s. 10(6) is not relevant to the present discussion). Laddie J attempted to find a meaning for the proviso that was consistent both with s. 10(3) of the Act (equivalent to Article 9(1)(c) of the CTMR) and with the proviso to s. 11(2) of the Act (equivalent to Article 12 of the CTMR). He agreed with counsel that, first, the onus rests with the trade mark proprietor to show that the criteria for the proviso are met (thereby removing the protection of the defence) and, secondly, the wording of the phrase as a whole imports an objective standard:

> This part of the proviso simply means that if the use is considered honest by members of a reasonable audience, it will not infringe. . . . Honesty has to be gauged against what is reasonably to be expected by the relevant public of advertisements for the goods or services in issue ([1996] RPC 307 at 315–16).

Although delivered in the context of alleged infringement by comparative advertising, such interpretation would seem equally applicable to Article 12 of the CTMR, thus requiring the *Mercury* decision to be accorded extreme caution.

In the later case of *Kimberly-Clark v Fort Sterling Ltd* [1997] 7 EIPR D-185, concessions by counsel resulted in the scope of the proviso to s. 10(6) of the United Kingdom Trade Marks Act 1994 not being given further analysis. The lack of discussion is particularly unfortunate in view of the fact that the defendant's offer to replace their rolls of toilet tissue with those of the ANDREX brand if the consumer was not satisfied was held to amount to passing-off. If such conduct amounted to passing-off, then logically it should have amounted to trade mark infringement. Factors which were taken into account in deciding that passing-off had been made out included the size and colouring of the word ANDREX on the defendant's product, coupled with the near-invisible size of the lettering pointing out that ANDREX was the plaintiff's brand. The overall impact was to make consumers think that the plaintiffs were responsible for the defendant's promotion. The case has much in common with the older decision in *Newton Chambers & Co. Ltd v Neptune Waterproof Paper Co. Ltd* (1935) 52 RPC 399, where over-prominent use of the plaintiff's mark for disinfectants was held to take the case outside the scope of the descriptive use defence and which points yet again to the conclusion that the proviso to Article 12 of the CTMR should be given an objective meaning.

It may be noted in conclusion that a recent reference to the Court of Justice by the Hoge Raad der Nederlanden (*BMW AG v Deenik* (case C-63/97) [1997] OJ C 108/14) has asked a series of questions seeking guidance on the scope of fair use under the Directive. An answer cannot realistically be expected before 1999.

Acquiescence (Article 53 CTMR)
Article 53 of the CTMR, which provides for acquiescence as a limitation on the rights of the CTM owner, has its counterpart in Article 9 of the Directive.

However, the two provisions are not identical in their wording and there is no equivalent to Recital 11 of the Directive (which explains acquiescence) in the CTMR.

Article 53 of the CTMR has to be understood in the context of Article 52 of the CTMR, which, in general terms, provides for a CTM to be declared invalid, either upon application to OHIM or by way of counterclaim to infringement proceedings, because it was registered in breach of Article 8 of the CTMR (relative grounds for refusal). Article 53 of the CTMR contemplates two different scenarios:

(a) where the owner of an earlier CTM wishes to object to a later CTM under Article 52 of the CTMR; and

(b) where the owner of an earlier national mark (whether registered or unregistered) wishes, on the basis of the same Article, to object to a later CTM.

Article 53 of the CTMR provides in each case that where the proprietor of the earlier trade mark has acquiesced for a period of five successive years in the use of the later mark while being aware of such use, he can no longer apply for a declaration of invalidity in respect of the later mark, or, what is more important for the purposes of the present discussion, oppose the use of the later mark in respect of the goods or services for which it has been used, unless registration of the later mark was obtained in bad faith.

The elements of acquiescence   The key ingredients of Article 53 of the CTMR are as follows:

(a) There must be an earlier CTM or international, Benelux or national trade mark, though the last mentioned may be registered (within the meaning of Article 8(2) of the CTMR) or unregistered (within the meaning of Article 8(4) of the CTMR).

(b) There must be a later CTM, which by definition must have achieved registration in the face of the earlier right, whether this occurred because the owner of the senior right was unsuccessful in opposition proceedings or was negligent in failing to take steps to object to the junior mark.

(c) The junior mark must have been used within the Community for a period of five successive years (the wording of Article 53 of the CTMR may be contrasted here with s. 48 of the United Kingdom Trade Marks Act 1994, which, in incorporating Article 9 of the Directive, uses the phrase 'for a continuous period of five years'). It is reasonable to assume that, in accordance with statement 10 of the Council and Commission in the minutes of the Council Meeting at which the CTMR was adopted (explaining Article 15 of the CTMR) (see OHIM OJ 5/96, p. 615), use in one Member State will suffice.

(d) The owner of the senior right must have known of the use of the junior mark. Knowledge of its registration alone is not sufficient, what is required is knowledge of use. Reference to the similar provision in the Directive and in particular Recital 11 thereto suggests that what is required is actual knowledge rather than any form of constructive knowledge being attributed to the owner because of negligence (Recital 11 to the Directive contains the words 'knowingly tolerated').

These requirements suggest that acquiescence under Article 53 of the CTMR has some affinity with the common law doctrine of estoppel, as explained by Oliver J in *Taylors Fashions Ltd* v *Liverpool Victoria Trustees Co. Ltd* [1982] QB 133 at pp. 151–2:

> Furthermore the more recent cases indicate, in my judgment, that the application of the *Ramsden* v *Dyson* principle — whether you call it proprietary estoppel, estoppel by acquiescence or estoppel by encouragement is really immaterial — requires a very much broader approach which is directed rather at ascertaining whether, in particular individual circumstances, it would be unconscionable for a party to be permitted to deny that which . . . he has allowed or encouraged another to assume to his detriment than to inquiring whether the circumstances can be fitted within the confines of some preconceived formula serving as a universal yardstick for every form of unconscionable behaviour.

What is unclear, however, is where acquiescence (or 'knowing toleration') lies on the spectrum of unconscionable behaviour referred to by Oliver J. Inequitable conduct may range from actual consent (whether tacit or otherwise), through some form of inducement or encouragement (which again may be active or passive, as in the recent United Kingdom copyright case of *Film Investors Overseas Services SA* v *Home Video Channel Ltd* (1996) *The Times*, 2 December 1996), to inordinate delay in bringing infringement proceedings (such as occurred in *Cluett Peabody & Co. Inc.* v *McIntyre Hogg Marsh & Co. Ltd* [1958] RPC 335 (29 years) and *Vine Products Ltd* v *Mackenzie & Co. Ltd* [1969] RPC 1 (100 years)). Whilst Article 53 of the CTMR lays down a precise time limit for acquiescence, it is the degree of inequitable conduct which will require explanation by the Court of Justice.

Onus of proof   It would seem logical to assume that the burden of proving knowledge of use of the later mark will lie with the party raising the plea of acquiescence, and that such burden may be difficult to discharge. However, where the use of the later mark is extensive and the two proprietors are in the same line of business, it may be that the court would agree that a prima facie case of awareness has been made out, thus shifting the burden of proof to the earlier proprietor.

Bad faith   The plea of acquiescence cannot be raised where the later CTM was 'applied for in bad faith'. This gives rise to several questions concerning the meaning of 'bad faith' and the period of time covered by the phrase 'applied for'.

In relation to 'bad faith', it will be recalled that unlike Article 3(2)(d) of the Directive, this objection does not appear in the list of absolute grounds for the refusal of a CTM application in Article 7 of the CTMR but instead is listed as one of the grounds for a declaration of invalidity under Article 51(1)(b) of the CTMR. Little guidance is to be found in either the CTMR or the Directive on the meaning of the phrase. Indeed the linguistic evidence concerning its meaning has been described as 'tenuous and contradictory' (*Road Tech Computer Systems Ltd* v *Unison Software (UK) Ltd* [1996] FSR 805). United Kingdom trade mark lawyers might be tempted to equate it to the phrase 'bona fide' as it appeared in the 1938 Act. However, as pointed out in *Imperial Group Ltd* v *Philip Morris & Co. Ltd*

[1982] FSR 72, the phrase 'bona fide' was used in two quite separate senses in that piece of legislation, namely, in a narrow, subjective way to mean 'dishonesty' in s. 8 (see *Baume & Co. Ltd v A.H. Moore Ltd* [1958] RPC 226) and in a wider, objective manner importing the test that the conduct in question must be 'genuine' in s. 26 (the *Imperial Group* case itself). This hardly helps to decide, therefore, whether the CTMR imposes a subjective or an objective standard.

What is also unclear is whether the bad faith on the part of the junior proprietor must relate to their conduct generally or only their conduct in relation to the senior mark. General bad faith might include stockpiling, wrongful entitlement or deliberate choice of two CTMs with a view to partitioning the market. If bad faith relates solely to the senior registration, again there is uncertainty surrounding its meaning. It will be remembered from chapter 3 that the CTM applicant is furnished with the OHIM search report and to some extent national search reports, but is well-advised to carry out prior searches of all national or regional trade mark registries and national companies registries. Would persisting with a CTM application in the light of such official and private search reports constitute 'bad faith' or would the later applicant have to have gone further, such as contacting the owner of the earlier right?

It must also be considered whether the phrase 'applied for' is limited to the time of the filing of the application, so that subsequent knowledge of earlier rights acquired during opposition proceedings would not amount to bad faith within the meaning of the Article, or whether the phrase refers to the whole period of time during which the later CTM application is being processed by OHIM up to the point of entry on the Register. Some guidance here may be gleaned from Article 51(1)(b) of the CTMR which makes bad faith *at the time of filing* a ground for invalidity and from the OHIM brochure which describes bad faith as 'unfair practices involving lack of good faith on the part of the applicant *at the time of filing*' (emphasis added).

Effect of acquiescence   The effect of acquiescence is to prevent the owner of the earlier right suing the owner of the later right for infringement, but only in respect of the goods or services for which the later mark has been used. There is nothing to stop the owner of the earlier mark seeking partial revocation of the later mark for non-use, nor indeed is there anything to stop the owner of the earlier mark seeking to have the later mark revoked on any of the other grounds found in Article 50(1)(b) and (c) of the CTMR (generic or deceptive use, though this might prove to be a hostage to fortune) or seeking to have the later mark declared invalid under Article 51 of the CTMR on one of the absolute grounds for refusal.

Article 53(3) of the CTMR means that the holder of the later CTM is equally powerless to prevent the use of the earlier mark by suing *its* proprietor for infringement, but again is not prevented from seeking revocation of the earlier mark under Article 50 of the CTMR or a declaration of invalidity under Article 51 of the CTMR. Acquiescence thus serves as a defence to infringement but does not give better rights. The result of acquiescence is a potential stalemate, with both marks coexisting in the Community.

The one difference between the CTMR and the Directive concerning acquiescence is that the latter gives Member States the option to allow the plea of acquiescence to be raised against the owner of other intellectual property rights (specifically a right to a name, a right of personal portrayal, a copyright or 'other forms of industrial property', which phrase must be taken to refer to registered or unregistered designs). On the other hand, Article 53(2) of the CTMR is limited to earlier national, regional or international trade marks which are either registered, applied for or well known in accordance with Article 8(2) of the CTMR, or which, although unregistered, have acquired sufficient rights to enable the proprietor to stop subsequent marks under the criteria laid down in Article 8(4) of the CTMR.

Prior rights (Articles 106 and 107 CTMR)

Although there is no express saving (and hence no defence) for prior rights, as mentioned in chapter 4 above, one of the unique features of the CTM system (the so-called 'Emmental cheese' characteristic) is the ability for earlier national rights and earlier CTMs to exist alongside a later CTM thus undermining its unitary character. This is made possible by Articles 106 and 107 of the CTMR.

Earlier rights (Article 106 CTMR)   Article 106 of the CTMR permits the owners of earlier rights to sue under national law for infringement of their rights by a later CTM, in addition to opposing the registration of such mark under Article 8 of the CTMR or seeking to have it cancelled for invalidity under Article 52 of the CTMR. The effect of a successful action under Article 106 of the CTMR is to prevent the use of the later CTM in a particular Member State or States. 'Earlier rights' are stated without qualification to be those within Article 8 or Article 52(2) of the CTMR and therefore comprise the following:

(a)   CTM or national, Benelux or international trade mark registrations or applications for them (provided they mature into registrations) which meet the criteria laid down by Articles 8(1) or 8(5) of the CTMR;

(b)   well known trade marks which meet the criteria laid down by Article 8(1) or (5) of the CTMR;

(c)   the rights of the 'proprietor' of a CTM which has been unjustifiably registered in the name of the proprietor's agent or representative contrary to Article 8(3) of the CTMR;

(d)   unregistered national trade marks or other national signs used in the course of trade of more than mere local significance which meet the conditions of Article 8(4) of the CTMR; and

(e)   rights to a name, rights to personal portrayal, copyrights or other industrial property rights which meet the conditions of Article 52(2) of the CTMR.

Article 106(2) of the CTMR creates the fiction that for the purposes of the prior rights provision, the CTM is deemed to be a national trade mark, in that its proprietor is to rely on rights granted by national law rather than under the CTMR.

Examples have already been given in chapter 4 of the way in which Article 106 of the CTMR could be relied on by the owners of prior rights to destroy the unitary character of the later CTM.

Apart from prior rights falling within Article 8(3) of the CTMR (unjustifiable registration by an agent) or Article 52(2) of the CTMR (other forms of prior rights), Article 106 of the CTMR is subject to the defence of acquiescence under Article 53 of the CTMR, as explained above.

Prior rights applicable in particular localities (Article 107 CTMR)   The right to oppose the use of a later CTM is given by Article 107 of the CTMR to the owner of a used but unregistered and localised mark. Whether such a right is recognised will depend on the national law of the Member State in question. The right to sue under national law to prevent the use of the junior CTM registration is subject to any plea of acquiescence under Article 53 of the CTMR, although if acquiescence is proved, the proprietor of the later CTM is equally debarred from opposing the use of the local prior right.

Defence 'as to the merits' (Article 95(3) CTMR)

Article 95(3) of the CTMR provides for a limited defence (as opposed to a counterclaim) to be raised by the defendant in actions brought under Articles 92(1)(a) and (c) of the CTMR (respectively, actions for infringement or threatened infringement of a CTM and actions for matters occurring between the date of publication of the CTM application and the date of publication of its registration). The Article permits a limited plea 'relating to revocation or invalidity of the CTM otherwise than by way of counterclaim' to be raised. Such a plea is only admissible where the defendant argues that the CTM could be revoked for non-use or could be declared invalid under Article 52(1) of the CTMR on account of an earlier right of the defendant. No other grounds of revocation or invalidity may be pleaded, and in particular it should be noted that the relative grounds are limited to those earlier rights owned by the defendant and no one else.

From the conditional wording used in Article 95(3) of the CTMR, it may be inferred that the defendant does not have to discharge the normal burden of proof relating to counterclaims (see below) but merely has to satisfy the court that an arguable case has been made out. Unlike a counterclaim, the defence will not operate to remove the CTM from the Register of CTMs but will simply shield the defendant from liability for infringement.

Exhaustion of rights

The statement of principle (Article 13 CTMR)

Article 13 of the CTMR (which has its counterpart in Article 7 of the Directive) provides that a CTM shall not entitle the proprietor to object to its use in relation to goods which have been put on the market in the Community by him or with his consent, unless there exist legitimate reasons to oppose the further commercialisation of the goods, especially where the condition of the goods is changed or impaired.

Article 13 reflects the body of case law developed by the Court of Justice of the European Communities since its seminal decision in *Deutsche Grammophon GmbH* v *Metro-SB-Grossmärkte GmbH & Co. KG* (case 78/70) [1971] ECR 487, in which it laid down for the first time the distinction between the existence and exercise of intellectual property rights. The case law should be seen as the Court's attempt to reconcile the territorial nature of national intellectual property rights with the concept of what was initially the common market, later the single market, and ultimately the European Economic Area (EEA). Whichever of these three concepts is under discussion, the touchstone is that all the Member States are treated as a single trading area without internal national boundaries.

In creating the doctrine of Community-wide exhaustion of national intellectual property rights, the Court of Justice has had to strike a balance between, on the one hand, the absolute prohibition found in Article 30 of the Treaty of Rome (hereafter Article 30 EC Treaty) on restrictions on imports and, on the other, the limited derogations found in Article 36 of the Treaty of Rome (hereafter Article 36 EC Treaty) for the protection of 'industrial and commercial property' and in Article 222 of the Treaty concerning Member States' rights to determine their own laws concerning property. It has justified the concept of exhaustion of rights by saying that the specific aim of intellectual property (whether patents, copyright or trade marks) is to allow the owner to control the first marketing of the relevant goods covered by that right:

> The specific subject matter of a trade mark is in particular to guarantee to the owner that he has the exclusive right to use that trade mark for the purpose of putting a product on the market for the first time and therefore to protect him against competitors wishing to take advantage of the status and reputation of the trade mark by selling products bearing it illegally (*Bristol-Myers Squibb* v *Paranova A/S* (cases C-427, 429 and 436/93) [1996] ECR I-3457, para. 44)

Once that first marketing has occurred, anywhere in the EEA, the proprietor of the right should not be able to object to subsequent dealings in the goods unless they are tampered with in some way.

Application of the doctrine of exhaustion to CTMs
It is readily apparent that, because of the unitary and pan-European character of the CTM (Article 1 CTMR), not all of the case law created by the Court of Justice will be relevant to an appreciation of Article 13 of the CTMR. As is explained in chapter 9, a CTM cannot be transferred to different parties in different Member States, although there can be partial transfer as to particular goods and services (Articles 16 and 17 of the CTMR). There can, however, be partial licensing of CTMs (either as to some of the goods or services and/or as to part of the Community) subject to the obligation to record the transaction (Article 22 CTMR). The modified doctrine of exhaustion of rights as it applies to CTMs therefore operates as follows:

Parallel and infringing imports Where the proprietor of a CTM wishes to rely on it in a particular Member State to resist the importation of goods from another Member State, it is still necessary (as is the case when discussing Community-wide exhaustion of national trade mark rights) to determine whether the goods in question should be treated as parallel or infringing imports.

Parallel imports are those goods which originated with the CTM proprietor in another Member State, that is, they were marketed by the proprietor, or with his consent, or by a member of the same corporate group, or by a licensee, in the exporting Member State. In such a situation, Article 13 of the CTMR dictates (in line with the early decision of the Court of Justice in *Centrafarm BV* v *Sterling Drug Inc.* (case 15/74) [1974] ECR 1147 and *Centrafarm BV* v *Winthrop BV* (case 16/74) [1974] ECR 1183) that the CTM right is exhausted unless the conduct of the importer brings the case within the scope of the derogation in Article 13(2) of the CTMR (see below). Just as in the case of national trade mark rights, it is not possible to grant parallel licences of a CTM which attempt to partition the right along national boundaries, with the objective of protecting a local distributor or subsidiary (*Établissements Consten SA* v *Commission* (cases 56 and 58/64) [1966] ECR 299).

Where, however, the goods originate from an unconnected third party, who has no legal or economic links with the CTM owner, the CTM right can always be used to keep out the third party's products (*Terrapin (Overseas) Ltd* v *Terranova Industrie C.A. Kapferer & Co.* (case 119/75) [1976] ECR 1039; *Deutsche Renault AG* v *Audi AG* (case C-317/91) [1993] ECR I-6227). In other words, *infringing imports* touch upon the *existence* of the trade mark right and can always be enjoined, whereas *parallel imports* relate to its *exercise* and can never be enjoined unless the facts of the case fall within the derogation found in Article 13(2) of the CTMR.

Limited application of the doctrine of exhaustion   Given the unitary character of the CTM, the following areas of the Court's jurisprudence will not be germane to Article 13(1) of the CTMR:

(a)   Cases, whether decided under Article 85 of the Treaty of Rome (hereafter Article 85 EC Treaty) (such as *Sirena Srl* v *Eda Srl* (case 40/70) [1971] ECR 69) or under Article 30 EC Treaty (such as *IHT Internationale Heiztechnik GmbH* v *Ideal-Standard GmbH* (case C-9/93) [1994] ECR I-2789), where, because of an earlier assignment, whether voluntary or involuntary, national trade mark rights in different Member States have ended up in the hands of different proprietors. Transfers of CTMs have to be for the whole of the Community. It is, however, possible to envisage a scenario where the proprietor of a 'family' of CTMs chooses to transfer one or more of the marks to a third party, whilst retaining others, possibly with a view to partitioning the market. This arguably would not fall within the terms of Article 17(4) of the CTMR, which gives OHIM limited power to object to deceptive transfers. However, it may safely be presumed that the reservation made by the Court in the *Ideal-Standard* case to object to transfers which are not for legitimate business reasons would come into play and that such transfers would be invalid under Article 85 EC Treaty.

(b)   Cases (such as *Merck and Co. Inc.* v *Stephar BV* (case 187/80) [1981] ECR 2063 and *Merck and Co. Inc.* v *Primecrown Ltd* (case C-267/95 [1997] 1 CMLR 83) where it has been unsuccessfully argued by the intellectual property owner that absence of legal protection in the exporting Member State means that there can be no consent to marketing. Article 1 of the CTMR ensures that the CTM has uniform force throughout the EC. The only issue is the factual one of whether the CTM proprietor consented to the placing of the product on the market somewhere within the 15 Member States. By parity of reasoning, also irrelevant are those cases where the infringer has tried to rely on the lack of legal protection in the exporting Member State as a justification for his conduct (*EMI Electrola GmbH* v *Patricia Im- und Export* (case 341/87) [1989] ECR 79 and *Warner Bros Inc.* v *Christiansen* (case 158/86) [1988] ECR 2605, both cases involving copyright and related rights).

(c)   Cases which have pleaded disparity of national laws as a justification permitting infringing imports, arguing that such national laws are contrary to

Article 30 EC Treaty (*Thetford Corporation v Fiamma SpA* (case 35/87) [1988] ECR 3585; *Industrie Diensten Groep BV v Beele* (case 6/81) [1982] ECR 707; and *Keurkoop BV v Nancy Kean Gifts BV* (case 144/81) [1982] ECR 2853). The CTM is a supranational right.

(d)   Cases (concerned primarily with patents) where the intellectual property owner is treated as not having consented to first marketing because of national laws on compulsory licensing (*Pharmon BV v Hoechst AG* (case 19/84) [1985] ECR 2281). There can be no compulsory licensing of trade marks, whether national or Community (TRIPs, Article 21).

The exception to exhaustion (Article 13(2) CTMR)
Article 13(2) of the CTMR (reflecting Article 7(2) of the Directive) provides that the doctrine of exhaustion is not to apply where there exist legitimate reasons for the proprietor to oppose further commercialisation of the goods, especially where the condition of the goods is changed or impaired after they have been put on the market.

This derogation is based on a specific group of cases decided in the late 1970s by the Court of Justice dealing with the repackaging of pharmaceutical products. These cases have now been supplemented by more recent decisions.

In *Hoffmann-La Roche & Co. AG v Centrafarm Vertriebsgesellschaft Pharmazeutischer Erzeugnisse mbH* (case 102/77) [1978] ECR 1139 tranquilliser tablets sold in the United Kingdom were repackaged so as to make them acceptable to the German market, the importer reaffixing the trade mark together with its own name and address to the outside of the repackaged product. Such conduct was held by the Court of Justice to undermine the function of the trade mark in guaranteeing the quality of the goods, so that they became infringing imports. The Court went on, however, to provide guidelines for the parallel importer who wishes to repackage goods without incurring liability for trade mark infringement:

(a)   the marketing system adopted by the trade mark owner must contribute to the artificial partitioning of the markets between Member States;

(b)   the repackaging must not adversely affect the condition of the goods;

(c)   the owner of the trade mark must receive prior notice before the re-packaged product is put on sale;

(d)   it must be stated on the new packaging by whom the product has been repackaged.

These guidelines were followed by the parallel importer in *Pfizer Inc.* v *Eurim-Pharm GmbH* (case 1/81) [1981] ECR 2913 with the result that the trade mark proprietor could not object.

The importer in *Centrafarm BV v American Home Products Corporation* (case 3/78) [1978] ECR 1823 not only repackaged the goods, but changed the trade mark from that registered by the trade mark owner in the country of export to that registered in the country of import. The importer was held to infringe the latter registration. The Court accepted that the trade mark owner had good reason to have different marks in different Member States, but added the warning that if different marks were chosen simply to partition the single market, the parallel importer would be at liberty to change the marks without incurring liability.

Bristol-Myers Squibb v *Paranova A/S* (cases C-427, 429 and 436/93) [1996] ECR I-3457 concerned a series of references from Danish and German courts, in which the Court of Justice was asked to clarify the *Hoffmann-La Roche* and *American Home Products* rulings concerning the repackaging of parallel imports of pharmaceuticals in the subsequent light of Article 7 of the Directive. The Court ruled that Article 7 (and, by inference, Article 13 of the CTMR) has to be interpreted in the light of Article 36 EC Treaty. Although Article 7(1) of the Directive (Article 13(1) of the CTMR) recognises the principle of exhaustion of rights, Article 7(2) of the Directive (Article 13(2) of the CTMR) allows the trade mark owner legitimately to oppose the further marketing of a pharmaceutical product where there had been repackaging and reaffixing of the trade mark. However, the Court went on to qualify this statement in several important respects:

(a)   Repackaging cannot be challenged where the trade mark owner has chosen different forms of packaging for different Member States so that repackaging is necessary to market the product in the country of importation (that is, an additional burden is placed on the importer).

(b)   What matters is whether the reliance on trade mark rights would have the effect of artificially partitioning the common market; it need not be proved that the trade mark owner deliberately sought to do this (thus clarifying whether the *American Home Products* ruling involved a subjective or objective assessment of the trade mark proprietor's motives in choosing different marks for different Member States).

(c)   Repackaging cannot be challenged where the original condition of the goods is not affected, for example, merely by placing the contents in new external packaging, by affixing sticky labels or by adding new user instructions. It is for the national court to decide whether the condition of the goods is indirectly affected, for example, if the new user instructions omit vital information or are inaccurate, or if an article (such as an inhaler for an anti-asthma drug) inserted by the importer does not comply with the method of use envisaged by the original manufacturer.

(d)   Repackaging cannot be challenged as long as the new packaging states clearly the name of the manufacturer and the name of the repackager, but it is again for the national court to decide whether the poor quality of the repackaging damages the reputation of the trade mark.

(e)   In all cases, notice of repackaging must be given to the trade mark owner, and, if demanded, samples of the repackaged product must be supplied; but consent to repackaging is not required.

More recently, Advocate-General Jacobs has delivered his advisory opinion to the Court of Justice in *Parfums Christian Dior SA* v *Evora BV* (case C-337/95) 29 April 1997, a case concerned with luxury goods rather than pharmaceuticals. In addition to the right given by the *Paranova* ruling to oppose defective, poor quality or untidy repackaging, he has recommended that a trade mark owner should have the right under Article 7(2) of the Directive (equivalent to Article 13(2) of the CTMR) to oppose the use of the mark by a reseller in advertising, where such advertising is liable to damage significantly the reputation of the trade mark and of its owner. In the case of luxury goods such as perfumes (or, say, fashion garments) the harm may consist in tarnishing the up-market image associated with the goods. However, the risk of significant damage to the reputation of the trade mark owner must be properly substantiated. The same principles apply under Articles 30 and 36 EC Treaty where the trade mark owner seeks to rely on trade marks or copyright in the bottles or packaging to prevent such harmful advertising.

This may be contrasted with his opinion in *Loendersloot* v *George Ballantine & Son Ltd* (case C-349/95) 27 February 1997, where the trade mark owner was using labels affixed to bottles of alcoholic drinks as a means of identifying bottles which had been the subject of parallel importing. Advocate-General Jacobs advised the Court of Justice that the trade mark owner cannot exercise his trade mark rights to oppose the *removal* and subsequent reapplication of labels once the goods have been placed on the market where it is established that the use of the trade mark right will contribute to the artificial partitioning of the market. However, three conditions must be observed in order for the parallel importer to be able to continue with the relabelling, namely, that the guarantee of origin is not impaired, that the original condition of the product is not adversely affected and the reputation of the trade mark owner is not damaged. The same principles apply where the word 'pure' is omitted from the original labels, where the importer's name is replaced with that of another, and where the importer removes hidden identification marks placed underneath the labels.

Non-EEA goods and the question of international exhaustion

In *EMI Records Ltd* v *CBS United Kingdom Ltd* (case 51/75) [1976] ECR 811, again decided in the context of *national* trade mark rights, the Court of Justice said that Article 30 EC Treaty did not apply to goods coming from outside the Community. Consequently, domestic trade mark law could be used to stop parallel imports of goods from a non-EEA Member State such as the USA or Japan. The decision appeared to create a 'fortress Europe' situation, as exhaustion of rights only applied to goods having an EC origin moving *between* Member States. Since then the Court has explained in *Phytheron International SA* v *Jean Bourdon SA* (case C-352/95) [1997] ECRI-1729 that where goods have been manufactured outside the Community but then marketed in a Member State with the trade mark owner's consent, they are subject to Community-wide exhaustion.

Reference to the commentary on the 1984 drafts of the Directive and CTMR (see COM (84) 470 final of 31 July 1984) reveals that the Commission decided against any policy of international exhaustion of rights, and settled instead for Community-wide exhaustion (a policy since reiterated by the Commission in response to questions by the European Parliament). Indeed such policy is to be found in various provisions in Council Directive 91/250/EEC on the Legal Protection of Computer Programs [1991] OJ L 122/42 and in Council Directive 92/100/EEC on Rental Rights and Lending Rights and on Certain Rights Related to Copyright in the Field of Intellectual Property [1992] OJ L 346/61. Despite this, it has been argued that the wording of Article 7(1) of the Directive (Article 13(1) of the CTMR) gives the courts in Member States a discretion whether or not to recognise the concept of international exhaustion of rights in respect of non-EEA goods. It should be noted that Article 6 of TRIPs is neutral on this point.

There is no uniform pattern to Member States' post-harmonisation domestic laws at present. In the United Kingdom it is unclear, in the light of Jacob J's remarks in *Northern & Shell* v *Condé Nast & National Magazine Distributors Ltd*

[1995] RPC 117, which of two previous Court of Appeal pre-harmonisation decisions would be followed, *Revlon Inc.* v *Cripps & Lee Ltd* [1980] FSR 87 (in favour of international exhaustion) or *Colgate-Palmolive Ltd* v *Markwell Finance Ltd* [1989] RPC 497 (against it). It must be said, though, that the latter case involved imports which were qualitatively different from the domestic product, whereas the former did not. In Germany, the Bundesgerichtshof has declared that it will no longer apply the principle of international exhaustion in the light of Article 7 of the Directive (decision of 14 December 1995 in *1 ZR 210/93 (Dyed Levi Jeans)* [1996] GRUR 271). There have been similar decisions in the Netherlands (*Braun AG* v *Elbeka Electro BV*, District Court of Breda, 26 June 1996); France (*Société Ocean Pacific Sunwear et Société Mercure International of Monaco* v *Société Eximin et Société Carrefour France*, Cour de Paris, 12 May 1995); and Italy (*Samsonite Co. and Samsonite Italia* v *Rio SpA*, Tribunale di Torino, 11 July 1994). Other Member States have not yet decided the matter in the light of the Directive. The one exception, permitting international exhaustion, would appear to be Belgium (*Sebago Inc.* v *GB-UNIC*, Brussels Commercial Court, 11 October 1996, RK 291/96).

The question of whether the Directive imposes an obligation on Member States to exclude international exhaustion of national trade mark rights will be resolved when the Court of Justice gives its preliminary ruling in a reference from the Austrian Supreme Court in *Silhouette International Schmied GmbH & Co. KG* v *Hartlauer Handelsgesellschaft mbH)* (case C-355/96) [1996] OJ C 388/6, but an answer cannot realistically be expected before the end of 1998. It is to be hoped that the Court will also make clear whether exhaustion of rights in Article 13 of the CTMR is limited to Community-wide exhaustion.

Counterclaims for revocation and declarations of invalidity

The defendant to an action for infringement of a CTM may, besides relying on one or more of the limitations explained above, raise before a CTM court a counter-claim that the CTM should either be revoked or should be the subject of a declaration of invalidity. However, it should be noted at the outset that a counterclaim which relies on revocation will normally have effect only from the date of the counterclaim (Article 54(1) CTMR and see further below) and so will not operate to remove liability for previous acts of infringement. A counterclaim for a declaration of invalidity, on the other hand, means that the CTM never existed (Article 54(2) CTMR) and so liability for infringement will be wiped out. A defendant wishing to escape liability for infringement needs to be precise about which category of counterclaim to use.

Jurisdiction to hear counterclaims (Article 92(d) CTMR)
Exclusive jurisdiction to hear counterclaims in the context of infringement proceedings is conferred on designated CTM courts (explained below) by Article 92(d) of the CTMR. It should be noted that the validity of a CTM cannot be put in issue in an action for a declaration of non-infringement pursuant to Article 92(b) of the CTMR (Article 95(2) CTMR). The CTMR contains no provision permitting an application for revocation or for a declaration of invalidity to be brought by way of pre-emptive strike before a CTM court. Such matters can only be raised by way

of counterclaim to infringement proceedings. If it is desired to 'knock out' a CTM before its proprietor takes steps to enforce it, then cancellation proceedings must be brought before OHIM (see chapter 5).

Presumption of validity (Article 95 CTMR)

CTM courts having jurisdiction under Article 92 of the CTMR are directed by Article 95(1) of the CTMR to treat the CTM as valid unless validity is put in issue by the defendant by way of counterclaim. This means that the onus of proof rests with the defendant to show that the grounds of revocation or invalidity have been made out. Chapter 5 has already drawn attention to the fact that there is no equivalent provision regarding cancellation proceedings before OHIM; and to the fact that where the owner of an earlier CTM or Benelux, international or national trade mark seeks to oppose a later mark or have it declared invalid, the onus of proving use of the earlier mark will be placed on its proprietor if the applicant for or owner of the junior mark so requests (Articles 43(2) and 56(2) and (3) CTMR). The inference from the wording of Article 95(1) of the CTMR must be that the onus of proving non-use outside the specific instances covered by Article 56(2) and (3) of the CTMR rests with the party raising the counterclaim. There is no equivalent to s. 100 of the United Kingdom Trade Marks Act 1994, which places the onus of proving use of a trade mark on the registered proprietor, unless that can be extrapolated from the obligation to use a CTM found in Article 15 of the CTMR.

It may be noted in passing that a similar presumption of validity is imposed by Article 103 of the CTMR on courts having jurisdiction in disputes relating to CTMs other than the categories of action listed in Article 92 of the CTMR.

Rejection of counterclaim (Article 96(2))

A CTM court is required by Article 96(2) of the CTMR to reject the counterclaim if a decision by OHIM covering the same subject matter and cause of action and involving the same parties has already become final. This reflects the unitary character of the CTM and is in the interests of procedural economy.

Cooperation with OHIM (Articles 96(4), (6) and (7) and 100 CTMR)

Another feature of the unitary character of the CTM is the obligation placed on a CTM court to liaise with OHIM. Such a court is required:

(a)   to notify OHIM of the date on which the counterclaim was filed, which fact is to be recorded by OHIM on the Register of CTMs (Article 96(4) CTMR);

(b)   to send a copy of the final judgment on the counterclaim to OHIM, which is to mention the judgment on the Register of CTMs (Article 96(6) CTMR);

(c)   upon application by the proprietor of the CTM and after hearing the other parties, to stay the proceedings and request the defendant to seek cancellation of the mark before OHIM: failure by the defendant to observe any time limit set by the court will mean that the counterclaim is deemed to be withdrawn (Article 96(7) CTMR) (under Article 100(3) of the CTMR, such stay of proceedings empowers the court to award such provisional and protective measures as it thinks fit);

(d)   when dealing with any action under Article 92 of the CTMR (other than an application for a declaration of non-infringement), to stay the proceedings either of its own motion or at the request of the parties (in each case after hearing the parties) if the validity of the CTM is already in issue before another CTM court or before OHIM. A stay of proceedings may be refused where there are special grounds for continuing with the hearing, but where a stay is granted provisional and protective measures may be ordered (Article 100(1) and (3) CTMR). There is no requirement in Article 100(1) of the CTMR that the dispute before the other CTM court should be between the same parties or involve the same subject matter.

Conversely, by the terms of Article 100(2) of the CTMR, OHIM is required, when dealing with cancellation proceedings, to stay the proceedings where the validity of the CTM is already in issue on account of a counterclaim before a CTM court. Such stay of proceedings may be made by OHIM either of its own motion or at the request of one of the parties, but in each case the decision to stay must be taken after a hearing. The parties also have the option of requesting a stay of the proceedings before the CTM court to enable OHIM to conclude the cancellation proceedings.

In relation to Articles 96(7) and 100 of the CTMR, the proprietor of the CTM which has been challenged will need to consider carefully which of the two forums, the CTM court or OHIM, is likely to deal more favourably with the response to the counterclaim. This will depend to a certain extent on the prevailing attitude of the CTM court in question, but an informed decision will only be possible once OHIM has developed a sufficient body of case law.

Grounds for revocation or invalidity (Articles 50 to 52 CTMR)
Article 96(1) of the CTMR declares that a counterclaim for revocation or for a declaration of invalidity can only be based on the grounds mentioned in the CTMR. The grounds have already been explained in detail in chapter 5 and are merely listed here for the sake of convenience.

Grounds of revocation (Article 50(1) CTMR)   The grounds of revocation (which may have partial effect — Article 50(2) CTMR) are:

    (a)   that the CTM has not been put to genuine use in the Community (contrary to the obligation to use a CTM found in Article 15 of the CTMR) in connection with the goods or services in respect of which it is registered within a continuous period of five years, unless there were proper reasons for non-use (Article 50(1)(a) CTMR);

    (b)   that in consequence of the acts or inactivity of the proprietor, the CTM has become the common (that is, generic) name in the trade for the product or service in respect of which it is registered (Article 50(1)(b) CTMR);

    (c)   that in consequence of the use made of it by the proprietor or with his consent, the CTM is liable to mislead the public, particularly as to the nature, quality, or geographical origin of the goods or services (Article 50(1)(c) CTMR);

    (d)   that the proprietor no longer satisfies the conditions of Article 5 of the CTMR as regards entitlement (see chapter 2) (Article 50(1)(d) CTMR).

Grounds for a declaration of invalidity (Articles 51(1) and (2) and 52(1) and (2) CTMR)   The grounds on which a CTM may be declared invalid mirror the absolute and relative grounds for refusal of an application (again, these may have partial effect only, Article 51(3) CTMR). They are:

(a) that the CTM was registered in breach of Article 5 of the CTMR (entitlement) or Article 7 of the CTMR (absolute grounds for refusal), although an objection that the mark was registered in breach of Article 7(1)(b), (c) or (d) of the CTMR may be met by the argument that it has acquired distinctiveness by reason of use after registration (Article 51(1)(a) and (2) CTMR);

(b) that the applicant was acting in bad faith when he filed the application for the CTM (Article 51(1)(b) CTMR);

(c) that the CTM was registered despite the existence of relative grounds for refusal. The relative grounds are:

(i) an earlier trade mark, being either a CTM or a Benelux, international or national registration, or an application for such a registration (provided that it matures to registration) which meets the criteria laid down in Article 8(1) or (5) of the CTMR (Article 52(1)(a) CTMR);

(ii) an earlier well known mark (within the meaning of Article 6 of the Paris Convention) which meets the criteria laid down in Article 8(1) or (5) of the CTMR (Article 52(1)(a) CTMR);

(iii) a mark unjustifiably registered by the agent or representative of the proprietor in his own name, contrary to Article 8(3) of the CTMR (Article 52(1)(b) CTMR);

(iv) an unregistered mark or other sign used in the course of trade of more than mere local significance, the use of which entitles its owner to prohibit the use of the later CTM under Article 8(4) of the CTMR (Article 52(1)(c) CTMR); and

(v) a right to a name, a right of personal portrayal, a copyright or an industrial property right (Article 52(2) CTMR).

The relative grounds for invalidity are all subject to a plea of express consent on the part of the earlier proprietor to the later CTM (Article 52(3) CTMR) and to a plea of issue estoppel (Article 52(4) CTMR).

Examination of the application to revoke (Article 96(5) CTMR)
By virtue of Article 96(5) of the CTMR, the provisions of Article 56(3), (4), (5) and (6) of the CTMR apply to counterclaims raised before CTM courts. This immediately raises a difficulty of interpretation. Article 56(3) of the CTMR (the owner of an earlier Benelux, international or national mark which operates as a relative ground of invalidity is to be put to proof of use, if the owner is a party to the proceedings) is itself dependent on Article 56(2) of the CTMR (the owner of an earlier CTM which operates as a relative ground of invalidity is to be put to proof of use, if a party to the proceedings), and yet Article 56(2) of the CTMR is not expressly incorporated by Article 96(5) of the CTMR. Does this mean a different burden of proof of use if the defendant to the infringement proceedings is coincidentally the owner of the earlier right, depending on whether that right is a CTM or not?

Be that as it may, the remaining provisions of Article 56 of the CTMR (which have already been explained in chapter 5) are straightforward. Article 56(4) of the CTMR empowers the court, at its discretion, to invite the parties to reach a friendly settlement. Article 56(5) of the CTMR provides for the outcome of the case: either total or partial cancellation of the CTM, or rejection of the counterclaim. Article 56(6) of the CTMR (in duplication of Article 96(6) of the CTMR) provides for the outcome of the case to be entered on the Register of CTMs once the decision is final (that is, once the time limit for lodging an appeal has expired).

Locus standi

When cancellation proceedings are brought before OHIM, Article 55 of the CTMR provides detailed rules about *locus standi*. In effect these mean that whereas any natural or legal person, or any trade or consumers' association can bring proceedings for revocation or for a declaration of invalidity based on Article 5 of the CTMR (entitlement), Article 7 of the CTMR (absolute grounds) or bad faith, only the owner of an earlier trade mark (as defined in Article 52(1) of the CTMR) or the owner of an earlier right (as defined in Article 52(2) of the CTMR) can seek a declaration of invalidity based on relative grounds. No such restriction appears in the provisions of the CTMR dealing with counterclaims. This means that a defendant could raise by way of counterclaim the existence of an earlier CTM or Benelux, international or national mark or some other earlier right which belongs to a third party.

But what if the plaintiff then wishes to put in issue the non-use of the earlier trade mark belonging to the third party? The owner of it will not necessarily be party to the proceedings (it will be up to national procedural rules dealing with joinder of parties or intervention to decide this point). If the owner of the earlier trade mark is not so joined, on whom will fall the burden of proving that it has been used, bearing in mind the comments made above concerning burden of proof in counterclaims and the lack of incorporation of Article 56(2) of the CTMR into Article 96(5) of the CTMR?

Consequences of revocation or invalidity (Article 54 CTMR)

As explained in chapter 5, Article 54 of the CTMR draws a clear-cut distinction between the effects of revocation and the effects of invalidity. Under Article 54(1) of the CTMR, revocation (whether total or partial — Article 50(2) CTMR) operates only from the date of the application to revoke or the date of the counterclaim. However, an earlier date may be fixed at the request of one of the parties subject to the savings found in Article 54(3) of the CTMR. By contrast, a successful application to have a CTM declared invalid (which again may be total or partial — Articles 51(3) and 52(5) CTMR) means that the mark is deemed not to have had any effect from the outset.

This means that revocation cannot shield a defendant from liability for acts of infringement committed before the effective date of revocation, but a declaration of invalidity can (see the United Kingdom decision of *Second Sight Ltd* v *Novell UK Ltd* [1995] RPC 423).

Acquiescence (Article 53 CTMR)

A counterclaim for a declaration that a CTM is invalid on relative grounds may be met by a plea of acquiescence under Article 53 of the CTMR. This has been explained above.

Enforcing the CTM

When an action may be brought (Article 9(3) CTMR)

Under Article 9(3) of the CTMR, the rights conferred by a CTM will only prevail against third parties from the date of publication of the *registration* in the *Community Trade Marks Bulletin* (see chapter 3). Article 9(3) of the CTMR in its second sentence, nevertheless, permits the proprietor retrospectively to claim reasonable compensation for 'matters' occurring between the date of publication of the *application* and the date of publication of the registration if the relevant conduct would amount to infringement after the latter date. By way of emphasis, the same Article provides that the court seised of the case may not decide on the merits of the case until after publication of the registration. It is unclear whether this wording contemplates the commencement of infringement proceedings before the grant of registration (which would contradict the wording of Article 6 of the CTMR) or between the grant of and publication of registration.

Title to sue (Articles 9(1), 17(6), 22(3) and (4) and 96(3) CTMR)
The opening words of Article 9(1) of the CTMR make clear that it is the proprietor of the CTM alone who has title to sue. Where the mark has been transferred, Article 17(6) of the CTMR states that the successor in title may not invoke the rights arising from the registration 'as long as the transfer has not been entered on the Register'. It is therefore vitally important, as explained in chapter 9, that any transfer of a CTM be entered promptly on the Register of CTMs, otherwise there may be a successful application to strike out the infringement proceedings.

Under Article 22(3) of the CTMR, the licensee of a CTM may only bring infringement proceedings in his own name with the consent of the proprietor, unless the wording of the licence agreement provides otherwise or unless he is an exclusive licensee. An exclusive licensee is entitled to give formal notice to the proprietor requesting that infringement proceedings be brought and can then commence such proceedings in his own name if the proprietor does not take action 'within an appropriate period'. It may be assumed that the words 'formal notice' imply some sort of written communication (the details of which may well be spelled out in the licence agreement) but there is no clarification of what amounts to an 'appropriate period'. This might be the period stipulated by the parties in the licence agreement, or it might be the period provided by the relevant national law. An example of the latter would be s. 30(2) of the United Kingdom Trade Marks Act 1994, which lays down a period of two months within which the proprietor must respond to the licensee's request to commence proceedings. However, it should be noted that this domestic provision applies only to non-exclusive licensees, as under s. 31 of the 1994 Act, an exclusive licensee is entitled to bring proceedings in his own name.

The inability of the exclusive licensee to commence infringement proceedings in respect of a CTM in his own name until the procedure in Article 22 of the CTMR is exhausted should be contrasted with the position under the national laws of other Member States, most of whom confer better rights on an exclusive licensee than does the CTMR (for a useful summary see Kur, 'Harmonization of the trademark laws in Europe — an overview' (1997) 28 IIC 1). The Directive does not touch on procedural rights accorded to licensees.

In cases where the infringement proceedings are brought in the name of the proprietor, a licensee is entitled to intervene for the purpose of obtaining compensation for damage sustained by the licensee's business (Article 22(4) CTMR). Conversely, where it is the licensee who brings infringement proceedings and a counterclaim for revocation or declaration of invalidity is raised, the proprietor must be informed and may be joined as a party to the action in accordance with the conditions set out in national law (Article 96(3) CTMR).

Enforcement is left to national law (Articles 14 and 97 CTMR)
Rather than create a special Community court to deal with litigation concerning a CTM, the CTMR leaves the enforcement of the CTM right to national law, subject to the applicable law being that of the CTMR itself (Articles 14 and 97 CTMR). In so doing the CTMR adopts the relevant provisions of the Brussels Convention on Jurisdiction and the Enforcement of Judgments in Civil and Commercial Matters 1968 as amended (hereafter 'the Brussels Convention') (Article 90 CTMR). The CTMR overcomes the problem caused by the fact that the same text of the Brussels Convention is not necessarily in force in all the Member States by declaring in Article 104 of the CTMR that the provisions of the Convention which are rendered applicable by the provisions of the CTMR 'shall have effect in respect of any Member State solely in the text of the Convention which is in force in respect of that State at any given time'.

In incorporating the terms of the Brussels Convention, the CTMR draws a distinction between actions brought under Article 92 of the CTMR (basically, infringement actions and counterclaims) and any other disputes concerning CTMs (such as licensing disputes). Disputes which do not fall within Article 92 of the CTMR are assigned to those national courts which would normally have jurisdiction over trade mark disputes *ratione loci* and *rationi materiae* under the Brussels Convention, in which case the national court is to apply whichever version of the Convention is operative in its Member State (Articles 102(1) and 104 CTMR). The national court is directed to treat the CTM as valid (Article 103 CTMR). Where no national court has jurisdiction by virtue of the Brussels Convention, disputes not falling within Article 92 of the CTMR may be heard by Spanish courts.

In relation to disputes falling within Article 92 of the CTMR, however, the text of the Brussels Convention is modified as follows:

(a) Article 2 (domicile of the defendant to be the principal criterion for choice of jurisdiction), Article 4 (in the absence of the defendant's domicile, national law is to determine choice of jurisdiction), and Article 5(1), (3), (4) and (5) of the Convention (special jurisdiction) are all excluded (Article 90(2)(a) CTMR). This is because the provisions of those Articles are displaced by the rules in Article 93(1) to (3) of the CTMR for determining jurisdiction over CTM infringement actions.

(b) Article 24 of the Brussels Convention (provisional and protective measures) is excluded (Article 90(2)(a) CTMR). Article 99 of the CTMR contains its own version of the provision.

(c) Articles 17 and 18 of the Brussels Convention (dealing respectively with jurisdiction based on the agreement of the parties and jurisdiction based on the defendant's having entered an appearance) are to apply subject to the modification that the court in question must be a CTM court (Articles 90(2)(b) and 93(4) CTMR).

(d) Title II of the Brussels Convention (jurisdiction to be based on domicile in a Member State) is extended so that jurisdiction may also be based on establishment in a Member State (Article 90(2)(c) CTMR).

Designation of 'CTM courts' (Article 91 CTMR)
A preliminary requirement is that each Member State, under Article 91 of the CTMR, must designate 'as limited a number as possible' of first and second-

instance courts to deal with CTM litigation brought under Article 92 of the CTMR, this to be communicated to the Commission within three years of the effective date of the CTMR. In the event of a CTM court not being designated by a Member State, the courts of that State which would have jurisdiction over trade mark disputes are deemed to have the power to act as CTM courts. The Commission is required to publish the list of CTM courts in the *Official Journal of the European Communities*.

Despite the exhortation to appoint as limited number as possible of first-instance courts, practice between the Member States has varied enormously, with the United Kingdom merely designating the High Court as the CTM court of first instance in England, Wales and Northern Ireland and the Court of Session as the CTM court for Scotland (The Community Trade Mark Regulations 1996 (SI 1996/1908); by contrast, and because of its federal structure, Germany has designated all of its district courts (Landgericht) as CTM courts of first instance. It may be noted in passing that the United Kingdom does not appear to have designated the Court of Appeal and the Court of Session (Inner House) as its second-instance CTM courts in SI 1996/1908, though further appeals therefrom are a matter of national law under Article 101 of the CTMR.

The CTM courts are required by Article 97 of the CTMR to apply the substantive provisions of the CTMR to actions brought under Article 92 of the CTMR and only apply their own national law to matters not covered by the CTMR. Matters which are not covered by the CTMR include rules of procedure (Article 97(3) CTMR), sanctions other than injunctions for trade mark infringement (Article 98 CTMR), interim measures other than those having international effect (Article 99(1) CTMR) and appeals (Article 101 CTMR). All of these issues are therefore left to national law to determine.

Jurisdiction of CTM courts (Article 92 CTMR)
The designated CTM courts are given exclusive jurisdiction, by Article 92 of the CTMR, to deal with the following:

(a)   all infringement actions and — if permitted under national law — acts in respect of threatened infringement relating to CTMs;
(b)   actions for declarations of non-infringement (if recognised by national law);
(c)   claims for damages brought under the terms of Article 9(3) of the CTMR (conduct committed by the defendant between the date of publication of the CTM application and the date of publication of its registration); and
(d)   counterclaims for revocation or for a declaration of invalidity of a CTM. As noted above, such courts are to treat the CTM as valid unless validity is put in issue by the defendant (Article 95 CTMR).

Any other dispute relating to a CTM falls to be heard by a national court under the terms of Article 102 of the CTMR.

Determining international jurisdiction over infringement actions: the basic rule (Articles 93(1), (2) and (3) and 94(1) CTMR)
Article 93 of the CTMR contains detailed rules for determining which of the CTM courts should hear actions covered by Article 92 of the CTMR. They mirror the

basic principles laid down in the Brussels Convention, but (as already stated) are somewhat modified to take account of the nature of the CTM right. Once the appropriate CTM court is chosen, it will have jurisdiction, by virtue of Article 94(1) of the CTMR, to hear claims of infringement committed anywhere in the Community, that is, there is international jurisdiction. A CTM court which has exclusive jurisdiction under Article 93 of the CTMR can also grant international interlocutory injunctions under Article 99(2) of the CTMR. Jurisdiction for actions not covered by Article 92 of the CTMR fall to be determined in accordance with the Brussels Convention under Articles 102 and 104 of the CTMR.

The basic rules for determining the correct CTM court for actions covered by Article 92 of the CTMR are:

(a)   proceedings should be brought in the courts of the Member State in which the defendant is domiciled (Article 93(1) CTMR);

(b)   if the defendant is not domiciled in any of the Member States, proceedings should be brought in the courts of the Member State in which the defendant has an establishment (Article 93(1) CTMR);

(c)   if the defendant is neither domiciled nor established in any of the Member States, proceedings should be brought in the courts of the Member State in which the plaintiff is domiciled (Article 93(2) CTMR);

(d)   if the plaintiff is not domiciled in any of the Member States, proceedings should be brought in the court of the Member State in which the plaintiff has an establishment (Article 93(2) CTMR);

(e)   if neither defendant nor plaintiff is domiciled or has an establishment in any of the Member States, proceedings are to be brought in the Spanish courts (Article 93(3) CTMR).

The criterion of 'establishment' (which is not found in the Brussels Convention) appears to be derived from Article 3 of the Paris Convention, which accords protection to nationals of States which are not parties to the Union if they have 'a real and effective industrial or commercial establishment' in the territory of one of the countries of the Union. It will be recalled that the phrase 'real and effective establishment' also appears in Article 5 of the CTMR, where it governs entitlement to apply for a CTM (see the detailed explanation in chapter 2). Unless decided differently by the Court of Justice of the European Communities, it must be assumed that the single word 'establishment' in Article 93 of the CTMR bears the same meaning.

Alternative rules for international jurisdiction (Articles 93(4) and 94(1) CTMR)
Despite the apparently stringent conditions of Article 93(1) to (3) of the CTMR, there are two other means whereby a CTM court can be given exclusive international jurisdiction under Article 94(1) of the CTMR. They are:

(a)   where there is an agreement between the parties that a different CTM court will hear the dispute (Article 93(4)(a) CTMR, reflecting, with modifications, Article 17 of the Brussels Convention); and

(b)   where the defendant enters an appearance before a different CTM court (Article 93(4)(b) CTMR, reflecting, with modifications, Article 18 of the Brussels Convention).

Even where these alternative rules are applied, the CTM court will still have jurisdiction over acts of infringement committed anywhere in the Community (Article 94(1) CTMR).

National jurisdiction (Articles 93(5) and 94(2) CTMR)
The final possibility for choice of jurisdiction is found in Article 93(5) of the CTMR, which provides that actions under Article 92 of the CTMR (other than one for a declaration of non-infringement) may also be brought before the CTM court of the Member State where the act of infringement was committed. However, in this instance the court's jurisdiction relates only to acts of infringement committed or threatened within that Member State or acts of infringement committed between the date of publication of the application and the date of publication of registration within that Member State (Articles 93(5) and 94(2) CTMR).

Sanctions (Article 98 CTMR)
Although CTM courts are directed by Article 97(2) and (3) of the CTMR to apply national law in matters not covered by the CTMR, Article 98(1) of the CTMR, by way of derogation, states that where a CTM court finds that the defendant has infringed or threatened to infringe, it *shall* issue an order prohibiting the defendant from continuing with such conduct. This appears to make the award of a final injunction mandatory. Such final injunction will, where the CTM court has international jurisdiction by virtue of Article 93(1) to (4) of the CTMR, have Community-wide effect. The only means whereby the award of a final injunction could be regarded as discretionary is if the phrase 'unless there are special reasons for not doing so' can be interpreted as bringing into play equitable concepts, such as those employed by the Chancery Division of the High Court in London when awarding injunctive relief.

In granting final injunctive relief, the CTM court is also required, by the same Article, to take such other measures in accordance with its national law as are aimed at ensuring the defendant's compliance. That apart, the CTM court is to apply the law of the Member State (Article 98(2) CTMR). This will cover not only the award of damages or other monetary compensation for infringement (such as the award of an account of profits found in common law jurisdictions), but other remedies (such as those found in ss. 15, 16 and 19 of the United Kingdom Trade Marks Act 1994) concerned with the erasure of the infringing sign, and delivery up or destruction of infringing goods. It will presumably also extend to those provisions of national law which impose criminal liability for trade mark infringement.

Interim relief (Article 99 CTMR)
Article 99 of the CTMR, based on Article 24 of the Brussels Convention, deals with the award of 'provisional and protective measures'. It draws a distinction between:

(a)   applications for such relief which are made to 'the courts of a Member State including CTM courts', even though a CTM court of another Member State has jurisdiction as to the substance of the matter; and
(b)   applications made to CTM courts which have exclusive international jurisdiction by virtue of Articles 93(1) to (4) and 94(1) of the CTMR.

In the latter instance, such provisional and protective measures are, subject to the provisions on enforcement in Title III of the Brussels Convention, to be applicable in the territory of any Member State (Article 99(2) CTMR). Courts falling into the former category can grant such interim relief in respect of the CTM as may be available in respect of national trade marks but (by inference) this will not have international effect.

Stay of proceedings (Articles 100 and 105 CTMR)

Two particular Articles of the CTMR provide for proceedings to be stayed in certain circumstances. Article 100 of the CTMR deals with stay of proceedings where the issue of validity is before another CTM court or OHIM. Article 105 of the CTMR, based on Articles 21 and 22 of the Brussels Convention, contains detailed rules for determining which CTM court should decline to hear a case where two causes of action, involving the same parties, are brought in different Member States, one based on a CTM and the other based on a national mark.

Stay of proceedings where validity is in issue elsewhere (Article 100 CTMR)   As explained above in the context of counterclaims, Article 100 of the CTMR deals with the situation where counterclaims for revocation or for a declaration of invalidity are before two CTM courts or before a CTM court and OHIM. In summary, under Article 100(1) of the CTMR, a CTM court, when dealing with any action under Article 92 of the CTMR (other than an application for a declaration of non-infringement), is obliged to stay the proceedings, either of its own motion or at the request of the parties (in each case after hearing the parties), if the validity of the CTM is already in issue before another CTM court or before OHIM. A stay of proceedings may be refused where there are special grounds for continuing with the hearing, but where a stay is granted, provisional and protective measures may be ordered (Article 100(1) and (3) CTMR). There is no requirement in Article 100(1) of the CTMR that the dispute before the other CTM court should be between the same parties or involve the same subject matter. Evidence that there is a counterclaim pending before another CTM court will be apparent from the inspection of the Register of CTMs (Article 96(4) CTMR).

Conversely, by the terms of Article 100(2) of the CTMR, OHIM is required, when dealing with cancellation proceedings, to stay the proceedings where the validity of the CTM is already in issue on account of a counterclaim before a CTM court. Such stay of proceedings may be made by OHIM either of its own motion or at the request of one of the parties, but in each case the decision to stay must be taken after a hearing. The parties also have the option of requesting a stay of the proceedings before the CTM court to enable OHIM to conclude the cancellation proceedings. The inference must be that cancellation proceedings before OHIM take priority over counterclaims before CTM courts.

Stay of proceedings when there are civil actions on the basis of more than one trade mark (Article 105 CTMR)   Article 105 of the CTMR contemplates the scenario of a proprietor suing in more than one Member State for trade mark infringement on the basis of parallel CTM and national registrations. It does not apply to applications for provisional and protective measures. It provides for a court to decline jurisdiction as follows:

(a)   Where *simultaneous* actions are brought in two different Member States, one based on a CTM and one on a national trade mark and they involve the same cause of action and the same parties:

(i)   the court other than the one first seised must decline jurisdiction in favour of the other court if the CTM and national trade mark are identical and valid and are for the same goods or services, unless the jurisdiction of the court first seised of the matter is contested;

(ii)   the court other than the one first seised may decline jurisdiction in favour of the other court if the CTM and national trade mark are identical and valid but are for similar goods and services, and where the marks are similar and valid but are for identical or similar goods or services (Article 105(1) CTMR).

(b)   Where *successive* actions are brought in two different Member States, one based on a CTM and one on a national trade mark and they involve the same cause of action and the same parties:

(i)   the court hearing the action for the infringement of the CTM must reject the action if final judgment has already been given on the basis of an identical national mark valid for identical goods or services (Article 105(2) CTMR);

(ii)   the court hearing the action for the infringement of the national trade mark must reject the action if final judgment has already been given on the basis of an identical CTM valid for identical goods or services (Article 105(3) CTMR).

Forum shopping
There has been some debate about the desirability of forum shopping under the above provisions of the CTMR in order to achieve the best result in an action for the infringement of a CTM. Arguably, the jurisdiction rules in Article 93(1) to (4) of the CTMR do not possess the flexibility that is often claimed for them. Close examination of the wording indicates that the primary rule for choice of jurisdiction (in line with Article 2 of the Brussels Convention) is the defendant's domicile, determined in accordance with Articles 52 and 53 of the Brussels Convention (which provide, respectively, rules for determining the domicile of natural and legal persons). Only if the defendant does not have a domicile in any of the Member States will it be possible to choose jurisdiction on the basis of the defendant's establishment (for example, by considering in which Member States a New York company has branch offices and so on). Again, choice of jurisdiction based on the plaintiff's domicile or establishment is only possible if jurisdiction cannot be based on the previous paragraphs of Article 93 of the CTMR.

The only possibility for forum shopping appears to be if jurisdiction is chosen on the basis of Article 93(5) of the CTMR, but that has the drawback that the CTM court can only deal with events occurring within the territory of its own Member State. It must therefore be a commercial decision whether to choose a CTM court having international or national jurisdiction under, respectively, Article 94(1) or Article 94(2) of the CTMR.

In the event that a CTM proprietor is able to forum shop, the following factors will need to be considered:

(a)   the cost and speed of proceedings, including national rules on legal representation and the willingness of the court to accept survey evidence as proof of infringement;

(b)   the likelihood of the defendant raising a counterclaim before the CTM court, that court's likely response to it and whether the proprietor would fare any better in cancellation proceedings before OHIM;

(c)   the attitude of the CTM court to key concepts in the CTMR such as 'likelihood of association' in Article 9 of the CTMR (contrast the approaches of Benelux courts with those of other Member States);

(d)   the desirability of choosing a CTM court which does have exclusive international jurisdiction as a result of the combined effects of Articles 93 and 94 of the CTMR, particularly in relation to the award of provisional and protective measures under Article 99 of the CTMR and final injunctive relief under Article 98 of the CTMR, in addition to any further national remedies which might be available;

(e)   should the mark and the alleged infringing sign not be identical, linguistic considerations (for example, what may seem confusingly similar to a German-speaking consumer may not appear so to an English-speaking one); and

(f)   until uniform guidelines are developed by the Court of Justice on the assessment of similarity of goods and services, how different CTM courts approach this issue.

References to the Court of Justice of the European Communities for preliminary rulings

The jurisdiction to give preliminary rulings (Article 177 EC Treaty)
As explained above, the task of hearing actions for the infringement of CTMs is allocated to specifically designated CTM courts in each of the Member States. Whilst national law will govern procedural matters, such courts are to determine substantive issues by reference only to the terms of the CTMR (Article 14 CTMR). The one unifying factor implicit in the CTMR is that any questions about its interpretation can only be determined by the Court of Justice of the European Communities by virtue of its jurisdiction under Article 177 of the Treaty of Rome (hereafter Article 177 EC Treaty). This makes the Court of Justice the only body which can give an authoritative interpretation of the substantive elements of the CTMR. When the meaning of a particular provision in the CTMR is unclear, a CTM court should avail itself of the preliminary ruling procedure found in Article 177 EC Treaty. Designated CTM courts and lawyers using them should be aware of the desirability of referring such questions to the Court of Justice, so that the CTMR can maintain its uniform effect throughout the Community.

Article 177 EC Treaty
Article 177 EC Treaty provides as follows:

The Court of Justice shall have jurisdiction to give preliminary rulings concerning:
(a)   the interpretation of this Treaty;
(b)   the validity and interpretation of acts of the institutions of the Community and of the [European Central Bank];

(c) the interpretation of the statutes of bodies established by an act of the Council, where those statutes so provide.

Where such a question is raised before any court or tribunal of a Member State, that court or tribunal may, if it considers that a decision on the question is necessary to enable it to give judgment, request the Court of Justice to give a ruling thereon.

Where any such question is raised in a case pending before a court or tribunal of a Member State against whose decisions there is to be no judicial remedy under national law, that court or tribunal shall bring the matter before the Court of Justice.

Purpose of a preliminary ruling

Right from the outset the Court of Justice has stated that Article 177 EC Treaty is 'an instrument of uniformity' (*De Geus* v *Robert Bosch GmbH* (case 13/61) [1962] ECR 45 at 51). It has consistently adopted on 'open-door policy', encouraging national courts to make references. It has therefore stated that the discretion to refer given by Article 177(2) EC Treaty to courts other than those of last instance should not be fettered by any system of precedent (*Rheinmühlen Düsseldorf* v *EVGF* (case 166/73) [1974] ECR 33) and that even if the matter has been decided before, the national court is free to refer it again (*Da Costa en Schaake NV* v *Nederlandse Belastingenadministratie* (case 28-30/62) [1963] ECR 31). There are very few instances of the Court's declining a reference for a preliminary ruling, but it has refused to give a ruling where it considered the reference to be contrived (*Foglia* v *Novello (No. 1)* (case 104/79) [1980] ECR 745; *Foglia* v *Novello (No. 2)* (case 244/80) [1981] ECR 3045); or where the facts of the case were unclear or the questions asked by the national court were thought to be hypothetical (*Wienand Meilicke* v *ADV/ORGA F.A. Meyer AG* (case C-83/91) [1992] ECR I-4871).

However, what should be remembered is that Article 177 EC Treaty is not an appeal procedure. A referral is not instigated by either of the parties, rather it is a decision taken by the domestic court itself as an interlocutory step in the main proceedings. A case should be referred to the Court of Justice by a domestic court or tribunal before final judgment in the case is given. If final judgment has been given and leave to appeal has been refused, then it is not possible to make a referral as the national court is *functus officio* (*Chiron Corporation* v *Murex Diagnostics Ltd* [1995] All ER (EC) 88).

The role of the Court of Justice is to act in partnership with the national court by offering its guidance on the interpretation of the Treaty or of secondary legislation (such as the Directive or the CTMR) made pursuant to the Treaty. The Court of Justice does not find facts, nor interpret national law, nor rule on the compatibility of national law with Community law, although it can provide the national court with sufficient guidance on the meaning of Community law that the national court can determine the question of compatibility for itself (*Prantl* (case 16/83) [1984] ECR 1299). Once the preliminary ruling has been given, it is for the national court to utilise it in reaching its own decision on the facts of the case.

Court or tribunal

Much case law has been devoted to the issue of what is a 'court or tribunal' for the purposes of Article 177(2) EC Treaty, most of the difficulties being encountered in the context of quasi-public administrative tribunals and arbitration. The question is one to be determined by Community not national law. Suffice it to say that there can be no doubt that CTM courts empowered to decide questions of infringement under Article 92 of the CTMR and other national courts empowered by Articles 90(1) and 102 of the CTMR to deal with other disputes involving CTMs meet the relevant criteria laid down by the Court of Justice (see *Broekmeulen* v *Huisarts Registratie Commissie* (case 246/80) [1981] ECR 2311). The only problem which might be encountered is where a licence agreement relating to a CTM provides for any disputes to be settled by arbitration, in which case there can be no referral to the Court of Justice unless and until the arbitrator's decision is itself appealed to a national court (see *Nordsee Deutsche Hochseefischerei GmbH* v *Reederei Mond Hochseefischerei Nordstern AG & Co. KG* (case 102/81) [1982] ECR 1095; *Bulk Oil (Zug) AG* v *Sun International Ltd* (case 174/84) [1986] ECR 559).

If the tribunal is competent to refer under Article 177 EC Treaty, the Court of Justice will not question whether it was properly constituted or whether it observed its own rules of procedure (*Reina* v *Landeskreditbank Baden-Württemberg* (case 65/81) [1982] ECR 33).

Has a question of Community law been raised?

A precondition of Article 177(2) EC Treaty is that Community law must be relevant to the case. This is a matter for the national court to decide, but in cases brought before CTM courts by virtue of their jurisdiction under Article 92 of the CTMR, it will automatically be the case that Community law is in issue.

Is a decision on Community law necessary?

A more contentious issue has been whether a decision on Community law is necessary. United Kingdom lawyers will no doubt be familiar with the overly restrictive approach of Lord Denning MR in *H.P. Bulmer Ltd* v *J. Bollinger SA* [1974] Ch 401, in which he stated that 'necessary' meant that the answer from the Court of Justice must be conclusive of the case. No such limitation has been placed on the word by the Court of Justice itself, and subsequent United Kingdom cases have demonstrated a more liberal view of what amounts to 'necessity' (see *R* v *International Stock Exchange of the United Kingdom and the Republic of Ireland Ltd, ex parte Else [1982] Ltd* [1993] QB 534).

Discretion of the National Court under Article 177(2) EC Treaty

A court or tribunal governed by Article 177(2) EC Treaty, once it perceives that Community law is relevant and that a decision thereon is necessary, still has a discretion to refer. Use of the Article 177 EC Treaty procedure in the United Kingdom may initially have been restricted because of the 'guidelines' on the exercise of the discretion put forward by Lord Denning in *H.P. Bulmer Ltd* v *J. Bollinger SA* [1974] Ch 401. The factors which he thought should be taken into account included: the need to decide the facts first; the time it will take to get a ruling; the need to avoid overloading the Court of Justice; the need to formulate the question clearly; the difficulty and importance of the point; the expense of getting a ruling; the wishes of the parties; and the desirability of not referring if the matter is reasonably clear and free from doubt.

Lord Denning's views should be contrasted with those of the Court of Justice itself in its recently published Notes for Guidance on References by National

Courts for Preliminary Rulings (Bulletin of Proceedings 34/96, reprinted at [1997] All ER (EC) 1). These notes do not have binding effect and are intended to offer practical information to all interested parties with a view to removing some of the difficulties previously encountered.

The Notes state that the order of the national court or tribunal referring a question to the Court of Justice may be in any form allowed by national procedural law (for example, for the United Kingdom see Order 114 of the Rules of the Supreme Court). Reference of a question normally involves a stay of the national proceedings, but such a decision is for the national court to take in accordance with its own national law. As the order for reference has to be translated into all the official languages of the Community, and as the other Member States and the Community institutions are entitled to make observations to the Court of Justice thereon, national courts should try to draft references as clearly and precisely as possible. The order for a reference should contain a statement of reasons which is sufficient to enable the Court of Justice, the other Member States and the Community institutions to obtain a clear understanding of the factual and legal context of the main proceedings. This statement of reasons should include:

(a)   a statement of the facts which are essential to a full understanding of the legal significance of the main proceedings;

(b)   an exposition of the national law which may be applicable (a point not necessarily relevant to cases under the CTMR);

(c)   a statement of the reasons which have prompted the referral; and

(d)   where appropriate, a summary of the arguments of the parties.

The aim of all of this is to put the Court of Justice in a position to give the national court an answer which will be of assistance to it.

The notes conclude with a statement that the national court may refer a question to the Court of Justice as soon as it finds that a ruling on the point of interpretation is necessary to enable it to give judgment. Even so, because the Court of Justice neither decides issues of fact nor interprets national law, it is desirable that the decision to refer should not be taken until the main proceedings have reached a stage when the national court is able to define, if only as a working hypothesis, the factual and legal context of the question. The administration of justice is best served if the reference is not made until both sides have been heard. Proceedings for a preliminary ruling before the Court of Justice are free of charge. The Court does not rule on costs, which are determined by the outcome of the national proceedings.

Duty to refer under Article 177(3) EC Treaty

The scope of Article 177(3) EC Treaty and in particular the phrase 'against whose decisions there is to be no judicial remedy under national law' are not entirely free from doubt. It is not clear whether the phrase refers to courts whose decisions can *never* be appealed (such as the House of Lords for the United Kingdom legal system) or the highest court in the case itself where there is no automatic right of appeal. The Court of Justice appears to favour the latter interpretation (see *Costa* v *ENEL* (case 6/64) [1964] ECR 585), with confirmation being awaited should the Court of Justice agree with the opinion of Advocate-General Jacobs in *Parfums Christian Dior SA* v *Evora BV* (case C-337/95) 29 April 1997.

Apart from this point, it would seem that a final court is not always required to refer. Under the doctrine of *acte claire* explained in *Srl CILFIT* v *Ministry of Health* (case 283/81) [1982] ECR 3415, the Court of Justice stated that there is no duty placed on a court of last instance to refer where:

(a)   the question of Community law is irrelevant; or

(b)   the provision in question has already been interpreted by the Court of Justice; or

(c)   the correct application is so obvious as to leave no room for doubt.

However, the Court went on to state that when considering whether a point of Community law is 'obvious', the national court must ask itself whether the matter is equally obvious to the courts of other Member States and must bear in mind the following factors:

(a)   that Community legislation is drafted in every official language of the EC, each version being equally authentic;

(b)   that Community law has its own terminology, so that legal concepts in Community law have different meanings from similar concepts found in national law; and

(c)   that the provisions of Community law must be placed in the context of and interpreted in the light of the objectives of Community law and its state of evolution at the date of the application of the provision.

These factors have the effect of limiting considerably the power of a national court of last instance to decline to make a reference.

Effect of preliminary ruling
The Court of Justice has made clear that any ruling it gives providing an interpretation of Community law must be operative from the moment of the entry into force of the provision (see *Amministrazione delle Finanze dello Stato* v *Srl Meridionale Industria Salumi* (cases 66, 127 and 128/79) [1980] ECR 1237), in other words its rulings are retrospective. Rulings on interpretation of the CTMR will be operative from 14 March 1994 (60 days after the date of its publication in the *Official Journal of the European Communities*) (Article 43 CTMR); rulings on the interpretation of the IR will be operative from 22 December 1995 (seven days from the date of publication in the *Official Journal of the European Communities*) (Article 3 IR).

Only in exceptional cases will the Court of Justice make a prospective ruling (as it did in *Defrenne* v *SABENA (No. 2)* (case 43/75) [1976] ECR 455) but limiting the temporal effect of its ruling is something the Court will do only where a retrospective ruling would have major economic consequences for the Member States and businesses in the Community. It can hardly be expected that this will be so in the context of the CTMR. Whether a ruling is to be prospective only is a matter for the Court of Justice at the time of the ruling itself, not subsequently (*Gravier* v *City of Liège* (case 293/83) [1985] ECR 593).

Chapter Eight
Appeals

Introduction

Decisions pertaining to a Community trade mark (CTM) can be challenged, by appeals within OHIM itself, and appeals from OHIM to the Court of First Instance by way of judicial review under Article 63 of the CTMR, which in part mirrors Article 173 of the Treaty of Rome (Article 173 EC Treaty). References by Community trade mark courts (CTM courts) to the Court of Justice of the European Communities for a preliminary ruling under the procedure found in Article 177 of the Treaty of Rome (Article 177 EC Treaty) should not be considered as appeal proceedings, as the decision to refer (which must be made before final judgment is given in the case) rests with the CTM court hearing the main action, and not the parties themselves. Accordingly, the ability of a CTM court to make a reference for a preliminary ruling in the context of hearing a claim for the infringement of a CTM was dealt with in chapter 7.

OHIM Boards of Appeal

Appeals from first-instance departments (Article 57 CTMR)
The decision-making competence of OHIM rests with its individual examiners plus a number of Divisions (specifically the Opposition Divisions, the Administration of Trade Marks and Legal Division, and the Cancellation Divisions) (Article 125 CTMR and see chapter 1). These will be referred to collectively as 'first-instance departments'. Each first-instance department is allocated specific tasks by the CTMR.

Thus by Article 126 of the CTMR, examiners are charged with taking decisions under Article 36 of the CTMR (conditions of filing), Article 37 of the CTMR (conditions relating to entitlement), Article 38 of the CTMR (absolute grounds for refusal) and Article 66 of the CTMR (refusal of a Community collective mark because it is contrary to Articles 64 or 65 cf the CTMR or contrary to public policy). By Article 127 of the CTMR, Opposition Divisions are responsible for taking decisions on any opposition brought pursuant to Articles 42 to 44 of the CTMR; and by Article 129 of the CTMR, the Cancellation Divisions are to be responsible for decisions in relation to applications before OHIM to revoke or declare invalid CTMs under the terms of Articles 50 to 56 of the CTMR. Finally, under Article 128 of the CTMR, the Administration of Trade Marks and Legal Division is to deal with any matter not specifically assigned to the other two Divisions, and in particular is to be responsible for decisions in respect of entries in the Register of CTMs. This includes the making of entries relating to dealings in CTMs (Articles 16 to 23 CTMR and Rules 31 to 35 IR — see chapter 9), as well as matters relating to conversion (Article 108 CTMR and Rules 44 to 47 IR), surrender (Article 49 CTMR and Rule 36 IR), renewal (Article 47 CTMR and Rules 29 and 30 IR), alteration of the CTM (Article 48 CTMR and Rule 25 IR) and change of name or address of the proprietor or of the proprietor's registered representative (Rule 26 IR).

Article 57 of the CTMR, supplemented by the IR, the FR and the AR, accordingly provides that an appeal shall lie from any first-instance department to OHIM Boards of Appeal.

Similarity to the European Patent Office Boards of Appeal

The Articles in the CTMR dealing with the OHIM Boards of Appeal draw much of their inspiration from the equivalent articles in the European Patent Convention (EPC) dealing with the Boards of Appeals of the European Patent Office (EPO) in Munich. Many of the provisions in the CTMR will therefore appear familiar to practitioners conversant with the workings of the EPO and, where appropriate, this chapter will cross-refer to established case law from the EPO Boards of Appeal on the meaning of the equivalent EPC Articles.

Nevertheless, differences exist between the two systems. First, OHIM Boards of Appeal are not subdivided into Legal and Technical Boards. Further, because overall judicial control of OHIM's decisions rests with the Court of First Instance, there is no provision in the CTMR equivalent to Articles 22 and 23 of the EPC for an Enlarged Board of Appeal to deal with references from Boards of Appeal on points of law.

Despite this, it has been frequently held that the legal function of appeals within the EPO is to render a judicial decision on the correctness of first-instance decisions (see *UNILEVER/Viscosity reduction* (T 34/90) [1992] OJ EPO 454 and *PROCTER & GAMBLE/Detergent composition* (T 369/91) [1993] EPOR 497). Accordingly, the EPO Boards of Appeal have been recognised as possessing the characteristics of judicial tribunals (see *Merrill Lynch's Application* [1988] RPC 1 at 12; *Lenzing AG's European Patent (UK)* [1997] RPC 245; and see further Singer, ed. Lunz, *The European Patent Convention* (London, 1995), pp. 67–8; Stephens-Ofner, 'The Boards of Appeal: policemen or umpires?' [1997] 4 EIPR 167). If such an approach is equally applicable to OHIM Boards of Appeal, this means that the legal and factual framework of an appeal must be the same or closely similar to that on which the first-instance decision was given. This in turn will have a bearing on the conduct of the case, both at first instance and on appeal, and in particular on the introduction of new evidence at the appeal stage (see below).

Appointment of members of OHIM Boards of Appeal (Articles 130 and 131 CTMR)

Members of OHIM Boards of Appeals, which are charged by Article 130 of the CTMR with the responsibility for deciding all appeals within OHIM, are treated as senior officials and hence are appointed under the special procedure established under Article 120 of the CTMR (Article 131 CTMR). This means that, like the President and Vice-Presidents of OHIM, they are appointed by the EU Council of Ministers from a shortlist prepared by the OHIM Administrative Board, and hold office for a term of five years renewable. Unlike the President, however, their removal from office during such term (which can only be on a complaint by the body which appointed them) is under the control of the Court of Justice and not the EU Council of Ministers (Article 131(1) CTMR), thus stressing the judicial nature of their appointment.

Exclusion and objection (Article 132 CTMR and Article 3 AR)
Members of the Boards of Appeal are required to be independent and, in particular, may not be examiners or members of any of the Divisions of OHIM. As in the case of examiners and members of the Divisions, members of the Boards of Appeal may not take part in any proceedings if they have any personal interest therein, or if they have previously acted as representatives of one of the parties, or if they participated in the decision under appeal (Article 132(1) CTMR). Although the onus rests on the individual member to withdraw from a particular case, any of the parties can object to a Member of the Board of Appeal, either on one of the grounds listed in Article 132(1) of the CTMR or on the ground of suspected partiality (Article 132(3) CTMR). However, such an objection will be inadmissible if the party concerned takes a procedural step while being aware of a reason for the objection. No objection can be based on the nationality of any of the examiners or members of the Divisions or Boards of Appeal. Further (and this must be considered a remote possibility) a Board of Appeal can, of its own initiative and on the same grounds, decide that one of its members is precluded from taking part in a case, such intervention having the effect of suspending proceedings until the member is replaced by an alternate (Article 3 AR and Article 132(4) CTMR).

Article 132 of the CTMR in its essential elements closely resembles Article 24 of the EPC, in particular with regard to the ability of one of the parties to object to a particular Board member. It is unclear from EPO case law whether it is sufficient if the party objecting believes there is a risk of partiality (for example, if the Board member is a former employee of the other party) or if there must be evidence of actual partiality (contrast the opinion of the Enlarged Board of Appeal in *DISCOVISION/Appealable decision* (G 5/91) [1992] OJ EPO 617 with the decision of the Board of Appeal in *DISCOVISION/Appealable decision* (T 261/88) (16 February 1993)).

Organisation of the Boards of Appeal (Articles 1, 2, 4 and 5 AR)
Article 1 of the AR provides that, before the beginning of each working year, an Authority composed of the President of OHIM, the OHIM Vice-President responsible for the Boards of Appeal, the Chairmen of the Boards and three other Board of Appeal members elected by the full membership of the Boards, shall allocate duties to each Board according to objective criteria, resolve any conflicts regarding the allocation of duties, and shall also allocate the members and their alternates to each Board. Provision is also made for such arrangements to be altered during the year if necessary (Article 1(1) AR). The circumstances when alternate members are to be used is spelled out in Article 2 of the AR. The Authority has a quorum

of five, has autonomy over its own internal procedure and acts by majority vote. However, at the time of writing, it is anticipated that only three Boards of Appeal will be constituted. Ironically, this will trigger Article 1(4) of the AR, which contemplates a smaller Authority, having one rather than three elected positions and a quorum of three.

Article 5 of the AR requires OHIM to establish a Registry for each Board of Appeal, with one of the Registrars acting as Senior Registrar. The Registries are given specific responsibility for dealing with questions of admissibility (Article 61(1) CTMR, Rule 49 IR and Article 5(3) AR) and with the preparation of minutes of oral proceedings and of the taking of evidence (Articles 75 and 76 CTMR, Rules 56 to 60 inclusive IR and Article 5(4) AR).

Article 4 of the AR requires the Chairman of each Board of Appeal to designate a member of the Board as rapporteur for each appeal. The rapporteur is responsible for communications with the parties to the appeal, the preparation of meetings of the Board and of any oral proceedings, and the drafting of the Board's decisions prior to its secret deliberations (Articles 4 and 12 AR). A useful comparison may be made here with Article 4 of the Rules of Procedure of the EPO Boards of Appeal and with the role of the judge-rapporteur at the Court of Justice of the European Communities.

What can be appealed

Decisions of OHIM (Article 57 CTMR and Rules 52 to 55 IR)
Article 57 of the CTMR simply states that decisions subject to appeal are those of the examiners, the Opposition Divisions, the Administration of Trade Marks and Legal Division and the Cancellation Divisions. In the case law of the Court of Justice of the European Communities under Article 173 EC Treaty, the word 'decision' has a well-developed meaning, namely, 'a measure, the legal effects of which are binding on and capable of affecting the interests of, the applicant by bringing about a distinct change in his legal position' (see *SA Cimenteries CBR Cementbedrijven NV* v *Commission* (cases 8–11/66) [1967] ECR 75 and *Demo-Studio Schmidt* v *Commission* (case 210/81) [1983] ECR 3045). Accordingly, whether or not any document issued by OHIM amounts to a decision will depend on its content, not its form.

Incidental communications
Incidental communications from OHIM in the course of proceedings which are preparatory to reaching a decision will not be appealable (see, by way of analogy, *IBM* v *Commission* (case 60/81) [1981] ECR 2639, concerned with the decision-making powers of the EC Commission under Community competition policy; and the EPO ruling in *GEBRÜDER SULZER AG/Frottierwebmaschine* (T 520/89) (19 February 1990)).

The need for writing (Rule 52 IR)
Under Rule 52 of the IR all decisions of OHIM (except those given during the course of oral proceedings) must be in writing and must state the reasons on which they are based. Even decisions given during the course of oral proceedings have

to be confirmed in writing. Rule 52(2) of the IR also requires all decisions to be accompanied by a written communication, drawing attention to the addressee's right of appeal laid down in Articles 57 to 59 of the CTMR and stating the time limit for filing an appeal. If the approach of the EPO is followed, the fact that a communication is not labelled 'decision' will not affect the right of appeal; equally, failure by OHIM to attach a notice setting out the right of appeal will not change the communication's characteristic as a decision (see *MCWHIRTER/PCT form* (J 26/87) [1989] OJ EPO 329). Non-compliance with Rule 52(2) of the IR by failing to attach the text of Articles 57 to 59 of the CTMR to a decision will not render it invalid. This is because of the last sentence of Rule 52(2) of the IR, which indicates that the parties cannot invoke the omission of the written communication of the possibility of an appeal (see *EXXON/Alumina spinel* (T 42/84) [1988] OJ EPO 251 on the parallel provision in EPO Rule 68(2)).

Loss of rights (Article 77 CTMR and Rule 54 IR)

Decisions which are capable of being appealed under Article 57 of the CTMR must be distinguished not only from incidental communications from OHIM, but from notifications made by OHIM pursuant to Article 77 of the CTMR and Rule 54 of the IR, which is in similar form to EPO Rule 69.

In particular, it should be noted that Rule 54 of the IR provides that where OHIM finds that a loss of any rights results *without any decision having been taken* (for example, because a CTM applicant has failed to act within a given time limit), it shall communicate this to the person concerned under Article 77 of the CTMR, drawing attention to Rule 54(2) of the IR. In turn, Rule 54(2) of the IR gives that person the right to question the accuracy of OHIM's findings by applying for a decision within two months of the notification. This request for a decision does not reactivate the relevant time period which the applicant has breached, but does have the effect of getting OHIM to consider whether its original communication was correct.

The net result of these provisions is that an appeal cannot be brought in respect of notification of loss of rights (see by way of confirmation EPO decision *LEMONNIER/Requête pour publication anticipée* (J 13/83) [1987-92] CLBA 156), but only in respect of the decision made in response to the questioning of the loss of rights. In cases such as this, the person concerned is advised both to lodge an appeal and seek *restitutio in integrum* under the provisions of Article 78 of the CTMR (see below).

If no request for a decision is made in accordance with Rule 54 of the IR, the notification of loss of rights has irreversible legal effect at the end of the two-month period, even if the notification was erroneous.

Interlocutory appeals (Article 57(2) CTMR)

To return to the basic provision in Article 57 of the CTMR, paragraph 2 thereof makes clear that interlocutory decisions which leave outstanding the rights of any one party cannot be appealed on their own, but only as part of a final decision, unless stated otherwise. This is in similar form to Article 106(3) of the EPC. Matters which may be the subject of interlocutory decisions include those relating to procedure and evidence. The possibility of an interlocutory appeal in relation to such issues is important if proceedings would otherwise be protracted. It is unclear from EPO case law whether an appeal against an interlocutory decision, in cases where a separate appeal is expressly allowed, must always be filed within the two-month time limit or whether the issue can later be challenged in conjunction with the final decision. Common sense would suggest that the interlocutory appeal should be governed by its own time limit. However, what is clear is that if an interlocutory decision is the subject of a separate appeal, it cannot be challenged a second time in combination with the final decision.

Effect of an appeal

Suspensive effect

Any appeal brought under Article 57 of the CTMR has suspensive effect, which ensures that a challenged decision does not take effect until an appeal has been decided. This presupposes that during the period for filing an appeal, no steps are taken by OHIM to put the first-instance decision into effect. OHIM will only take action after the decision has come into full effect with the expiry of the time limit for any possible appeal. By analogy with EPO case law, should OHIM take action before the time limit for an appeal has expired, this will be deemed to have no legal effect (see *LELAND STANFORD/Approval — disapproval* (T 1/92) [1993] OJ EPO 685 and *SOLVDIA/Suspensive effect* (J 28/94) (7 December 1994)).

Ineffective appeals

When the time limit for lodging an appeal has expired, there is only suspensive effect if an effective appeal has been filed, but not if there is an ineffective appeal, for example, because the appellant did not pay the appeal fee (see Rule 49(3) IR). Whether any of the other grounds on which an appeal may be treated as inadmissible (see Rule 49 of the IR discussed below) has the effect of destroying the suspensive nature of an appeal remains to be seen, but future case law may well draw a distinction between factors which render an appeal automatically inadmissible and factors where the appellant is given an opportunity of correction under Rule 49(2) of the IR. In the latter case, the appeal may be deemed to have suspensive effect until it becomes clear that the appellant is not going to comply with the Board of Appeal's request within the prescribed time limit.

Relationship with restitutio in integrum

Restitutio in integrum in respect of a late-filed appeal can be awarded under Article 78 of the CTMR. In such a case, the suspensive effect will operate from the grant of *restitutio*.

Joinder of appeals

If several appeals are filed against a decision, Article 7(1) of the AR provides for them to be dealt with in the same proceedings; where appeals are filed against separate decisions and all are designated to be dealt with by one Board having the same composition, the Board can deal with them all in joined proceedings, subject to the consent of the parties (Article 7(2) AR).

Making an appeal

Notice of appeal (Rule 48 IR)
Under Rule 83 of the IR, OHIM is to make available free of charge the form for lodging an appeal. An appellant may use the OHIM notice of appeal form (which may be freely photocopied and which is also obtainable from Benelux and national trade mark registries) or may use forms of a similar structure or format, such as those generated by computer, as long as they contain the same information as the official form.

Rule 48 of the IR prescribes the content of the notice of appeal. It shall contain:

(a)   The details of the appellant given in accordance with Rule 1(1)(b) of the IR. As explained in chapter 3 in the context of CTM applications, Rule 1(1)(b) requires the name, address and nationality of the appellant and the State in which he is domiciled or has his seat or is established. Names of natural persons must be indicated by the person's family name and given name. Names of legal entities must be given in full although their official designation (Ltd, plc, GmbH) may be abbreviated. The law of the State governing the legal entity must also be given.

(b)   Where the appellant has appointed a representative, the name and the business address of the representative given in accordance with Rule 1(1)(e) of the IR. As explained in chapter 3, again in the context of CTM applications, non-Community appellants must appoint a qualified representative to act for them in proceedings before OHIM (Article 88(2) CTMR), whilst Community appellants may choose to represent themselves or to act through a qualified representative (Article 88(1) and (3) CTMR). Chapter 2 has already explained who may act as a representative (Articles 89 and 88(3) CTMR) and the need for the representative to file a general or specific authorisation to act (Rule 76 IR). Under Rule 1(1)(e) of the IR, the representative must supply his name and business address in accordance with Rule 1(1)(b) of the IR described above.

(c)   A statement identifying the decision which is contested and the extent to which amendment or cancellation of the decision is requested. The identification of the contested decision and the request for its amendment or cancellation should be distinguished from the statement of the grounds for appeal, which can be filed in accordance with Article 59 of the CTMR four months after the contested decision, as opposed to the notice of appeal, which must be lodged within two months. The subsequent filing of the grounds of appeal should not, however, be regarded as a mere formality. The grounds of appeal involve a presentation of the appellant's case and should state the legal and/or factual reasoning which form the basis of the challenge.

In addition, the notice of appeal must be filed in the language of the proceedings in which the contested decision was taken, determined in accordance with Article 115 of the CTMR (see chapter 3 for a detailed explanation of the language rules).

Locus standi (Article 58 CTMR)
The right to file an appeal is limited to those who were parties to the previous proceedings. Accordingly, Article 58 of the CTMR provides that any party adversely affected by a decision may appeal against it. Thus a person whose

application is rejected by an examiner, whether pursuant to Articles 36, 37, 38 or 66 of the CTMR, or a person who has made an unsuccessful application to the Administration of Trade Marks and Legal Division, concerning the making of an entry on the Register (in the circumstances outlined above) has an automatic right of appeal. If there are joint applicants for or joint proprietors of the CTM, each has the right to appeal. Further, any other parties to proceedings before OHIM are parties to any appeal as of right, so that those who have been successful before the Opposition or Cancellation Divisions have their interests protected in any appeal brought by the unsuccessful party.

Whether a person is 'adversely affected' by a decision of OHIM will depend on a comparison of the original request made by the appellant and the extent to which that request has been granted by the decision. In conformity with the practice of the EPO, it is submitted that the adverse effect on the appellant must apply both at the time when the original decision is issued and when the appeal is actually heard, that is, it must be satisfied during the whole of the appeal procedure. Adverse effect therefore goes to admissibility.

By virtue of Article 41 of the CTMR, any natural or legal person or representative body which, after publication of a CTM application, has made written observations to OHIM concerning the effect on that application of the absolute grounds listed in Article 7 of the CTMR does not become a party to the proceedings and thus has no right of appeal under Article 58 of the CTMR. In the event of a CTM application subsequently proceeding to registration despite the making of written observations, the only form of redress available to such third parties will be to seek a declaration of invalidity before a Cancellation Division of OHIM pursuant to Article 51 of the CTMR.

Time limits (Article 59 CTMR and Rules 70 to 73 IR)

In keeping with the time limit prescribed by Article 173 EC Treaty for judicial review of any of the acts of the Community institutions, Article 59 of the CTMR lays down a period of two months after the date of notification of the decision appealed from for an appeal to be lodged. The notice of appeal is deemed to have been filed only when the fee has been paid (ECU 800, Article 2 FR) but as noted already the appellant has an additional two months in which to file a written statement setting out the grounds of the appeal (Article 59 CTMR).

The two-month time limit prescribed by Article 59 of the CTMR will be calculated in accordance with Rules 70 and 71 of the IR, subject to the derogations in Rule 72 of the IR, but taking into account the detailed rules found in Rules 61 to 69 of the IR concerning the ways in which decisions of OHIM are to be notified. The general principles concerning the calculation of time limits were set out in chapter 1. The consequences of failing to comply with the time limits prescribed by Article 59 of the CTMR are subject, however, to the principle of *restitutio in integrum* found in Article 78 of the CTMR and explained next.

Restitutio in integrum

Influenced by Article 122 of the EPC, Article 78 of the CTMR creates a procedure which provides for the restoration of a party's rights in certain circumstances.

Who may apply for restitutio

The procedure is open to the applicant for or proprietor of a CTM or (unlike Article 122 of the EPC) any other party to proceedings before OHIM who has been unable to observe a time limit in spite of all due care having been taken, provided that the non-observance has had the direct consequence of causing the loss of any right or means of redress. This wider availability of the restoration procedure is no doubt influenced by the EPO Enlarged Board of Appeal decision in *VOEST ALPINE/Re-establishment of opponent* (G 1/86) [1987] OJ EPO 447, in which Article 122 of the EPC was extended to an opponent on the basis of the general principle of law that all parties in legal proceedings before a court ought to be given the same procedural rights unless there is an objective and logical reason for treating them otherwise.

Conditions for restoration

The specific wording of Article 78 of the CTMR should be noted. It will apply only where the following three conditions are all satisfied:

(a) There was a failure to observe a time limit vis-à-vis OHIM. It matters not whether the time limit is set by the CTMR itself, or by the IR, or whether it is a time limit specified by OHIM, for example under Rule 9(3), Rule 11, Rule 28(2), Rule 31(6) of the IR and so on. However, the restoration procedure is not available in the case of a failure to observe the time limit for claiming priority under Article 29 of the CTMR, nor for filing an opposition under Article 42 of the CTMR, nor, self-evidently, where there is a failure to observe the time limit prescribed by Article 78 of the CTMR for the restoration procedure itself. The exclusion of the filing of an opposition under Article 42 of the CTMR from the restoration procedure extends to the payment of the fee for such opposition, because such omission means that the opposition is deemed never to have been filed (see Guidelines Concerning Proceedings before OHIM, OHIM OJ 12/96, p. 1806). Further, by virtue of Article 74(2) of the CTMR, which empowers OHIM to disregard facts or evidence not submitted in due time by the parties concerned, it would seem that the restoration procedure cannot be used to remedy such an omission (see the same Guidelines, OHIM OJ 12/96, p. 1806).

(b) The failure to comply with the time limit had the direct consequence of a loss of rights for the applicant for restoration.

(c) The failure to comply with the time limit was despite all due care having been taken.

Application for restitutio

Under Rule 83 of the IR, OHIM is to make available, free of charge, a form for applying for *restitutio in integrum*. At the time of writing, none has been published. However, it is clear from Article 78 of the CTMR that the application for restoration must be filed in writing (communicated by any of the methods stipulated in Rule 79 of the IR) and must state the grounds on which it is based and the facts on which the applicant relies. The statement of grounds will need to identify who was responsible for ensuring compliance with the time limits, when and why this person was prevented from dealing with the matter on time, when the cause of non-compliance ceased to exist, and must show that all due care had been exercised (see *BROWN BOVERI/Statement of grounds of appeal* (T 13/82) [1983] OJ EPO 411 for an illustration). The application will only be deemed to have been filed on payment of the relevant fee (ECU 200, Article 2 FR). As with appeals, the obligation to pay the fee for the restoration procedure is absolute.

Time limit for applying for restitutio

An application for restoration of rights must be filed within two months beginning with the time of the removal of the cause of non-compliance with the original time limit. In practice this will often be the date on which the party receives notification of loss of rights under Rule 54 of the IR. The omitted act must also be completed within the two-month period. Further, and in the interests of legal certainty, the application for restoration must be made within an absolute and overall limit of one year from the expiry of the first unobserved time limit. In the case of the period of grace provided for by Article 47(3) of the CTMR for the late renewal of a CTM, the further period of six months is to be deducted from the one-year period.

Failure to comply despite all due care

The onus is on the party seeking restoration to show, objectively, that all due care was taken. In *BRUNSWICK/Re-establishment of rights refused* (T 287/84) [1985] OJ EPO 333, the EPO Board of Appeal stressed that the presence of the word 'all' in Article 122 of the EPC indicated that all the surrounding circumstances of a particular case ought to be taken into account. Thus natural disasters and other unforeseeable events (equating in English law to the concept of *force majeure*) which could not be avoided by the exercise of all due care will usually justify *restitutio*, but pressure of work, organisational problems or errors of law will normally not. Under EPO case law, it is not just the conduct of the applicant for restoration which is in issue, but that of the applicant's representative and the office assistants which both employ. For a fuller discussion of the extensive EPO case law on this important topic, the reader is referred to Singer, *The European Patent Convention* (London, 1995).

Effect of restitutio

The application for *restitutio* is determined by whichever first-instance department or Board of Appeal was competent to decide on the omitted act. The effect of a successful application is that the applicant's rights are re-established and the procedure in question is continued as if the time limit had been met.

Article 78 of the CTMR does provide protection for third parties who may be adversely affected by the restoration. Where the applicant for or proprietor of a CTM has rights re-established, these may not be invoked against a third party who has put goods on the market or supplied services under a sign which is identical with or similar to the restored mark in the period between the loss of rights and the publication of their restoration (Article 78(6) CTMR). Further (and in contrast to Article 122 of the EPC), such third party can, within two months from the date of publication of the restoration, seek to challenge that decision (Article 78(7) CTMR).

Member States are free to provide the *restitutio in integrum* procedure in respect of time limits laid down by the CTMR which are to be observed in dealings with their authorities (Article 78(8) CTMR).

Steps in an appeal

Interlocutory revision (Article 60 CTMR and Rule 51 IR)
In the interests of procedural economy, once an appeal has been lodged, the department whose decision is being contested can, if it considers the appeal to be admissible and well-founded, immediately rectify the decision, thus saving the parties the expense of continuing with the matter before the Board of Appeal (Article 60(1) CTMR). Interlocutory revision is therefore possible only in the most clear-cut of cases: if the matter is not beyond doubt, then the matter must be referred to the Board of Appeal.

If an interlocutory revision occurs, the relevant first-instance department (which will have been notified of the appeal) is required by Rule 51 of the IR to order the reimbursement of the appeal fees, subject to the four-year period for extinguishment of rights against OHIM prescribed in Article 80 of the CTMR. No interlocutory revision is permitted where the appellant is being opposed by another party to the proceedings, and hence will not be available in the case of a contested decision of the Opposition or Cancellation Divisions. Any decision which is not so revised by the relevant department within one month after the receipt of the statement of grounds is automatically remitted to the Board of Appeal without delay, and without comment on its merits (Article 60(2) CTMR).

Examination of the Appeal (Articles 61 and 62 CTMR and Rules 49 to 50 IR)
Article 61 of the CTMR, reflecting both the case law under Article 173 EC Treaty and the principles found in Article 110 of the EPC, draws a clear-cut distinction between whether an appeal is admissible and whether it is allowable.

Admissibility (Rule 49 IR)   Admissibility is dealt with in further detail by Rule 49 of the IR, which draws a distinction between automatic grounds of inadmissibility and grounds of inadmissibility which can be rectified within a time period to be specified by the Board. Rule 49(1) of the IR (which may be compared with EPO Rule 65) obliges the Board of Appeal to reject an appeal in certain circumstances unless the deficiencies are remedied within the relevant original time limits prescribed by Article 59 of the CTMR. The defects which thus render an appeal automatically inadmissible are:

(a)   seeking to challenge an act of OHIM which is not a reviewable decision under Article 57 of the CTMR;
(b)   not being a party who is adversely affected by a decision within the terms of Article 58 of the CTMR;
(c)   not complying with the provisions of Article 59 of the CTMR concerning the time limit for lodging an appeal, paying the requisite fee or lodging the statement of grounds of appeal;
(d)   failure to comply with Rule 48(1)(c) of the IR in not providing a statement identifying the decision which is contested; and
(e)   not complying with Rule 48(2) of the IR by filing the notice of appeal in a language which does not comply with the choice of language rules in Article 115 of the CTMR.

A further particular form of automatic inadmissibility should be noted, namely, that if the appeal fee is paid out of time, the appeal is deemed not to have been filed at all and the fee will be returned to the appellant (Rule 49(3) IR). As previously indicated, failure to pay the fee will mean that there can be no suspensive effect.

The relevant time limit within which the above defects must be remedied in order to avoid a preliminary finding of automatic inadmissibility will, with one exception, be the period of two months from the date of notification of the contested decision. The exception relates to the filing of the statement of the grounds for the appeal, which must be effected within four months of this date. The clear message from Rule 49(1) of the IR therefore is that it is better to file an appeal sooner rather than later so that as much as possible of the original two-month time limit is available for dealing with any of these problems of automatic inadmissibility. Cynicism suggests, however, that most appeals will be lodged extremely close to the two months' deadline.

Further, under Rule 49(2) of the IR, there are other defects which, although they do not render the appeal automatically inadmissible, entitle the Board of Appeal to demand the appellant to take steps to correct them: failure to do so within the period to be stipulated by the Board will then lead to a finding of inadmissibility. These further defects are:

(a)   not providing the name and address of the appellant in conformity with Rule 1(1)(b) of the IR; and
(b)   where the appellant has appointed a representative, not supplying the name and address of the representative in accordance with Rule 1(1)(e) of the IR.

The effect of inadmissibility, whether under Rules 49(1), 49(2) or 49(3) of the IR, may be overcome, however, if it is possible to plead *restitutio in integrum* as explained above.

If the practice of the EPO is followed, the appeal must remain admissible throughout the whole of the appeal proceedings.

Allowability (Article 61 CTMR)   If the appeal is admissible, Article 61 of the CTMR obliges the Board of Appeal to consider whether it is allowable. Rule 50 of the IR, though not in the same language as EPO Rule 66, states that all the provisions (presumably of the CTMR and the IR) which governed the first-instance proceedings are to be applicable to the appeal proceedings *mutatis mutandis*. This means that the Board of Appeal is subjected to the general provisions found in Title IX, Procedure, of the CTMR (Articles 73 to 80) and to the general provisions set out in Title XI of the IR (Rules 52 to 83 IR).

Conduct of the appeal
As in the conduct of oppositions under Article 43 of the CTMR and reflecting the general principle of law that a party has the right to make his views known, the Board is empowered by Article 61(2) of the CTMR to invite the parties, as often as necessary, to file observations within periods to be fixed by the Board, in response to the Board's own communications or to those from other parties.

When deciding on the appeal, the Board can exercise any power within the competence of the first-instance department which issued the contested decision or can remit the case to that department for further prosecution (Article 62(1) CTMR). This means that the Board need not only confirm or annul and remit a first-instance decision, but can decide the case for itself. If the case is remitted for further prosecution (and such reference back is entirely within the discretion of the Board of Appeal), the first-instance department is bound by the *ratio decidendi* of the Board of Appeal so far as the facts are the same (Article 62(2) CTMR). This means that although such department is given an opportunity to consider the issues again, it will be bound by those questions of principle already determined by the Board of Appeal. One of the grounds for referring the matter back to the first-instance department is if there has been a serious procedural irregularity, such as a failure to give one of the parties an opportunity to comment (Article 8 AR) (see below).

The decision of the Board will only take effect two months from the date of notification, unless a further appeal has been brought before the Court of First Instance, in which case the Board's decision only becomes effective once the further appeal is rejected (Articles 62(3) and 63(5) CTMR).

When issuing its decision, the Board of Appeal is bound by the formalities prescribed by Rule 50(2) of the IR, which closely resembles Article 63 of the Rules of Procedure of the Court of Justice [1991] OJ L 176/7. Apart from setting out such mundane requirements as the date, names of the members of the Board, the name of the registry official responsible for handling the case, the names of the parties and of their representatives and the actual ruling of the Board, Rule 50(2) of the IR specifies in particular that from a substantive point of view the decision must contain a statement of the issues to be decided, a summary of the facts and the reasons for the decision. Where necessary, a decision on costs must also be given.

Internal management of the appeal (Articles 9 to 13 AR)

As regards the internal management of the appeal, reference should be made to Articles 9 to 13 inclusive of the AR. The collective effect of these provisions is to ensure that the initiative for the conduct of the appeal rests very much with the Board, and in particular with the rapporteur for the case. Thus, if the Board decides that oral proceedings are appropriate (as will be explained below, they are viewed as an exception to the standard means of conducting a case before OHIM) then the Board may, when it issues the summons to attend, add a communication drawing the parties' attention to the matters which it considers are particularly significant or no longer contentious, or 'containing other observations that may help to concentrate on essentials during the oral proceedings' (Article 9 AR, containing wording similar to that found in Article 11 of the Rules of Procedure of the EPO Boards of Appeal). Communications from the Board during the course of an appeal are to be framed in such a way as not to imply that the Board is in any way bound (Article 10 AR), and the Board has the ability to refer to the President of OHIM questions of general importance which arise during the course of pending proceedings; only once the President has given his views may the parties make observations thereon (Article 11 AR). Finally, Articles 12 and 13 of the AR contain detailed rules concerning the secret deliberations of the Board (which are set in motion by the draft decision prepared by the rapporteur) and the order in which its votes are to be cast.

Oral Proceedings (Article 75 CTMR, Rules 56 and 60 IR and Article 9 AR)
The procedure of OHIM, whether at first instance or on appeal, is essentially in writing. Under Article 75 of the CTMR oral proceedings may be held either at the instance of OHIM or at the request of any party to the proceedings, provided OHIM considers that such proceedings would be expedient (the wording of Article 75 of the CTMR is subtly yet significantly different from the principal provision in Article 116 of the EPC which grants a European patent applicant an absolute right to oral proceedings). Oral proceedings are therefore to be regarded as exceptional.

Oral proceedings before the Boards of Appeal are public, like those of the Cancellation Divisions, unless the first-instance department decides that the admission of the public could have 'serious and unjustified disadvantages', for example, because they might disclose confidential information about one of the parties or one of the witnesses (Article 75(3) CTMR). By contrast, oral proceedings before examiners, the Opposition Divisions and the Trade Marks and Legal Division are always in camera (Article 75(2) CTMR). Oral proceedings in whatever forum must be distinguished from any informal or unofficial contact with the parties, such as interviews or telephone conversations (see Guidelines Concerning Proceedings before OHIM, OHIM OJ 12/96, p. 1798).

Oral proceedings before the Boards of Appeal are governed by the general provisions on oral hearings in Rules 56 and 60 of the IR. Rule 56 provides for the parties to be summoned to the oral proceedings (by at least one month's notice unless agreed otherwise) (Rule 56(1) IR). Failure to appear does not prevent the proceedings continuing (Rule 56(3) IR), so that a party who fails to appear must bear the consequences of such failure. Again, the role of the Boards of Appeal in controlling the proceedings is evidenced by Rule 56(2) of the IR, which provides for the parties' attention to be drawn to matters which need to be discussed in order for a decision to be taken, and by Article 9(2) of the AR (noted already above), which provides for the Boards to make observations to the parties 'that may help to concentrate on essentials during the oral proceedings'.

Rule 60 of the IR deals with the matter of record keeping. Minutes of the oral proceedings and evidence given thereat are to be kept. In particular, any testimony is to be minuted so that the witness, expert or party can examine the record and approve or reject it, the fact of approval itself being minuted, as is any objection to the formal record. Copies of the minutes, signed by the relevant OHIM employees, are to be provided to the parties, but a full transcript is only available on request and subject to the payment of the costs incurred in making the transcript (which may be in typescript or other machine-readable form).

Any oral proceedings before the Boards of Appeal are to be the last step before a decision is taken. Article 9(3) of the AR requires the Board to ensure that the case is ready for decision at the conclusion of the oral proceedings. The Board's decision may be given orally (Rule 52(1) IR), although it must be notified to the parties in writing subsequently. It is only the written notification which has any effect regarding the calculation of time limits for subsequent action by the parties (Rule 70(2) IR).

Taking of evidence (Article 76 CTMR and Rules 57 to 60 IR)
Article 76(1) of the CTMR provides for OHIM to collect evidence by a variety of means. It is almost identical to Article 117 of the EPC save that there is no

provision for evidence gathering by inspection, nor does it provide for an individual (whether party, witness or expert) to give evidence before a competent court in his or her country of residence. Evidence can therefore only be given directly to OHIM. (It may be noted in passing, however, that although Article 76(1) of the CTMR does not refer to obtaining evidence by inspection, Rule 57 of the IR does contain such a reference, which must be an oversight.)

Briefly, the means of obtaining evidence are (Article 76(1) CTMR):

(a) by hearing the parties;
(b) by issuing requests for information;
(c) by the production of documents and other items;
(d) by hearing witnesses;
(e) by hearing the opinion of experts; and
(f) by receiving statements in writing sworn or affirmed or having a similar effect under the law of the State in which the statement is drawn up.

The list in Article 76(1) of the CTMR is not exhaustive owing to the presence of the words 'shall include'. There is no indication that any one means of obtaining evidence has more probative value than any other means. In relation to categories (a) and (d) (which according to EPO case law are mutually exclusive), there is no means of compelling the giving of evidence and no sanction for refusal.

OHIM may commission one of its members to examine the evidence (Article 76(2) CTMR) thus reflecting the EPO principle of the free evaluation of evidence (see below): in the case of a Board of Appeal, this task will fall to the rapporteur. Where necessary, an individual may give his or her evidence orally, in which case the parties are to be informed of the witness hearing before OHIM and have the right to attend and put questions to the witness (Article 76(3) and (4) CTMR).

Further detail is added to Article 76(1)(a), (d) and (e) of the CTMR (dealing with evidence to be given by individuals) by Rules 57 to 60 of the IR, which have their counterparts in the Rules made pursuant to the EPC. These latter Rules in turn drew their inspiration from Articles 21 to 29 of the Protocol on the Statute of the Court of Justice of the European Communities and Articles 45 to 53 of the Court's Rules of Procedure. The wording of Rules 57 to 60 of the IR again illustrates how the initiative in evidence gathering rests with OHIM.

Thus under Rule 57 of the IR, if OHIM (that is, on appeal, a Board of Appeal) considers it necessary to hear oral evidence, it shall take a decision to that end. If one of the parties requests oral evidence from a witness or expert, again it is OHIM which determines the details. In either case, however, at least one month's notice must be given, such notice indicating the facts regarding which the individual is to be heard.

Equally, under Rule 58 of the IR, where OHIM decides to commission an expert (in contrast to one of the parties calling an expert witness), it is for OHIM to decide the expert's terms of reference and the form which the report is to take (though the parties can object to the expert on the same grounds as they may object to a member of a Board of Appeal under Article 132 of the CTMR).

Rule 59 of the IR deals with the costs of taking of evidence. Witnesses and experts summoned by OHIM are entitled to reimbursement of reasonable travel and subsistence expenses and to be compensated for loss of earnings, at rates to be determined by the President of OHIM in the light of EC Staff Regulations. Witnesses and experts who appear without being summoned are entitled merely to the reimbursement of expenses. Expenses and compensation may be paid in advance. Liability for such costs rests with OHIM where it decided of its own initiative that it was necessary to hear the oral evidence of witnesses or experts. Otherwise liability rests with the party requesting such oral evidence. OHIM has the discretion to demand a deposit (that is, security for costs) from such a party as a condition of taking oral evidence. Such provision clearly enables OHIM (and in particular a Board of Appeal) to penalise a party through the costs mechanism where it is sought to adduce evidence on appeal when such evidence could have been raised before a department of first instance.

Rule 60 of the IR, dealing with the minuting of oral proceedings and the giving of oral evidence, has already been noted above.

If the approach of the EPO is adopted, the burden of proof in proceedings before OHIM (whether at first instance or on appeal) will be the normal one of the balance of probabilities (see *RESEARCH CORPORATION/Publication* (T 381/87) [1990] OJ EPO 213). Reference was also made above to the principle of the free evaluation of evidence adopted by the EPO, a principle which may not be familiar to English lawyers. If OHIM adopts this rule (and there is every reason to suppose that it will), any person may be heard as a witness and any documents may be adduced as evidence without restriction. There is no question of compelling an individual to give evidence, nor is there any sanction for refusal, except that in the case of a party to the proceedings, such a refusal can lead to adverse inferences being drawn. It is presumed, therefore, that the tribunal has such discernment as to be able to form an assessment of the probative value of all the evidence that is put before it (see generally on the principle of free evaluation of evidence *TELEMECHANIQUE/Power supply unit* (T 482/89) [1992] OJ EPO 646).

Remission (Article 8 AR)

Article 8 of the AR empowers the Board to set aside any appealed decision of a department of first instance where the proceedings have been 'vitiated by funda-mental deficiencies', a phrase which by reference to EPO case law on the equivalent provision in EPO Rule 67 means 'substantial procedural irregularities'. In such a case, the Board can either remit the case to the original department of first instance or can decide the matter itself.

As with interlocutory revision, Rule 51 of the IR requires the Board of Appeal, if it considers reimbursement to be equitable by reason of a substantial procedural violation, to order reimbursement of the appeal fees, again subject to the four-year period for extinguishment of rights against OHIM prescribed in Article 80 of the CTMR. In contrast, however, to the case of interlocutory revision, where reim-bursement of fees is mandatory, in a case arising under Article 8 of the AR the repayment must be considered by the Board of Appeal to be 'equitable' in the light of the irregularities, thereby implying an element of discretion. Examples from EPO case law where repayment has been ordered include failure to give an applicant a decision within a reasonable period of time (*PACCAR/Excess claims fees* (J 29/86) [1988] OJ EPO 84), failing to give an applicant the opportunity to submit observations (*CATALDO/Cause of non-compliance* (J 7/82) [1982] OJ EPO 391) or failing to give adequate reasons for a decision *KUREHA KAGAKU/*

Unreasoned decision (J 27/86) [1988] EPOR 48). By contrast, no repayment was ordered where Examination Guidelines had not been adhered to or where the applicant had not been informed of its right of appeal *(EXXON/Alumina spinel* (T 42/84) [1988] OJ EPO 251).

The only other circumstance in which the appeal fee is returned to the appellant is when the fee for the appeal is paid out of time (Rule 49(3) IR). In other cases of inadmissibility or if an appeal, which though otherwise in order, is subsequently withdrawn, there can be no refund of fees.

General principles (Article 79 CTMR)

Article 79 of the CTMR, which is in substantially identical terms to Article 125 of the EPC, provides that in the absence of procedural provisions in the CTMR itself, in the IR, in the FR or in the rules of procedure of the Boards of Appeal, OHIM shall take into account the principles of procedural law generally recognised in the Member States. A similar reference to general principles of law common to the Member States can be found in Article 215 of the Treaty of Rome (in the context of the non-contractual liability of the Community for the behaviour of its institutions). Further reference should be made to the substantial jurisprudence of the Court of Justice concerning the general principles of Community law, developed ostensibly under the authority of Article 164 of the Treaty of Rome, albeit in Article 173 EC Treaty actions for judicial review or in Article 177 EC Treaty references questioning the validity of Community measures. Such general principles of Community law have been created by the Court as a means of adding detail to the framework of the Treaty of Rome by reference to 'constitutional traditions common to the Member States' (see *Nold* v *Commission* (case 4/73) [1974] ECR 491 at 507 (judicial review proceedings) and *R* v *Kirk* (case 63/83) [1984] ECR 2689 (Article 177 EC Treaty proceedings)). The seemingly simple provision in Article 79 of the CTMR therefore requires further comment.

First, it should be noted that the scope of Article 79 of the CTMR is limited to procedural not substantive matters: as regards the latter, the CTMR itself is to be regarded as conclusive. Secondly, before general principles of law can be referred to, it must be established that there is an absence of procedural provisions in the CTMR or its secondary legislation. Reference to the EPC experience indicates that there is likely to be little use of Article 79 of the CTMR to fill in procedural gaps (see *RIKER/Withdrawal* (J 6/86 [1988] OJ EPO 124). Indeed, the CTMR and its secondary legislation, which are drafted in wide language, already enshrine the traditional notions of natural justice.

If, however, resort to Article 79 of the CTMR is proved to be necessary, the presence of the word 'principle' suggests that the Board of Appeal will not have to concern itself with the details of national procedural law but only with universal precepts. Reference to the case law of the Court of Justice concerning general principles of Community law shows that a particular principle does not have to be found in the legal system of every Member State. And if found in only one or two Member States' legal systems, it does not have to be acceptable to all other Member States, as long as it is in accord with the aims and objectives of the Community's legal system (see *AM & S Europe Ltd* v *Commission* (case 155/79) [1982] ECR 1575, where the Court adopted the procedural principle of legal professional privilege even though it was well-established only in Member States having a common law tradition).

In their rare use of Article 125 of the EPC, the EPO Boards of Appeal have recognised the principle of legitimate expectations, which is already well-established in Community law (see *MEDTRONIC/Administrative agreement* (G 5, 7, 8/88) [1991] OJ EPO 137) but more importantly have stated that the relationship between the EPO and European patent applicants is governed by the principle of good faith (see *MOTOROLA/Admissibility* (J 2/87) [1988] OJ EPO 330 and *MEMTEC/Membranes* (J 3/87) OJ EPO 3). The consequence is that communications addressed to those dealing with the EPO must be worded clearly and unambiguously so as to rule out any misunderstanding on the part of an addressee. Communications containing erroneous information which misleads the addressee are to be treated as void and of no effect in their entirety. There is every reason to suppose that such a general principle governing the relationship between OHIM and all those who are parties before it will be adopted by the OHIM Boards of Appeal in due course.

Costs (Articles 81 and 82 CTMR and Rule 94 IR)

The basic principle governing costs established by Article 81 of the CTMR is that the losing party in opposition, revocation, invalidity or appeal proceedings is to bear the fees and costs of the other party unless otherwise decided, in other words, costs follow the event. This should be contrasted with the principle established under the EPC under which each party bears its own costs unless otherwise decided.

Article 81(1) of the CTMR and Rule 94(6) and (7) of the IR limit fees and costs to those actually incurred by the winning party which are essential to the appeal proceedings, although these may include the travel, subsistence and remuneration of one agent, adviser or advocate (but not more than one — Rule 94(7)(g) IR) within the limits of the scales set for each category of costs by Rule 94(7) of the IR. As in the case of proceedings before the Opposition or Cancellation Divisions, the Board of Appeal can apportion costs in cases where each party succeeds on some and fails on other points, and can also apportion costs 'if reasons of equity so dictate' (Article 81(2) CTMR). The decision concerning the award of costs under Articles 81(1) and (2) of the CTMR will be made by the Board of Appeal as part of its substantive decision (Rule 94(1) IR).

The liability of the losing party to bear the costs applies also to any party which terminates proceedings by withdrawing the appeal (Article 81(3) CTMR). There is also a discretion to decide on costs if an appeal does not proceed to judgment (because, for example, the parties reach a friendly settlement) (Article 81(4) CTMR). In both of these instances, Rule 94(2) of the IR provides for a decision on costs alone to be made by the Board of Appeal. Where the parties conclude a settlement of costs which differs from the above principles, the Board of Appeal is required to note such agreement (Article 81(5) CTMR).

The parties can request the Registry of the Board of Appeal to decide on the amount of costs, which decision can be reviewed by the Board of Appeal (but without oral proceedings) provided that this is requested by the parties within one month of the date of notification of the award of costs by the Registry (Rule 94(4) and (5) IR).

Appeals from OHIM to the Court of First Instance

Judicial control of OHIM (Article 63 CTMR)
Article 63 of the CTMR provides that:
1. Actions may be brought before the Court of Justice against decisions of the Boards of Appeal on appeals.
2. The action may be brought on grounds of lack of competence, infringement of an essential procedural requirement, infringement of the Treaty, of this Regulation or of any rule of law relating to their application or misuse of power.
3. The Court of Justice has jurisdiction to annul or alter the contested decision.
4. The action shall be open to any party to proceedings before the Board of Appeal adversely affected by its decision.
5. The action shall be brought before the Court of Justice within two months of the date of notification of the decision of the Board of Appeal.
6. The Office shall be required to take the necessary measures to comply with the judgment of the Court of Justice.

The Court of First Instance
Despite the reference in the wording of Article 63 of the CTMR to the 'Court of Justice', Recitals 12 and 13 to the CTMR make clear that it is the Court of First Instance of the European Communities which is to have jurisdiction over appeals from the OHIM Boards of Appeal. The Court of First Instance was established as part of the reforms to the Community generated by the Single European Act 1987, by virtue of Council Decision 88/591/ECSC/EEC/Euratom ([1988] OJ L 319/1 and corrigendum in [1989] OJ L 241/17) as amended by Council Decision 93/350/ Euratom/ECSC/EEC ([1993] OJ L 144/16). Although its jurisdiction was confined initially to staff cases and the review of the competition decisions of the EC Commission, the Court of First Instance now has jurisdiction to hear all cases brought under Articles 173 and 175 of the Treaty of Rome by non-privileged applicants (that is, anyone other than Community institutions or Member States). It was therefore logical to add to this the judicial control over OHIM in relation both to CTMs and (when operative) Community designs.

The Rules of Procedure of the Court of First Instance are to be found at [1991] OJ L 136/1, with subsequent corrigendum at [1991] OJ L 317/34 and with further amendments at [1994] OJ L 249/17, [1995] OJ L 44/64 and [1997] OJ L 102/7. Council Decision 95/208/EC Treaty amending the Protocol on the Statute of the Court of Justice of the European Communities (which is the constitutional document governing both courts) now provides for further amendments to be made to the Rules of Procedure which are to 'take account of the specific features of litigation in the field of intellectual property' (see [1995] OJ L 131/33).

Procedure of the Court
It is beyond the scope of this work to deal in detail with the operation of the Court of First Instance and the reader is referred to specialist texts such as D. Vaughan (ed.), *Butterworths Guide to European Court Practice* (1990); K. P. E. Lasok, *The European Court of Justice Practice and Procedure* (Butterworths, 1994); and R. Plender, *European Courts: Practice and Precedents* (Sweet & Maxwell, 1996).

Suffice it to say that the Court (composed of 15 judges, one drawn from each Member State) is divided for operational purposes into chambers of three or five. It was originally intended (under Article 12 of the Rules of Procedure) that the chambers of three would deal with staff cases with all other cases allocated to a five-judge chamber, but now cases are allocated to chambers on criteria determined by the Court itself (see [1994] OJ L 249/17). Only in special circumstances will a case be heard by the plenary Court.

The Court operates in all the official languages of the Community. Article 35(2) of the Rules of Procedure provides for the language of the case to be chosen by the applicant, although this can be varied for part or all of the proceedings to any other official Community language at the discretion of the Court following either a joint request of all the parties or a request of one of the parties (in the latter case there must be a hearing of the application to vary the language of the case). The language of the case must be used throughout the entire written and oral proceedings, with any relevant documents which are in another language being translated into the language of the case.

Private parties appearing before the court must be legally represented (though legal aid is available). Under Article 17 of the Protocol on the Statute of the Court of Justice as amended by Council Decision 94/993/EC ([1994] OJ L 379/1), only lawyers authorised to practise before a court of a Member State or of a State which is party to the EEA Agreement (at present Norway, Iceland and Liechtenstein) can represent or assist a party before the court.

The Court has wide-ranging powers to order the conduct of the case and the collection of evidence. Its procedure is essentially written, with oral proceedings forming the last (brief) stage before the Court makes its decision. The Court's deliberations are secret and it will deliver a single, collegiate judgment in open court.

If the winning party so requests, costs follow the event, although the Court has discretion to apportion costs where a party wins on some points and loses on others. It can penalise a party whose conduct it considers has caused the other party to incur unreasonable costs. A party who discontinues proceedings is liable for the other party's costs if they have been requested in the pleadings. The parties are free to reach an agreement on costs. If costs are not claimed in the written pleadings, each party is to bear its own costs.

A further appeal, but on a point of law only, is available to the Court of Justice itself.

What can be challenged (Article 63(1) CTMR)

Article 63(1) of the CTMR states simply that actions may be brought against decisions of the Boards of Appeal on appeals. This statement merits two observations.

First, the use of the word 'decision' raises exactly the same issues as were discussed above in detail in relation to Article 57 of the CTMR. A decision of the Board of Appeal (that is, one which changes the applicant's legal position) must be distinguished from incidental communications during the conduct of the case before the Board of Appeal and from a notification of loss of rights under Article 77 of the CTMR.

Secondly, although Article 63(1) of the CTMR uses the term 'appeals', this should be understood in the light of Article 63(2) of the CTMR which sets out the grounds of appeal. The grounds of appeal are such that the procedure is essentially one of judicial review rather than an appeal on the merits of the case.

Who can challenge (Article 63(4) CTMR)
The standing to bring an action under Article 63(4) of the CTMR should be contrasted with that of non-privileged applicants under Article 173(4) EC Treaty. Whilst the latter permits a private party to challenge a Community act only if that act is in substance a decision and then only if that decision is either addressed to them or of 'direct and individual concern' to them, the former grants *locus standi* to any party to proceedings before the Board of Appeal who is 'adversely affected' by its decision. The use of the phrase 'adversely affected' raises the identical issues discussed above in relation to the meaning of Article 58 of the CTMR.

In *inter partes* cases which are appealed from the Board of Appeal, the party which was successful before the Board will obviously be a party before the Court. Articles 115 and 116 of the Rules of Procedure of the Court also give rights of intervention (in support of one or other of the parties) although in the case of an intervener who is not a Member State or Community institution, an application to intervene must set out a statement of interest in the result of the case. The decision to allow an intervention rests with the President of the Court.

Grounds of Challenge (Article 63(2) CTMR)
With one minor addition, the grounds of appeal listed in Article 63(2) of the CTMR repeat verbatim the four grounds of annulment found in Article 173(2) EC Treaty. The additional ground is the reference to an infringement of the CTMR. Historically, the grounds are derived from French administrative law but in the 40 years since the Treaty of Rome became operative, both German and English administrative law have contributed considerably to the wealth of case law concerning Community judicial review.

The extensive jurisprudence developed under Article 173 EC Treaty reveals that the Court does not always specify which ground it is relying upon to annul a Community measure. Indeed, there is a degree of overlap between the grounds of appeal and one or more may be pleaded in the alternative or in combination. Thus, for example, were a Board of Appeal to issue a decision which was not properly reasoned, this could be challenged both under the heading of infringement of an essential procedural requirement or infringement of the CTMR.

The grounds of appeal will now be discussed in turn.

Lack of competence   Lack of competence would be applicable where the Board of Appeal has acted in a way which exceeds the powers given to it by the CTMR. There are few examples where the ground of lack of competence has been upheld in Article 173 EC Treaty proceedings and it is difficult to envisage how it would arise in the context of the CTMR.

Infringement of an essential procedural requirement   Procedural challenges are much more common under Article 173 EC Treaty and it can be anticipated that in time they will form a sizeable proportion of appeals from the OHIM Boards of Appeal. Thus a party may seek to show that the Board of Appeal has failed to comply with the detailed requirements of Title IX of the CTMR or with Title XI of the IR. A technical failure to comply with procedural rules will not, however, suffice: the appellant will have to show that the requirement was essential, in that it had an adverse effect on the conduct of the case before the Board of Appeal.

By far the most common illustration of infringement of an essential procedural requirement is lack of reasoning. It was noted above that Article 73 of the CTMR and Rule 50(2) of the IR both require that a Board of Appeal must give a reason for its decision. However, the giving of a statement of reasons is of itself not enough: this ground of review enables the Court to evaluate the quality of the reasoning and to consider whether it is internally consistent. Consequently, the statement of reasons must not be vague or contradictory, rather it 'must disclose in a clear or unequivocal fashion the reasoning followed by the Community authority which adopted the measure in question' (see *Nippon Seiko KK v Council* (case 258/84) [1987] ECR 1923 at 1966 and *Rewe-Handelsgesellschaft Nord mbH v Hauptzollamt Kiel* (case 158/80) [1981] ECR 1805).

Infringement of the Treaty, the CTMR and any rule of law   This ground of review overlaps considerably with the previous one, as infringement of an essential procedural requirement will of itself be an infringement of the CTMR. The most important aspect of this ground of review, however, is the reference to 'any rule of law'. In the context of Article 173 EC Treaty the phrase has enabled the Court of Justice to develop and utilise general principles of Community law (derived from the laws common to the Member States) as a means of controlling the conduct of Community institutions. These general principles include proportionality, legal certainty, legitimate expectations, non-discrimination, adherence to the rules of natural justice and respect for legal professional privilege. At first glance, the CTMR and its secondary legislation would appear to incorporate most of these. However, as was noted in the discussion of Article 79 of the CTMR above, there is the EPO precedent of the general principle of good faith governing the relationship between the EPO and European patent applicants which would seem suitable for adoption in this context.

Misuse of power   This ground of review has generated few cases under Article 173 EC Treaty and it is difficult to imagine how, given the wording of the CTMR and its secondary legislation, it could be raised in relation to a decision of the Board of Appeal.

Time limits (Article 63(5) CTMR)
In common with Article 59 of the CTMR as well as Article 173(5) EC Treaty, Article 63(5) of the CTMR lays down the standard period of two months within which a decision of the Board of Appeal must be appealed.

The two-month time limit prescribed by Article 63 of the CTMR will be calculated in accordance with Rules 70 and 71 of the IR, subject to the derogations in Rule 72 of the IR, but taking into account the detailed rules found in Rules 61 to 69 of the IR concerning the ways in which decisions of OHIM are to be notified. The general principles concerning the calculation of time limits were set out in chapter 1.

Powers of the Court (Article 63(3) CTMR)
In one sense, Article 63 of the CTMR goes beyond the concept of judicial review found in Article 173 EC Treaty, because it confers on the Court of First Instance the ability not only to annul the decision of the Board of Appeal, but also to alter it. Thus, if an appeal is successful, the case is not remitted to OHIM (which is directed merely by Article 63(6) of the CTMR to ensure that the necessary measures to comply with the judgment of the Court are taken) but instead the rights of the parties will be determined by the Court.

The extent to which the Court will be prepared to alter a contested decision remains to be seen, as this will be a novel experience for the Court. The impact of Article 63 of the CTMR on the workload of the Court must also be a matter of some speculation. Jurisdiction under Article 63 of the CTMR entails additional Rules of Procedure for the Court, which will take time to become a matter of routine. Further, delays in hearing actions are already considerable and it has been estimated that the Court will receive some 400 appeals annually from OHIM (see *The European Advocate*, Summer 1997, p. 7).

Chapter Nine
Transactions in a Community Trade Mark

Property rights

One of the chief attributes of any intellectual property right is the ability of the owner to exploit it commercially. This is as true of trade marks as it is of patents and copyright. The CTMR accordingly contains provisions relating to the proprietor's rights of exploitation in a Community trade mark (CTM). However, it should never be forgotten that any voluntary form of exploitation, in order to be valid, must comply with the stringent provisions of EC competition policy.

Mechanism for determining property rights (Article 16(1) and (2) CTMR)
Because of the unitary effect of the CTM declared by Article 1 of the CTMR, some mechanism is required for determining which system of property rights should govern such a mark. The Treaty of Rome itself does not deal with rules of ownership and indeed declares in Article 222 that the property laws of Member States are not to be prejudiced by the Treaty itself.

Article 16(1) of the CTMR provides the mechanism. It states that a CTM is to be dealt with in its entirety and for the whole area of the Community as if it were a national trade mark registered in the Member State where:

   (a) the proprietor has his seat or his domicile on the relevant date; or
   (b) if the foregoing does not apply, the proprietor has an establishment on the relevant date.

In cases not covered by Article 16(1) of the CTMR, the CTM is treated as if it were a Spanish national registration (Article 16(2) CTMR).

The word 'establishment' in Article 16(1)(b) of the CTMR would appear to equate to the phrase 'real and effective industrial or commercial establishment' found in Article 3 of the Paris Convention. It will be recalled that this is used as one of the criteria for entitlement to a CTM in Article 5 of the CTMR and was explained in chapter 2.

To illustrate the application of Article 16(1) of the CTMR, a CTM owned by a German company will attract the German property rules applicable to German national registrations; a CTM owned by an Irish enterprise will be treated as if it were an Irish national registration. It seems that corporate proprietors of CTMs who are not incorporated under the laws of one of the Member States but who have several branch offices in the Community may have a choice of which Member State's laws to apply, given OHIM's stated intention of liberally interpreting the phrase 'real and effective industrial or commercial establishment'. Alternatively, since, as explained in chapter 2, there is no requirement in Article 5 of the CTMR that the proprietor of a CTM own the business in which the CTM is to be used, a non-EC parent company may wish to designate one particular subsidiary based in one Member State as the holder of all its CTM rights.

Joint ownership (Article 16(3) CTMR)

Article 16(3) of the CTMR provides that where two or more persons are mentioned in the Register of CTMs as joint proprietors, it is necessary to see whether the first-mentioned one has a domicile or establishment in the Community, in which case the law of the Member State of the first-named proprietor will apply; if not, the status of the second-named proprietor is examined to see if he gets the benefit of Article 16(1) of the CTMR, and so on. Only if none of the joint proprietors is within Article 16(1) of the CTMR will the mark be treated as a Spanish national mark.

It may be noted in passing that s. 23 of the United Kingdom Trade Marks Act 1994 creates a tenancy-in-common of a United Kingdom national mark which is the subject of co-ownership. By contrast, Article 16(3) of the CTMR refers expressly to 'joint proprietors'. This raises the possibility that a CTM which attracts the operation of United Kingdom law by virtue of Article 16 of the CTMR would be subject to a joint tenancy, whilst a purely national United Kingdom mark would attract the opposite regime under s. 23.

CTM applications (Article 24 CTMR)

Article 24 of the CTMR states that the provisions of Article 16 and all other Articles in the CTMR dealing with property rights in CTMs are to apply equally to pending applications for the same. Article 24 of the CTMR therefore creates a fiction (for the sake of commercial convenience, enabling pending applications to be dealt with alongside marks which have matured to registration) that there can be property rights in a CTM application. Such wording, however, flies in the face of Article 6 of the CTMR, which makes plain that a CTM (and therefore any proprietary rights conferred by it) can only be obtained by registration.

Transfer of a CTM

The ability to transfer (Article 17 CTMR)

Article 17 of the CTMR governs the transfer of ownership of a CTM. The use of the word 'transfer' in Article 17 of the CTMR is intended to cover both voluntary assignments and transfers by way of inheritance. Although Recital 10 to the CTMR and Article 17 of the CTMR do not suggest any restriction on the freedom to transfer, it must be remembered that a CTM which has been acquired by a natural or legal person who does not meet the entitlement criteria in Article 5 of the CTMR (see chapter 2) is liable to be rejected by OHIM when the application to register the transfer is made (see Rule 31(3) IR and the explanation below on the procedure for registering transfers). Even if the transfer is registered (in error), the CTM is still liable to be revoked under Article 50(1)(d) of the CTMR, either in cancellation proceedings before OHIM (see chapter 5) or by way of a counterclaim to infringement proceedings under Article 92 of the CTMR (see chapter 7).

Article 17(1) of the CTMR declares that a CTM can be transferred separately from any transfer of the undertaking, that is, it can be transferred with or without the goodwill of the business in which it has been used. The Article also provides a presumption for the converse situation. Where an undertaking is transferred as a whole, this is deemed to include a transfer of the CTM as well, unless, in accordance with the law governing the transfer, there is an express agreement to the contrary, or circumstances clearly dictate otherwise (Article 17(2) CTMR). The same principle applies to contracts to transfer the undertaking.

By virtue of Article 24 of the CTMR, explained above, the provisions of the CTMR and the IR dealing with the transfer of CTM registrations are equally applicable to the transfer of pending CTM applications.

Total or partial transfers

Article 17(1) of the CTMR also declares that the transfer of the CTM may be total or partial, that is, it can be in respect of some or all of the goods or services for which the mark is registered. This provision must be understood in the light of Recital 10 to the CTMR and of Article 17(4) of the CTMR. Recital 10 to the CTMR (which does not have an equivalent in the Directive, reflecting the fact that the Directive has only achieved partial harmonisation of national laws) declares that a CTM is to be regarded as an object of property and therefore capable of transfer. This, however, is subject, according to the same Recital, to the overriding need to prevent the public being misled as a result of the transfer.

In consequence, Article 17(4) of the CTMR gives OHIM the right to refuse to register the transfer where it is clear from the transfer documents that, because of the transfer, the CTM is likely to mislead the public. OHIM's objections can only be overcome by the successor agreeing to limit the registration to goods or services in respect of which it will not mislead.

The deception produced by the partial transfer must be as to the nature, quality or geographical origin of the goods or services in respect of which the CTM is registered (Article 17(4) CTMR). Similar wording appears in Article 50(1)(c) of the CTMR as one of the grounds of revocation of a CTM (see chapter 5, and in particular the illustrations given therein of deception as to the nature of the goods (*Fratelli Graffione SNC* v *Fransa* (case C-313/94) [1996] ECR I-6039); deception as to quality (*K. SABATIER Trade Mark* [1993] RPC 97); and deception as to geographical origin (*TONINO Trade Mark* [1973] RPC 568)). Nevertheless, what is contemplated by Article 17(4) of the CTMR is such deception being caused by the partial transfer itself. Moreover, the risk of deception must be ascertainable from the documents of transfer. Should OHIM not identify the deceptive nature of the partial transfer at the time of the application to record it, either or both of the resulting CTMs remain at risk of revocation, either in cancellation proceedings before OHIM or by way of a counterclaim to infringement proceedings.

Article 17(4) of the CTMR does not include in its list of deceptive circumstances confusion as to the commercial origin of the goods or services. It remains to be seen whether the Court of Justice uses Recital 7 to the CTMR (which in essence states that *in particular* the function of the CTM is to act as an indicator of origin) as a means of reading source confusion into the list of grounds upon which OHIM may object to a transfer.

It cannot be stressed too much that the partial transfer contemplated by Article 17(1) of the CTMR is only as to goods and services. The unitary character of the CTM, established in Article 1(2) of the CTMR and reiterated in the opening words of Article 16(1) of the CTMR, means that there can never be a partial assignment as to territory (contrast s. 24(2)(b) of the United Kingdom Trade Marks Act 1994 in relation to national trade marks).

Transfer of a mark registered in the name of an agent (Article 18 CTMR)
The assignment of a CTM to its rightful 'owner' can be demanded where it has been registered without authorisation by the agent or representative of the proprietor unless the agent justifies his action (Article 18 CTMR). This should be seen as the correlative right to Article 8(3) of the CTMR, which gives the rightful proprietor the right to oppose the agent's application, to Article 11 of the CTMR, which gives the rightful proprietor the right to oppose the use of the mark unjustifiably registered by the agent, and to Article 106 of the CTMR, which gives the proprietor the right to have the agent's mark prohibited under national law. Such transfer will be subject to the provisions of Article 17 of the CTMR and to the procedure for registering transfers (explained below).

Formalities for transfer (Article 17(3) CTMR)
Article 17(3) of the CTMR requires that a voluntary assignment of a CTM must be made in writing, and must be signed by both parties. Failure to comply with this renders the purported transfer void. The clear-cut wording of Article 17(3) of the CTMR would appear to abrogate the rule (found in common law jurisdictions) that an agreement to assign, if made for value, is specifically enforceable even in the absence of writing.

Need for registration (Article 17(5) CTMR)
Article 17(5) of the CTMR requires that any transfer must be entered in the Register of CTMs and published in the *Community Trade Marks Bulletin*. The application to record the transfer can be at the request of either of the parties.

The consequences of not recording a transfer are as follows:

(a)   The successor in title will not be able to invoke the rights arising from the registration and hence will not be able to sue for acts of infringement (Articles 17(6) and 9 CTMR).

(b)   The transfer will not have any effect vis-à-vis third parties in all the Member States, except to the extent that they acquired rights in the CTM after the date of the transfer but before the date of its registration with knowledge of the transfer (Article 23(1) CTMR). It is unclear whether the knowledge of the transfer on the part of the third party must be actual or constructive, but given the commercial nature of the dealings involved, one may assume that the criterion will be actual knowledge. The binding effect of the transfer on those with knowledge of it does not apply to anyone who acquires the CTM under the terms of Article 17(2) of the CTMR (transfer of the mark along with the whole undertaking) or by any other form of universal succession (Article 23(2) CTMR).

(c)   Notifications from OHIM will continue to be sent to the person registered as proprietor (Article 17(8) CTMR). This means that the successor runs the risk of not receiving notification of subsequent CTM applications under Article 39(6) of the CTMR nor a renewal reminder under Article 47(1) of the CTMR. The repercussions are self-evident.

However, there is no time limit stated within which the transfer should be registered and hence no further sanction for late registration other than the consequences outlined above (contrast s. 25(4) of the United Kingdom Trade Marks Act 1994 which removes the ability to claim a pecuniary remedy if an assignment is not recorded within six months, or, if this is not possible, as soon as practicable thereafter).

Procedure for registering the transfer (Rules 31 and 32 IR)

General requirements   Under Rule 83(1)(d) of the IR, OHIM is to make available free of charge a form for applying for the registration of a transfer of a CTM. At the time of writing none has been published, but when the form is available it is expected to contain the essential elements set out in Rule 31 of the IR. In the meantime, applicants are advised to make written application to OHIM requesting the transfer of a CTM, containing the information specified by Rule 31 of the IR.
     The general requirements for recording the transfer of a CTM registration are to apply *mutatis mutandis* to an application to record the transfer of a CTM application (Rule 31(8) IR). The transfer of more than one CTM can be included on a single form, provided that the registered proprietor and the successor in title are the same in each case (Rule 31(7) IR).
     Under Rule 31(1) of the IR, the application to register a transfer must contain:

(a)   the registration number of the CTM;
(b)   particulars of the new proprietor, set out in accordance with Rule 1(1)(b) of the IR (see chapter 3);
(c)   where not all the registered goods or services are included in the transfer, particulars of those to which the transfer relates;
(d)   documents which constitute proof of the transfer (see below).

Optionally, the application may contain details of the successor's professional representative, set out in accordance with Rule 1(1)(e) of the IR (see chapter 3).
     In addition, the appropriate fee must be paid (ECU 200 per entry, but where multiple requests are submitted, whether for CTM registrations or applications, the maximum fee is ECU 1,000) (Article 2 FR). The application to register the transfer is deemed not to have been filed unless and until the fee is paid in full, although OHIM will notify the applicant of this omission (Rule 31(4) IR). Equally, if any of the requirements of Article 17(1) to (4) of the CTMR or if any of the requirements of Rule 31 of the IR are not met, OHIM will notify the applicant giving a time period (in principle, two months — see Guidelines Concerning Proceedings before OHIM, OHIM OJ 12/96, p. 1790) within which the deficiency must be remedied. If the deficiency is not remedied within the time limit, the application to register the transfer will be rejected (Rule 31(6) IR). One particular

ground of rejection has already been noted above, namely, that the successor in title does not meet the requirements of Article 5 of the CTMR concerning entitlement (see chapter 2).

Proof of transfer As stated above, besides supplying certain basic details, the applicant for registration of the transfer must supply OHIM with satisfactory proof of the transfer. Rule 31(5) of the IR (which appears somewhat contradictory when read in conjunction with Rule 31(1) and Rule 83(1)(d) of the IR) provides three alternative means of supplying this proof to OHIM:

(a)   the application for registration of the transfer may be signed by the registered proprietor or his representative and by the successor in title or his representative; or

(b)   if the application to register the transfer is submitted by the successor in title, it may be accompanied by a declaration signed by the registered proprietor or his representative to the effect that he agrees to the registration of the successor in title; or

(c)   the application may be accompanied by a completed transfer form or document, as specified in Rule 83(1)(d) of the IR, signed by the registered proprietor or his representative and by the successor in title or his representative.

The net effect of these somewhat circular provisions is that although Article 17(5) of the CTMR states that *one* of the parties can apply for the transfer, for there to be satisfactory proof of the transfer, the registered proprietor must participate in the registration process. In the case of corporate acquisitions, therefore, it is particularly important to ensure that the requisite formalities are completed promptly. Delay may mean that the registered proprietor may have been wound up, in which case it would be impossible to comply with Rule 31(5) of the IR.

Partial transfers (Rule 32 IR)

Besides the general requirements found in Rule 31 of the IR, Rule 32 of the IR imposes extra conditions for partial transfers. Nevertheless, Rule 32 of the IR begins by declaring that Rule 31 of the IR is to apply *mutatis mutandis* to partial transfers and then repeats the requirement found in Rule 31(1)(c) of the IR, namely, that the application to register must indicate to which goods and services the partial transfer relates. Under Rule 32(2) of the IR, the remaining goods and services are to be distributed between the original and new registrations so as to ensure that the two do not overlap. Clearly, it will be necessary to see how practice develops under Rule 32(2) of the IR.

From a practical point of view, Rule 32(4) of the IR empowers OHIM to allocate a new registration number to the partially transferred mark and to open a new file, which is to contain details of the original registration and the application for the partial transfer. A copy of this application is also to be included in the file relating to the original registration.

Pending CTM applications may be partially transferred, with the resultant 'split' applications being continued in the names of both parties. The successor in title is not liable to make payments where any fees have already been paid by the registered proprietor (sic) (Rule 32(5) IR).

Licensing of a CTM

The ability to license (Article 22 CTMR)
Article 22 of the CTMR, in like manner to Article 8 of the Directive, provides that a CTM can be licensed for some or all of the goods or services for which it is registered and for the whole or part of the Community. Such licence may be exclusive or non-exclusive. By virtue of Article 24 of the CTMR, explained above, the provisions of the CTMR and the IR dealing with the licensing of CTM registrations are equally applicable to the licensing of pending CTM applications. Licences of CTMs which are partial as to territory will be subject to EC competition policy, explained below.

Unlike transfers of CTMs, there are no provisions in the CTMR laying down any particular formalities for licences of CTMs. It must therefore be inferred that a licence can be entered into verbally. Indeed, such inference is consistent with the wording of Article 15(3) of the CTMR which provides that any use of a CTM with the consent of the proprietor shall be deemed use by the proprietor. Nevertheless, prudence dictates that any licence of a CTM should be in writing, not just for evidential reasons, but to assist the proprietor in making use of the rights conferred by Article 22(2) of the CTMR and for the purposes of effective quality control, as explained below.

Rights of the proprietor (Article 22(2) CTMR)
Article 22(2) of the CTMR provides that where the licensee breaches the terms of the licence with regard to its duration, the form covered by the registration in which the trade mark may be used, the scope of the goods or services for which the licence is granted, the territory in which the trade mark may be affixed or the quality of the goods manufactured or of the services provided by the licensee, the proprietor can invoke the rights conferred by the registration against the licensee. The use of the phrase 'invoke the rights conferred by the registration' indicates that the proprietor will be able to bring infringement proceedings against the licensee under the terms of Article 9 of the CTMR rather than just an action for breach of contract. However, reference to the proprietor being able to object to the licensee's use of the mark in breach of territorial restrictions should be understood in the light of EC competition policy as it applies to trade mark licences (see below).

Rights of the licensee (Article 22(3) CTMR)
As indicated in chapter 7, the procedural status of the licensee of a CTM may not be as advantageous as that conferred on the licensee of a national mark under the laws of the Member States (see Kur, 'Harmonization of trademark laws in Europe — an overview' (1997) 28 IIC 1).

The licensee of a CTM can only bring infringement proceedings in his own name where the owner consents, unless the terms of the licence provide otherwise. However, an exclusive licensee can bring infringement proceedings where the owner, after a formal request, does not bring such proceedings within an appropriate period (Article 22(3) CTMR). The wording of Article 22(3) of the CTMR does not make clear whether an exclusive licence can confer on the licensee the right to bring proceedings in his own name, although it would be illogical were such right to be given to a non-exclusive licensee but not to an exclusive licensee.

Further, no guidance is given on what should be regarded as an 'appropriate' period for the registered proprietor's response (contrast s. 30 of the United Kingdom Trade Marks Act 1994, albeit dealing with non-exclusive licensees).

The generalised wording of Article 22(3) of the CTMR is yet another reason why (from the licensee's point of view) a written licence agreement is preferable, so as expressly to confer on the licensee, whether exclusive or non-exclusive, the right to commence proceedings in his own name, or to give further detail of the rights of the exclusive licensee to call on the proprietor to take steps to protect the mark. Conversely, the CTM proprietor will want to rely on the express terms of a written agreement to prevent the licensee having such procedural rights. The non-interventionist approach to licences of the CTMR means that such issues are a matter for negotiation between the parties.

Other rights of the licensee (Article 22(4) and (5) CTMR and Rule 34(2) IR)
Where it is the proprietor of the CTM who commences infringement proceedings, the licensee is entitled to intervene in order to obtain compensation for any damage which he has suffered (Article 22(4) CTMR). Again, this is a matter which can usefully be dealt with under the terms of the licensing agreement.

By inference from the wording of Article 22(5) of the CTMR, a licensee is able to transfer the licence, although common sense dictates that this must be subject to the terms of the licence agreement. Also, by inference from Rule 34(2) of the IR, sub-licences may be granted, but again this must be dependent on the terms of the head licence.

Need for registration (Articles 22(5) and 23(1) CTMR)
Article 22(5) of the CTMR provides that on request of one of the parties, the grant or transfer of a licence in respect of a CTM shall be entered on the Register of CTMs and published in the *Community Trade Marks Bulletin*. The wording of Article 22(5) of the CTMR is virtually the same as that of Article 17(5) of the CTMR, which would suggest that registration of the grant or transfer of a licence is mandatory. Nevertheless, as chapter 5 has already explained, failure to record the licence does not prevent the benefit of the use of the trade mark by the licensee accruing to the proprietor under Article 15(3) of the CTMR.

The only formal consequence of not recording a licence, therefore, seems to be that the licence will not have any effect vis-à-vis third parties in all the Member States, except to the extent that they acquired rights in the CTM after the date of the licence but before the date of its registration with knowledge of the licence (Article 23(1) CTMR). As stated above, it is presumed that 'knowledge' in Article 23(1) of the CTMR refers to actual knowledge. The binding effect of the licence on those with knowledge of it does not apply to anyone who acquires the CTM under the terms of Article 17(2) of the CTMR (transfer of the mark along with the whole undertaking) or by any other form of universal succession (Article 23(2) CTMR).

As with the registration of transfers, there is no time limit stated within which the licence should be registered, assuming, that is, that Article 22(5) of the CTMR makes the registration of licences compulsory.

The more relaxed approach to the form and registration of licences of CTMs should be contrasted with that prevailing under ss. 25 and 28 of the United Kingdom Trade Marks Act 1994.

Procedure for registration (Rule 33 IR)

General requirements As with the registration of transfers, Rule 83(1)(e) of the IR anticipates that OHIM will eventually make available free of charge a form for applying for the registration of a licence of a CTM. None has yet been published, but it can be expected to contain the essential elements set out in Rules 31 and 33 of the IR. Those desirous of registering licences in the meantime may make written application to OHIM, furnishing the information required by Rule 33 of the IR.

Rule 33(1) of the IR states that the requirements of Rule 31(1)(a), (b) and (c) and (2) of the IR apply *mutatis mutandis* to the registration of the grant or transfer of a licence of a CTM. Equally applicable are Rule 31(4) of the IR (payment of fees) and Rule 31(7) of the IR (multiple marks). By Rule 33(4) of the IR, the provisions dealing with licences of CTM registrations are to apply to pending CTM applications.

Accordingly, when seeking to register the licence of a CTM, the applicant must furnish:

(a)   the registration number of the CTM;
(b)   particulars of the licensee, set out in accordance with Rule 1(1)(b) of the IR (see chapter 3); and
(c)   where not all the registered goods or services are included in the licence, particulars of those to which the licence relates.

The application may also contain details of the licensee's professional representative, set out in accordance with Rule 1(1)(e) of the IR (see chapter 3).

Because Rule 33(1) of the IR does not by cross-reference incorporate Rule 31(1)(d) of the IR in its procedure for the registration of licences, it would seem that there is no requirement to furnish any details of the licence agreement. Equally, because Article 5 of the CTMR applies only to *proprietors* of CTMs, and because Rule 31(3) of the IR is not incorporated by reference into Rule 33(1) of the IR, the licensee need not be a natural or legal person who complies with the terms of that Article. Further, and in contrast to Article 17(4) of the CTMR, there is no power granted to OHIM to object to licensing arrangements which may render the mark deceptive.

The appropriate fee is ECU 200 per entry, but where multiple requests are submitted, whether for CTM registrations or applications, the maximum fee is ECU 1,000 (Article 2 FR). The application to register the licence is deemed not to have been filed unless and until the fee is paid in full, although OHIM will notify the applicant of this (Rule 31(4) and 33(1) IR). If any of the other requirements of Article 22 of the CTMR or of Rule 33(1) and (2) of the IR are not met, OHIM will notify the applicant giving a time period within which the deficiency must be remedied (as stated above, this will be two months — see Guidelines Concerning Proceedings before OHIM, OHIM OJ 12/96, p. 1790). If the deficiency is not remedied within the time limit, the application to register the licence will be rejected (Rule 33(3) IR).

Special requirements for licences Rule 33(2) of the IR deals with the registration of the details of partial licences, and requires additional information to be given.

Where the partial licence is limited as to the range of goods and services, such goods and services must be indicated. Likewise, where the licence is limited as to part of the Community or as to a period of time, the geographical or temporal limitations must be notified to OHIM. In addition, paragraphs (1) and (2) of Rule 34 of the IR enable the existence of an exclusive licence and a sub-licence, respectively, to be entered on the Register of CTMs. Paragraphs (3) and (4) of Rule 34 of the IR repeat (arguably unnecessarily) the effect of Rule 33(2) of the IR.

Cancellation or modification of the registration of a licence (Rule 35 IR)
Rule 35(1) of the IR provides for the cancellation of the entry of a licence on the Register of CTMs, whether the entry relates to a CTM registration or a pending application (Rule 35(7) IR). Although the title of the Rule indicates that it also deals with the registration of changes to licences, modification is only dealt with by means of a cross-reference to the earlier provisions of Rules 33 and 35.

Rule 83(1) of the IR does not contemplate a specific form for the purposes of Rule 35 of the IR, although OHIM has a general power to issue such a form under Rule 83(2) of the IR. In the absence of such a form, written notification to OHIM containing the requisite information will suffice.

The application to cancel the registration or modification of a licence can be made at the request of one of the persons concerned, and must contain the following:

(a) the registration number of the CTM;
(b) particulars of the licence which is to be cancelled or modified; and
(c) either documents showing that the licence no longer exists or a statement by the licensee to the effect that he consents to the cancellation or change of the licence (Rule 35(1) and (4) IR).

The application to cancel or modify the licence is deemed not to have been filed unless and until the fee (ECU 200 per entry subject to a maximum of ECU 1,000 where there are multiple entries, Article 2 FR) is paid in full, although OHIM will notify the applicant of such non-payment (Rule 35(3) IR). Equally, if any of the remaining requirements of Rule 35(1) and (4) of the IR are not met, OHIM will notify the applicant giving the usual time period of two months (see Guidelines Concerning Proceedings before OHIM, OHIM OJ 12/96, p. 1790) within which the failure must be remedied. If nothing further is done, then the application to cancel or modify the registration of the licence will be rejected (Rule 33(5) IR).

Need for quality control by the proprietor
From the above, it will be readily apparent that the CTMR takes a fairly low-key approach to the question of trade mark licensing. No formalities are required for licence agreements, failure to register appears to have few harmful consequences and even if it is decided to register a licence, the details of the agreement do not have to be furnished to OHIM. No power is given to OHIM to object (in the context of the registration procedure found in Rule 33 of the IR) to licences which render the mark deceptive.

It should not be assumed, however, that to get the benefit of Article 15 of the CTMR, all a CTM proprietor needs to do is to select one or more licensees and then sit back. Arguably, the exercise of effective quality control over licensees is vital to the well-being of the CTM for the following reasons:

(a) If a trade mark owner indulges in the uncontrolled licensing of a CTM, the registration is open to revocation proceedings before OHIM under Article 50(1)(c) of the CTMR or to a counterclaim for revocation when infringement proceedings are brought against a third party under Article 92 of the CTMR. This will be because, owing to the conduct of the proprietor, the mark has become deceptive as to the nature, quality or geographic origin of the goods. Allowing a licensee to use the mark on poor quality merchandise would fall within this provision.

(b) Uncontrolled licensing of the CTM may also expose the mark to cancellation proceedings or a counterclaim based on Article 50(1)(b) of the CTMR. This will be because, owing to the acts or inactivity of the proprietor, the mark has become the common name in the trade for a product or service in respect of which it is registered. Trade mark owners need to adopt the strategies outlined in chapter 5 to ensure that the mark does not become generic.

(c) Although there is no express provision in the CTMR, there is the risk that uncontrolled use of a CTM by a licensee may not count as *genuine* use for the purposes of Article 15 of the CTMR. This is because of the emphasis given to the function of a trade mark as an indicator of origin (see Recital 7). Non-existent quality control may therefore render the contractual arrangement between the parties little more than a bare licence, so that the connection between the trade mark and its proprietor is non-existent. Support for this proposition can be found in the United Kingdom decision of *JOB Trade Mark* [1993] FSR 118 and in Article 19(2) of TRIPs, which states that '*When subject to the control of its owner*, use of a trade mark by another person shall be recognised as use of the trade mark for the purpose of maintaining the registration' (emphasis added).

CTMs as security

Security interests (Article 19(1) CTMR)

Article 19(1) of the CTMR declares that a CTM can be given as security (that is, as a charge to secure debts) independently of the undertaking owning it, or be the subject of other rights *in rem*. By inference from the wording of Rule 33(1) of the IR, a chargee is able to transfer the right *in rem* to another. Article 19 of the CTMR applies to both CTM registrations and applications (Article 24 CTMR).

By virtue of the opening words of Article 16(1) of the CTMR (explained above), security interests must be over the CTM in its entirety and for the whole area of the Community. The formalities governing the creation (and, by inference, the transfer) of such security rights will be governed by the relevant national law determined in accordance with the same Article.

Need for registration (Article 19(2) CTMR)

Article 19(2) of the CTMR provides (with wording similar to Articles 17(5) and 22(5) of the CTMR) that on the request of one of the parties, rights *in rem* over a CTM shall be entered on the Register of CTMs and published in the *Community Trade Marks Bulletin*.

In line with what has already been said about registering licences of CTMs, the only effect of not recording a security interest will be that such interest will not have any effect vis-à-vis third parties in all the Member States, except to the extent that they acquired rights in the CTM after the date of the execution of the security but before the date of its registration with knowledge of the right *in rem* (Article 23(1) CTMR). As stated above, it is presumed that 'knowledge' in Article 23(1) of the CTMR refers to actual knowledge. The binding effect of the right *in rem* on those with knowledge of it does not apply to anyone who acquires the CTM under the terms of Article 17(2) of the CTMR (transfer of the mark along with the whole undertaking) or by any other form of universal succession (Article 23(2) CTMR).

Procedure for registration (Rule 33 IR)
Yet again, Rule 33(1) of the IR states that the requirements of Rule 31(1)(a), (b) and (c) together with that of Rule 31(2) of the IR dealing with the transfer of the CTM apply *mutatis mutandis* to the registration of the creation or transfer of a right *in rem* in respect of a CTM. Likewise the provisions on payment of fees (Rule 31(4) IR) and multiple marks (Rule 31(7) IR) are stated to apply to security interests. Pending CTM applications are also subject to the same procedure (Rule 33(4) IR).

Unlike the registration of transfers or licences, Rule 83(1) of the IR does not contemplate a specific form for the registration of security interests, although one may be issued by virtue of OHIM's authority to do so under Rule 83(2) of the IR. In the absence of such a form, written notification to OHIM containing the requisite information will suffice.

Rule 33 of the IR states that when seeking to register the creation or transfer of a security right over a CTM, the applicant must furnish:

(a)   the registration number of the CTM; and
(b)   particulars of the chargee, set out in accordance with Rule 1(1)(b) of the IR (see chapter 3).

The application may also contain details of the chargee's professional representative, set out in accordance with Rule 1(1)(e) of the IR (see chapter 3).

There is apparently (from the wording of Rule 33(1) of the IR) no requirement to furnish any details of the security agreement, nor (in view of the non-incorporation of Rule 31(3) into Rule 33(1) of the IR) need the chargee be a natural or legal person who complies with the terms of Article 5 of the CTMR. This, however, leaves unresolved the question of what happens if the charge becomes absolute so that the chargee becomes the legal owner of the CTM.

The appropriate fee is ECU 200 per entry, with a maximum of ECU 1,000 where the application relates to multiple CTM registrations or applications (Article 2 FR). The application to register the security interest is deemed not to have been filed unless and until the fee is paid in full. OHIM will notify the applicant of any failure to pay the fees (Rule 31(4) and 33(1) IR) and of any failure to comply with any of the other requirements of Article 19 of the CTMR or Rule 33(1) and (2) of the IR. The usual period of two months to remedy any failing will be granted (see Guidelines Concerning Proceedings before OHIM, OHIM OJ 12/96, p. 1790). In the event of non-compliance after the two-month period, the application to register the security interest will be rejected (Rule 33(3) IR).

Cancellation or modification of the registration of the security interest (Rule 35 IR)
Rule 35(1) of the IR (already explained in relation to the cancellation of licences) provides also for the removal of the entry of a right *in rem* from the Register of CTMs, whether the entry relates to a CTM registration or a pending application (Rule 35(7) IR) and, by means of cross-reference, to the modification of a security interest (Rule 35(6) IR).

No form for the cancellation or modification of a right *in rem* is listed in Rule 83(1) of the IR. In the absence of OHIM providing a form pursuant to Rule 83(2) of the IR, written notification to OHIM containing the requisite information will suffice.

The application to cancel or modify the registration of a security interest can be made at the request of one of the persons concerned, and must contain the following:

    (a)   the registration number of the CTM;
    (b)   particulars of the charge which is to be cancelled or modified; and
    (c)   either documents showing that the charge no longer exists or a statement by the chargee to the effect that he consents to the cancellation or modification of the security interest (Rule 35(1) and (4) IR).

The application to cancel the security interest is deemed not to have been filed unless and until the fee is paid in full, the requisite fee being ECU 200 per entry subject to a maximum of ECU 1,000 in the case of multiple entries (Article 2 FR). The applicant will be notified by OHIM of this and of any other failure to comply with the requirements of the CTMR or of Rule 35(1) and (4) of the IR. If the failure is not corrected within the standard period of two months (see Guidelines Concerning Proceedings before OHIM, OHIM OJ 12/96, p. 1790) then the application to cancel the registration of the right *in rem* will be rejected (Rule 33(5) IR).

Levy of execution

Rights of judgment creditors (Article 20 CTMR)
By virtue of Article 20 of the CTMR, a CTM can be levied in execution, that is, seized by a judgment creditor of the proprietor in satisfaction of a debt.

The opening words of Article 16(1) of the CTMR (explained at the start of this chapter) make clear that the levy of execution must be over the CTM in its entirety and for the whole area of the Community. The formalities relating to the levy of execution will be governed by the relevant national law determined in accordance with the same Article (Article 20(2) CTMR). Levy of execution can also occur in relation to CTM applications (Article 24 CTMR).

Need for registration (Article 20(3) CTMR)
Article 20(3) of the CTMR provides (with wording similar to Articles 17(5) and 22(5) of the CTMR) that on the request of one of the parties, a levy of execution against a CTM shall be entered in the Register of CTMs and published in the *Community Trade Marks Bulletin*. However, the provisions of Article 23(1) of the CTMR dealing with the effect of failure to register on third parties do not apply in this instance.

Procedure for registration (Rule 33 IR)
The requirements of Rule 31(1)(a), (b) and (c) and (2) of the IR must be complied with in relation to the registration of a levy of execution in respect of a CTM (Rule 33(1) IR) as must the requirements of Rule 31(4) of the IR concerning the payment of fees and of Rule 31(7) of the IR dealing with multiple entries. By Rule 33(4) of the IR, the provisions dealing with the levy of execution over CTM registrations are to apply to pending applications.

OHIM has a general discretion under Rule 83(2) of the IR to issue the appropriate form for the registration of a levy of execution, but in the event that none is made available, written notification to OHIM containing the requisite information will suffice.

According to Rule 33 of the IR, when seeking to register a levy of execution over a CTM, the applicant must furnish:

(a)   the registration number of the CTM; and
(b)   particulars of the judgment creditor, set out in accordance with Rule 1(1)(b) of the IR (see chapter 3).

The application may also contain details of the judgment creditor's professional representative, set out in accordance with Rule 1(1)(e) of the IR (see chapter 3). There is apparently (from the wording of Rule 33(1) of the IR) no requirement to furnish any details of the judgment.

Under Article 2 of the FR, the fee for such registration is ECU 200 per entry, subject to a maximum of ECU 1,000 where multiple requests are submitted. Failure to pay the fee in full means that the application to register the levy of execution is deemed not to have been filed. OHIM will notify the applicant of this (Rules 31(4) and 33(1) of the IR). If any of the other requirements of Article 20 of the CTMR or of Rule 33(1) and (2) of the IR are not met, the applicant will be told and given the standard two-month period in which to correct matters. If no action is taken, the application to register the levy of execution will be rejected (Rule 33(3) IR).

Cancellation or modification of the registration of the levy of execution (Rule 35 IR)
Rule 35(1) of the IR provides for the cancellation or modification of the entry of a levy of execution on the Register of CTMs, whether the entry relates to a CTM registration or a pending application (Rule 35(7) IR).

In the absence of a form published by OHIM pursuant to its general powers found in Rule 83(2) IR, written notification containing the information required by Rule 35 of the IR should be made in order to cancel or modify the levy of execution. Such notification can be made at the request of one of the persons concerned, and must contain the following:

(a)   the registration number of the CTM;
(b)   particulars of the entry which is to be cancelled or modified; and
(c)   either documents showing that the levy no longer exists or a statement by the judgment creditor to the effect that he consents to the cancellation of the entry (Rule 35(1) and (4) IR).

Failure to pay the requisite fee in full (ECU 200 subject to the maximum of ECU 1,000 for multiple entries, Article 2 FR) means that the cancellation or modification is deemed not to have been filed. Non-paying applicants will be notified (Rule 35(3) IR), as will applicants who fail to comply with any of the other requirements of Rule 35(1) and (4) of the IR. The normal period of two months will be given for putting right any omission, otherwise the application to cancel the entry will be rejected (Rule 33(5) IR).

Bankruptcy

CTMs when the proprietor is insolvent (Article 21 CTMR)

Until the Community creates common rules for bankruptcy proceedings, a CTM can be the subject of bankruptcy proceedings, but only in the Member State in which such proceedings are first brought against the CTM proprietor (Article 21(1) CTMR). Therefore, when multiple proceedings for bankruptcy are brought in different Member States but based on the same facts, the CTM can only be claimed once by whoever commences the first proceedings.

It is for the competent national authority (such as the trustee in bankruptcy or liquidator) to apply to OHIM to request an entry on the Register of CTMs indicating this. Such entry must be published in the *Community Trade Marks Bulletin* (Article 21(2) CTMR). The provisions of Article 23(1) CTMR (concerned with the effect of failure to register on third parties) do not apply where there is failure to register the outcome of bankruptcy proceedings against the CTM proprietor. By virtue of Article 24 of the CTMR, Article 21 of the CTMR applies to pending CTM applications as it applies to CTMs.

Procedure for registration (Rule 33 IR)

Rule 33(1) of the IR applies the provisions of Rule 31(1)(a), (b) and (c) and (2) of the IR *mutatis mutandis* to the registration of an order of bankruptcy against the proprietor of a CTM, as it does with Rule 31(7) of the IR (multiple marks) and Rule 33(4) of the IR (pending CTM applications). However, by Rule 33(1) of the IR no fee is payable by the relevant national authority upon the application to register the bankruptcy.

The competent national authority should send written notification of the bankruptcy to OHIM, supplying the relevant information, in the absence of any form having been issued by OHIM pursuant to Rule 83(2) of the IR. The information which must be furnished comprises:

(a) the registration number of the CTM; and
(b) particulars of the relevant national authority, set out in accordance with Rule 1(1)(b) of the IR (see chapter 3).

The application may also contain details of the trustee in bankruptcy's or liquidator's professional representative, set out in accordance with Rule 1(1)(e) of the IR (see chapter 3). There is apparently (from the wording of Rule 33(1) of the IR) no requirement to furnish any details of the bankruptcy judgment.

Cancellation or modification of registration of the entry (Rule 35 IR)

By inference, Rule 35 of the IR (which deals with cancellations or modification of licences and other transactions) applies equally to the cancellation of an entry in the Register of CTMs relating to the bankruptcy of the CTM proprietor, as Rule 35(3) IR states that no fee is to be charged to the relevant national authority where such entry is cancelled. That apart, the provisions of Rule 35 of the IR are stated to apply in like manner to such a cancellation as they apply to the cancellation of other rights affecting CTMs.

Competition law considerations

Introduction

Mention has already been made in chapter 7 of how the defence of exhaustion of rights was developed, in the context of national intellectual property rights, by the Court of Justice in its attempt to reconcile the principle of the free movement of goods with Article 36 of the Treaty of Rome (Article 36 EC Treaty).

Property dealings in CTM registrations are of significance, both under Article 30 of the Treaty of Rome (Article 30 EC Treaty) (which prohibits restrictions on imports), and, more importantly, in the context of EC competition policy. Article 30 EC Treaty will be relevant where a proprietor or licensee wishes to stop the importation of trade-marked goods from another Member State. Competition policy will be relevant as regards the content of agreements relating to trade marks and as regards the issue of whether the ownership of a CTM is anti-competitive.

Free movement of goods

Article 30 EC Treaty (together with Article 34 of the Treaty of Rome) contains one of the 'four freedoms' of the Community, namely, the free movement of goods. In the case of infringing imports, Article 30 EC Treaty gives way to Article 36 EC Treaty, thereby enabling the trade mark owner or licensee to prevent the import-ation of a competitor's product (*Terrapin (Overseas) Ltd* v *Terranova Industrie C.A. Kapferer & Co.* (case 119/75) [1976] ECR 1039; *Deutsche Renault AG* v *Audi AG* (case C-317/91) [1993] ECR I-6227).

In the case of parallel imports, where a CTM is the subject of parallel licences in different Member States, Article 13 of the CTMR applies so as to prevent either the proprietor or licensees from relying on the rights conferred by Article 9 of the CTMR. Thus they are unable to object to the importation of goods put on the market in another Member State with the consent of the trade mark owner (*Centrafarm BV* v *Winthrop BV* (case 16/74) [1974] ECR 1183).

The significance of the *Winthrop* case is the willingness of the Court of Justice to treat a corporate group as a single entity. The outcome, however, is the same whether the goods are marketed by the parent company, by a local subsidiary, by another licensee or by a distributor. In every instance, the goods have been put in circulation in the Community *with the trade mark owner's consent.* The same principle applies where the goods are manufactured outside the Community, but subsequently sold within the Community with consent (*Phytheron International SA* v *Jean Bourdon SA* (case C-352/95) [1997] ECR I-1729).

The only instance of when the proprietor or a licensee of a CTM can object to parallel imports is where the circumstances fall within the derogation contained in Article 13(2) of the CTMR, that is, there exist legitimate reasons for the proprietor (or licensee) to oppose the further commercialisation of the goods, especially where the condition of the goods is changed or impaired after they have been put on the market. The proprietor or licensee can therefore object to defective, poor-quality or untidy repackaging (*Bristol-Myers Squibb* v *Paranova A/S* (cases C-427, 429 and 436/93) [1996] ECR I-3457) or to advertising which undermines the high-class image of luxury goods (Opinion of Advocate-General Jacobs in *Parfums Christian Dior SA* v *Evora BV* (case C-337/95) 29 April 1997).

In view of the unitary character of the CTM (described above) the case law of the Court of Justice on whether a subsequent proprietor of a national trade mark can object to goods put on the market by the original owner is not relevant. However, as mentioned in chapter 7, there remains the possibility of a proprietor of a group of CTM registrations transferring some whilst retaining others with a view to partitioning the market. The Court of Justice has already reserved to itself the right to object to transfers which are not for legitimate business reasons (*IHT Internationale Heiztechnik GmbH* v *Ideal-Standard GmbH* (case C-9/93) [1994] ECR I-2789).

Competition law

The competition law provisions of the Treaty of Rome, namely, Articles 85 and 86 (Article 85 EC Treaty and Article 86 EC Treaty), outlaw two forms of conduct which could distort competition within the single market, namely, restrictive agreements and the abuse of a dominant position. These will be considered in turn as they apply to property dealings in CTMs.

Article 85 EC Treaty   This renders void any agreement, decision or concerted practice between undertakings which may affect trade between Member States and which has the object or effect of preventing, restricting or distorting competition within the common market.

The Article also provides for the Commission to grant exemption to any agreement which satisfies the pro-competitive criteria in Article 85(3) EC Treaty. Secondary legislation made under the Treaty confers powers on the EC Commission to investigate breaches of competition policy, to make formal decisions and to impose fines and other sanctions on those who breach Articles 85 and 86 EC Treaty. Where parties to an agreement wish to have it declared compatible with competition policy (so-called negative clearance) or to have it exempted under Article 85(3) EC Treaty because it has pro-competitive benefits, they must notify the agreement to the Commission.

To ease the administrative burden of dealing with notifications, over the years the Commission has legislated (by virtue of powers conferred on it by the Council of Ministers under Article 87 of the Treaty of Rome) to produce a number of Regulations containing so-called block exemptions. These provide a series of guidelines to parties who want to enter common forms of agreement, such as exclusive distribution and exclusive purchasing agreements, by indicating which contractual provisions are acceptable and which are not. The block exemptions do not provide 'boilerplate' clauses to be inserted into agreements. Rather, it is up to the parties to negotiate terms in the light of what is permissible. Should an agreement consist only of clauses which are unobjectionable, then it will be exempted from the effects of Article 85 EC Treaty. If, however, the contract cannot comply with the terms of a block exemption, it still has to be individually notified to the Commission and may be declared contrary to Article 85 EC Treaty.

It was originally assumed that Article 85 EC Treaty was targeted at horizontal agreements, that is, at cartels existing between independent undertakings occupying similar positions in the market, for example, price-fixing agreements between manufacturers, or market-sharing agreements between distributors. It was also assumed that vertical restraints, such as agreements between a manufacturer and distributor, were not inimical to the objective of free competition and so were outside the scope of Article 85 EC Treaty.

Most forms of intellectual property licences, including CTM licences, are vertical restraints. It therefore came as a surprise when the Court of Justice of the European Communities ruled in 1966 that Article 85 EC Treaty did indeed apply to vertical restraints, the ruling occurring in the context of a trade mark agreement (*Établissements Consten SA* v *Commission* (cases 56 and 58/64) [1966] ECR 299).

Since then, intellectual property agreements, particularly patent licences, have come under a great deal of scrutiny by the Commission and the Court, and are specifically the subject of block exemptions dealing with technology transfer agreements (relating to patents and know-how) and franchise agreements (which are relevant to CTMs). Although the number of Court and Commission decisions on trade mark agreements is relatively small when compared with those on patent licences, it is nevertheless necessary to consider such agreements in the context of both vertical and horizontal restraints on competition.

Vertical Restraints   In *Établissements Consten SA* v *Commission* (cases 56/64 and 58/64) [1966] ECR 299 the Court accepted the Commission's argument that a distribution agreement which:

(a)   obliged the distributor to sell minimum quantities of the manufacturer's goods and to refrain from selling competing brands;
(b)   conferred exclusive territorial protection on the distributor; and
(c)   permitted the distributor to register the manufacturer's trade mark and use it to keep goods from other distributors out of its territory;

infringed Article 85 EC Treaty. Trade mark rights were being used to obstruct parallel imports and the parties' conduct was an abuse of trade mark legislation. Although decided in the context of national trade mark rights, the message from the case for CTM owners is obvious. Licensees of CTMs cannot be given exclusive territorial protection against parallel imports.

However, the Commission has since been prepared to accept that sometimes (depending on the nature of the product) it may be acceptable for a limited degree of territorial exclusivity to be conferred on a trade mark licensee, although absolute territorial protection can never be granted (*Re Davide Campari-Milano SpA Agreement* [1978] 2 CMLR 397).

Although the Commission and Court of Justice have often examined the contents of patent licences to see if individual clauses (other than territorial restrictions) are anti-competitive, this has rarely happened with trade mark licences, possibly because trade marks are not perceived by the Commission to be as monopolistic as patents.

One trade mark licence which was examined by the Commission was that in *Moosehead/Whitbread* [1991] 4 CMLR 391. The agreement contained a no-challenge clause in respect of the trade mark, meaning that the licensee could not question the validity of the trade mark without being in breach of contract. Such clauses were at one time prohibited in patent licences as being anti-competitive (though they now receive more favourable treatment in the Technology Transfer Block Exemption). However, the Commission decided in this case that the clause was outside the scope of Article 85 EC Treaty. The trade mark was relatively new and unknown to the United Kingdom market (as was the product, Canadian lager) and hence was not a barrier to entry to other firms in what was a highly competitive market anyway.

Horizontal restraints   One type of horizontal agreement involving trade marks is that known as a trade mark delimitation agreement. Such an agreement may come about where two rival concerns (often from different Member States — see, for example the facts of *Terrapin (Overseas) Ltd* v *Terranova Industrie C.A. Kapferer & Co.* (case 119/75) [1976] ECR 1039 and *Deutsche Renault AG* v *Audi AG* (case C-317/91) [1993] ECR I-6227) own the same or similar marks for the same or similar products. Rather than litigate to determine which undertaking has the better right, they agree to compromise the dispute by drawing up a contract laying out their respective trade mark rights. The EC Commission and the Court of Justice have had occasion to consider such agreements several times, so that their legal standing is fairly clear. The rules can be summarised thus:

(a)   Where the two companies are unconnected and where each has independently acquired trade mark rights, the marks being identical or similar and for competing goods, so that there is a genuine dispute, then the Commission may view such an agreement as outside the scope of Article 85 EC Treaty (*Re Penney's Trade Mark* [1978] 2 CMLR 100).

(b)   Where, however, the trade mark has a common origin and the two owners agree to divide trade mark ownership along national boundaries, then Article 85 EC Treaty will be infringed (*Re the PERSIL Trade Mark* [1978] FSR 348).

(c)   Even where the parties are unconnected, a trade mark delimitation agreement may still fall foul of Article 85 EC Treaty if it completely prevents the parties from marketing their goods in the other's territory. Instead, they should be free to sell their goods in the other's territory as long as a different brand name is chosen (*Re the Agreement of Sirdar Ltd* [1975] 1 CMLR D93).

(d)   The trade mark rights relied on by the parties to the delimitation agreement must be valid, so that, for example, an agreement based on a dormant registration which is liable to revocation for non-use will infringe Article 85 EC Treaty (*BAT Cigaretten-Fabriken GmbH* v *Commission* (case 35/83) [1985] ECR 363).

Care, therefore, needs to be taken when drafting a trade mark delimitation agreement to ensure that the rights on which it is based are valid and that it is not in effect a market sharing agreement in which trade mark rights are used to partition the single market. Delimitation agreements concluded as the result of a 'friendly settlement' of opposition or cancellation proceedings before OHIM, or as a means of settling an infringement action or counterclaim before CTM courts, or as a means of reconciling earlier national rights with later CTM rights under Articles 106 and 107 of the CTMR will all need to be checked to ensure compliance with the foregoing.

Franchise agreements   Franchising is a particular type of licence involving trade marks and other intellectual property rights, such as know-how and designs, which has developed considerably in recent years, to the extent that it is now the subject of a block exemption under Article 85 EC Treaty, to be found in Commission Regulation 4087/88.

Franchising is a method of distributing goods or supplying services by a series of individual agreements governing a common business format. A product of standard appearance and which is easily identifiable (for example, because of a brand name) is sold in uniform premises using the same business methods; or a service is provided relying on standardised procedures. These arrangements are encountered frequently, for example, in the hotel and catering industries, vehicle hire, hairdressing and photocopying.

The Court of Justice in *Pronuptia de Paris GmbH* v *Pronuptia de Paris Irmgard Schillgalis* (case 161/84) [1986] ECR 353 identified the basis of the franchise system. It enables the franchisee to operate as an independent business while using the name, trade marks and know-how of the franchisor. It can be distinguished from a distribution agreement because in addition to the licensing of trade marks, it involves the transfer of other intellectual property rights (usually know-how), for which the franchisee pays.

In order for a franchise agreement to function properly, it is essential that the franchisor is able to lay down a common business format to which all franchisees should adhere, and that obligations relating to the integrity of the intellectual property rights (know-how, copyright and trade marks) should be imposed. As a result of this analysis, the EC Commission has basically adopted a benevolent attitude to this type of contract, because it is capable of stimulating economic activity. Franchising improves distribution without the need for major investment by the franchisor, and provides incentives for the franchisee because it enables ready entrance to the market under a name which has already achieved public recognition through the promotion of a trade mark. This results in a benefit to consumers, again through improved distribution coupled with the existence of traders personally interested in the efficient operation of their business.

Regulation 4087/88 permits agreements which:

(a)   exclude the franchisor from granting rights to third parties within the contract territory (in other words, the franchisee is an exclusive licensee of the trade mark within the geographical area of the agreement);

(b)   oblige the franchisee to operate only from the licensed premises;

(c)   prevent the franchisee from soliciting customers outside the contract territory (though 'passive' sales, whereby the customer approaches the franchisee, can be dealt with, by analogy to parallel imports); and

(d)   oblige the franchisee not to deal in competing goods and services.

Other restrictions may be permitted in so far as they are necessary to protect the above-mentioned intellectual property rights or to maintain the reputation of the network. This category of clause includes an obligation not to engage in a similar competing business, to use best endeavours to sell the goods, to offer minimum ranges of the goods, to achieve minimum turnover, to meet objective quality control standards and to pay a fixed proportion of revenue towards advertising.

Banned clauses are those which:

(a)   prevent the franchisee from using know-how after termination of the contract where such information has become generally known (though of course were the franchisee to continue using the trade marks this would amount to infringement);

(b)   allow the franchisor to determine selling prices (as opposed to recommending them);

(c)   prevent the franchisee from challenging the validity of the intellectual property rights (though the franchisor can treat such conduct as a breach of contract);

(d)   stop the franchisee supplying goods to customers because of where they live.

The block exemption only applies to franchises for the distribution of goods or the supply of services (including master franchises), but does not apply to industrial franchises, where the franchisee produces goods, nor to wholesale franchises.

Distribution and service franchises will of necessity involve the licensing of trade marks, whether these are CTM or national registrations. Where a CTM proprietor therefore wishes to set up a series of franchise agreements, whether in one Member State or throughout the EC, the provisions of the Block Exemption will need to be borne in mind.

Article 86 EC Treaty   This prohibits any conduct which is an abuse of a dominant position within the common market or a substantial part of it, if that conduct affects trade between Member States.

The Article envisages an undertaking which has market power (that is, the ability to behave independently of its competitors, the size of market share not being conclusive) in the relevant product or service market. The finding of market power depends on a detailed economic analysis, but could result from the success of a particular brand name where it has been the subject of extensive promotion (see, for example, the analysis of the power of the ANDREX brand in *Kimberly-Clark/Scott* [1996] OJ L 183/1). An undertaking which finds itself in such a position has a special responsibility not to allow its conduct to impair genuine undistorted competition in the single market, and any failure to discharge this responsibility will amount to an abuse.

The Court of Justice has stated on several occasions that the mere ownership of intellectual property rights is not caught by Article 86 EC Treaty (*Parke Davis and Co. v Probel* (case 24/67) [1968] ECR 55; *AB Volvo v Erik Veng (UK) Ltd* (case 238/87) [1988] ECR 6211, decided respectively in relation to patents and industrial designs, but equally applicable to CTMs). However, patents, copyright and trade marks may be combined with other factors leading to market power, in which case their exploitation may be anti-competitive. Exploitation in this context includes a decision by the intellectual property owner *not* to grant licences (at least where the right in question is *de minimis*) as well as granting licences on excessive terms (*Radio Telefis Eireann v Commission* (cases C-241 and 242/91P) [1995] ECR I-743).

Most of the cases involving intellectual property rights and Article 86 EC Treaty have related to patents or copyright, but there are a few involving trade marks.

In *OSRAM/AIRAM* (11th Report on Competition Policy) the Commission hinted that it might be abusive for a firm in a dominant position to register a trade mark knowing that a competitor already uses that mark. Today, such a finding would be over and above the ability of the competitor to have the mark declared invalid, were it a CTM, on the grounds of bad faith in accordance with Article 51(1)(b) of the CTMR. In *Chiquita/Fyffes* (Commission Press Release of 4 June 1992) the Commission took the view that an agreement between Fyffes and Chiquita that Fyffes would not use its trade mark on mainland Europe for 20 years infringed both Articles 85 and 86 EC Treaty. The breach of Article 86 EC Treaty lay in the fact that its inability to use the mark would hinder Fyffes in its competition with Chiquita in the banana market. Such an agreement today would have the effect of stopping a party from obtaining a CTM or, if a CTM is already registered, from using the CTM in accordance with Article 15 of the CTMR.

Most recently, in *Warner Lambert Co. v Gillette Co.* [1993] 5 CMLR 559, the Commission found that an agreement concerning the transfer and delimitation of trade mark rights infringed Article 86 EC Treaty and ordered divestiture of the mark. In that case, the worldwide rights to the WILKINSON SWORD trade mark had been purchased in a management buy-out funded by Gillette, the manufacturer of the rival product. The purchaser and Gillette then divided the WILKINSON SWORD trade mark rights so that the mark was owned by the purchaser in the EC and the United States of America and by Gillette elsewhere (such a division of ownership would still be possible were the EC trade mark a CTM).

The Commission's objection to the deal under Article 86 EC Treaty was based not on the strength of the WILKINSON SWORD trade mark but on the fact that it had been acquired by a company (Gillette) which controlled 70 per cent by volume of the market in wet-shaving products in the EC as a whole. The abuse of dominant position was because Gillette had acquired a substantial shareholding in its principal competitor. Further, the terms of the funding agreement enabled Gillette to restrict the purchaser's ability to use the trade mark to advertise its products outside America or the EC. Such conduct, were it to occur today, would not have any effect on (say) the WILKINSON SWORD CTM registration as such. Rather, what is of concern is whether the ownership of the CTM enables or prevents worldwide inter-brand competition.

Gillette was ordered to sell its equity interest in the purchaser to an unconnected third party and to reassign to the purchaser the trade mark rights for the rest of Europe outside the EC. Although decided in the context of national trade mark rights, the decision would apply equally to a CTM proprietor who uses the market power of a brand name to coerce a weaker competitor into structuring its business activities and trade mark ownership to the commercial advantage of the CTM owner.

Mergers   Council Regulation 4064/89 [1989] OJ L 365/1 as amended (the Merger Regulation) confers on the EC Commission the power to investigate and if necessary object to mergers over a certain size which it considers to be 'incompatible with the common market'. Often the Commission will approve a merger on terms and, on occasion, it has demanded the divestiture of national brand names as a condition of its approval where the merger would otherwise have the effect of eliminating inter-brand rivalry.

The most recent example of divestiture of trade marks to promote competition is the Commission's decision in *Kimberly-Clark/Scott* [1996] OJ L 183/1. Approval of the merger between the owners of the KLEENEX brand and the owners of ANDREX for toilet tissue was granted on condition that the KLEENEX mark was transferred or licensed to third parties for certain items within the proprietor's product range.

The decision, although concerned with the value of national brand names in the United Kingdom and Irish markets for toilet tissue would be equally applicable to CTMs. The Commission's strategy in ordering assignment and/or licensing of particular national trade marks would have to be modified, however, to take account of the unitary nature of any CTMs, so that any divestiture of ownership would have to be for the whole of the Community. In such a scenario, the compulsory licensing of CTMs might prove to be the more attractive solution where a merger has the effect of reducing inter-brand rivalry. Compulsory licensing of CTMs appears to be a novel solution to anti-competitive behaviour and would pose the interesting question of whether the CTM owner could object to parallel imports from the compulsory licensee, by analogy with the patent case of *Pharmon BV* v *Hoechst AG* (case 19/84) [1985] ECR 2281. Such compulsory licence would appear, however, to be in breach of Article 21 of TRIPs.

Chapter Ten
The Madrid System

Introduction

The 'Madrid system' collectively refers to two separate treaties:

(a)   the Madrid Agreement Concerning the International Registration of Marks, which was concluded in 1891, entered into force in 1892 and was last revised at Stockholm in 1967 (the Madrid Agreement); and

(b)   the Protocol Relating to the Madrid Agreement which was adopted in 1989, entered into force on 1 December 1995 and came into operation on 1 April 1996 (the Madrid Protocol).

Each treaty provides for the international registration of marks for goods and services (that is, trade and service marks) and is essentially a *filing system.*

On the basis of a 'home' registration or application for registration a trade mark owner can apply to the International Bureau of the World Intellectual Property Organisation (WIPO) in Geneva, which administers the system, for a so-called international registration specifying the countries where protection is required. The mark is registered and published by the International Bureau in the *WIPO Gazette of International Marks.* Details of the mark are forwarded to the trade mark offices of the countries in which protection is sought, who then 'register' (or refuse) the mark according to the rules existing in their countries at the time.

The advantages to the trade mark owner are that by filing a single application at one office in one language with one international registration fee paid in one currency, he can obtain a single registration with one registration number and one renewal date covering a number of jurisdictions.

The Community trade mark (CTM) offers its proprietor similar advantages to international registration over a series of national trade marks. But there are, inter alia, three important differences between the CTM and the Madrid systems:

(a)   CTM registration results in a supranational trade mark while international registration is a procedural short cut often described as a bundle of national or (regional) applications or registrations;

(b)   CTM registration can be applied for directly while international registration must be based on a national (or regional) registration or application for registration; and

(c)   the geographical coverage of the CTM is limited to the territory of the European Community while Madrid has the potential to extend to all the Contracting States of the Paris Convention (at the time of writing 143 States, see appendix 1).

The above differences, particularly the third, mean that the CTM and Madrid systems are complementary rather than exclusive of one another.

The aims of the present chapter are therefore:

(a)   to provide the trade mark owner and his representative with an overview of the Madrid system (for a fuller account see *Guide to the International Registration of Marks under the Madrid Agreement and the Madrid Protocol*, published by WIPO); and

(b)   to describe the Commission of the European Communities Proposals for linking the CTM with the Madrid system.

A chart comparing features of the CTM and international registration (including a cost comparison) is at appendix 12.

Why two separate treaties?

The Madrid Agreement

The Madrid Agreement is generally regarded as successful and relatively inexpensive. Since it came into force in 1892 over 600,000 international registrations have been made with each registration covering an average of 10 countries. At the beginning of 1997 over 280,000 registrations under the Madrid Agreement were in force.

Nevertheless only 47 States are party to the Madrid Agreement (see appendix 3). Important trading nations like the United Kingdom, the United States of America, Japan and the Nordic countries have never joined. Features of the Madrid Agreement which are unattractive to those countries include (as described below) 'central attack', the 12-month period for a designated country to refuse protection and the fee paid to national trade mark offices, which is not enough to cover full examination.

The Madrid Protocol

The Madrid Protocol contains a number of innovations which are designed to facilitate membership of non-Agreement countries — thereby extending the geographical coverage of the Madrid system — and to provide links between the Madrid and the CTM systems.

At the time of writing 22 countries have ratified or acceded to the Madrid Protocol including 15 countries which are also party to the Madrid Agreement (see appendix 4). All contracting States to the European Economic Area Treaty (1992) are bound to adhere to the Madrid Protocol. The European Community will accede to the Madrid Protocol in 1998.

In May 1994, the United States of America stated that it would not join the Madrid Protocol because it objected to voting rights being given to participating intergovernmental organisations, for example the European Community, in addition to Member States of those organisations.

Parallel systems

At least until 1 December 2005 the Madrid Agreement and Protocol will continue to operate in parallel. Article 9*sexies*(2) of the Madrid Protocol means that (unless before that date all Madrid Agreement countries join the Protocol) there will be three groups of members of the Madrid Union:

(a)   countries party only to the Madrid Agreement;
(b)   countries party to the Madrid Agreement and Protocol; and
(c)   countries or organisations party only to the Madrid Protocol.

And see 'The safeguard clause' below.

Common regulations

Despite its innovations, the Madrid Protocol is based upon the Madrid Agreement and shares some common numbering of articles. Reference below to 'Article' is to the article of the same number in both the Madrid Agreement and Protocol unless otherwise indicated (by **A** for the Madrid Agreement; and by **P** for the Madrid Protocol) .

In addition the Madrid Agreement and Protocol have the same set of 'Common Regulations' (adopted on 18 January 1996 with effect from 1 April 1996) and references below to 'Rule' are to these Common Regulations unless otherwise stated.

The United Kingdom

The Madrid Protocol has been implemented in the United Kingdom by the Trade Marks (International Registration) Order 1996 (SI 1996/714) and by the Trade Marks (Fees) Rules 1996 (SI 1996/1942) made under s. 54 and ss. 54 and 79 of the Trade Marks Act 1994 respectively.

A United Kingdom application for international registration may designate for territorial extension of protection Contracting Parties to the Madrid Protocol only.

International registration has not received the same degree of interest from United Kingdom trade mark owners as the CTM. In the period April 1996 to March 1997 the International Bureau of WIPO received only 50 international applications from the United Kingdom Patent Office. By contrast in the same period the International Bureau recorded over 2,000 requests for protection in the United Kingdom of international registrations originating in other Contracting Parties, notably Germany.

Who may become a party to the Madrid Agreement or Protocol?

Contracting Parties (Article 14, Rule 1(iii))

The Madrid Agreement is open to States party to the Paris Convention (**A** Article 14(2)(a)).

The Madrid Protocol is similarly open to States party to the Paris Convention (**P** Article 14(1)(a)) but also to intergovernmental organisations where (**P** Article 14(1)(b)):

(a)   at least one member State of the organisation is a party to the Paris Convention; and

(b)   the organisation has a regional office for the purpose of registering marks with effect in the territory of the organisation (provided that such office has not been notified as a common office under **P** Article 9*quater* (see below)).

The European Community is one such intergovernmental organisation. The Organisation Africaine de Propriété Industrielle (OAPI, covering the former French colonies in west and central Africa) might be another but the OAPI has so far shown no interest in joining the Madrid Protocol.

The Benelux is unlikely to qualify as an intergovernmental organisation for reasons stated below.

The term 'Contracting Party' is defined in the Common Regulations to include any country party to the Madrid Agreement or any State or intergovernmental organisation party to the Madrid Protocol (Rule 1(iii)).

Common office of several States (Article 9quater)
Article 9*quater* provides that where several States are all party to the Madrid Agreement or all party to the Madrid Protocol and have unified their domestic laws on trade marks, they may notify WIPO that a common trade mark office is to be substituted for the national offices of each of them and that the whole of their respective territories is to be regarded as one State for the purposes of the Madrid Agreement or Protocol.

Where such a notification is made under the Madrid Protocol, the common office is not regarded as a regional office of an intergovernmental organisation under **P** Article 14(1)(b). In other words, the respective States are the Contracting Parties to the Protocol and not the organisation under which the common office has been established.

No notification of a common office has been made by any group of States presently party to the Madrid Protocol. The Benelux has made an Article 9*quater* notification under the Madrid Agreement (to which organisations cannot in any event be party) and might be expected to make a similar notification under the Madrid Protocol once its member countries have deposited their instruments of ratification.

Who may obtain international registration?

*The applicant (**A** Articles 1(2) and 2, **P** Article 2(1))*
An application for international registration ('international application') may be made by any national of a Contracting State or of a State member of a Contracting Organisation, or any other natural or legal person domiciled or having a real and effective industrial or commercial establishment in a Contracting State or in the territory of a Contracting Organisation.

Basic registration or basic application for registration in the office of a Contracting Party — the 'office of origin' (**A** Article 1(2) and (3), **P** Article 2(1), Rule 1(viii)–(x) and (xxvi))
A mark for which international registration is sought must be the subject of a prior national or regional registration made by, or an application for registration filed with, the trade mark office of one of the Contracting Parties (the 'office of origin') (**A** Article 1(2), **P** Article 2(1)).

Whereas under the Madrid Agreement an international application can be based only upon a prior national or regional *registration* ('basic registration'), one of the innovations of the Madrid Protocol is that an international application can be based on a prior national or regional registration or *application for registration* ('basic application'). The international application may relate only to goods and services covered by the basic registration or basic application.

An international application may be based on several registrations (under the Madrid Agreement) or on several registrations and/or applications for registration (under the Madrid Protocol) which together cover the goods and services listed in the international application. The basic registrations and/or applications must be in the same ownership and with the same office.

The office of origin depends on which treaty governs the international application (Rule 1(xxvi)) which in turn depends on which Contracting Parties are to be designated (Rule 1(viii)–(x)):

(a)   Where the international application is governed by the Madrid Agreement the office of origin must be (**A** Article 1(3)):

(i)   the office of the country in which the applicant has a real and effective industrial or commercial establishment; or
(ii)   if none, the office of the country in which the applicant has his domicile; or
(iii)   if none, the office of the country of which the applicant is a national;

provided in each case that the country is a party to the Madrid Agreement. The applicant has no discretion as to the office of origin but must follow this so-called 'cascade'.

(b)   Where the international application is governed by the Madrid Protocol the cascade does not apply. The applicant may choose his office of origin which must be one of the following:

(i)   the office of the country of which the applicant is a national, or in which the applicant has a real and effective industrial or commercial establishment (**P** Article 2(1)(i)); or
(ii)   the office of the organisation, if the applicant is a national of a country party to the organisation, or where the applicant is domiciled or has a real and effective industrial or commercial establishment in the territory of the organisation (**P** Article 2(1)(ii));

provided in each case that the country or the organisation is a party to the Madrid Protocol.

(c) Where the international application is governed by both the Madrid Agreement and Protocol the applicant must follow the cascade of the Agreement as there can only be one office of origin. Alternatively the applicant may decide to cancel his designations under the Agreement and proceed under the Protocol where he has a choice of office of origin.

Where the registration resulting from an international application is transferred (see below), the office of a Contracting Party with respect to which the transferee fulfils the conditions (of nationality, domicile or establishment as above) to be the holder of the international registration is called an 'interested office'.

Representation

The applicant for or the holder of an international registration may choose to be represented before the International Bureau (Rule 3(1)(a)). But there is no requirement for representation as there is for non-Community applicants in proceedings before OHIM relating to a CTM (see chapter 2).

The person appointed need not be the same representative the applicant or holder uses before the office of origin or any other interested office. For example, the applicant may need to instruct a local agent because protection of the international mark is refused in one of the designated Contracting Parties. Only one representative may be appointed to act on behalf of the applicant or the holder before the International Bureau (Rule 3(1)(c)).

The address of the representative must be:

(a) in the case of an international application governed by the Madrid Agreement, in a country bound by the Agreement (Rule 3(1)(b)(i));

(b) in the case of an international application governed by the Madrid Protocol, in a country or in the territory of an organisation bound by the Protocol (Rule 3(1)(b)(ii));

(c) in the case of an international application governed by the Madrid Agreement and Protocol, in a country bound by the Agreement or the Protocol, or in the territory of an organisation bound by the Protocol (Rule 3(1)(b)(iii));

(d) in the case of an international registration, in a country bound by the Madrid Agreement or Protocol or both, or in the territory of an organisation bound by the Protocol (Rule 3(1)(iv)).

A representative may be appointed in the international application by inserting his name and address in the appropriate place on the application form. No authorisation to act or power of attorney need be supplied. The same is true where a representative is appointed on the presentation of a subsequent designation or a request for a change to be recorded (for example, a change of ownership or a change of name and address of the holder or a representative), but only if the official form is submitted through the office of origin or an interested office (that is, not directly to the International Bureau) (Rule 3(2)(a)). Otherwise the appointment must be made in a separate communication for which an unofficial form (MM12) is made available by the International Bureau.

Alternatively a representative may be appointed at any time in a separate communication (Rule 3(2)(b)). The communication may be presented to the International Bureau by:

(a) the applicant, holder or representative, in which case it must be signed by the applicant or holder; or

(b) by the office of origin or an interested office (if that office so allows), in which case it must be signed by the applicant or the holder or by the office concerned.

Except in certain cases (for example, notification of renewal) all communications are sent by the International Bureau to a duly appointed representative and not to the applicant or the holder. Similarly the representative may sign communications and carry out other procedural steps in the place of the applicant or holder (Rule 3(5)).

Procedure on international application

Filing through the office of origin (A Article 1(2), P Article 2(2), Article 8(1), Rules 9(1) and 11(7))
An international application must be filed with the office of origin (that is, the office in charge of the basic registration or application) who will transmit it to the International Bureau of WIPO in Geneva (A Article 1(2), P Article 2(2), Rule 9(1)). The office of origin may charge a fee for the handling of international applications (Article 8(1)). The United Kingdom Patent Office charges a submission fee of £40 (Trade Marks (Fees) Rules 1996 (SI 1996/1942)).

If an international application is submitted direct to the International Bureau, it is returned to the sender unconsidered (Rule 11(7)).

Language of the international application (Rule 6(1) and (2))
An international application which is governed by the Madrid Agreement must be in French (Rule 6(1)(a)). That becomes the working language of the application or the international registration resulting from it (Rule 6(2)(a)).

An international application which is governed by the Madrid Protocol, or by the Madrid Agreement and Protocol, may be in French or English (Rule 6(1)(b)). Those become the working languages of the application or the international registration resulting from it (Rule 6(2)(b)). The office of origin may specify that such an international application be either in English or in French (Rule 6(1)(b)). An international application filed through the United Kingdom Patent Office must be in English.

Application form (Article 3(1)–(3), Rule 9(2) and (4)–(7))
An international application must be in the prescribed form (Article 3(1), Rule 9(2)). There are three different application forms depending on whether the application is governed by the Madrid Agreement or Protocol, or both. The form for use in the United Kingdom is Form MM2 reproduced at appendix 7. Application forms must be completed using a typewriter or other machine; handwritten forms are not acceptable to the International Bureau of WIPO (Rule 2(1)(a)).

The international application must contain, inter alia, the name and address of the applicant and of any representative, details of entitlement to file, details of the basic registration or the basic application, details of any Convention priority claimed under Article 4(2), a reproduction of the mark (capable of fitting in an 8 cm × 8 cm box), particulars of any colour claimed, a list of goods and services and a list of Contracting Parties where protection is required (Article 3(1)–(3), Rule 9(4)–(7)).

Priority (Article 4(2))   Priority (under Article 4 of the Paris Convention) may be claimed for the international registration from the application out of which the basic registration resulted or from the basic application. Convention priority may also be claimed from an application filed with an office other than the office of origin (for example, from an earlier application from which the basic application claims priority). In either case the application from which priority is claimed must have been filed in the six-month period prior to the date of the international registration. The applicant need not submit a copy of the earlier application in support of his priority claim.

Specification of goods and services (Article 3(2), Rule 9(4)(a)(xiii))   The goods and services for which international registration of the mark is sought must be grouped in the appropriate Nice Agreement classes. Each group must be preceded by the number of the class and the list must be presented in the Nice Classification order. The words used in the Alphabetical List should be used to describe the goods and services wherever possible.

Designation of Contracting Parties (Articles 3bis and 3ter(1))   The applicant must specify or 'designate' the Contracting Parties in which protection for his mark is requested. All Contracting Parties have declared this to be a requirement under the Madrid Agreement. The requirement is automatic under the Madrid Protocol.

Where the applicant's office of origin is party to the Madrid Agreement only, the applicant may designate Contracting Parties to the Agreement only. If it is party to the Madrid Protocol only, the applicant may designate Contracting Parties to the Protocol only. If it is party to both the Agreement and the Protocol, the applicant may designate Contracting Parties to the Agreement and Protocol.

An applicant cannot designate the Contracting Party whose office is his office of origin.

Declaration of intent to use (Rule 7(2))   An applicant may be required to supply a declaration of intention to use the mark in the territory of a Contracting Party which he has designated for protection. The requirement can only apply in a Contracting Party which is designated under the Madrid Protocol and must be notified by that Party to WIPO. The United Kingdom has made such a notification under Rule 7(2). The declaration of intention to use may be incorporated in the official application form (as is the case for the United Kingdom) or may, at the request of the Contracting Party, need to be filed in a separate document. No Contracting Party has so far requested the separate filing of a declaration of intention to use.

Signature (Rule 9(2)(b))   The international application must be signed by the office of origin (see below). The office of origin may additionally require (or allow) the international application to be signed by the applicant or his representative. A United Kingdom applicant must sign the international application.

Certification and signature by the office of origin (Article 3(1), Rule 9(5)(b), (6)(b) and (7))

Before transmitting an international application to the International Bureau of WIPO the office of origin must check and certify:

(a)   the date of receipt;

(b)   that the applicant named in the international application is the same as the holder of the basic registration or the applicant named in the basic application;

(c)   that the mark in the international application is identical with the mark in the basic registration or basic application;

(d)   that if colours are claimed in the international application, the claim for colour is the same as in the basic registration or basic application;

(e)   that where the international application contains indications that the mark is a three-dimensional mark, a sound mark or a collective, certification or guarantee mark, the same indications appear in the basic registration or basic application;

(f)   that where the international application contains a description in words of the mark, the same description appears in the basic registration or basic application;

(g)   that the goods and services indicated in the international application are covered by the list of goods and services appearing in the basic registration or basic application.

Any discrepancies must be notified to the applicant and corrected before the international application can be forwarded to the International Bureau of WIPO.

Fees (Article 8, Rule 10)
The standard fee structure is the same for both treaties (Article 8(2), Rule 10):

(a)   a basic fee (currently Swiss francs 653 or Swiss francs 903 where the mark is in colour);

(b)   a supplementary fee for each class of goods and services over three (currently Swiss francs 73); and

(c)   a complementary fee in respect of each Contracting Party designated (also Swiss francs 73).

Net annual receipts from basic fees (after deduction of expenses and charges of the International Bureau) are distributed equally between the Contracting Parties (Article 8(4)). The total revenue derived from supplementary and complementary fees is divided amongst the Contracting Parties in proportion to the number of designations made in each of them (Article 8(5) and (6)).

A further innovation of the Madrid Protocol is that a Contracting Party may declare that it wishes to receive an 'individual fee' where it is designated under the Protocol instead of a share in the proceeds of the supplementary and complementary fees. The individual fee declared may not exceed the amount which the Contracting Party's office is entitled to receive from an applicant for a 10-year registration in the register of that office minus the amount of any savings gained from operating the international procedure (**P** Article 8(7), Rule 10(2) and (3)). Eight Contracting Parties to the Madrid Protocol (China, Denmark, Finland,

Iceland, Norway, Sweden, United Kingdom, Switzerland) have so far declared individual fees. The introduction of individual fees substantially increases the cost of international registration for Protocol users. For example, the total amount of the supplementary and complementary fees for an international application in four classes designating four countries under the Madrid Agreement is Swiss francs 365. The total amount of individual fees for an international application in four classes designating, say, Denmark, Finland, Norway and Sweden under the Madrid Protocol is Swiss francs 2,490.

Fees are payable in Swiss francs (Rule 35(1)) in advance of the registration of the mark by the International Bureau (Article 8(2)). Fees may be paid direct to the International Bureau or through the office of origin provided that office agrees to collect and forward such fees (Rule 34(1)). In the case of a United Kingdom applicant fees should be paid direct to the International Bureau (that is, not submitted with the international application) or may be charged to a deposit account held with the United Kingdom Patent Office.

Examination (Article 3(2) and (4), Rules 11–13)
The International Bureau of WIPO examines the international application in order to ascertain whether it meets the applicable requirements (that is, examination is as to formality only). Any irregularities in the international application are communicated both to the applicant or his representative and to the office of origin. Responsibility for remedying the irregularity depends upon its nature.

For example, the office of origin must remedy any defect relating to the applicant's entitlement to file (Rule 11(4)(a)(iii)) while responsibility for supplying a clear reproduction of the mark rests with the applicant (Rule 11(2)(a)). A shortfall in fees paid directly to the International Bureau must be remedied by the applicant (Rule 11(2)(a)). But where fees are paid through the office of origin any missing amounts may be paid by the office of origin or the applicant (Rule 11(3)).

The International Bureau has the final say regarding the correct classification and grouping of goods and services listed in an international application (Article 3(2) and see above). It tries to resolve any disagreement with the office of origin (Rule 12).

Registration, notification and publication (Article 3(4), Rules 14 and 32(1)(a)(i))
If, or when, the international application is in order, the International Bureau registers the mark and sends a certificate to the holder. It also notifies the offices of the designated Contracting Parties of the international registration and informs the office of origin. The international registration is published in the *WIPO Gazette of International Marks*, in French where it results from an application governed exclusively by the Agreement, otherwise in English and French (Rule 6(3)).

Date of the international registration (Article 3(4), Rule 15)
The date of the international registration is normally the date on which the international application was received by the office of origin, provided that the office of origin forwards the international application, and the International Bureau receives it, within two months of its date of receipt by the office of origin. If not, the date of international registration is normally the date on which the International Bureau receives the international application (Article 3(4)).

The date of the international registration may be affected by certain key irregularities (omissions of items such as the date and number of the basic registration or the basic application, a reproduction of the mark or a list of goods and services or designated Contracting Parties) found by the International Bureau to exist in an international application. This is not the case where the irregularities are remedied within two months of receipt of the application by the office of origin. If key irregularities remain outstanding after that two-month period, the international registration bears the date on which the final irregularity is remedied (Rule 15(1)(a)). If key irregularities are not remedied within three months of their notification by the International Bureau, the international application is deemed to be abandoned.

Other irregularities (including those relating to the payment of fees or to the classification of goods and services) do not affect the date of the international registration (Rule 15(1)(b) and (2)). However, such irregularities must be remedied within the time specified by the International Bureau, otherwise the international application is deemed to be abandoned.

Protection of an international registration (Articles 4(1) and 5, Rules 16–18)
From the date of the international registration, each designated Contracting Party must afford the mark the same protection as if it had been filed directly in the office of that Contracting Party. If no refusal of protection is notified to the International Bureau within the prescribed time limit, or if such refusal is subsequently withdrawn, the mark becomes protected in the Contracting Party, as from the date of the international registration, as if the mark had been registered in the office of that Contracting Party (Article 4(1)).

Each designated Contracting Party has the right to refuse protection to an international registration in its territory. But such refusal may only be on the grounds in the Paris Convention (Article 6*quinquies*(B)) which would apply under the legislation of that Contracting Party if the mark had been filed directly with the office of that Contracting Party (Article 5(1)).

The normal time limit for notifying refusal is one year from the date on which the International Bureau notifies the international registration to the designated Contracting Party (Article 5(2)). However, under the Protocol a Contracting Party may declare that the time period for refusal is to be extended to 18 months (**P** Article 5(2)(b)) or even longer where a refusal may result from an opposition, provided that (**P** Article 5(2)(c)):

(a) before the expiry of the 18-month period, the office of the Contracting Party notifies the International Bureau that oppositions may be filed outside the 18-month period; and

(b) notification of refusal based on an opposition is made no later than seven months after the opposition period begins or one month after the end of the opposition period, if earlier.

The United Kingdom has made such a declaration.

An international registration which designates the United Kingdom is examined for the absolute and the relative grounds for refusal in ss. 3 and 5 of the Trade Marks Act 1994 and, if accepted by the Registrar, is advertised in the *Trade Marks*

Journal. It is then open to opposition by third parties within three months of the date of advertisement. Assuming no third-party opposition the mark becomes protected in the United Kingdom as 'a protected international trade mark (UK)' after the three-month opposition period has expired, whether or not the 18-month period for notifying refusal has also expired. Protection is effective from the date of the international registration. 'Actual registration' of the mark for the purposes of the Trade Marks Act 1994 is deemed to be when the mark becomes protected in the United Kingdom (note that the international mark is not entered on the United Kingdom Register), which means, inter alia, that the right to sue for infringement and the five-year period within which the mark must be put to genuine use in the United Kingdom run from the protection and not the effective date of the protected international trade mark (UK) (Articles 9–13, Trade Marks (International Registration) Order 1996 (SI 1996/714)).

Subsequent designation

The protection of an international registration can be extended to further countries by making a 'subsequent designation' (Article 3*ter*(2), Rule 24(1)). That is, new countries can be added to an international registration after it has been obtained.

The Common Regulations enable the holder of an international registration which resulted from an international application governed by the Madrid Agreement to designate Contracting Parties to the Madrid Protocol but not the Agreement, provided that at the time of that designation:

(a)   the Contracting Party whose office is the office of origin; or
(b)   where the international registration has been transferred, a Contracting Party with respect to which the transferee fulfils the conditions to be the holder of an international registration,

is bound by the Madrid Protocol (Rule 24(1)(b)).

The same applies in the converse situation. The holder of an international registration which resulted from an international application governed by the Madrid Protocol can designate Contracting Parties to the Madrid Agreement but not the Protocol, where the Contracting Party whose office is the office of origin or an interested office is, at the time of the designation, bound by the Madrid Agreement. But, where the international application was based on a basic application, the designation of a Contracting Party to the Agreement cannot be made until that basic application has matured to registration (Rule 24(1)(c)).

Where any Contracting Party is designated under the Agreement, the subsequent designation must be presented through the office of origin (or another interested office). The subsequent designation must also be presented through the office of origin of a Contracting Party who has made a declaration to that effect under Rule 7(1). Otherwise a subsequent designation may be presented directly to the International Bureau (Rule 24(2)(a)). A United Kingdom applicant may present his subsequent designation either through the United Kingdom Patent Office or directly to the International Bureau.

The official form for use in making a subsequent designation is Form MM4 reproduced at appendix 8 (Rule 24(2)(b)). The procedure on subsequent designation is similar to that on international application outlined above (and see Rule

24(3)–(9)). The fees payable on a subsequent designation are a basic fee (currently Swiss francs 300) and a complementary fee (currently Swiss francs 73) for each Contracting Party designated. An individual fee may be payable instead of the complementary fee where a Contracting Party who has declared such a fee is designated under the Madrid Protocol (Rule 24(4) and see above).

The fees paid for a subsequent designation last only until the next renewal date of the international registration. Care must therefore be taken over the timing of making a subsequent designation.

Subsequent dealings

An international registration may be transferred (by assignment, testamentary disposition or operation of law) in whole or in part as to goods and services or as to territory, but only to a transferee who is entitled to file international applications as regards the Contracting Parties designated in the international registration (**A** Article 9*bis* and 9*ter*, **P** Article 9). In other words, the transferee must have a real and effective industrial or commercial establishment or domicile in, or be a national of, a Contracting Party or Parties to the Madrid Agreement and/or Protocol as the case may be. The office of the latter Party or Parties is an interested office (which may or may not include the office of origin).

The transfer is effected by recording in the International Register. A request for recording of change of ownership must be in the prescribed form (MM5) (Rule 25(1)(a)(i)) and, where any of the designated Contracting Parties in respect of which a change of ownership is to be recorded was designated under the Madrid Agreement, presented to the International Bureau through the office of origin or another interested office (Rule 25(1)(b)(i)). The latter is also the case where the request is presented by someone other than the holder (transferor), for example, the transferee (Rule 25(1)(b)). Otherwise the request may be presented to the International Bureau by the holder directly or through the office of origin or another interested office, if that office so allows.

The request must contain the number of the international registration being transferred, the name of the holder, the name and address of the transferee, details of the transferee's entitlement to hold the international registration and indications of the goods and services and the designated Contracting Parties to which the transfer relates (Rule 25(2)). The request must be signed by the holder if it is presented directly to the International Bureau. Where the request is presented through an office that office (but not necessarily the holder) must sign it. The office concerned may require or allow the holder to sign the request (Rule 25(1)(c)). A fee of Swiss francs 177 is payable for recording of the transfer.

Any irregularities in the request must be remedied within three months of their notification by the International Bureau, otherwise the request is considered abandoned (Rule 26).

Assuming the request is in order, the change of ownership is recorded by the International Bureau in the International Register. The International Bureau informs the holder, any office through which the request was presented and the designated Contracting Parties for which the international registration is transferred (Rule 27(1)). The change of ownership is published in the *WIPO Gazette of International Marks*.

The office of a designated Contracting Party which is notified of a change of ownership affecting that Contracting Party may declare the transfer ineffective according to its domestic law (Rule 27(4)). A Article 9*ter*(1) particularly mentions the case of a partial transfer where the goods and services transferred are similar to those remaining in the name of the holder. The effect of a declaration by a designated Contracting Party that a change of ownership has no effect is that, with respect to that Contracting Party, the international registration remains in the name of the holder (the transferor).

Dependence, central attack and transformation

Five years' dependency on the national or regional mark (Article 6(3))
For a period of five years from the date of the international registration, the validity of an international registration is dependent on the fate of the basic application, the registration resulting therefrom or the basic registration. The international registration ceases to be effective in all the Contracting Parties in which it had effect if, or to the extent that, the basic application is withdrawn or is the subject of a final decision of rejection, or the registration resulting therefrom or the basic registration lapses or is renounced, or is the subject of a final decision of revocation, cancellation or invalidation either within the five-year period or as a result of an action commenced within that period (Article 6(3)).

Note that it is irrelevant whether the basic application, the registration resulting therefrom or the basic registration is lost voluntarily, through a trade mark office decision or through a court order. Equally it is irrelevant that the grounds or the circumstances leading to the refusal or cancellation are unique to the legislation of the Contracting Party whose office is the office of origin. Moreover, the dependence is unaffected by any change of ownership of the international registration.

Procedure on cessation of effect of the basic application, the registration resulting therefrom or the basic registration (Article 6(4), Rule 22)
The office of origin must notify the International Bureau if the basic application, the registration resulting therefrom or the basic registration ceases to have effect during the five-year period of dependency. It must also inform the International Bureau of any action commenced within the five-year period of dependency which might result in the basic application, the registration resulting therefrom or the basic registration ceasing to have effect after the expiry of that period. Once a final decision is taken in the action the office of origin must inform the International Bureau of the result. The office of origin must, where appropriate, request the International Bureau to cancel the international registration to the extent applicable.

The International Bureau records any notification in the International Register and sends copies of the notification to the holder and to the offices of the designated Contracting Parties. It also complies with any request by the office of origin to cancel the international registration in whole or in part and notifies the holder and the designated Contracting Parties accordingly. Cancellations and notifications of pending actions are published in the *WIPO Gazette of International Marks* (Rule 32(1)(a)(viii) and (xi)).

Central attack and independence (Article 6(2))
The possibility of destroying an international registration in the first five years through a single action against the basic mark in the Contracting Party whose office is the office of origin is known as 'central attack'. It is a powerful weapon in the hands of the owner of a conflicting mark in several designated Contracting Parties.

After the initial five years, the international registration becomes independent of the basic application, the registration resulting therefrom or the basic registration (Article 6(2)). The validity of the international registration then depends on the domestic trade mark law of each of the Contracting Parties in which it has effect. Cancellation of the international mark for one of those Contracting Parties does not automatically lead to its cancellation for the other Contracting Parties (with the obvious exception of the Benelux countries).

*Transformation (**P** Article 9quinquies)*
The dangers of central attack are exacerbated under the Madrid Protocol where an international application can be based on an application for registration filed with the office of origin. An important innovation of the Madrid Protocol is that an international registration which is cancelled by the International Bureau at the request of the office of origin (see above) can be transformed into a series of national or regional trade mark applications, with a filing date corresponding to the date of the international registration, and enjoying the same priority under the Paris Convention as claimed by the international registration.

An application for transformation must be filed with the offices of the designated Contracting Parties within three months of the date of cancellation of the international registration and can only be made in respect of goods and services covered by the international registration.

Transformation is not available under the Madrid Agreement. Moreover, it is not available under the Madrid Protocol where the international registration is cancelled by the International Bureau at the request of the holder.

A transformation application made to the United Kingdom Trade Marks Registry must be on Form TM3 and costs £100. The procedure is governed by Articles 19 and 20 of the Trade Marks (International Registration) Order 1996 (SI 1966/714).

Replacement

Where a mark which is the subject of an international registration having effect in a Contracting Party is already registered in the office of that Contracting Party, in the name of the same holder and for the same goods and services, the international registration is deemed to replace the national or regional registration (note, not the 'home' registration). Such replacement is without prejudice to any rights acquired by virtue of the earlier national or regional registration (Article 4*bis*(1)).

One of the main advantages of replacement is that it obviates the need for renewal of concurrent national or regional registrations. However, for the first five years of the international registration it is advisable to maintain a concurrent national or regional registration because of dependency and central attack.

Replacement is automatic but the holder may require the office in whose register the national or regional mark is registered to take note in its register of the international registration (Article 4*bis*(2)). Where the office of a designated

Contracting Party has taken note in its register, following a request made by the holder with that office, that a national or regional registration has been replaced by an international registration, that office must notify the International Bureau accordingly. The International Bureau records the indications so notified in the International Register and informs the holder accordingly (Rule 21). The notified indications are published in the *WIPO Gazette of International Marks.*

In the United Kingdom replacement is governed by Article 21 of the Trade Marks (International Registration) Order 1966 (SI 1996/714). Rights in the protected international trade mark (UK) run from the date of registration (that is, the date of application) of the United Kingdom registered trade mark taking into account any priorities claimed in respect of that registered trade mark.

Duration and renewal

An international registration lasts initially for a period of 10 years (Article 6(1)) and needs renewing every 10 years thereafter (Article 7(1)). Renewal fees comprise a basic fee (currently 653 Swiss francs), a supplementary fee for each class of goods and services over three (currently 73 Swiss francs) and a complementary fee for each Contracting Party designated (again 73 Swiss francs) or, to the extent that the international registration is governed by the Madrid Protocol and the designated Contracting Parties have declared individual fees, the basic fee and those individual fees (Article 7(1)).

Technically speaking, under the Madrid Agreement an international registration lasts for an initial period of 20 years and is renewable for periods of 20 years (**A** Articles 6(1) and 7(1)). However under the Common Regulations the fees payable for an international application governed by the Agreement must be paid in two instalments of 10 years each and the second instalment is treated as a renewal fee (Rule 10(1)). Subsequent renewals may only be for 10 years (Rule 30(4)).

Renewals are effected by the International Bureau. A request for renewal (no official form is prescribed but an unofficial form is sent by the International Bureau to the holder or his representative before the renewal date) accompanied by the renewal fees should be sent direct to the International Bureau or via the office of origin or another interested office which has agreed to handle such renewals. The United Kingdom Patent Office charges a handling fee of £20 for renewals (Trade Marks (Fees) Rules 1996 (SI 1996/1942)).

The International Bureau records the renewal in the International Register, notifies the designated Contracting Parties of the renewal and sends a renewal certificate to the holder (Rule 31(1) and (3)). It also publishes the renewal in the *WIPO Gazette of International Marks* (Rule 32(1)(a)(iv)).

The safeguard clause

The fact that Contracting Parties can be members of both the Madrid Agreement and Protocol raises the question of which treaty is binding between them. The position is governed by Article 9*sexies*(1) of the Madrid Protocol to the effect that where, with regard to a given international application or registration, the office of origin is the office of a State party to both the Madrid Agreement and Protocol, that international application or registration is, with respect to any other State also party to the Madrid Agreement and Protocol, governed exclusively by the Agreement.

Linking the CTM to Madrid

It has been stated that one of the objectives of the Madrid Protocol was to provide mechanisms to link the Madrid system to the CTM. That objective was achieved by **P** Article 14(1)(b) (in conjunction with **P** Article 2(4)), which sets out two preconditions for an organisation to become party to the Madrid Protocol:

(a)   at least one of the member States of the organisation is a party to the Paris Convention; and

(b)   the organisation has a regional office for the purpose of registering marks with effect in the territory in which the constituting treaty of that organisation applies.

Since 1 April 1996 the European Community has satisfied both these conditions. (All the Member States are party to the Paris Convention and OHIM opened its doors for business on 1 April 1996.) In July 1996, the Commission presented proposals for a Council Decision approving the accession of the European Community to the Madrid Protocol (COM(96) 367 final of 22 July 1996) and for a Council Regulation modifying the CTMR (COM(96) 372 final of 24 July 1996) in order to give effect to such accession. The Commission notes, in particular, that:

(a)   the Madrid Agreement is popular with the nine Member States (Austria, Benelux, France, Germany, Italy, Portugal and Spain) who are party to the Agreement;

(b)   the establishment of a link between the CTM system and the Madrid system facilitates trade between the European Community and third countries; and

(c)   the failure to establish such a link is detrimental to the CTM system because trade mark owners must continue to use national trade marks to obtain protection in third countries.

The Commission's Proposals have been endorsed by the Economic and Social Committee ([1997] OJ C 89/6) and the Legal Affairs Committee of the European Parliament (European Parliament Press Release, 19 March 1997) and are expected to be approved by the Council in late 1997. On that timetable, the European Community will accede to the Madrid Protocol in January 1998, with effect from April 1998.

Accession of the European Community to the Madrid Protocol (COM(96) 367 final of 27 July 1996)
The Commission proposes that the European Community accedes to the Madrid Protocol under Article 235 of the Treaty (that is, the same legal basis as for the CTMR). Only one declaration will be made — under Article 8(7) of the Protocol — for an individual fee in connection with designation of, and renewal of protection in, the European Community, in an amount slightly less than the basic and class fees charged for the application and registration, and the renewal of a CTM respectively.

No declaration will be made to extend the normal 12-month period allowed by **P** Article 5(2)(a) for notifying the refusal of protection to an international mark. OHIM considers that it is able to communicate any provisional refusal of protection before the expiry of the time limit of one year from the date on which the notification of extension to the European Community has been sent to OHIM by the International Bureau. Furthermore since there will be no declaration under **P** Article 14(5), holders of existing international registrations will be able subsequently to extend protection for their marks to the European Community. This means that international registrations effected under the Madrid Agreement can be extended to the European Community provided that the holder is a national of, or domiciled or established in, a State which has also become a party to the Madrid Protocol.

Another important consequence of the accession is that trade mark owners in Member States which have not yet ratified the Madrid Protocol will be able to take advantage of the Protocol through filing with OHIM an application for the registration of a CTM.

A Regulation modifying the CTMR (COM(96) 372 final of 24 July 1996)

Since an international registration designating the European Community under the Madrid Protocol is in principle equivalent to a CTM, the draft measures for giving effect to the accession are proposed as a new Title to the CTMR — Title XIII (the existing Title XIII (final provisions) becomes Title XIV). Likewise the IR, FR and Boards of Appeal Regulation would apply in principle *mutatis mutandis* to international registrations (Draft Article 140 CTMR).

The proposed new Title XIII deals first with the filing of international applications through OHIM as the office of origin (that is, where the basic application or basic registration is in respect of a CTM). The deemed date of receipt of an international application based on a CTM may be deferred until the outcome of the CTM application is known. An international application may be in any of the languages of the Madrid Protocol provided that it is one of the languages of OHIM (to cope with a possible expansion in the number of Protocol languages). The language of the international application is the language of proceedings before OHIM. A subsequent designation under **P** Article 3*ter*(2) may be made via OHIM and must be in the language of the international application. International fees are payable directly to the International Bureau (draft Articles 141–5 CTMR).

The proposed new Title then goes on to deal with the effects of an international registration designating the European Community in terms of **P** Article 4(1)(a) (see above). OHIM intends to publish in the *Community Trade Marks Bulletin* limited particulars of international registrations designating the European Community (the date of the international registration or the date of the subsequent designation, the international registration number and the date of publication of the international registration in the *WIPO Gazette of International Marks*). OHIM will also publish the fact that no refusal of protection for an international registration designating the European Community has been notified at the expiry of the relevant 12–month period, or that refusal has been withdrawn. The right to sue for infringement of an international registration designating the European Community runs from the date of the second publication; a claim for damages from the first publication (Draft Articles 146 and 147 CTMR).

The applicant for or the holder of an international registration designating the European Community may claim, in respect of his mark, the seniority of earlier trade marks which are registered or are having effect under the Madrid Agreement or Protocol in one or more Member States (including the Benelux). Seniority may be claimed in the international application or directly before OHIM. Note that the seniority of an earlier international mark includes the rights in a national or regional trade mark that has been replaced by the international mark under **A/P** Article 4*bis* (Draft Article 148 CTMR).

An international registration designating the European Community is subject to the same search procedure and examination on absolute grounds as a CTM application. However, there is a nine-month opposition period for international registrations designating the European Community, running from the date of publication of the international registration in the *Community Trade Marks Bulletin* (the first publication above). The reason for the nine-month opposition period is to ensure timely notification to OHIM of any refusal of protection. Where a final decision to refuse protection to an international registration is taken, or protection in respect of the European Community is renounced by the holder of an international registration in consequence of an opposition, OHIM refunds to the holder part of the individual fee (draft Articles 149–51 CTMR).

OHIM will, at the request of the holder, enter a notice in the Register of CTMs that a CTM has been replaced by an international registration designating the European Community (draft Article 152 CTMR). An international trade mark having effect in the Community may be revoked under Article 50 of the CTMR or declared invalid on absolute grounds under Article 51 of the CTMR. No provision appears to have been made for relative invalidity under Article 52 of the CTMR (draft Article 153 CTMR).

Where an international registration designating the European Community is refused protection, or ceases to have effect, it may be converted into national trade mark applications in Member States (including the Benelux), retaining for that purpose the date of the international registration and any priority or seniority claimed for the international registration. The proposed new Title further provides for the holder of the international registration to 'opt back' into the Madrid system by converting his international registration into subsequent designations in Member States (depending on whether the holder is entitled to make designations under the Madrid Protocol only or the Madrid Agreement and the Protocol). However, any such opting back requires amendment of the Madrid Protocol, the Madrid Agreement or the Common Regulations (draft Article 154 CTMR).

The use requirements for an international registration designating the European Community are the same as for a CTM. The five-year period within which the international mark must be put to use in the Community runs from the date of publication of the fact that there has been no notification of refusal or that refusal has been withdrawn (the second publication above) (draft Article 155 CTMR).

In accordance with **P** Article 9*quinquies* the proposed new Title deals with the transformation of an international registration designating the European Community into a CTM application following a successful 'central attack' on the basic application, the registration resulting therefrom or the basic registration. Transformation needs to be differentiated from conversion described above (draft Article 156 CTMR).

Finally, the language in which an international application was filed (at present necessarily either English or French) designating the European Community is the language of proceedings where the holder of the international registration is the sole party to proceedings before OHIM. A second language must be specified in the international application which must be one of the languages of OHIM. The second language may become the language of opposition, revocation or invalidity proceedings before OHIM. If a second language is not specified in the international application, the second language will be the language into which the International Bureau translated the international application (again, at present, necessarily English or French). The same language rules apply where the European Community is designated through a request for subsequent territorial protection pursuant to **P** Article 3*ter*(2) (draft Article 157 CTMR).

Chapter Eleven
Community Collective Marks

What is a Community collective mark?

The CTMR follows Article 7*bis* of the Paris Convention in providing for the filing and protection of collective marks. A Community collective mark is defined by Article 64(1) of the CTMR as:

> a Community trade mark which is described as such when the mark is applied for and is capable of distinguishing the goods or services of the members of the association which is the proprietor of the mark from those of other undertakings.

The key feature of a Community collective mark is that it is a mark belonging to an association the purpose of which is to distinguish the goods or services of the members of that association from the goods or services of other undertakings.

Although a Community collective mark may imply a guarantee to the consumer that goods or services bearing the mark derive from a certain country or region, or possess certain common characteristics or qualities, there is no requirement for a guarantee function as such. In consequence Article 64(1) of the CTMR contains no prohibition on the proprietor of a Community collective mark using the mark himself.

The CTMR neither provides for nor recognises certification marks (compare Article 15 of the Directive).

The definition of a Community collective mark is considered to be met where the association which is the proprietor of the mark consists of several member associations and it is the members of those member associations who use the mark to distinguish their goods or services (Joint statements by the Council and the Commission of the European Communities entered in the minutes of the Council meeting, at which the Regulation on the Community Trade Mark is adopted on 20 December 1993, OHIM OJ 5/96, p. 619).

Who may apply for a Community collective mark?

A Community collective mark may be applied for by (Article 64(1) CTMR):

> Associations of manufacturers, producers, suppliers of services, or traders which, under the terms of the law governing them, have the capacity in their own name

to have rights and obligations of all kinds, to make contracts or accomplish other legal acts and to sue and be sued, as well as legal persons governed by public law.

The essential criteria are that the applicant is an *association*, with *legal personality*. Some unincorporated bodies will not qualify to be the holders of Community collective marks.

Article 7*bis* of the Paris Convention imposes an obligation on its member States 'to accept for filing and to protect collective marks belonging to associations . . . even if such associations do not possess an industrial or commercial establishment [anywhere in the world]'. Nevertheless, since a Community collective mark is a Community trade mark (CTM) described as a Community collective mark when the conditions of Article 64(1) of the CTMR apply, the applicant must satisfy the entitlement criteria of Article 5 of the CTMR by having nationality, domicile or establishment in the Community or in a country party to the Paris Convention or the World Trade Organisation (see chapter 2).

Application of the CTMR and the IR to Community collective marks

Article 64(3) of the CTMR states that the provisions of the CTMR apply to Community collective marks subject to Articles 65 to 72 inclusive. In the same manner, Rule 42 of the IR states that the provisions of the IR apply to Community collective marks subject to Rule 43.

This chapter describes only the additional provisions in the CTMR and the IR which relate to Community collective marks.

Registrability of a Community collective mark

Application for a Community collective mark (Rule 1(1)(i) IR)
A CTM application must state if it is for a Community collective mark (Rule 1(1)(i) IR). The applicant indicates that a Community collective mark is applied for by checking box 68 on the OHIM application form.

Grounds for refusal (Articles 64(1) and (2) and 66 CTMR)
A Community collective mark must be capable of distinguishing the goods or services of the association, rather than any one undertaking, from the goods or services of other undertakings. The absolute ground for refusal in Article 7(1)(a) of the CTMR must be read subject to the definition of a Community collective mark in Article 64(1) of the CTMR (Article 66(1) CTMR).

As an exception to the absolute ground for refusal in Article 7(1)(c) of the CTMR, a sign which serves in trade to designate the geographical origin of goods or services may be registered as a Community collective mark. However, the proprietor is not then entitled to prevent third parties from using the sign in the course of trade, provided that such use is in accordance with honest practices in industrial or commercial matters. In particular, other traders are free to use, within those limits, a geographical name which is the subject of a Community collective mark (Article 64(2) CTMR). Furthermore, any person whose goods or services originate in the geographical area concerned must be allowed to become a member of the association which owns the Community collective mark (Article 65(2) CTMR and see below).

In addition to the absolute grounds for refusal listed in Article 7(1) of the CTMR, a Community collective mark must be refused registration if it is liable to mislead the public as regards the character or the significance of the mark, in particular, if the public are likely to take the mark as something other than a collective mark (Article 66(2) CTMR). The following example is given:

> The Council and the Commission consider that a collective mark which is available for use only by members of an association which owns the mark is liable to mislead within the meaning of Article 66(2) if it gives the impression that it is available for use by anyone who is able to meet certain objective standards (Joint statements by the Council and the Commission of the European Communities entered in the minutes of the Council meeting, at which the Regulation on the Community Trade Mark is adopted on 20 December 1993, OHIM OJ 5/96, p. 619).

An objection under Article 66(2) of the CTMR may be overcome by amending the applicant's regulations governing the use of the mark (Article 66(3) CTMR and see below).

An application for a Community collective mark must also be refused if (Article 66(1) CTMR):

(a)   the applicant fails to meet the entitlement conditions of Articles 5 and 64(1) of the CTMR;

(b)   regulations governing use of the mark are not submitted by the applicant to OHIM in accordance with Article 65 of the CTMR and Rule 43 IR (see below); or

(c)   the regulations governing use of the mark are contrary to public policy or to accepted principles of morality. The OHIM Examination Guidelines state that, for example, rules which discriminate on the grounds of sex, creed or race could be unacceptable (Guideline 11.5.2, OHIM OJ 9/96, p. 1334). Again, amendment of the regulations may overcome an objection on this ground (Article 66(3) CTMR).

Regulations governing use of the Community collective mark (Article 65 CTMR, Rule 43 IR)

Regulations governing use must be filed with the application for a Community collective mark or submitted to OHIM within two months of the filing of that application (Article 65(1) CTMR, Rule 43(1) IR). The two-month period for filing the regulations is extendible in accordance with Rule 71(1) of the IR. The regulations must specify (Article 65(2) CTMR and Rule 43(2) IR):

(a)   the name of the applicant and his office address;

(b)   the object of the association or the object for which the legal person governed by public law is constituted;

(c)   the bodies authorised to represent the association or the said legal person;

(d)   the conditions for membership;

(e)   the persons authorised to use the mark;

(f)   where appropriate, the conditions governing use of the mark, including sanctions;

(g)   where the geographical origin of goods or services is the subject of the application for a Community collective mark, an authorisation that any person whose goods or services originate in the geographical area concerned may become a member of the association.

Observations (Article 67)

Observations pursuant to Article 41 of the CTMR may be submitted on the additional grounds for refusal of an application for a Community collective mark mentioned above.

Publication (Rule 12(j) IR)

The publication of the CTM application in the *Community Trade Marks Bulletin* must contain a statement that the application is for a Community collective mark. The number code (551) has been allocated to this item (see chapter 3).

Fees (Article 2(3), (4), (9) and (10) FR)

The basic fee for an application for a Community collective mark is ECU 1,675. A class fee of ECU 400 is payable for each class of goods and services over three in the application.

The basic fee for the registration of a Community collective mark is ECU 2,200. A class fee of ECU 400 is payable for each class of goods and services over three in the registration.

Registration (Rule 84(2)(m) IR)

An indication that the mark is a Community collective mark must be entered in the Register of CTMs.

Maintenance of a Community collective mark

Renewal (Article 2(14) and (15) FR)

The fees payable on the renewal of a Community collective mark are a basic fee of ECU 5,000 and a class fee of ECU 1,000 for each class of goods and services exceeding three.

Use (Article 68 CTMR)

Use of a Community collective mark by any person with authority to use it satisfies the use requirements of the CTMR, provided that the other conditions in the CTMR regarding use of a CTM are met.

Amendment to the regulations (Article 69 CTMR)

Any amendment to the regulations governing use of a Community collective mark must be submitted to OHIM (Article 69(1) CTMR). The amendment cannot be recorded in the Register of CTMs if the amended regulations (Article 69(2) CTMR):

(a)   no longer comply with the requirements of Article 65(2) of the CTMR (which requires the regulations to specify the persons authorised to use the mark, the conditions of membership and, where appropriate, the conditions of use of the mark including sanctions, and, where appropriate, to authorise third parties whose goods or services originate in the geographical area concerned to become members of the proprietor association); or

(b)   involve a ground for refusal of a Community collective mark as mentioned above.

Amendments to the regulations governing use of a Community collective mark are subject to the observation procedure in Article 41 of the CTMR as amended by Article 67 of the CTMR (Article 69(3) CTMR). Presumably such amendments are published in the *Community Trade Marks Bulletin* although there appears to be no express provision for this in the CTMR or the IR.

Revocation (Article 71 CTMR)
In addition to the grounds for revocation of a CTM in Article 50 of the CTMR, a Community collective mark may be revoked in proceedings before OHIM or on the basis of a counterclaim in infringement proceedings, if:

(a)   the proprietor does not take reasonable steps to prevent the mark being used in a manner incompatible with any conditions of use in the regulations (taking into account any amendments entered in the Register of CTMs);

(b)   the proprietor has used the mark in a way which renders it liable to mislead the public as regards the character or the significance of the mark, in particular, if it is likely to be taken to be something other than a collective mark; or

(c)   an amendment of the regulations governing use has been entered in the Register in breach of Article 69(2) of the CTMR (see above), unless the proprietor of the mark by further amending the regulations complies with the requirements of that paragraph.

Invalidity (Article 72)
Apart from the grounds for invalidity of a CTM in Articles 51 and 52 of the CTMR, a Community collective mark may be declared invalid in proceedings before OHIM or on the basis of a counterclaim in infringement proceedings, if the mark was registered in breach of the grounds for refusal in Article 66 of the CTMR (see above), unless the proprietor of the mark, by amending the regulations governing use, overcomes those grounds.

Infringement

A person with authority to use a Community collective mark has the rights conferred on a licensee of a CTM by Article 22(3) and (4) of the CTMR (Article 70(1) CTMR). Subject to contract and the proprietor's consent, an authorised user can bring proceedings for infringement of a Community collective mark. If his authority is exclusive, the authorised user may bring such proceedings if the proprietor, after formal notice, does not himself bring infringement proceedings within an appropriate period. An authorised user can intervene in infringement proceedings brought by the proprietor in order to claim compensation for damage suffered by him.

The proprietor of a Community collective mark is entitled to claim compensation on behalf of persons who have authority to use the mark where those persons have sustained damage in consequence of unauthorised use (Article 70(2) CTMR).

Appendix 1
List of Contracting Parties to the Paris Convention for the Protection of Industrial Property (1883)

At 24 October 1997 — 143 States.

Albania
Algeria
Argentina
Armenia
Australia
Austria
Azerbaijan
Bahamas
Bahrain
Bangladesh
Barbados
Belarus
Belgium
Benin
Bolivia
Bosnia and Herzegovina
Brazil
Bulgaria
Burkina Faso
Burundi
Cameroon
Canada
Central African Republic
Chad
Chile
China
Colombia
Congo
Costa Rica

Côte d'Ivoire
Croatia
Cuba
Cyprus
Czech Republic
Democratic People's Republic of Korea
Democratic Republic of the Congo
Denmark
Dominican Republic
Egypt
El Salvador
Equatorial Guinea
Estonia
Finland
France
Gabon
Gambia
Georgia
Germany
Ghana
Greece
Guinea
Guinea-Bissau
Guyana
Haiti
Holy See
Honduras
Hungary

Iceland
Indonesia
Iran (Islamic Republic of)
Iraq
Ireland
Israel
Italy
Japan
Jordan
Kazakstan
Kenya
Kyrgyzstan
Latvia
Lebanon
Lesotho
Liberia
Libya
Liechtenstein
Lithuania
Luxembourg
Madagascar
Malawi
Malaysia
Mali
Malta
Mauritania
Mauritius
Mexico
Monaco
Mongolia
Morocco
Netherlands
New Zealand
Nicaragua
Niger
Nigeria
Norway
Panama
Paraguay
Peru
Philippines
Poland
Portugal
Republic of Korea

Republic of Moldova
Romania
Russian Federation
Rwanda
Saint Kitts and Nevis
Saint Lucia
Saint Vincent and the Grenadines
San Marino
Senegal
Sierra Leone
Singapore
Slovakia
Slovenia
South Africa
Spain
Sri Lanka
Sudan
Suriname
Swaziland
Sweden
Switzerland
Syria
Tajikistan
The former Yugoslav Republic of
  Macedonia
Togo
Trinidad and Tobago
Tunisia
Turkey
Turkmenistan
Uganda
Ukraine
United Arab Emirates
United Kingdom
United Republic of Tanzania
United States of America
Uruguay
Uzbekistan
Venezuela
Viet Nam
Yugoslavia
Zambia
Zimbabwe

Appendix 2
List of Members of the World Trade Organisation

At 1 November 1997 — 132 members.

Angola
Antigua and Barbuda
Argentina
Australia
Austria
Bahrain
Bangladesh
Barbados
Belgium
Belize
Benin
Bolivia
Botswana
Brazil
Brunei Darussalam
Bulgaria
Burkina Faso
Burundi
Cameroon
Canada
Central African Republic
Chad
Chile
Colombia
Congo
Costa Rica
Côte d'Ivoire
Cuba
Cyprus
Czech Republic
Democratic Republic of the Congo

Denmark
Djibouti
Dominica
Dominican Republic
Ecuador
Egypt
El Salvador
European Communities
Fiji
Finland
France
Gabon
Gambia
Germany
Ghana
Greece
Grenada
Guatemala
Guinea Bissau
Guinea
Guyana
Haiti
Honduras
Hong Kong, China
Hungary
Iceland
India
Indonesia
Ireland
Israel
Italy

Jamaica
Japan
Kenya
Korea
Kuwait
Lesotho
Liechtenstein
Luxembourg
Macau
Madagascar
Malawi
Malaysia
Maldives
Mali
Malta
Mauritania
Mauritius
Mexico
Mongolia
Morocco
Mozambique
Myanmar
Namibia
Netherlands — for the Kingdom in
   Europe and for the Netherlands
   Antilles
New Zealand
Nicaragua
Niger
Nigeria
Norway
Pakistan
Panama
Papua New Guinea
Paraguay
Peru

Philippines
Poland
Portugal
Qatar
Romania
Rwanda
Saint Kitts and Nevis
Saint Lucia
Saint Vincent and the Grenadines
Senegal
Sierra Leone
Singapore
Slovak Republic
Slovenia
Solomon Islands
South Africa
Spain
Sri Lanka
Suriname
Swaziland
Sweden
Switzerland
Tanzania
Thailand
Togo
Trinidad and Tobago
Tunisia
Turkey
Uganda
United Arab Emirates
United Kingdom
United States
Uruguay
Venezuela
Zambia
Zimbabwe

Appendix 3
List of Contracting Parties to the Madrid Agreement Concerning the International Registration of Marks (1891)

At 1 November 1997 — 47 States.

States whose names appear in italics are party also to the Madrid Protocol.

Albania
Algeria
Armenia
Austria
Azerbaijan
Belarus
Belgium
Bosnia and Herzegovina
Bulgaria
China
Croatia
Cuba
Czech Republic
Democratic People's Republic of Korea
Egypt
France
Germany
Hungary
Italy
Kazakstan
Kyrgyzstan
Latvia
Liberia
Liechtenstein

Luxembourg
Monaco
Mongolia
Morocco
Netherlands
Poland
Portugal
Republic of Moldova
Romania
Russian Federation
San Marino
Sierra Leone
Slovakia
Slovenia
Spain
Sudan
Switzerland
Tajikistan
The former Yugoslav Republic of Macedonia
Ukraine
Uzbekistan
Viet Nam
Yugoslavia

Appendix 4
List of Contracting Parties to the Protocol Relating to the Madrid Agreement Concerning the International Registration of Marks (1989)

At 1 November 1997 — 22 States.

States whose names appear in italics are party also to the Madrid Agreement.

China
Cuba
Czech Republic
*Democratic People's Republic
 of Korea*
Denmark
Finland
France
Germany
Hungary
Iceland
Lithuania

Monaco
Norway
Poland
Portugal
Republic of Moldova
Russian Federation
Slovakia
Spain
Sweden
Switzerland
United Kingdom

Appendix 5
Community Trade Mark Application Form

OHIM-form
1.1 FN   Office for Harmonisation
in the Internal Market

Avenida de Aguilera, 20
E-03080 Alicante
Tel. +34-6-5 13 91 00
Fax +34-6-5 13 13 44

**Application
for a Community Trade Mark**

	For receiving office	Date of receipt	Number of pages	Applicant's/Representative's reference number
This area is reserved - for receiving office (if member state or the Benelux Office) - for OHIM	For receiving office			
	For OHIM			

Language of application

[X]	1 *Indicate one of the following languages*	First language	1 [ ] ES [ ] DA [ ] DE [ ] EL [ ] EN [ ] FR [ ] IT [ ] NL [ ] PT [ ] FI [ ] SV
	2 *Indicate one of the following languages which must be different from the first*	Second language	2 [ ] ES [ ] DE [ ] EN [ ] FR [ ] IT

Applicant

3 *If ID number is given, no other information except the name relating to applicant need be given unless there are changes as compared to information supplied under ID number; if necessary give the complete address on address page*

3 [ ] given _____

4 [ ] not given, complete address page

5 Name for verification _____

Representative

4 *Check this box if a representative has been appointed*

Representative   6 [ ] appointed

7 *If ID number is given, no other information except the name relating to representative need be given unless there are changes as compared to information supplied under ID number; if necessary give the complete address on address page*

ID number of representative   7 [ ] given _____

8 [ ] not given, complete address page

Name for verification   9 _____

ID number of authorisation   10 [ ] given _____

11 *Check one of these boxes*   Authorisation   11 [ ] attached   [ ] to follow

Fees

12 *For fees see current table of fees*

Basic filing fee   12 _____ ECU

Class fee for each class exceeding three   13 [classes exceeding three] X _____ class fee = _____ ECU

Total of fees   14 _____ ECU

15 *If payment is to be withdrawn from account with OHIM indicate account number*

Payment of fees   15 [ ] to be withdrawn from account of applicant/ representative with OHIM _____

16 *If payment is remitted indicate account and date of remittance*   16 [ ] remitted to account of OHIM _____

17 [ ] cheque attached   [ ] payment will be made later

Signature

18 *Date optional*   Signature and date   18 _____

19 *Optional; if application is made by an employee of the applicant the indication of the name is mandatory*   Name of person signing   19 _____

20 [ ] application made by employee of applicant

Employee authorisation   21 [ ] attached   [ ] to follow

ID number of authorisation   22 [ ] given   1.1

OHIM-Form
1 2 EN

Application for a Community Trade Mark

Addresses of applicant(s)

23 *Indicate one*	**Applicant**	23 ☐ Legal person	☐ Natural person

The information on this page need only be given either if ID number is not given or, if there are changes as compared to information supplied under ID number

Name of legal person	24
Nature of legal person	25
State where legal entity has its seat	26
Surname	27
First name	28
Street and house number or equivalent	29
City and postal code where available	30
Country	31

32 *If different from above, such as P.O.Box, city and postal code*

Postal address	32
Telephone number/s	33
Telefax number/s	34
Electronic mail ID	35
Other information	36
Nationality	37

Multiple applicants

38 *Where there is more than one applicant check the box and indicate on attachment the required information for all additional applicants; absent any other information, the name and address of the applicant indicated on the form will be used as an address for correspondence with regard to all applicants*

Multiple applicants	38 ☐

39 *If an employee of a legal person having economic connections with the applicant check this box and attach details of name, address etc.*

Economic connections	39 ☐

12

OHIM-Form
1.3 EN

Application for a Community Trade Mark

Addresses of representative(s)

40 Indicate one, but only if representative is appointed

Representative   40 ☐ Association of representatives   ☐ Natural person

The information on this page need only be given either if ID number is not given or, if there are changes as compared to information supplied under ID number

41	Name of association	
42	Surname	
43	First name	
44	Street and house number or equivalent	
45	City and postal code where available	
46	Country	

47 If different from above, such as P.O.Box, city and postal code

47 Postal address

44 Telephone number/s

49 Telefax number/s

50 Electronic mail ID

51 Other information

52 Check one of these boxes

Nature of representative   52 ☐ Legal practitioner   ☐ Professional representative

53 Indicate number on the list of professional representatives

53 Number on the list of professional representatives

Multiple representatives

54 Where there is more than one representative, check the box and indicate on attachment the required information for all additional representatives; absent any other information, the name and address of the representative indicated on the form will be used as an address for correspondance with regard to all representatives

Multiple representatives   54 ☐

13

Application for a Community Trade Mark

Representation of the mark

Type of mark

55 [ ] word mark

Representation of the word mark   54

52 *Representation of mark on separate sheet no larger than A4*

57 [ ] figurative mark

58 [ ] three-dimensional

59 *If other mark state what type*

59 [ ] other

Specification of the other type of mark 60

61 *Check this box if colour is claimed and*

Colour   61 [ ] claimed

62 *Indicate the colours making up the mark*

Indication of colours   62

63 *Optional*

Translation into second language   63 [ ] attached   [ ] to follow

64 *Optional*

Description of the mark   64

65 *Optional*

Translation into second language   65 [ ] attached   [ ] to follow

66 *Statement as to the element(s) of the mark in respect of which no exclusive rights are claimed (disclaimer) (optional)*

Statement (disclaimer)   66

67 *Optional*

Translation into second language   67 [ ] attached   [ ] to follow

Collective mark   68 [ ] collective mark

Regulations   69 [ ] attached   [ ] to follow

14

OHIM-Form
1.5 EN

Application for a Community Trade Mark

List of goods and services

70 Goods/services should preferably be grouped in the numerical order of the classification (Nice Classification), indicating the number of the class, and preferably using the terminology of the Nice classification including the Alphabetical List; if the space provided is not sufficient, use attachment instead

70   Class No.   List

71 Optional

| Translation into second language | 71 ☐ attached | ☐ to follow |

Priority

72 Check this box if convention priority (Paris Convention and TRIPS Agreement) is claimed

| Convention priority | 72 ☐ claimed |

Country of first filing   73

Date of first filing   74

Filing number   75

76 If priority is not claimed for all of the goods/services of the first filing, list goods/services of the first filing for which priority is claimed; if the space is not sufficient use attachment instead

List of goods/services of first filing   76   Class No.   List

77 Check one of these boxes

Priority documents
Certified copy of first filing   77 ☐ attached   ☐ to follow

78 The OHIM languages are ES, DE, EN, FR, IT

Translation of first filing in one of the OHIM languages   78 ☐ attached   ☐ to follow

79 If multiple priorities are claimed, check this box and make the corresponding statements for the additional priorities on attachment

Multiple priorities   79 ☐ claimed

80 Check this box if claimed and attach details

Exhibition priority   80 ☐ claimed

15

OHIM-Form
1.6 EN

Application for a Community Trade Mark

Seniority

81 *Check this box if seniority is claimed*	**Seniority**	**81** ☐ claimed
82 *Check one of these boxes*	Nature of registration	**82** ☐ national registration in member state ☐ international registration with effect in member state
83 *Indicate member state and*	Member state	**83** _____
84 *Indicate the registration number and date or, where applicable,*	Registration number and date	**84** _____
85 *Number and date of international registration*	Number and date of international registration	**85** _____
86 *Check one of these boxes*		**86** ☐ seniority is claimed for all the goods/services in the previous registration ☐ seniority is not claimed for all the goods/services in the previous registration

87 *If Seniority is not claimed for all goods/services indicate the goods/services in the previous registration in respect of which seniority is claimed; if the space provided is not sufficient, use attachment instead*

List of goods/services in the previous registration

87 Class No. | List

Seniority documents

88 *Check one of these boxes* Certified copy of previous registration **88** ☐ attached   ☐ to follow

89 *If multiple seniorities are claimed, check this box and make the corresponding statements for the additional seniorities on attachment* **Multiple seniorities** **89** ☐ claimed

---

Number of attachments **90** _____

16

**OFFICE FOR HARMONIZATION IN THE INTERNAL MARKET
(TRADE MARKS AND DESIGNS)**

NOTES ON THE APPLICATION FORM

<u>General Remarks</u>

The Application Form is made available by the Office for Harmonization in the Internal Market pursuant to Rule 83 of the Regulation Implementing the Regulation on the Community Trade Mark. The form may be obtained free of charge from the Office and from the industrial property offices of the Member States, including the Benelux Trade Mark Office. It may also be copied free. Applicants or their representatives may use forms of a similar structure or format, such as forms generated by computers on the basis of the information contained in the Application Form. Where such electronically generated forms are used, the use of attachments may be avoided by simply continuing in the text of the form where the Application Form does not provide sufficient space. Applicants may also use the electronic application form on 3.5" diskette available without charge from the Office and from the central industrial property offices of the Member States, including the Benelux Trade Mark Office.

The Application Form consists of three columns. The left column contains instructions, the middle column indicates the information required, and the right column must be completed by providing the required information. When certain information may be supplied later, it is nevertheless recommended that the Application Form be completed as far as possible and the necessary information be supplied at the time of filing the application. This will facilitate and expedite the handling of the application.

<u>Completed Application Forms should be sent</u> directly to the Office in Alicante or, at the applicant's choice, to one of the central industrial property offices of the Member States (for Belgium, Luxembourg, and The Netherlands the Benelux Trade Mark Office). Applications as well as any other communication relating to procedures before the Office <u>sent by mail</u> should be addressed as follows:

> Office for Harmonization in the Internal Market
> Receiving Unit
> Apartado de Correos 77
> E-03080 Alicante, Spain.

Communications by <u>special delivery</u> (such as courier services) should be addressed as follows:

> Office for Harmonization in the Internal Market
> Receiving Unit
> Avenida de Aguilera, 20
> E-03080 Alicante, Spain.

Communications by <u>telefax</u> should be sent to the following OHIM fax number only:

> + 34-6-513 1344.

Where communications are sent by fax, communication of the original (confirmation) is not necessary and not recommended. The Office will issue receipts, as far as applications are concerned, and will invite further communications should the communication by telefax be insufficient.

For information, call OHIM at the following telephone number:
> + 34-6-513 9333.

1.12.95

Pages 1, 2 and 3

Page 1 deals with languages, the applicant, the representative, the fees and the signature

The applicant or his representative may indicate his own reference number in the space provided at the top of page 1. The Office will use this reference number, which should occupy no more than 20 spaces, in any communications sent by the Office.

The applicant must select the language of the application proceedings ("first language"), which may be any of the eleven official languages of the European Community (Spanish - ES, Danish - DA, German - DE, Greek - EL, English - EN, French - FR, Italian - IT, Dutch - NL, Portuguese - PT, Finish - FI, Swedish - SV). The applicant must also select a second language, which must be one of the five languages of the Office (Spanish, German, English, French, Italian) and which must be different from the first language. The second language must also be selected when the first language is one of the languages of the Office. The second language will be used by the Office in communicating with the applicant or his representative when the first language is not one of the five languages of the Office. The second language is also the language, or one of the languages, available for opposition and cancellation proceedings. Any language version of the Application Form may be used, as long as the textual elements, in particular the list of goods and services, are completed in the language of the application proceedings.

If the applicant has previously been allocated an ID number by the Office, it is sufficient to indicate that ID number and the name. Otherwise, page 2 must be completed with all the necessary information. Providing all available means of communication is recommended as this will facilitate communication between the Office and the applicant. Where the applicant has an address for delivery (street, house number, etc.) and a different address for postal service (such as P.O. box etc.) both addresses should be given, and the Office will use both of these addresses as appropriate. When there is more than one applicant, the box on page 2 should be checked and the necessary information for all applicants should be provided on an attachment.

The above remarks apply to representatives as well. Where necessary, the required information should be supplied on page 3.

Representation - except for the filing of the application - is mandatory for applicants having neither their domicile or principal place of business nor a real and effective establishment in the European Community. Where the application is filed by the applicant directly in these cases, any further communication by the Office or with the Office will have to be through a representative. Any other applicant is free to appoint a representative.

Representation before the Office may be exercised only by professional representatives falling into one of the two following categories:

-   legal practitioners qualified in the Member State who are entitled to act in that Member State as representative in trade mark matters and who have their place of business in the European Community,

-   professional representatives entered on the list maintained by the Office.

Representatives must file an authorisation (power of attorney). Authorisations may be given in the form of General Authorisations or Individual Authorisations. Authorisation Forms are available from the Office and from the central industrial property offices of the Member States including the Benelux Trade Mark Office. Where an ID number has been allocated to an authorisation already on record at the Office, it is sufficient to indicate that ID number without supplying a further copy of the authorisation.

18

Natural or legal persons may act through an employee. The information on page 3 on representatives should not be completed by employee representatives. Rather, the Office will communicate with the applicant under the applicant's address. Employee representatives must also file an authorisation. The Authorisation Form made available by the Office may be used for appointing an employee representative.

Employees of legal persons with their domicile or principal place of business or an establishment within the European Community may represent other legal persons provided there exist economic connections between the two legal persons, such as common ownership or control. This also applies when the applicant is a legal person from outside of the European Community. In these cases, the box on page 2 should be checked and the appropriate information relating to the legal person whose employee acts on behalf of the applicant (name, address, etc.) should be provided on an attachment. The authorisation in these cases must be given by the applicant. The authorisation should contain the necessary information about the legal person giving the authorisation, the person authorised and the legal person employing the employee representative with whom the applicant has economic connections. The Office may require further evidence.

The basic application fee for a Community trade mark is ECU 975 which covers up to three classes of goods and services. Each additional class will cost ECU 200. The basic fee for a Community collective mark is ECU 1,675. Each class above three will cost ECU 400.

Payments must be made in ECU. Payment can be effected by

> an instruction to debit a current account held with the Office, providing the number of that account,

> making a transfer to a bank account of the Office,

> enclosing a cheque or similar instrument, such as a banker's draft, in ECU, noting the name, address and reference number of the applicant or representative and the application to which it refers.

Current accounts may be opened by making written application to the Office at the following address:

> Office for Harmonization in the Internal Market
> Financial Services
> Avenida de Aguilera, 20
> E-03080 Alicante, Spain
> Telephone: +34-6-513 9340
> Telefax: +34-6-513 9113

Money transfers may be made to the following acounts of the Office at the following banks:

> Banco Alicante,   Account No. 0127-2001-30/82000044-954
> Banco Bilbao Vizcaya, Account No. 0182-5596-201-222222-8
> BNP Españ,   Account No. 0058.1700.21.0252388002

indicating the name, address and reference number of the applicant or representative and the application to which the payment refers.

The application must be signed at the bottom of page 1. If an employee signs, his name must also be given.

19

Page 4

Page 4 deals with the <u>mark</u> to be registered. An attachment must be used for the representation of any mark which is not a word mark.

The - optional - translation of information relating to the mark will facilitate and expedite the handling of applications by the Office because, where the language of the application is not one of the five languages of the Office, the Office will have to communicate with the applicant concerning these translations. Even where the first language is one of the languages of the Office, such translations are useful.

Page 5

Page 5 deals with the <u>goods and services</u> for which the mark is to be registered and with <u>priority</u>.

For the list of <u>goods and services</u>, the Office recommends that the terminology of the Nice Classification including that of the Alphabetical List established under that classification be used. This will facilitate and expedite the handling of the application, especially as concerns any required translations.

For <u>priority</u>, while much of the required information may be supplied after the filing, it is recommended that as much information be supplied together with the application. This will facilitate and expedite the handling of the application. The mandatory elements are the indication of the country of first filing and the date.

In cases of <u>partial priority</u>, the list of goods and services for which priority is claimed may be given in the language of the application proceedings (the "first language" indicated on page 1) or in any of the five languages of the Office. The language chosen must be the same as that in which the translation of the first filing is (or will be) filed.

Page 6

Page 6 deals with <u>seniority</u>.

In addition to the registration number, the relevant date must be indicated. This is always the date from which the earlier registration was effective as an earlier mark. This will generally be the filing date, or any priority date claimed for the earlier registration, and not the registration date where that date is different from the filing date. Where the earlier registration is an international registration pursuant to the Madrid Agreement or the Protocol to the Madrid Agreement, the international registration date (or any priority claimed for the international registration) should be indicated.

In case of <u>partial seniority</u>, the list of goods and services for which seniority is claimed may be given in the language of the application proceedings (the "first language" indicated on page 1). Instead of choosing that language, the list may also be provided in the language of the registration whose seniority is claimed.

20

Appendix 6
Notice of Opposition to a CTM

Office for Harmonization in the Internal Market

Avenida de Aguilera, 20
E - 03080 Alicante
Apartado de Correos 77

Tel. + 34 - 6 - 513 93 33
Fax + 34 - 6 - 513 13 44

OHIM-Form
2.1 EN

Notice of Opposition

		Date of receipt	Number of pages	Opponent's /Representative's reference number
This area is reserved for OHIM	**For OHIM**			

	Language		
[1] *Check one of these boxes*	Language of opposition	1	☐ ES ☐ DE ☐ EN ☐ FR ☐ IT

	Opposed application	
[2] *Mandatory*	Application number	2
[3] *Mandatory*	Applicant	3
[4] *Optional*	Date of publication	4

	Opponent	
[5] *Indicate ID number if available; if not, complete page 2*	ID number of opponent	5 ☐ given
[6] *Mandatory*	Name of opponent	6
[7] *Mandatory; check the appropriate box*	Entitlement	7 ☐ proprietor ☐ authorised licensee ☐ person authorised under national law
	Evidence of entitlement	8 ☐ attached ☐ to follow

	Professional representative	
[9] *Check the box if a professional representative is appointed*	Professional representative	9 ☐ appointed
[10] *Indicate ID number if available; if not, complete page 3*	ID number of professional representative	10 ☐ given
[11] *Mandatory*	Name	11

	Authorisation	
[12] *Check this box if OHIM is already in possession of authorisation and*	Authorisation on file	12 ☐ already on file
[13] *indicate ID number of authorisation if available*	ID number of authorisation	13 ☐ given
[14] *Check one of these boxes if authorisation is not on file*	Authorisation not on file	14 ☐ attached ☐ to follow

	Fees	
[15] *For fees see current table of fees*	Opposition fee	15 ECU
[16] *Payment will automatically be deducted from current account unless one of the following boxes is checked or a specific instruction to the contrary is provided*	Payment Current account	16 ☐ current account No.
[17] *If payment is remitted indicate OHIM account number and*	Remittance to account of OHIM	17 ☐ OHIM account No.
[18] *indicate date of remittance of payment*	Date of remittance	18
	Cheque	19 ☐ attached

	Signature	
[20] *Optional*	Date of signing	20
[21] *Mandatory*	Signature	21
[22] *Indicate name of person signing*	Name	22
[23] *Check as appropriate if signature is by employee representative or professional representative*		23 ☐ employee ☐ legal practitioner ☐ professional representative

	Number of sheets	
[24] *Total number of sheets, including attachments*	Number of sheets	24

Notice of Opposition

OHIM-Form
2.2 EN

Complete this page only when indications on page 1 are insufficient

Opponent

25 *Check this box if applicable and*

26 *indicate name*

Nature   **25** ☐ legal person   ☐ natural person

Name   **26** _____

First name/s of natural person   **27** _____

Address

Street and house number or equivalent   **28** _____

City and postal code where available   **29** _____

Country   **30** _____

31 *If different from above, such as P.O. Box, city and postal code*

Postal address   **31**

Telephone number/s   **32** _____

Telefax number/s   **33** _____

Electronic mail ID   **34** _____

Other information   **35** _____

Multiple opponents

36 *Where there is more than one opponent, check the box, and indicate on this page the required information for all additional opponents; if the space provided is not sufficient, use attachment instead.*

Absent any other information, the name and the address of the opponent indicated above will be used as an address for correspondence with regard to all opponents

Multiple opponents   **36** ☐

Economic connections

37 *If an employee of a legal person having economic connections with the opponent is appointed to act on behalf of the opponent, check the box and provide the necessary details (name and address of legal person having economic connections with opponent, basis of economic connections); if the space provided is not sufficient, use attachment instead.*

Economic connections   **37** ☐

Notice of Opposition

	Professional representative(s)	
Complete this page only when indications on page 1 are insufficient	**Type**	
38 *Check this box*	Association of representatives	38 ☐ association of representatives
and 39 *indicate name of association*	Name of association	39 _____
or		
40 *check this box and*	Natural person	40 ☐ natural person
41 *indicate name of representative and*	Surname of representative	41 _____
	First name of representative	42 _____
43 *check one of these boxes*	Nature of representative	43 ☐ legal practitioner ☐ professional representative
	Address	
	Street and house number or equivalent	44 _____
	City and postal code where available	45 _____
	Country	46 _____
47 *If different from above, such as P.O. Box, city and postal code*	Postal address	47 _____
	Telephone number/s	48 _____
	Telefax number/s	49 _____
	Electronic mail ID	50 _____
	Other information	51 _____

	Multiple representatives	
52 *Where there is more than one representative, check the box, and indicate on this page the required information for all additional representatives; if the space provided is not sufficient, use attachment instead.*	Multiple representatives	52 ☐

Absent any other information, the name and the address of the representative indicated above will be used as an address for correspondence with regard to all representatives

Notice of Opposition

OHIM-Form
2.4 EN

Basis of opposition

53 Check the appropriate box/es and provide the required information hereafter; if opposition is based on more than one earlier mark or sign, additional sheets (copies of this page and page 5) must be completed, if necessary, for each earlier mark or sign

Opposition is based on

53 ☐ earlier mark (registration or application)

54 ☐ earlier registered mark with reputation

55 ☐ earlier well-known mark

56 ☐ earlier non-registered mark

57 ☐ earlier other sign used in the course of trade

58 ☐ mark filed by an agent

Earlier mark (registration or application)

59 Check one of these boxes

Type of mark

59 ☐ Community mark   ☐ national mark   ☐ international registration with effect in a Member State

60 If national mark or international registration, check the appropriate box

Member State/s

60 DK | DE | GR | ES | FR | IE | IT | AT | PT | FI | SE | GB | BENELUX

61 Indicate word mark; if other type of mark, provide a representation on attachment

Representation of the mark

61 _____

62-65 Complete as appropriate; if priority is invoked , provide details on attachment

Filing date   62 _____

Filing No.   63 _____

Registration date   64 _____

Registration No.   65 _____

66 Copy required only when earlier mark is a national mark or international registration

Copy of registration/application

66 ☐ attached   ☐ to follow

67-68 Check and complete as appropriate; indicate goods/services on which opposition is based; if the space provided is not sufficient, use attachment instead

Opposition is based on

67 ☐ all the goods/services for which earlier mark is registered/applied for

68 ☐ less than all the goods/services, namely:

Earlier registered mark with reputation

69 If opposition is based on earlier registered mark with reputation, complete lines 61-64-65 and box 66 and check as appropriate one of the following boxes

Reputation

69 ☐ in the Community   ☐ in a Member State (including Benelux)

70 Check the appropriate box

Member State

70 DK | DE | GR | ES | FR | IE | IT | AT | PT | FI | SE | GB | BENELUX

71-72 Check one of the boxes and complete as appropriate; indicate only goods/services for which reputation is claimed; if the space provided is not sufficient, use attachment instead

Opposition is based on

71 ☐ all the goods/services for which earlier mark is registered

72 ☐ less than all the goods/services, namely:

Evidence of reputation

73 ☐ attached   ☐ to follow

Notice of Opposition

OHIM-Form
2.5 EN

Earlier well-known mark

74 *Indicate word mark; if other type of mark, provide representation on attachment*

Representation of the mark | 74 _____

75 *Indicate Member State/s where mark is well-known*

Member State/s | 75 | BE | DK | DE | GR | ES | FR | IE | IT | LU | NL | AT | PT | FI | SE | GB |

76 *If the space provided is not sufficient, use attachment instead*

Opposition is based on the following goods/services | 76 _____
_____
_____
_____

Evidence of mark being well-known | 77 ☐ attached   ☐ to follow

---

Earlier non-registered mark

78 *Indicate word mark; if other type of mark, provide representation on attachment*

Representation of the mark | 78 _____

79 *Indicate Member State where earlier non-registered mark is protected*

Member State | 79 | BE | DK | DE | GR | ES | FR | IE | IT | LU | NL | AT | PT | FI | SE | GB |

80 *If the space provided is not sufficient, use attachment instead*

Opposition is based on the following goods/services | 80 _____
_____
_____
_____

Evidence of protection | 81 ☐ attached   ☐ to follow

Earlier sign used in the course of trade

82 *Indicate sign; if the sign is not consisting of a word, provide representation on attachment*

Representation of the sign | 82 _____

83 *Indicate nature of rights claimed*

Nature of rights | 83 _____

84 *Indicate Member State where earlier sign is protected*

Member State | 84 | BE | DK | DE | GR | ES | FR | IE | IT | LU | NL | AT | PT | FI | SE | GB |

85 *Indicate goods/services, object of economic activity; if the space provided is not sufficient, use attachment instead*

Opposition is based on the following goods/services | 85 _____
_____
_____
_____

Evidence of protection | 86 ☐ attached   ☐ to follow

Mark filed by agent

87 *Indicate word mark; if other type of mark, provide representation on attachment*

Representation of the mark | 87 _____

88 *Indicate country/ies where opponent is proprietor of mark*

Country/ies | 88 _____

Evidence of ownership of mark | 89 ☐ attached   ☐ to follow

Notice of Opposition

OHIM-Form
2.6 EN

Extent of opposition

90-91 *Check one of these boxes*

Opposition is directed

90 ☐ against all goods/services in the application

91 ☐ against part of goods/services in the application, namely:

92 *Specify goods / services against which opposition is directed; if the space provided is not sufficient, use attachment instead*

92 _____

_____

_____

Grounds of opposition

93-94 *Check the appropriate box when opposition is based on earlier mark (registered or application) or earlier well-known mark*

Opposition is based on earlier mark and

93 ☐ identity of marks and goods/services

94 ☐ likelihood of confusion

95 *Check the box when opposition is based on earlier registered mark with reputation*

Opposition is based on earlier registered mark and

95 ☐ unfair advantage/ detriment to distinctiveness or repute

96 *Check the box when opposition is based on earlier non-registered mark*

Opposition is based on earlier non-registered mark and

96 ☐ right to prohibit use of later mark under national law

97 *Check the box when opposition is based on an earlier sign used in the course of trade*

Opposition is based on earlier sign and

97 ☐ right to prohibit use of later mark under national law

98 *Check the box when opposition is based on mark filed by an agent*

Opposition is based on mark filed by an agent and

98 ☐ mark was filed without authorisation of proprietor

99 *If the space provided is not sufficient, use attachment instead*

Explanations of grounds

99 _____

_____

_____

_____

_____

_____

_____

_____

_____

Check that form has been signed on page 1

OFFICE FOR HARMONIZATION IN THE INTERNAL MARKET (TRADE MARKS AND DESIGNS)

NOTES ON THE OPPOSITION FORM

<u>General Remarks</u>

The Opposition Form is made available by the Office for Harmonization in the Internal Market pursuant to Rule 83 of the Regulation Implementing the Regulation on the Community Trade Mark. The form may be obtained free of charge from the Office and from the industrial property offices of the Member States, including the Benelux Trade Mark Office. It may also be freely photocopied. Opponents or their representatives may use forms of a similar structure or format, such as forms generated by computer on the basis of the information contained in the Opposition Form. With such electronically generated forms the user may overcome the need for attachments by simply adapting the size of sections of the form to accommodate the data to be entered therein.

The Opposition Form consists of three columns. The left-hand column contains instructions, the middle column indicates the information required, and the right-hand column must be completed by providing the required information. While certain information may be supplied after filing the opposition, it is nevertheless recommended that the Opposition Form should be submitted in the most complete form possible, with all the necessary information being supplied at the time of filing the opposition. This will facilitate and expedite the handling of the opposition.

Completed Opposition Forms should be sent <u>directly to</u> the OHIM in Alicante.

When <u>sent by mail</u> Opposition Forms (as well as any other communication relating to facts, evidence or observations from parties involved in an opposition procedure) should be addressed as follows:

> Office for Harmonization in the Internal Market
> Mail Office (Opposition Divisions)
> Apartado de Correos 77
> E-03080 Alicante, Spain

Communications by <u>special delivery</u> (such as courier services) should be addressed as follows:

> Office for Harmonization in the Internal Market
> Mail Office (Opposition Divisions)
> Avenida de Aguilera, 20
> E-03080 Alicante, Spain

Communications by <u>telefax</u> should be sent to the following OHIM fax number:

> +34-6-513 13 44

Where communications are sent by fax, confirmation copies are not necessary and not recommended. The Office will issue receipts for oppositions which are filed, and should a faxed communication be deficient the Office will invite the opponent to remedy the deficiency.

It is strongly recommended to include the words "OPPOSITION DIVISIONS" at the beginning of all correspondence relating to an opposition.

For more information, you may call OHIM at the following telephone number:

> +34-6-513 93 33

Pages 1, 2 and 3

Page 1 deals with languages, the opposed application, the opponent, the representative, authorisation, fees and signature.

The opponent or his representative may indicate his own reference number in the space provided for this purpose at the top of page 1. The Office will use this reference number, which should occupy no more than 20 spaces, in all communications sent by the Office.

Language: The opponent must submit the opposition in one of the five languages of the Office (Spanish - ES, German - DE, English - EN, French - FR, Italian - IT). Any language version of the Opposition Form may be used, as long as the textual elements are completed in one of the five languages of the Office. The language chosen may be the first language of the opposed application if this is a language of the Office, or the second language which necessarily is a language of the Office. If the opposition is filed in one of these two languages it will facilitate and expedite the handling of the case. Should this not be the case the opponent must provide a translation of the opposition within one month of the expiration date of the opposition period.

Opposed Application: The following details must be provided on the form: the application number attributed by the Office, the name of the applicant and the date of publication of the opposed application in the Community Trade Marks Bulletin.

Opponent: If the opponent has previously been allocated an ID number by the Office, it is sufficient to indicate that ID number and the name. Otherwise, page 2 must be completed with all the necessary information. The provision of details regarding all available means of communication is recommended as this will facilitate communication between the Office and the opponent. Where the opponent has an address for delivery and a postal address both addresses should be given, and the Office will use them as appropriate.

The opponent must provide information regarding entitlement on page 1 (proprietor of the mark, licensee authorised by the proprietor or person authorised under national law) and provide the necessary evidence.

Where there are multiple opponents the appropriate box on page 2 must be checked, and the necessary information relating to each opponent shall be provided on this page or in an annex.

The above remarks apply to representatives, with the exception to those related to the entitlement of the opponent. Where necessary, the required information should be supplied on page 3.

Representation: This is mandatory for opponents who do not have either their domicile, principal place of business, or a real and effective establishment in the European Community. In such cases, where the Opposition Form is filed directly by the opponent, a representative must be appointed within a two month period fixed by the Office. Any further communication by the Office or with the Office will have to be through the representative. Any other opponent is free to appoint a representative.

Representation before the Office may be exercised only by professional representatives falling into one of the two following categories:

-    legal practitioners qualified in the Member State who are entitled to act in that Member State as representative in trade mark matters and who have their place of business in the European Community,

-    professional representatives entered on the list maintained by the Office.

Authorisation: Representatives must file an authorisation (power of attorney). Authorisations may be given in the form of General Authorisations or Individual Authorisations. Authorisation Forms are available from the Office and from the central industrial property offices of the Member States including the Benelux Trade Mark Office. Where an ID number has been allocated to an authorisation already on record at the Office, it is sufficient to indicate that ID number without supplying a further copy of the authorisation.

Employees: The opponents (natural or legal persons) may act through an employee. The information on page 3 relates to professional representatives only and must therefore not be completed by employee representatives. Rather, the Office will communicate with the opponent under the opponent's address. Employee representatives must however also file an authorisation. The Authorisation Form made available by the Office may be used for appointing an employee representative.

Employees of legal persons with their domicile or principal place of business or an establishment within the European Community may represent other legal persons if (and only if) economic connections exist between the two legal persons, such as common ownership or control. This also applies when the opponent is a legal person from outside of the European Community. In these cases, the box on page 2 must be checked and the appropriate information relating to the legal person whose employee acts on behalf of the opponent (name, address, telephone number, telefax number, e-mail), and the basis of economic connections (parent company or subsidiary etc.) should be provided on this page or on an attachment. The authorisation in these cases must be given by the opponent. The authorisation must contain the necessary information about the legal person giving the authorisation, the person authorised and the legal person employing the employee representative with whom the opponent has economic connections. The Office may require further evidence.

Fees : The opposition fee is ECU 350 regardless of the number of earlier rights (marks or signs) invoked in the opposition.

Payments must be made in ECU. Payment can be effected

- by means of a current account held with the Office, indicating the number of that account,
- by making a transfer to a bank account of the Office,
- by enclosing a cheque or similar instrument, such as a banker's draft, in ECU, noting the name, address and reference number of the opponent or representative and the opposition to which it refers.

If the opponent does not specify any form of payment, but has a current account held with the Office, this account will be debited directly. Otherwise, the Office will follow the form of payment indicated on the Opposition Form.

Current accounts may be opened by making written application to the Office at the following address:

Office for Harmonization in the Internal Market
Financial Services
Avenida de Aguilera, 20
E-03080 Alicante, Spain
Telephone: + 34-6-513 93 40
Telefax: + 34-6-513 91 13

Money transfers may be made to the following accounts of the Office at the following banks:

Banco Alicante   Account No. 0127-2001-3082000445-90
Banco Bilbao Vizcaya   Account No. 0182-5596-2012222228-95
BNP España   Account No. 0058-1700-0252388002-21

indicating the name, address and reference number of the opponent or representative and the opposition to which the payment refers.

Signature: The Opposition Form must be signed by the opponent, the professional representative or by the employee at the bottom of page 1. Following the signature the name of the signatory must be indicated, together with a basis of the entitlement for the signature. If the Opposition Form is signed by an employee of a legal person having economic connections with the opponent it is necessary to provide the necessary details on page 2.

3

Pages 4 and 5

Pages 4 and 5 deal with earlier rights invoked in the opposition. At the top of page 4 the six categories of earlier rights upon which the opposition can be based are listed. The relevant box(es) should be checked and the corresponding section(s) on page 4 to 5 should be completed taking into consideration the nature of the rights in question. The information required here is of two types: firstly information identifying the earlier right, and secondly information regarding the goods and services involved.

Earlier Rights:

For registered marks, for marks with a reputation or for applications for registration, indicate the name of the mark (for any mark which is not a word mark a representation must be supplied in an annex), indicate the geographic area of protection, and supply the registration or application number and the date of registration or application.

For well known-marks (Article 6bis of the Paris Convention) or for non-registered marks, indicate the name of the mark (for any mark which is not a word mark a representation must be supplied in an annex) and indicate the geographic coverage of the mark (i.e. the Member State where the mark is well-known or exists).

For earlier signs, indicate the name of the sign (for any sign which does not consist of a word, a representation must be supplied in an annex) and its geographic coverage (in which Member State the sign is protected), indicate also the nature of the right claimed (company name, trade name, etc.).

Although it is not obligatory at this stage, it is recommended that the opponent provides together with the notice of opposition, a copy of the earlier mark(s) or evidence of the earlier rights or signs, or any further information concerning such earlier rights (evidence of the reputation of the mark, of the mark as being well-known, of the existence of the non-registered mark or sign etc.). This will facilitate and expedite the handling of the opposition by the Office.

Goods and Services:

For each earlier right claimed, the opponent must provide a list of goods and services upon which the opposition is based.

For earlier registered marks including marks with reputation or for applications, when the opposition is based on all the goods and services registered or applied for, it is sufficient to indicate so on the form. Should this not be the case, the opponent must list the goods and/or services involved.

For well known marks (Article 6bis of the Paris Convention), non-registered marks and earlier signs, a complete list of goods and services on which the opposition is based must be provided.

An opposition can be based on more than one earlier right. It is necessary to provide a separate page for each earlier right claimed.Copies of pages 4 and 5 should be provided with all required information relating to each earlier right. If the earlier right is protected in several Member States for the same goods and services(for example, in the case of an international registration) it may be sufficient to provide this information, together with the indication of the respective Member States, on one page.

Page 6

Page 6 deals with extent and grounds of opposition.

For extent of opposition, if opposition is entered against all the goods and services of the opposed application it is not necessary to specify individually each product andservice. Should the opposition be partial, it is necessary to specify each product and service against which the opposition is directed. The indication of the class number is sufficient should the opposition concern all products and services in a class.

For grounds of opposition, it is necessary to indicate the grounds on which opposition is based and to provide at the bottom of this page (or in an annex) all information, arguments or explanations in support of the opposition. It is suggested that, as far as is possible, all the necessary information should accompany the notice of opposition as this will facilitate and expedite the handling of the opposition.

Appendix 7
Madrid Protocol Application Form MM2

**APPLICATION FOR INTERNATIONAL REGISTRATION
GOVERNED EXCLUSIVELY BY THE PROTOCOL
RELATING TO THE MADRID AGREEMENT**

MM2

For use by the applicant; this international application contains, in addition to the application form, the following number of sheets:	For use by the applicant/Office of origin Applicant's reference: Office's reference:	For use by the International Bureau: Total additional sheets received:

1 CONTRACTING PARTY WHOSE OFFICE IS THE OFFICE OF ORIGIN:

2 APPLICANT   Identification code
(where supplied by WIPO):

(a) Name:

(b) Address:

(c) Address for correspondence:

(d) Telephone: Fax:

(e) Preferred language for correspondence: English [   ]   French [   ]

(f) Other indications (as may be required by certain designated Contracting Parties)

  (i) if the applicant is a natural person, nationality of applicant:

  (ii) if the applicant is a legal entity:

    - legal nature of the legal entity:

    - State and, where applicable, territorial unit within that State, under the law of which the legal entity is organized:

3 ENTITLEMENT TO FILE

(a) Indicate in the appropriate box or space:

  (i) where the Contracting Party mentioned in item 1 is a State, whether the applicant is a national of that State; or

  (ii) where the Contracting Party mentioned in item 1 is an organization, the name of the State of which the applicant is a national; or

  (iii) whether the applicant is domiciled in the territory of the Contracting Party mentioned in item 1; or   [   ]

  (iv) whether the applicant has a real and effective industrial or commercial establishment in the territory of the Contracting Party mentioned in item 1.   [   ]

(b) Where the address of the applicant, given in item 2(b), is not in the territory of the Contracting Party mentioned in item 1, indicate in the space provided below:

  (i) if the box corresponding to paragraph (a)(iii) of the present item has been checked, the domicile of the applicant in the territory of that Contracting Party, or,

  (ii) if the box corresponding to paragraph (a)(iv) of the present item has been checked, the address of the applicant's industrial or commercial establishment in the territory of that Contracting Party.

4 REPRESENTATIVE (if any)

Identification code
(where supplied by WIPO):

Name:

Address:

Telephone: Fax:

5 BASIC APPLICATION OR BASIC REGISTRATION

Basic application number: Basic application date: (dd/mm/yyyy)

Basic registration number: Basic registration date: (dd/mm/yyyy)

6 PRIORITY CLAIMED

☐ The applicant claims the priority of the earlier filing mentioned below.

Office of priority filing:

Priority filing number (if available):

Priority filing date: (dd/mm/yyyy)

If the claiming of priority does not relate to all the goods and services listed in item 10 of this form, indicate in the space provided below the goods and services for which priority is claimed.

7 THE MARK

(a) Place the reproduction of the mark, as it appears in the basic application or the basic registration, in the square below.

(b) Where the reproduction in item (a) is in black and white and color is claimed in item 8 of this form, place a color reproduction of the mark in the square below.

(c) ☐ The applicant declares that he wishes the mark to be considered as a mark in standard characters.

Where the Office of origin has addressed this form by telefacsimile, the present space must be completed before addressing the original of this page to the International Bureau.
Basic application or basic registration number or Office reference number as shown on the first page of this form:

Signature by the Office of origin:

8   COLOR(S) CLAIMED

☐   The applicant claims color as a distinctive feature of the mark.

Color or combination of colors claimed:

Indication, for each color, of the principal parts of the mark that are in that color (as may be required by certain designated Contracting Parties):

9   MISCELLANEOUS INDICATIONS

(a) Transliteration of the mark (where applicable):

(b) Translation of the mark (as may be required by certain designated Contracting Parties)

   (i) into English:

   (ii) into French:

(c) Where applicable, check the relevant box or boxes below:

☐ Three-dimensional mark   ☐ Sound mark   ☐ Collective mark, certification mark, or guarantee mark

(d) Description of the mark where a description is contained in the basic application or the basic registration:

10   GOODS AND SERVICES FOR WHICH INTERNATIONAL REGISTRATION IS SOUGHT

Class   Goods and services

11 DESIGNATED CONTRACTING PARTIES

Check the corresponding boxes to designate Contracting Parties

☐ **CH** Switzerland

☐ **CN** China

☐ **CU** Cuba

☐ **CZ** Czech Republic

☐ **DE** Germany

☐ **DK** Denmark

☐ **ES** Spain

☐ **FI** Finland

☐ **GB** United Kingdom*

☐ **IS** Iceland

☐ **KP** Democratic People's Republic of Korea

☐ **MC** Monaco

☐ **NO** Norway

☐ **PL** Poland

☐ **PT** Portugal

☐ **SE** Sweden

Others:

* By designating the United Kingdom, the applicant declares that he has the intention that the mark will be used by him or with his consent in the United Kingdom in connection with the goods and services identified in this application.

12 SIGNATURE BY THE APPLICANT OR HIS REPRESENTATIVE
(If required or allowed by the Office of origin)

(dd/mm/yyyy)

13 CERTIFICATION AND SIGNATURE OF THE INTERNATIONAL APPLICATION BY THE OFFICE OF ORIGIN

(a) Certification

The Office of origin certifies

(i) that it received from the applicant a request to present this application, and that this request was received on

(dd/mm/yyyy).

(ii) that the applicant named in item 2 is the same as the applicant named in the basic application or the holder named in the basic registration mentioned in item 5; that the mark in item 7(a) is the same as in the basic application or the basic registration; that, where applicable, the claim for color in item 8 is the same as in the basic application or the basic registration; that all the indications given in item 9(c) and (d) also appear in the basic application or the basic registration; that the goods and services listed in item 10 are covered by the list of goods and services appearing in the basic application or the basic registration. (If the present international application is based on two or more basic applications and/or basic registrations of the same mark, the certification shall be deemed to apply to all those basic applications and basic registrations.)

(b) Office's signature:

Date of the signature: (dd/mm/yyyy)

FEE CALCULATION SHEET

(a) INSTRUCTIONS TO DEBIT FROM A CURRENT ACCOUNT

☐ The International Bureau is hereby instructed to debit the required amount of fees from a current account opened with the International Bureau (if this box is checked, it is not necessary to complete (b)).

Holder of the account: Account number:

Identity of the party giving the instructions:

(b) AMOUNT OF FEES; METHOD OF PAYMENT

Basic fee (653 Swiss francs if the reproduction of the mark is in black and white only; 903 Swiss francs if there is a reproduction in color)

Complementary and supplementary fees:

Number of designations
for which complementary   Total amount of the
fee is applicable   Complementary fee   complementary fees

              x   73 Swiss francs   =   =>

Number of classes of
goods and services   Total amount of the
beyond three   Supplementary fee   supplementary fees

              x   73 Swiss francs   =   =>

Individual fees (Swiss francs):

Designated Contracting Parties	Individual fee	Designated Contracting Parties	Individual fee

                                    Total individual fees   =>

                                         Grand total

Identity of the party effecting the payment:

		Holder of the account	Account number
Debit from a current account with WIPO	☐		
Payment received and acknowledged by WIPO	☐	WIPO receipt number	
Payment made by banker's check (attached)	☐	Check identification	dd/mm/yyyy
Payment made by banker's check (sent separately)	☐	Check identification	dd/mm/yyyy
Payment made to WIPO bank account N° 48 7080-81 with the Crédit Suisse, Geneva	☐	Payment identification	dd/mm/yyyy
Payment made to WIPO postal check account N° 12-5000-8, Geneva	☐	Payment identification	dd/mm/yyyy

Appendix 8
Madrid Protocol Subsequent Designation Form MM4

DESIGNATION SUBSEQUENT TO THE INTERNATIONAL REGISTRATION

MM4

For use by the holder; this subsequent designation contains, in addition to this form, the following number of sheets:	For use by the holder/Office Holder's reference: Office's reference:	For use by the International Bureau: Total additional sheets received:

1   INTERNATIONAL REGISTRATION NUMBER:

2   HOLDER (as recorded in the International Register)   Identification code
                                                           (where supplied by WIPO):

      Name:

      Address:

3   APPOINTMENT OF A REPRESENTATIVE
(A representative may be appointed in this form **only** if it is presented **through an Office**; if it is presented directly to the International Bureau, the appointment of a representative or of a new representative must be made in a separate communication.)

                                                        Identification code
                                                        (where supplied by WIPO):

      Name:

      Address:

      Telephone: Fax:

4   CONTRACTING PARTIES DESIGNATED IN THE PRESENT SUBSEQUENT DESIGNATION

Check the corresponding boxes to designate Contracting Parties

☐	**AL** Albania	☐	**DK** Denmark	☐	**KZ** Kazakstan	☐	**RO** Romania
☐	**AM** Armenia	☐	**DZ** Algeria	☐	**LI** Liechtenstein	☐	**RU** Russian Federation
☐	**AT** Austria	☐	**EG** Egypt	☐	**LR** Liberia	☐	**SD** Sudan
☐	**AZ** Azerbaijan	☐	**ES** Spain	☐	**LV** Latvia	☐	**SE** Sweden
☐	**BA** Bosnia and Herzegovina	☐	**FI** Finland	☐	**MA** Morocco	☐	**SI** Slovenia
☐	**BG** Bulgaria	☐	**FR** France	☐	**MC** Monaco	☐	**SK** Slovakia
☐	**BX** Benelux	☐	**GB** United Kingdom*	☐	**MD** Rep. of Moldova	☐	**SM** San Marino
☐	**BY** Belarus	☐	**HR** Croatia	☐	**MK** The former Yugoslav Rep. of Macedonia	☐	**TJ** Tajikistan
☐	**CH** Switzerland	☐	**HU** Hungary	☐	**MN** Mongolia	☐	**UA** Ukraine
☐	**CN** China	☐	**IS** Iceland	☐	**NO** Norway	☐	**UZ** Uzbekistan
☐	**CU** Cuba	☐	**IT** Italy	☐	**PL** Poland	☐	**VN** Viet Nam
☐	**CZ** Czech Republic	☐	**KG** Kyrgyzstan	☐	**PT** Portugal	☐	**YU** Yugoslavia
☐	**DE** Germany	☐	**KP** Democratic People's Republic of Korea				

      Others:

        *   By designating the United Kingdom, the holder declares that he has the intention that the mark will be used by him or with his consent in the United Kingdom in connection with the goods and services identified in the present subsequent designation.

5 GOODS AND SERVICES FOR WHICH THE PRESENT SUBSEQUENT DESIGNATION IS MADE

(a) ☐ The subsequent designation is for **all** the goods and services listed in the international registration identified in item 1 in respect of **all** the Contracting Parties designated in item 4.

(b) ☐ The subsequent designation is only for those goods and services listed in the continuation sheet in respect of **all** the Contracting Parties designated in item 4.

(c) ☐ The subsequent designation is only for those goods and services listed in the continuation sheet in respect of the Contracting Parties identified in the said continuation sheet; in respect of the other Contracting Parties designated in item 4, the subsequent designation is for all the goods and services listed in the international registration.

6 MISCELLANEOUS INDICATIONS

(a) Indications concerning the holder (as may be required by certain designated Contracting Parties)

   (i) if the holder is a natural person, nationality of the holder:

   (ii) if the holder is a legal entity:

     - legal nature of the legal entity:

     - State and, where applicable, territorial unit within that State, under the law of which the legal entity is organized:

(b) Translation of the mark (as may be required by certain designated Contracting Parties)

   (i) into English:

   (ii) into French:

(c) Indication, for each color, of the principal parts of the mark that are in that color (as may be required by certain designated Contracting Parties):

7 SIGNATURE BY THE HOLDER OR HIS REPRESENTATIVE
(where the subsequent designation is presented directly to the International Bureau or, where presented through an Office, if that Office requires or allows such a signature)

(dd/mm/yyyy)

8 DATE OF RECEIPT OF THE SUBSEQUENT DESIGNATION BY THE OFFICE AND SIGNATURE BY THE OFFICE
(where the subsequent designation is presented through an Office)

(a) Date of receipt by the Office: (dd/mm/yyyy)

(b) Signature:

FEE CALCULATION SHEET

(a)   INSTRUCTIONS TO DEBIT FROM A CURRENT ACCOUNT

☐   The International Bureau is hereby instructed to debit the required amount of fees from a current account opened with the International Bureau (if this box is checked, it is not necessary to complete (b)).

Holder of the account: Account number:

Identity of the party giving the instructions:

(b)   AMOUNT OF FEES; METHOD OF PAYMENT

Basic fee (300 Swiss francs)

Complementary fees:

Number of designations
for which complementary   Total amount of the
fee is applicable   Complementary fee   complementary fees

            x   73 Swiss francs   =   =>

Individual fees (Swiss francs):

Designated Contracting Parties	Individual fee	Designated Contracting Parties	Individual fee

                                        Total individual fees   =>

                                        Grand total

Identity of the party effecting the payment:

Debit from a current account with WIPO	☐ Holder of the account		Account number
Payment received and acknowledged by WIPO	☐ WIPO receipt number		
Payment made by banker's check (attached)	☐ Check identification		dd/mm/yyyy
Payment made by banker's check (sent separately)	☐ Check identification		dd/mm/yyyy
Payment made to WIPO bank account N° 48 7080-81 with the Crédit Suisse, Geneva	☐ Payment identification		dd/mm/yyyy
Payment made to WIPO postal check account N° 12-5000-8, Geneva	☐ Payment identification		dd/mm/yyyy

Appendix 9
CTM Registration Procedure

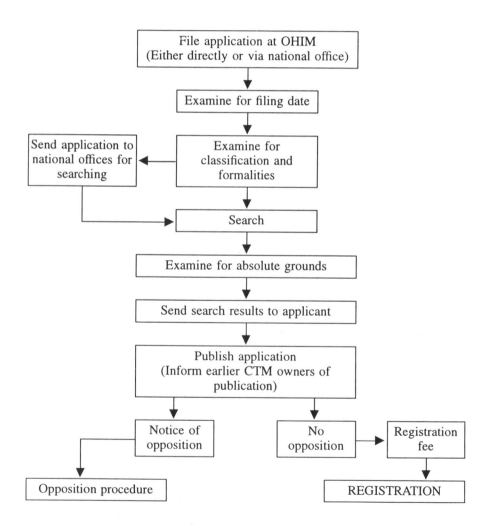

Appendix 10
CTM Opposition Procedure

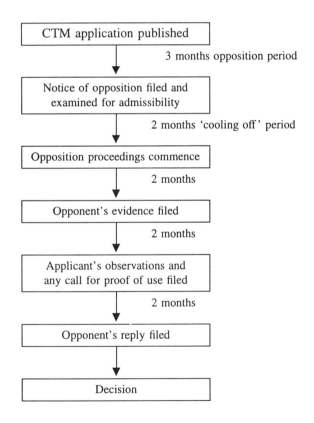

CTM application published

3 months opposition period

Notice of opposition filed and
examined for admissibility

2 months 'cooling off' period

Opposition proceedings commence

2 months

Opponent's evidence filed

2 months

Applicant's observations and
any call for proof of use filed

2 months

Opponent's reply filed

Decision

Appendix 11
International Application Procedure

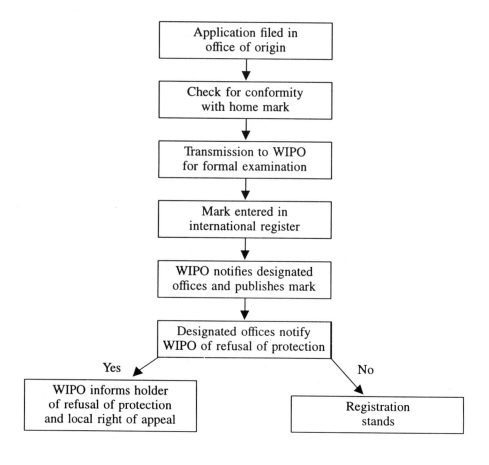

Application filed in
office of origin

Check for conformity
with home mark

Transmission to WIPO
for formal examination

Mark entered in
international register

WIPO notifies designated
offices and publishes mark

Designated offices notify
WIPO of refusal of protection

Yes

No

WIPO informs holder
of refusal of protection
and local right of appeal

Registration
stands

Appendix 12
Comparison of International and Community Trade Marks

	International TM	*Community TM*
Accessibility	Establishment or domicile in, or nationality of party to Agreement or Protocol	Establishment, seat or domicile in, or nationality of Member State or party to Paris Convention or WTO
Geographical coverage	Agreement or Protocol countries or both n.b. EC	EC
Choice of territories	Yes	No
Extension to new territories	Yes	No: new countries joining EC?
Preconditions for protection	Basic application or basic registration in office of origin	No – directly filed with OHIM
Dependence on basic application or registration	For first five years. Successful 'central attack' results in loss of international registration: but ability to *transform* under Protocol	No basic application or registration, therefore inapplicable

	International TM	*Community TM*
Examination	At national level after registration. Refusal only results in loss of protection in country concerned. N.b. need to appoint local agents	By OHIM on absolute grounds. Relative grounds available on opposition only. Refusal is for entire EC, but option to *convert*
Languages	French or French and English	OHIM official languages are Spanish, German, English, French and Italian. CTM application can be filed in any language of the EC, but opposition/ cancellation proceedings are in an OHIM language
Use	As per local law. Necessary to use in each designated party	Within five years of registration. Use in one Member State suffices
Assignment	May be partial as to territory	For entire EC only
Cancellation	Successful attack in designated party affects that territory only	Successful attack in one Member State knocks out CTM, but ability to *convert*
Enforcement of infringement rights	Separate national prosecutions	In a CTM court with jurisdiction for entire EC
Consolidation of existing national registrations	Replacement. N.b. not basic application/ registration	Seniority
Duration	10 years	10 years
Costs and renewal fees	Depends on how many protocol parties declare individual fees. N.b. agents' fees	Reasonable. N.b. opposition costs

Cost comparison
Protocol international application (no colour) in three classes based on UK application and designating Denmark, Finland, France, Germany, Portugal, Spain and Sweden.

		£
Basic UK application		325
WIPO basic fee		264
Denmark individual fee		241
Finland individual fee		205
Germany complementary fee		29
France complementary fee		29
Portugal complementary fee		29
Spain complementary fee		29
Sweden individual fee		158
	Total fees	1,309

CTM application in three classes for entire EC

Application fee		671
Registration fee		757
	Total fees	1,428

Rates of exchange prevailing 31 October 1997

Index